Parenting the Custodial Grandchild

BERT HAYSLIP, JR., received his doctorate in Experimental Developmental Psychology from the University of Akron in 1975. After teaching at Hood College in Frederick, MD, for 3 years, he joined the faculty at the University of North Texas, where he is now Regents Professor of Psychology. Dr. Hayslip is a Fellow of the American Psychological Association, the Gerontological Society of America, and the Association for Gerontology in Higher Education, and has held research grants from the National Institute on Aging, the Hilgenfeld Foundation, and the National Endowment for the Humanities. He is currently associate editor of *Experimental Aging Research,* editor of *The International Journal of Aging and Human Development,* and is on the Editorial Board of *Developmental Psychology.* His published research deals with cognitive processes in aging, interventions to enhance cognitive functioning in later life, personality-ability interrelationships in aged persons, grandparents who raise their grandchildren, grief and bereavement, hospice care, death anxiety, and mental health and aging. He is coauthor of *Hospice Care* (1992), *Psychology and Aging: An Annotated Bibliography* (1995), *Grandparents Raising Grandchildren: Theoretical, Empirical, and Clinical Perspectives* (Springer, 2000), *Adult Development and Aging* (Fourth Edition, 2007), *Working With Custodial Grandparents* (Springer, 2003), *Cultural Changes in Attitudes Toward Death, Dying, and Bereavement* (Springer, 2005), and *Diversity Among Custodial Grandparents* (Springer, 2006). He is Director of Undergraduate Instruction and chairs the doctoral program in Experimental Psychology at UNT, and teaches undergraduate courses in Death and Dying, Developmental Psychology, and Adult Development and Aging, and graduate courses in Gerontological Counseling, Human Development, and Life Span Development.

PATRICIA L. KAMINSKI, PhD, is an Associate Professor in the Department of Psychology's Counseling Program at the University of North Texas. She is a scientist-practitioner with specialized training in developmental psychology who has worked with clients and research participants ranging in age from 1 to 101 years. Dr. Kaminski earned her BA, *magna cum laude,* from Harvard University and her MS and PhD degrees in Psychology from Colorado State University, specializing in Counseling Psychology. She also completed a Postdoctoral Fellowship in Clinical Psychology at the Karl Menninger School of Psychiatry where she co-developed the Parent-Child Interaction Assessment (PCIA), a standardized procedure to observe dyadic interaction across contexts. Dr. Kaminski continued this work by devising scoring systems for the PCIA and PCIA-II to quantify and study relationship quality among caregivers and their children. Her research and clinical interests in caregiver-child relationships have resulted in over 50 professional papers, book chapters, and presentations, most with an emphasis on factors that may hinder or facilitate effective parenting and child adjustment. Her work has appeared in such peer-reviewed journals as *The Gerontologist, Marriage and Family Review,* and the *Bulletin of the Menninger Clinic.* Dr. Kaminski also serves on the Oxford University Press Advisory Panel for Counseling Psychology and is an editorial consultant for numerous peer-reviewed journals. In addition to her roles as researcher and teacher, Dr. Kaminski is clinically active as a practicum supervisor and pro bono counselor at UNT's Psychology Clinic. She is one of the few scientist-practitioners to study the contextual factors and relationship dynamics of custodial grandparents and grandchildren and apply her clinical expertise to understand the specific needs of grandfamilies.

Parenting the Custodial Grandchild

Implications for Clinical Practice

Bert Hayslip, Jr., PhD
Patricia L. Kaminski, PhD
Editors

SPRINGER PUBLISHING COMPANY
NEW YORK

Springer Publishing Company, LLC
11 West 42nd Street
New York, NY 10036
www.springerpub.com

Acquisitions Editor: Sheri W. Sussman
Production Editor: Julia Rosen
Cover design: Joanne E. Honigman
Composition: Apex Publishing, LLC

07   08   09   10/   5   4   3   2   1

Library of Congress Cataloging-in-Publication Data

Parenting the custodial grandchild : implications for clinical practice / [edited by] Bert Hayslip, Jr., Patricia Kaminski.
    p. cm.
  Includes bibliographical references and index.
  ISBN 978-0-8261-1685-7 (alk. paper)
  1. Grandparents as parents.   2. Caregivers.   3. Intergenerational relations.   4. Custody of children.   I. Hayslip, Bert.   II. Kaminski, Patricia.

HQ759.9.P37   2008
306.874'5—dc22   2007051944

Printed in the United States of America by Edwards Brothers, Inc.

To Gail, Stephen, Patrick, and June

BHJ

To my first teachers—my parents, Ruth L. and Norman G. Kaminski.
Any scholarly achievements I attain are inextricably rooted in my parents'
commitment to learning and passion for solving problems that, along with their
exceptional work ethic, they consistently modeled throughout my life.

PLK

Contents

Section 3: Intervention

Contributors

Elizabeth Barton, PhD
Center for Peace and Conflict Studies
Wayne State University
Detroit, MI

Sandra J. Bailey, PhD
Department of Health and
Human Development
Montana State University
Bozeman, MT

Navaz Bhavnagri, PhD
College of Education
Wayne State University
Detroit, MI

Lenora Campbell, DNS
Winston-Salem School of Nursing
Winston-Salem, NC

Penny Dahlen, EdD
Department of Health and
Human Development
Montana State University
Bozeman, MT

Linda Dannison, PhD
College of Education
Western Michigan University
Kalamazoo, MI

Megan L. Dolbin-MacNab, PhD
Department of Human Development
Virginia Polytechnic Institute and
State University
Blacksburg, VA

Jack W. Finney, PhD
Department of Psychology and
College of Science
Virginia Polytechnic Institute and
State University
Blacksburg, VA

Rebecca J. Glover, PhD
Department of Counseling, Human
Development, and Higher Education
University of North Texas
Denton, TX

Catherine Chase Goodman, DSW
Department of Social Work
California State University–Long
Beach
Long Beach, CA

John Hipple, PhD
Counseling and Testing Center
University of North Texas
Denton, TX

Lee Hipple, MSW
Department of Social Work (retired)
Texas Woman's University
Denton, TX

Jane L. Jooste, PhD
Department of Psychology
University of North Texas
Denton, TX

Jennifer K. King, PhD
Counseling and Testing Center
University of North Texas
Denton, TX

Stacey Kolomer, PhD
School of Social Work
University of Georgia
Athens, GA

Bethany L. Letiecq, PhD
Department of Health and
Human Development
Montana State University
Bozeman, MT

Robert J. Maiden, PhD
Department of Psychology
Alfred University
Alfred, NY

Rick Mauderer, MEd
Haltom High School
Haltom City, TX

Phillip McCallion, PhD
State University of New York
(SUNY)
Center for Excellence in
Aging Services
School of Social Welfare
Albany, NY

Mary McNamara, MSSA, LISW
Fairhill Center
Cleveland, OH

Margaret Shandor Miles, PhD
School of Nursing
University of North Carolina at
Chapel Hill
Chapel Hill, NC

Amy R. Murrell, PhD
Department of Psychology
University of North Texas
Denton, TX

Carol M. Musil, PhD
Bolton School of Nursing
Case Western Reserve University
Cleveland, OH

Ross D. Parke, PhD
Department of Psychology
University of California at Riverside
Riverside, CA

Vidya Ramaswamy, PhD
Center for Peace and Conflict
Studies
Wayne State University
Detroit, MI

Rhonda A. Richardson, PhD
College of Education, Health, and
Human Services
Kent State University
Kent, OH

Karen A. Roberto, PhD
Center for Gerontology
Virginia Polytechnic Institute and
State University
Blacksburg, VA

Stacey Rokoff, MSSA, LSW
Fairhill Center
Cleveland, OH

Heather L. Servaty-Seib, PhD
Department of Educational Studies
Purdue University
West Lafayette, IN

Andrea Smith, PhD
College of Education
Western Michigan University
Kalamazoo, MI

Gregory C. Smith, PhD
College of Education, Health, and
Human Services
Kent State University
Kent, OH

Dawn Turek, RN, DNP, CNP
Women's and Children's Health
Center
University Hospitals of Cleveland
Cleveland, OH

Cara Van Voorhis, MSW
School of Social Work
University of Georgia
Athens, GA

Camille B. Warner, PhD
Bolton School of Nursing
Case Western Reserve University
Cleveland, OH

Michael A. Wilkins, BS
Doctoral Student,
Counseling Psychology
Purdue University
West Lafayette, IN

Craig Zuckerman, EdD
Department of Psychology
Saint Bonaventure University
Allegany, NY

Foreword

Grandparents have long played important roles in the lives of their adult children and grandchildren in our own as well as many other cultures. In spite of their recognition in folklore, literature, art, and film, it has only been in the last 3 or 4 decades that grandparents have received the kind of academic scrutiny that other family members—especially mothers—have received for the past century.

A variety of changes in both the wider culture as well as in our theories of development and family adaptation have propelled the issue of grandparenting out of the shadows and into a more prominent place in both academic and social policy debates. Demographic changes including increased life expectancy make adults more likely to be available to assume grandparental roles. The increasing fragility of family arrangements is reflected in increased rates of divorce, and the decreased availability of parents for child care is due, in part, to the greater participation of women in the workforce, and has resulted in grandparents assuming parental roles more frequently. The increased recognition of the cultural variability in the United States, especially the appreciation of kith and kin in African American families, functioning in combination with the rising rate of immigration from places such as Mexico, Central America, and various Asian countries, has challenged the prevailing norm of the isolated nuclear family and reinvigorated the debate about the role of extended family members, including grandparents, in the lives of adult children and their offspring. On the academic side, several theoretical developments have made the study of grandparents and grandparenting more likely and more profitable since these new perspectives provide potentially useful theoretical foundations to guide investigation of this issue. The ecological systems theory of Urie Bronfenbrenner, with its call for viewing families not as isolated but as embedded in a range of nested social contexts, including extended families, set the stage for a serious examination of grandparents as socialization agents who could exert both direct and indirect influence on the development of grandchildren. Second, the rise of life course theory under the intellectual leadership of sociologist Glen Elder and developmental psychologist Paul Baltes, extending the earlier work of Robert Havighurst and Bernice Neugarten with its focus on the consequences of the timing of entry into various family and work roles throughout the life span and the links between individual lives across generations, emphasized the necessity of including grandparents in our theories of socialization. Moreover, this framework has provided a useful heuristic guide for beginning to unravel the complexity of cross-time and cross-generation family relationships, especially the concepts of on- and off-time events and normative and nonnormative change. As the contributors to this volume demonstrate, assuming a parental role in later life as a custodial grandparent is both off time and nonnormative and may, in part, explain the stresses and strains that are commonly found when unexpected demands are thrust upon grandparents. A further contribution to this perspective is its emphasis on the role of historical context in understanding development of family relationships. As seen in many chapters, the cross-time shifts in expectations about children's roles in the family, parents' own definitions of their roles and responsibilities, and the nature of grandparents' roles in different eras remind us of the importance of historical context and of the dynamic and changing nature of these relationships and roles. The current debates are clearly shaped by the specific values of our contemporary society and institutions. What is required is not only a description of the roles at present but the monitoring of how these roles have evolved and how they will shift in the future. Finally, family systems theory, a framework that developed from the family therapy work of Salvador Minuchin and others in the 60s and 70s, with its focus on the dynamic interdependence of individual, dyadic, triadic, and family levels of relationship analysis, has provided a helpful way of conceptualizing possible paths of influence not only within the family but between various family subsystems and extended family members, including grandparents. Together these theoretical perspectives provide useful starting points for understanding the role of grandparenting in the lives of children.

Considerable progress has been made in the last several decades involving movement beyond the initial descriptive stage of work in which the normative roles, contact patterns, and cultural images of grandparents were outlined. First, there is recognition that grandparents influence the physical, mental, and emotional well-being of grandchildren and their parents. Second, the impact of the grandparental role on the older adults in these roles is being documented as well. Third, a wider range of roles that grandparents can play in the lives of their adult children and their offspring has supplemented the initial work in which the supportive, teaching, and playful/recreational roles of noncustodial grandparents were the major focus (Furstenberg & Cherlin, 1988; Kornhaber, 1995).

As an early but lapsed contributor to this literature (Tinsley & Parke, 1984), I feel a little like Rip Van Winkle awakening after a period of solitude to realize how far the field has advanced in the last 25 years. This volume, under the able editorship of Bert Hayslip and Patricia Kaminski, is testimony to the changes that have taken place in the level of sophistication of our conceptualization of the issues, the methods employed, and the increased focus on intervention and education.

Let me briefly note some of these advances. Perhaps most important is the appreciation of the diversity of grandparental roles and responsibilities. Just as the field recognizes the increasing array of nuclear family forms, including single, step, adoptive, and same-gender parent family types, grandparent-headed households have joined the list of new family forms. Moreover, custodial grandparenting assumes a variety of forms, from co-parenting with an adult biological or stepchild, acting as a sole custodial parent for grandchildren, or dual parenting with a spouse. Not only are a range of family forms recognized, but the myriad of circumstances (parental death, incarceration, incapacitation, divorce, etc.) that lead to variations in parenting responsibilities for grandparents are documented as well. In addition, the implications of these variations for the caregiving role of grandparents and the differential effects of various antecedents on the adjustment of children in grandparent custody are outlined.

Diversity is evident not only in the structural arrangements of grandparental households but in the ethnicity of these families as well. Although African American women and to a lesser extent men have often assumed custodial grandparent roles, the number of White and Hispanic American adults in this role is increasing. The historical embrace of extended family arrangements by African Americans, and the relative success of this ethnic group in managing these often-custodial parental roles, is noteworthy and instructive for current cohorts of other cultural groups who are assuming these roles only in recent times. Moreover, in an age of rapid immigration, particularly from Latin regions such as Mexico and Central America, there is a ripe opportunity for members of the majority/host culture to learn from immigrant families with their strong commitment to the centrality of family and especially the role of extended family networks, including grandparents, as support systems.

A major advance is the increased focus on explanatory processes that aid in understanding the factors that account for variations in styles of grandparental parenting, and the impact of such parenting on grandchildren as well as the consequences for older adults who are custodial grandparents. Just as Belsky (1984), in a now-classic statement, argued that the quality of parenting is determined by three sets of factors including the personal resources of the caregivers, the characteristics of the child, and the contextual sources of stress and support, these same factors are useful for understanding variations in custodial grandparenting as well. Processes such as the mental, emotional, and physical health resources of the grandparents themselves, the positive and negative characteristics of the children under care, the social capital as expressed by the quality of the grandparent-grandchild relationship, the quality of the ties with the parents of the custodial grandchild, and the degree of community and social network support, in combination with the internal and external sources of stress, are all documented in this volume as relevant and meaningful processes for explaining grandparental behavior and outcomes.

A further advance is methodological. As the chapters in this volume illustrate, multiple methods are not just useful but necessary to unravel the complexities of grandparental caregiving. Not content to rely on single methods, the contributors use a wide range of both qualitative methods such as case studies and focus groups and quantitative strategies such as closed-ended surveys, structured interviews, standardized questionnaires and tests, and observational methods. Both sets of strategies play important and complementary roles in family research: qualitative approaches provide new insights, hunches, and hypotheses while quantitative methods permit formal testing of these hypotheses. In turn, qualitative work can aid in more accurately interpreting quantitative findings. Sampling strategies have improved as well. The small and unrepresentative samples of several decades ago, although still common and at times useful, are being supplemented by large representative national samples that permit evaluation of intra-cultural as well as social class, age, and regional variations.

In appreciation of the importance of capturing the dynamic and changing nature of grandparenting, cross-sectional designs are being joined by longitudinal designs that permit the evaluation of cross-time, bidirectional links between caregiving and both grandparent and grandchild adjustment. Moreover, the intervention studies that are reviewed in this volume can be viewed as short-term longitudinal studies that can begin to address the critical issue of direction of effects in this area. By altering children's behavior or by modifying grandparents' caregiving patterns, the plausibility of child-to-grandparent or grandparent-to-child effects can be more clearly established. These intervention efforts provide opportunities for theory testing and the evaluation of the reciprocal effects found in nonexperimental studies.

Just as the rest of the social sciences have abandoned deficit models of family functioning in favor of more positive approaches that focus on family strengths, the grandparent field has moved beyond the view of the custodial grandparent as an inferior model of parenting. Instead, as several authors in this volume stress, the strengths perspective with an emphasis on the positive assets of grandparents as custodial caregivers has become more common.

Rather than viewing custodial grandparents as deficient, inept, and struggling, portrayals of custodial grandparents as wise, nurturing, patient, and modeling prosocial behavior are increasingly embraced, a trend that is consistent with the recent rise of the "positive psychology" paradigm. In the same spirit, the potential positive impact of grandparental caregiving on grandparents themselves is being recognized just as recent work has underscored how maternal and paternal investment in the parenting role can increase adult generativity, as Erik Erikson theorized decades ago.

While the positive aspects of custodial grandparenting are being recognized, the negative side of the burdens, stresses, and strains on the well-being of grandparents continues to be a well-documented concern. The field has simply achieved a better balance by recognizing the interplay between risk and loss on the one hand and resilience and gain on the other hand; there is a more realistic and dynamic dialectic and a more mature conceptualization of the issues. The continued recognition of the downside of custodial grandparenting is the engine that drives the search for better intervention and support services for grandparents. In fact, one of the important take-home messages of this volume is the clear and unequivocal need for social and public policies devoted to assisting and supporting custodial grandparents. As chronicled in several chapters, these second-time parents not only play a central role in determining the developmental outcomes of the children in their care, but many barriers limit their effectiveness. The new and promising programs outlined in these pages suggest that the parenting practices of grandparents can be modified; grandchildren, in turn, can benefit; and the mental and physical well-being of the grandparents themselves can be improved. Particularly impressive is the extent to which the programs draw upon earlier basic research and theory as the guide to program development. As a result of this reliance, the programs are much more likely to succeed and in the long-term prove more economical and cost effective, since the program components were selected on the basis of earlier work concerning important determinants of caregiving. Second, as family systems theory suggests, the most successful intervention approaches are likely to be multilevel and include components to address the needs of both the grandparents and the children in their care. Third, as implied by ecological systems approaches and as this volume shows, a variety of contexts beyond the family, such as schools and probably religious and medical institutions, can be used as contexts for intervention. Fourth, the sensitivity of the contributors to the diversity of forms of custodial grandparenting is laudatory and a reminder that intervention programs need to take into account the unique needs of different types of custodial grandparents. Different family structures—single, co-parenting, or married skipped-generation arrangements—may each require common as well as unique interventions. Moreover, parenting girls or boys, toddlers or teens, or children with special needs may require specialized interventions to maximize effectiveness. Fifth, as several authors suggest, appreciation of ethnic variations needs to inform intervention efforts in order to improve their success in both recruitment and program effectiveness. Finally, the contributors stress the importance of rigorous evaluation of intervention efforts, a component that is sometimes neglected in the often well-intentioned but myopic rush to be helpful. The focus on intervention underscores the book's reminder of the malleability of family systems, including custodial grandparent systems, and leaves readers with a sense of optimism and hope about the viability of this new and growing family form.

In the final analysis, the volume is not merely a state-of-the-art report on the recent advances in this area, but an invitation to parents of many generations, researchers, and policy and intervention professionals to support new scholarship and novel intervention and evaluation efforts in this new domain of family life. Through our increased focus on understanding this new form of caregiving, these new repeat caregivers will be better accepted and potentially more effective. In turn, present and future generations of children who are in the care of these adults will benefit along with the caregivers themselves.

Ross D. Parke
November, 2007
University of California, Riverside

REFERENCES

Belsky, J. (1984). Determinants of parenting: A process model. *Child Development, 55,* 83–96.

Furstenberg, F. F., & Cherlin, A. (1988). *The new American grandparent.* New York: Basic Books.

Kornhaber, A. (1995). *Contemporary grandparenting.* Thousand Oaks, CA: Sage.

Tinsley, B. R., & Parke, R. D. (1984). The contemporary impact of the extended family on the nuclear family: Grandparents as support and socialization agents. In M. Lewis (Ed.), *Beyond the dyad* (pp. 161–194). New York: Plenum Press.

Preface

While previous texts targeting grandfamilies have examined custodial grand-parenting in either a generic sense, with regard to efforts at intervention, or with regard to diversity among grandparent caregivers, none has specifically focused upon the essence of what occurs in grandparents' efforts at parenting their grandchildren, as well as explored the nature of these interactions. Indeed, grandparents' views on the adequacy of their parenting skills and the nature of their relationships with their grandchildren are at the heart of many of the difficulties and satisfactions associated with the resumption of the parenting role in middle and later life, and are of central importance in the lives and well-being of both custodial grandparents and their grandchildren.

Parenting the Custodial Grandchild: Implications for Clinical Practice will be of great interest to family counselors, mental health practitioners, educators, school counselors, social workers, psychologists, and social service providers. It approaches the issue of parenting grandchildren from novel theoretical perspectives, presents new empirical data, and most importantly, provides valuable suggestions for therapists who are treating grandparent-grandchild dyads and their families. It is methodologically diverse, relying upon case studies, empirical findings, and national datasets. Additionally, it incorporates longitudinal work and focuses upon grandchildren, two elements that have been absent in research with grandparent caregivers to date.

The volume is organized in the following manner: the first section deals with intergenerational relationships, based on the assumption that parenting custodial grandchildren occurs in this larger context—this section therefore necessarily explores various aspects of such relationships between custodial grandparents and their grandchildren; the second section targets issues specific to parenting among custodial grandparents; and the final section focuses upon interventions, encompassing custodial grandparents and grandparent-grandchild relationships in this respect.

Parenting the Custodial Grandchild: Implications for Clinical Practice defines new areas of understanding pertaining to grandfamilies that are relevant to both researchers and practitioners, for example, dealing with grief and loss, focusing on grandchildren, grandparents' concerns about parenting, perceptions of grandchildren, parenting education, and intergenerational ambivalence, and therefore should provide fertile ground for work regarding these issues, which are so central to the lives of custodial grandparents and their grandchildren.

Bert Hayslip, Jr., and Patricia L. Kaminski
University of North Texas

SECTION 1

Intergenerational Relationships

This section deals with the understanding of factors that influence the larger context in which grandparents parent their grandchildren. Not only do relationships between generations form the backdrop against which grandparents raise their grandchildren, but as most grandparent caregivers will attest, their relationships with both their grandchildren and their adult children influence their roles as caregivers. In this context, this section addresses such questions as: What feelings arise when one takes on the role of grandparent caregiver? How does parenting a grandchild change the physical and mental health of grandparents? In what terms do grandparents perceive their grandchildren? What factors influence such perceptions? How does grandparents' own mental and physical health influence the well-being of their grandchildren?

CHAPTER 1

Ambivalence and Coping Among Custodial Grandparents

Bethany L. Letiecq, Sandra J. Bailey, and Penny Dahlen

INTERGENERATIONAL AMBIVALENCE AND CAREGIVER COPING AMONG CUSTODIAL GRANDPARENTS: IMPLICATIONS FOR CLINICAL INTERVENTION

One of the fastest growing family forms in the United States is grandparent-headed families, in which grandparents are providing the sole primary care of their grandchildren (U.S. Census Bureau, 2000). Absent from these families or on the periphery are the child's biological parents. Parents may be absent or marginally involved in their children's lives for a number of complex reasons including substance abuse, child abuse and neglect, mental illness, or military deployment (Fuller-Thomson, Minkler, & Driver, 1997). While there is a growing body of literature describing this emergent family form and examining the psychological well-being of and stressors experienced by grandparent caregivers (e.g., Bullock, 2004; Caputo, 2001; Hayslip, Jr., Emick, Henderson, & Elias, 2002; Kelley, Whitley, Sipe, & Yorker, 2000; Pruchno & McKenney, 2002), to date there is little research exploring intergenerational relations and the dynamics that emerge when multiple generations converge in the care of children.

Of particular interest when considering intergenerational relations is the concept of ambivalence. Many grandparents likely feel caught between two polarities—the desire to meet the needs of their adult children and their grandchildren (e.g., keeping their grandchildren in the family and thus avoiding foster care placement) on the one hand, and on the other, their reluctance to take on the parental role again while giving up plans for retirement. Because many of these grandfamilies form as a result of familial crisis (Fuller-Thomson et al., 1997), ambivalences may emerge as to what path to take to deal with the crisis. Should the grandparents, adult children, and grandchildren work to regain stability in the family or form a new family structure that will best meet the needs of individuals and family members? Ambivalence may also emerge among other family members, as other adult children and grandchildren in the family system might feel slighted because the grandparents are focusing attention and resources on the adult child in need and his or her offspring. These family members may recognize the urgent need for grandparents to step into the role of surrogate care provider, yet may feel ambivalent about how these shifting roles in the family will affect their lives.

Although it seems likely that many members affiliated with grandfamilies will experience ambivalence, there is little to no research exploring how ambivalence is experienced across generations, and how members of grandfamilies cope with such ambivalences over time. To explore the concept of intergenerational ambivalence, this chapter examines family life history data gathered from 26 grandfamilies where grandparents provided the sole care for their grandchildren. We draw from the recent literature concerning the conceptualization and operationalization of intergenerational ambivalence to guide this work.

CONCEPT OF AMBIVALENCE

The concept of ambivalence has its roots in both psychology and sociology (Lüscher, 2004). Psychological ambivalence has been defined as contradictory states of individuals, such as conflicting emotions or attitudes, or contradictory relationships between intimates (Willson, Shuey, & Elder, 2003). This ambivalence is the result of intrapersonal conflict and individual processes without consideration for social structural influences. As Spitze and Gallant (2004) suggest, psychological ambivalence may develop in part because of one's need for both autonomy and mutual support in one's family and how these conflicting needs change over the life course. Sociological ambivalence links individuals and social structures such that pressures imposed by contradictory demands or norms placed on an individual in a particular social structure (i.e., location, role, or relationship) may result in ambivalent feelings and attitudes (Willson et al., 2003). More recently, the concept of ambivalence has been used intergenerationally to refer to contradictions in relationships between parents and adult offspring (Connidis & McMullin, 2002; Lüscher & Pillemer, 1998; Pillemer & Lüscher, 2004).

Ambivalence as a concept to be used in the study of intergenerational family relations has begun to receive scholarly attention (e.g., Bengston, Giarrusso, Mabry, & Silverstein, 2002; Connidis & McMullin, 2002; Fingerman & Hay, 2004; Lüscher, 2002; Spitze & Gallant, 2004). As noted by Connidis and McMullin, ambivalence is "both a variable feature of structured sets of social relationships and a catalyst for social action" (p. 559). Lüscher (2004) adds that ambivalence should be understood as a consequence of competing perspectives oriented to one and the same object. These competing or polarized perspectives likely exist over time, thus adding a temporal dimension. And finally, it should be noted that intergenerational ambivalence as a concept differs from conflict. In Lüscher's (2002) view, "an awareness of a temporary or enduring irreconcilability is an important feature of ambivalence and a fundamental difference from conflict insofar as [conflicts] have, or can have, definite solutions" (p. 587). Lüscher posits that conflict and harmony may be common ways of dealing with ambivalence, suggesting both positive and negative valences.

OPERATIONALIZATION OF INTERGENERATIONAL AMBIVALENCE

The operationalization of intergenerational ambivalence is in its infancy; however, Lüscher (2002, 2004, 2005) has attempted to operationalize the concept using a two-dimensional model comprised of personal and institutional dimensions. On the personal dimension, relationships are experienced subjectively between two poles, where such contradictions create ambivalence. Lüscher (2002) uses the terms "convergence" or "divergence" to designate the dynamic nature of this personal dimension. On the institutional dimension, polar opposition may emerge between an insistence on a past social form or structure of relationships (referred to as reproduction) and a desire for dramatic change (referred to as innovation).

Lüscher (2005) then combines these polarized two dimensions to create a four-field module representing solidarity, emancipation, atomization, and captivation (see Figure 1.1). Each field can be interpreted as a typical way of coping with ambivalence. Lüscher's latest iteration of the module, which recognizes the dynamic nature of family development over the life course, includes a spiral around the four fields to suggest the possibility of people experiencing different modes of ambivalence as they move through different segments of their lives.

The four-field module, when applied to the lived experiences of grandparents raising grandchildren, can be demonstrated as follows. First, *solidarity* refers to "reliable support or the willingness of the generations to provide each other with services of a not necessarily reimbursable sort" (Lüscher, 2002, p. 589). When faced with ambivalences, family members may feel committed to upholding familial traditions and strive to experience harmony and unity within the family system. When applied to grandfamilies, solidarity may manifest across the generations, such that grandparents may work closely with their adult children to ensure that the grandchildren experience as little upheaval in their lives as possible. In this scenario, all family members likely work together to preserve or reproduce the family system in ways that are familiar and harmonious. The grandparents may maintain their identity as grandparents (rather than taking on the titles of "mom" and "dad") and facilitate relationships between the grandchildren under their care and the grandchildren's parents.

The second field, referred to as *emancipation,* suggests family members act in ways that support mutual emotional attachment (convergence) yet remain open to structural change (innovation). According to Lüscher (2002), relationships between parents and children are organized in such a way that the individual development and personal unfolding of all family members is furthered without losing sight of their mutual interdependence—in other words, the family members "mature reciprocally." When applying this field to grandparents raising their grandchildren, it is likely that grandparents negotiate with their adult children and reach a mutually agreed upon solution as to how the grandchildren will be reared. The grandparents may gain legal custody or adopt their grandchildren and may take on the identity of "mom" and "dad" with the full support of their adult children (i.e., the biological parents of the grandchildren).

Atomization is the third field. Here, the cohesiveness of the family is no longer ensured by their familial ties and histories. As Lüscher (2002) notes, "the concept clarifies the fragmentation of the family unit into its smallest components, specifically the individual family members. Apart from the unalterable fact that the participants are parents and children, they otherwise have very little in common" (p. 589). In grandfamily constellations, atomization may be experienced as family separation, where grandparents and adult children experience conflict and divergence, especially with regard to the grandchildren. Although the family members separate and come into conflict, an awareness of their generational bonds remains.

The remaining field, *captivation,* occurs when family members assert the primacy of the family institution over the claims of individual members, and conserve the institution with reluctance. Lüscher (2002) suggests that moral obligations and moral pressures are used by family members to exert their power. In other words, "one generation (predominantly the parental) attempts by invoking the institutional order to assert claims on the other or to bind it

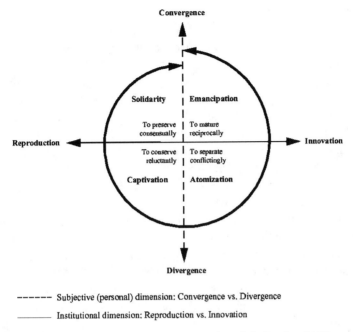

------ Subjective (personal) dimension: Convergence vs. Divergence

—— Institutional dimension: Reproduction vs. Innovation

FIGURE 1.1 Intergenerational ambivalence: A research module (Lüscher, 2005).

in moral terms without, however, basing its demands on a sense of personal solidarity" (p. 589). When considering grandfamilies, captivation may occur when grandparents assert their control over their adult children and take over the parenting of their grandchildren in order to preserve the family institution. The grandparents may attempt to facilitate relationships between their adult children and their grandchildren, yet may feel simultaneously reluctant about those ties.

Guided by Lüscher's (2005) work, this study uses qualitative methods to examine how ambivalences—as well as resolutions to ambivalences—manifest in the lives of grandparents rearing their grandchildren. Given the early stages of the conceptualization and operationalization of intergenerational ambivalence, this study is an exploration of the utility of applying the new framework to the lived experiences of custodial grandparents.

SAMPLE AND METHODS

The participants in this study were 26 grandfamilies who were the sole care providers of their grandchildren. Grandparents ranged in age from 36 to 71 years with a mean age of 56 years. At the time of the interview, 69% (*n* = 18) of the sample were married. The remainder were single, separated, divorced, or widowed. In this study, custodial grandparents reported a range of income levels, with annual household income from less than $15,000 to more than $70,000. Nearly 35% (*n* = 12) of the households received some type of government assistance (e.g., TANF child-only grants, Medicaid, food stamps). Education levels of grandparent caregivers were also diverse, with 4 participants in the sample having less than a high school diploma, 9 having a high school diploma or GED, and 20 having some postsecondary education. Grandparents had been the primary caregivers of their grandchildren for an average of 5.5 years, with a range from 4 months to 24 years. The sample was predominantly White, with the exception of one grandparent who was Native American.

This study conducted family life history interviews. Family life history interviewing is a method where the researcher obtains an individual's life story, offering an opportunity for immersion into the culture and meaning of the subject's world (Goodley, Lawthom, Clough, & Moore, 2004). In this study, family life histories were explored to better understand how the grandfamilies came to be and how the individuals made sense of their family configuration.

Grandparent caregivers were solicited through newspaper ads, local radio stations, and word of mouth. Interested grandparent caregivers made initial contact with a member of the research team, who then inquired to make sure the grandfamily met our inclusion criteria (that custodial grandparents were the primary caregivers of their grandchildren and that no parent was present in the home). Family life history interviews were conducted by two trained interviewers and all interviews were recorded for later transcription. The research team followed a semi-structured interview protocol, which began by generating a genogram of the family system. The interviewers proceeded to probe into the circumstances surrounding the grandparents' role as surrogate parents to their grandchildren. Next, questions turned to family relations and how the grandparents felt about their adult children and their grandchildren. Interviews concluded with questions about resource needs and social supports of the grandfamilies.

Data were analyzed using an analytic induction approach. According to Patton (2002), qualitative research can be deductive in nature when the researcher analyzes data to confirm or verify an existing theory. As Patton notes, qualitative analysis is sometimes at first deductive followed by (or alongside) an inductive process. Here, a researcher begins by examining the data in terms of "theory-derived sensitizing concepts" or applying an existing theoretical framework (p. 454). During this deductive phase, the researcher can simultaneously search for emergent patterns by using an inductive process.

We analyzed the data in light of Lüscher's (2005) four-field module. We also coded the data for emergent patterns of intergenerational ambivalence that fell outside the fields of solidarity, emancipation, atomization, and captivation; however, we only report the findings related to the module here.

RESULTS AND DISCUSSION

Guided by a new module of intergenerational ambivalence (Lüscher, 2005), this study attempted to expand our understanding of the ambivalences experienced by custodial grandparents. Because the new module reflects both agency between individuals and social structures as well as a time dimension, it is both dynamic and multifaceted. Below, each field of ambivalence is taken in turn, using direct quotes from grandparent caregivers to elucidate meanings. All names of participant grandparents have been changed to protect their identities.

Solidarity

As described earlier, solidarity refers to a willingness among the generations to "consensually preserve" the institution of the family and its traditions. While the family may experience ambivalence in how to move forward, the family members try to maintain harmony and unity within the system. An example of solidarity can be seen in the story of one grandfather, James (divorced, age 54), who currently is providing the sole care of his 17-year-old biological son and his grandson (age 8). His grandson was born to his adopted daughter, Sandy, when she was 17 years old. At age 15, Sandy had been diagnosed with bipolar disorder and, as the grandfather states, "with her condition and everything, she certainly was not responsible enough at the time of [my grandson's] birth to raise him, especially alone. There was really just no way." Thus, James and Sandy mutually agreed that he would raise his grandson. Since that decision was made, Sandy has relocated out of state to attend school and work, yet she maintains weekly contact with her son and visits several times a year. The biological father has no contact with his child, but does pay child support.

To date, James has not sought custody or legal guardianship over his grandson; however, he did consider adoption at one point. As he recalls, "I actually have thought about adopting, but his mother, even though she doesn't live here, is very much in his life." He goes on to say, "It's much easier now then it was some years ago. . . . But the last, I'm going to say, three years have been much much better. We have been real close and there is a lot of love there now."

We found five cases where solidarity emerged at some point during the family history, yet this was not a consistent theme in most families' responses to intergenerational ambivalence. James's family story emerged as a particularly poignant example of how we understand solidarity as a concept. This grand-family, when faced with intergenerational ambivalences, revealed a pattern of openness and a willingness to work together to preserve the institution of the family and the best interests of the child. Thus, as Lüscher (2002) notes, solidarity can manifest as a mode for dealing with ambivalences across the generations; however, this mode may be more covert than overt in its expression.

Emancipation

The second field, emancipation, occurs when family members act in ways that support mutual emotional attachment (convergence) yet remain open to institutional change (innovation). Emancipation was the most frequently coded type of intergenerational ambivalence in this study. All but three grand-families related stories about their familial history that revealed emancipation responses to intergenerational ambivalence. Again, not all families were in this field at the time of the interview, but most appeared to have worked toward emancipation as their response to ambivalence in their intergenerational re-lationships at some point in their history (primarily with the parents of the grandchildren in their care).

The concept of emancipation can be seen in the story of one 64-year-old grandmother, Marcy, who with her husband of 37 years has been raising her 14-year-old granddaughter and 10-year-old grandson on and off since birth. Marcy's adult son has a history of drug addiction—he would use for years, get clean for a while, and then "fall off the wagon again." Over the years, the son has maintained legal custody of the children, yet the grandparents have been the primary caregivers. The grandchildren call the grandmother "Mom" and the grandfather "Papa."

In this case, the grandparents have supported their son's role as father and have always maintained that one day—when their son was ready and able—the grandchildren would be returned to his care. In fact, at the time of the interview, the father had been clean for several years and had a stable job. He had been peripherally involved with the care of his children and had been paying some of the household expenses. He also was in a healthy (drug-free) relationship and was planning to get married. The grandmother noted that when he married, the grandchildren would be returned to their father. When asked how she felt about that, the grandmother said, "It's going to be hard for us, you know, it's kind of a bittersweet thing. It's going to be hard to let them go, because they're like ours. We've raised them, and yet, on the other hand, it's the best thing for them, you know, to have [their father] in their life." Reflecting over the years, the grandmother recalled, "You know, somebody said to me once, 'You have a choice,' but we really didn't have a choice. This is family."

Here, the family has been able to support the individual development of its members without, as Lüscher (2002) suggests, losing sight of their mutual interdependence. However, it should be noted that the dimension of time seems to be an important consideration in this case, as it is difficult to discern how supportive the mother was of her adult son while he was "off the wagon." It is likely that this family has moved through different fields of ambivalence over the years (such as captivation or atomization).

Atomization

Atomization, which refers to the loss of family cohesiveness, is exemplified by a conflicted separation. We found six examples of atomization in our sample. This was somewhat surprising given that approximately half of the grandfamilies in our study had an adult child who had a history of substance abuse. This finding may suggest that the grandfamilies in our sample were either not in conflict or had resolved their conflicts and had shifted to other fields in the model. It is also possible that the grandparents were reticent to share previous conflicts in their familial history.

However, a clear example of atomization emerged from the life history of a young married couple, Mike (age 36) and Jane (age 41), who recently adopted Jane's daughter's son Paul (age 5). Jane's daughter (from a previous marriage) suffers from bipolar disorder and had a history of neglecting her son. When Paul was 4 years of age, Jane confronted her daughter, suggesting she allow Jane and Mike to adopt Paul. As Jane relates,

> When she was in such a mental funk . . . I said, 'You know, this is ridiculous. We need to quit this' . . . and she said at the time she was willing to sign him over to us. . . . However we didn't force her into it. We discussed it with her in length before we showed her the papers. . . . And we held the [adoption] papers . . . for a full week [after the papers had been signed by the daughter] . . . because I was very torn because now I have these papers and I have them notarized with her signature on them and I am so heartbroken because I can't even begin to fathom how she could just coldly walk away from this child. . . . And on the fifth day . . . she came up to me and said, 'Did you turn in the paperwork?' and I said, 'No, I have not' and she said, 'You need to' and she walked away.

Shortly thereafter, Jane's daughter accused her of "stealing her son" and argued that what they did was illegal, but Jane feels like they did everything legally. Nevertheless, Jane remains ambivalent about her daughter's relationship with Paul. At the time of the interview, Jane's daughter had not had contact with Paul since the adoption. Jane noted that, on the one hand, she did not want her daughter to come around because Paul seemed to struggle emotionally for days after the visit. But on the other hand, Jane could not understand how her daughter could ignore Paul's birthday. Although the grandmother remains conflicted about her daughter's actions, she also recognizes that maintaining ties with her daughter may not be in the best interests of her adopted son or promote the well-being of the family system. Thus, her resolution was to diverge with her daughter and seek innovative solutions—solutions that radically altered the family structure.

Captivation

Lastly, captivation occurs when family members assert the primacy of the family institution over the wishes of individual members and conserve the institution with reluctance. In this study, we observed five examples of captivation as we coded the family life histories of participant grandfamilies. This field is exemplified by the story of Betsie (age 56) and her husband, Joe, who gained custody of their two granddaughters (ages 6 and 8) when they learned that their daughter-in-law, Jesse, a methamphetamine addict, was neglecting the girls and prostituting them in order to obtain more drugs. Betsie's son, Jack— the girls' biological father—had not been involved with the girls during their early years. Jack also had a history of alcohol and drug addiction and had been recently diagnosed with bipolar disorder. When the granddaughters arrived at Betsie and Joe's house, Jack was focused on getting his life stable, finding the right medication to regulate his disorder, and locating steady work.

However, this family's history is very complicated. When Betsie's granddaughters came to live with her, other family secrets began to emerge. Betsie's other adult children confronted their father Joe about his past alcohol addiction, depression, and physical abuse. And one of Betsie's daughters revealed that Jack had sexually abused her at 5 years of age. Jack then revealed that he too had been sexually abused by his caregiver when he was a toddler.

Clearly, this family had experienced numerous abuses, traumas, and stressors, and after the family secrets surfaced, Betsie's other adult children began to focus their attention on her. The adult children confronted her and asked her to leave her husband and put the granddaughters "up for adoption." But Betsie was reluctant. On the one hand, she understood the concerns of her children and questioned her own ability to care for the granddaughters. On the other, she wanted to preserve her family. As she said, "I was looking at it as one day at a time." Thus, she remained committed to Joe, facilitated weekly visits between Jack and the granddaughters, and, when Jesse got clean and sober, also allowed her to visit the granddaughters. At the time of the interview, Betsie's other adult children did not support any of those decisions, and although they kept in contact with Betsie, they remained distant. Yet Betsie felt that "it just takes time to work through . . . you know, all you can do is just keep saying, 'I'm sorry,' and that's what I've done is to just keep saying, 'I'm sorry.' " Betsie's goal was to preserve the family, even if reluctantly.

As these grandparents grapple with the initial crisis phase of taking in their grandchildren and taking over the surrogate parental function, grandfamilies must cope with their new functions and structures and often must shift their roles, identities, familial boundaries, and resources in order to adapt. It is perhaps not surprising that many intergenerational ambivalences emerge. How grandfamilies cope with ambivalences holds implications for how practitioners might intervene with grandfamilies. We conclude with a number of implications for clinicians working with grandfamilies, including therapists, educators, social workers, and other service providers.

CLINICAL IMPLICATIONS

All of the families in this study experienced ambivalences due to crises that resulted in shifting family structures and roles. Lüscher's module offers clinicians a clearer understanding of the challenges and resilience experienced by these families as they worked to find meaning in their situation and cope with their new family demands. Clinicians can assist these grandfamilies by first understanding the causes or genesis of grandfamily ambivalences, as well as the various pathways by which grandfamilies were formed and the complexity of family relationships. To assist grandparents in understanding family change, clinicians might discuss concepts such as role ambiguity and ambivalence. Clinicians may point out to grandfamilies that they may experience many ambivalences while they work to reestablish family equilibrium and clarify roles within the family system. It is likely that clinicians will need to join with the family in a way that may help reduce crisis and dysfunction and build healthier structures. Joining is a clinical process of bonding with the family so that therapeutic relationships can be built in an authentic manner (Haley, 1976; Minuchin, 1974). After joining, the clinician will want to assess the family in terms of where their ambivalences reside. Is the family converging or diverging? Is the family attempting to reproduce its traditional structure and functions or is it innovating?

Families that cope with ambivalences by converging and reproducing within the system will likely be easier for clinicians to assist in maintaining continuity within the intergenerational structure. When families exhibit solidarity, they often want to preserve the family institution and its traditions. Clinicians working within this frame can best serve the family by focusing on its strengths and finding ways in which the family can preserve its traditions and attachments should crisis happen again. Although solidarity appears to be the most stable field in the module, families in this field may be resistant to change. Clinicians might support families in exploring alternative ways of functioning that might produce more desirable outcomes.

Families in the field of emancipation also can be supported by identifying their strengths as well as their openness for structural and functional change and innovation. Clinicians working with these families might introduce the concept of reframing. Reframing does not always change the familial situation but changes the meaning of the situation for individual family members (Piercy & Sprenkle, 1986). Marcy, in the above case study, is a good example of the ability to reframe a family's situation. Sometimes therapists may need to help clients reframe the change in structure, especially if the family perceives the new structure as deficient or negative. Although families in emancipation are open to change and seem to be more fluid in role transition, the letting go of children by grandparents can also result in grief and loss issues. Therapists can help families express sadness over the loss or change in the system and help families remain connected through the promotion of positive communication skills and connecting rituals.

Families that tend toward divergence have much more difficult dynamics for clinical intervention. Such families often have complicated family histories, dysfunctional dynamics, and conflicted relationships. For families that fall in the atomization field, clinicians may need to understand substance abuse, mental disorders, and intervention strategies to help families cope. Clinicians may assume the role of the family change agent (Lee, Armstrong, & Brydges, 1996). In this role, intervention focuses on total system change. Not only must clinicians be skilled in interventions, but they need to be tolerant of the amount of time it takes to integrate changes, which can require an incredible amount of patience, persistence, and courage by the clinician.

Families that fall into the captivation field are more intolerable to change because they value the institution over the individual differences of family members. For families that have complicated abuse histories and mental disorders, the clinician will need to work slowly to break family secrets and create safety for all members. Because of the dominance of the institution and closed system, clinicians' abilities to join in the system may be delayed and interventions may be very slow. Because abusers and victims may be in the same family system, there need to be safeguards in place so that the abuse will not continue. Clinicians must also act ethically and report abuse to social services.

Intervening with grandparents rearing grandchildren likely poses many challenges for clinicians regardless of where the family is located in Lüscher's (2005) module. However, understanding the intergenerational ambivalences that emerge in grandfamily constellations may be useful as clinicians work to support healthy family functioning and promote positive adaptations to familial crises and change.

REFERENCES

Bengston, V., Giarrusso, R., Mabry, J. B., & Silverstein, M. (2002). Solidarity, conflict, and ambivalence: Complementary or competing perspectives on intergenerational relationships? *Journal of Marriage and Family, 64,* 568–576.

Bullock, K. (2004). The changing role of grandparents in rural families: The results of an exploratory study in southeastern North Carolina. *Families in Society: The Journal of Contemporary Human Services, 85,* 45–54.

Caputo, R. K. (2001). Depression and health among grandmothers co-residing with grandchildren in two cohorts of women. *Families in Society: The Journal of Contemporary Human Services, 82,* 473.

Connidis, I. A., & McMullin, J. A. (2002). Sociological ambivalence and family ties: A critical perspective. *Journal of Marriage and Family, 64,* 558–567.

Fingerman, K. L., & Hay, E. (2004). Intergenerational ambivalence in the context of the larger social network. In K. Pillemer & K. Lüscher (Eds.), *Intergenerational ambivalences: New perspectives on parent-child relations in later life* (pp. 133–151). Amsterdam: Elsevier.

Fuller-Thomson, E., Minkler, M., & Driver, D. (1997). A profile of grandparents raising grandchildren in the United States. *The Gerontologist, 37,* 406–411.

Goodley, D., Lawthom, R., Clough, P., & Moore, M. (2004). *Researching life stories: Method, theory, and analyses in a biographical age.* London: Routledge.

Haley, J. (1976). *Problem solving therapy.* San Francisco: Jossey-Bass.

Hayslip, B., Jr., Emick, M. A., Henderson, C. E., & Elias, K. (2002). Temporal variations in the experience of custodial grandparenting: A short-term longitudinal study. *The Journal of Applied Gerontology, 21*(2), 139–156.

Kelley, S. J., Whitley, D., Sipe, T. A., & Yorker, B. C. (2000). Psychological distress in grandmother kinship care providers: The role of resources, social support, and physical health. *Child Abuse and Neglect, 24*(3), 311–321.

Lee, C. C., Armstrong, K. L., & Bridges, J. L. (1996). The challenges of a diverse society: Counseling for mutual respect and understanding. *Counseling and Human Development 28*(5), 1–8.

Lüscher, K. (2002). Intergenerational ambivalence: Further steps in theory and research. *Journal of Marriage and Family, 64,* 585–593.

Lüscher, K. (2004). Conceptualizing and uncovering intergenerational ambivalence. In K. Pillemer & K. Lüscher (Eds.), *Intergenerational ambivalences: New perspectives on parent-child relations in later life* (pp. 23–62). Amsterdam: Elsevier.

Lüscher, K. (2005). Looking at ambivalences: The contribution of a "new-old" view of intergenerational relations to the study of the life course. *Advances in Life Course Research, 10,* 95–131.

Lüscher, K., & Pillemer, K. (1998). Intergenerational ambivalence: A new approach to the study of parent-child relations in later life. *Journal of Marriage and the Family, 60,* 413–425.

Minuchin, S. (1974). *Families and family therapy.* Cambridge, MA: Harvard University Press.

Patton, M. Q. (2002). *Qualitative research and evaluation methods* (3rd ed.). Thousand Oaks, CA: Sage.

Piercy, F. P., & Sprenkle, D. H. (1986). *Family therapy sourcebook.* New York: Guilford.

Pillemer, K. & Lüscher, K. (Eds.). (2004). *Intergenerational ambivalences: New perspectives on parent-child relations in later life.* Amsterdam: Elsevier.

Pruchno, R. A., & McKenney, D. (2002). Psychological well-being of black and white grandmothers raising grandchildren: Examination of a two-factor model. *Journal of Gerontology: Psychological Sciences, 57B*(5), 444–452.

Spitze, G., & Gallant, M. P. (2004). "The bitter with the sweet": Older adults' strategies for handling ambivalence in relations with their adult children. *Research on Aging, 26*(4), 387–412.

U.S. Census Bureau. (2000). *Profile of selected social characteristics: 2000.* Washington, DC: Author.

Willson, A. E., Shuey, K. M., & Elder, G. H. (2003). Ambivalence in the relationship of adult children to aging parents and in-laws. *Journal of Marriage and Family, 65*(4), 1055–1072.

CHAPTER 2

The Adjustment of Children and Grandparent Caregivers in Grandparent-Headed Families

Jane L. Jooste, Bert Hayslip, Jr., and Gregory C. Smith

Given the diversity among custodial grandparents (Hayslip & Hicks Patrick, 2006), it would not be surprising to find the influences on grandparent caregivers and those of their grandchildren to be multidimensional in nature. In this chapter, we explore the roles that ethnicity, family structure, and the developmental level of the grandchild play in impacting both caregiver and grandchild adjustment, key factors that impact the parenting demands faced by such grandparents in the context of raising their grandchildren.

THE ROLE OF ETHNICITY AMONG GRANDPARENT CAREGIVERS

Custodial grandparents range widely in age, health, economic levels, family structures, and ethnicities. Indeed, it is possible that differences in the family structure of grandparent-headed households may affect a grandchild's well-being (Casper & Bryson, 1998). The typical grandparent caregiver is a White married woman living above the poverty line (Fuller-Thomson, Minkler, & Driver, 1997). However, being African American (and single and living in poverty) increases the odds of becoming a grandparent caregiver (Roe & Minkler, 1998–1999). Fuller-Thomson and Minkler (2000) reported that African

17

Americans had 83% higher odds of being a grandparent caregiver than respondents from other races, while the majority of caregivers (62%) are non-Hispanic White.

Grandparent-headed families from different ethnic groups are likely to have varied expectations, traditions, and experiences (Dolbin-MacNab & Targ, 2003). While White American culture emphasizes individuality and democracy, African American and Hispanic cultures place much more emphasis on the family and are more accepting of extended family models. In this respect, Pruchno and McKenney (2002) reported that the caregiving role has greater centrality for African American grandmothers than White grandmothers, and Goodman and Silverstein (2001) reported that the African American grandmothers demonstrated greater life satisfaction and lower negative effect than either Hispanic or White grandmothers.

EDUCATION, SOCIOECONOMIC STATUS, AND GRANDPARENT AGE

While it is clear that ethnicity exerts a considerable influence in how families may adjust to being headed by a grandparent, the well-being of African American and Hispanic families is also likely to be influenced by lower income and less education. Moreover, a grandparent's age may be influenced in this respect. Younger grandparents appear to have poorer psychological well-being outcomes such as depression, while older grandparents tend to struggle more with their physical health. Concerning gender, grandmothers appear to be more at risk for depression than grandfathers, though very little is known about the experiences of grandfather caregivers.

THE GRANDCHILD'S DEVELOPMENTAL LEVEL

The age of the grandchild is also likely to be a factor in the adjustment of grandparent-headed households. Sawyer and Dubowitz (1994) found that those who entered kinship care as adolescents did better on math and reading tests than children who had entered kinship care before first grade. This suggests that the age at which a grandchild enters into the care of a grandparent may affect subsequent adjustment, at least in terms of educational outcomes, for the grandchild. One might reasonably expect that a child who joins a grandparent-headed household at birth may experience fewer adjustment difficulties than, for example, an older child who may have to change homes and schools in addition to experiencing the loss of a parent caregiver. From the grandparent's perspective, however, an infant requiring intensive round-the-clock care may be more demanding and taxing to care for than a school-aged child who is out of the house for a good deal of the day. While Hayslip and Kaminski (2006) have suggested that the relative age of both grandparent (see above) and grandchild is likely to affect the caregiving relationship (and thus the grandchild's subsequent development), there is a lack of research exploring these relationships or focusing on the developmental concerns of custodial grandchildren.

SCHOOL-RELATED DIFFICULTIES

Related to the grandchild's developmental level, grandchildren raised by grandparents may also manifest emotional, behavioral, and academic difficulties in their school environment (Edwards, 1998). Edwards reports a lack of communication between teachers and grandparent caregivers, which might exacerbate the difficulties of children in grandparent-headed households. Silverstein and Vehvilainen (2000) note that schools have changed a great deal since the grandparents' own children were in school, and they may not be aware of many of the resources available to their grandchildren. Edwards (2006) found that significantly more children raised by grandparents than children raised by parents demonstrated overall psychopathology. Silverstein and Vehvilainen (2000) found that a third of the grandparents they studied reported that their grandchildren needed to change schools when they moved in with them, suggesting that relocation may be a contributing factor to the well-being of children living with grandparents. In this study, 42% of such grandchildren had special needs, including learning disabilities, ADHD, depression, or developmental delays.

FAMILY STRUCTURE

Differences in the family structure of grandparent-headed households may also be related to the outcomes for grandparents and their grandchildren. Three-generation (or more) families, where grandparents are co-parenting, are likely to have special needs that differ from skipped-generation families. Stresses for co-parenting families could include role conflicts over the extent of shared parenting, in addition to conflict over child-rearing and parenting techniques themselves. Jendrek (1994) suggested that since the supplemental caregiver's role is less defined, these grandparents may experience stress related to their role ambivalence.

Overall, it seems that children in grandparent-headed households, like those in kinship families, do exhibit some difficulties in physical and psychological well-being. However, given the absence of data that considers their pre-grandparent caregiving arrangements, it is difficult to determine whether their difficulties might originate in their family of origin, the circumstances surrounding their transition to grandparent caregiving, or from actually residing with their grandparents. Some behavioral problems in grandchildren, for example, may be related to the family sociodemographic factors (Hayslip, Shore, & Henderson, 2000), and in this respect, Pinson-Millburn, Fabian, Schlossberg, and Pyle (1996) suggest that grandparent caregivers will provide the type of nurturance to offset some of the risk, albeit at a cost to their own well-being. Hayslip et al. (2000) found that having sought professional help for the grandchild was related to overall problem severity. Greater perceived overall problem grandchild severity was associated with poorer grandparent health, as well as the grandparent's desire to be a better parent and their personal obligation to raise the grandchild.

PURPOSE OF THE PRESENT STUDY

The present study, using a large national sample and various measures of well-being, including parental involvement, parental efficacy, and grandchild mental health, seeks to identify vulnerable subgroups of custodial grandchildren and their grandparent caregivers and the extent of their difficulties, in order to better inform agencies and social policy makers as to which groups are more likely to require what types of resources and interventions. This study uses an existing large national database, the National Survey of America's Families (NSAF), to describe the characteristics of grandparent-headed households in the context of comparing the differences in well-being of grandchildren and grandparent caregivers across several independent variables, including family type, ethnicity, gender, and age. While there have been studies to address the well-being of custodial and co-parenting grandparents in culturally diverse families (Goodman & Silverstein, 2002), to date there has been little focus on the well-being of children raised in differently structured and ethnically diverse grandparent-headed households, and few studies considering a variety of antecedents to the well-being of both grandparent caregivers and their grandchildren.

METHOD

This study used two of three waves of data, both independent samples, collected by the NSAF in 1997 and 2002. Given potential historical effects, they were analyzed separately. Overall, the 1997 and 2002 samples can be considered biased in favor of lower-income households, a disadvantage in that the sample cannot be considered truly representative of all households. However, the advantage of targeting lower-income households is that these are typically the households most at risk in terms of well-being and would thus be the households more likely to benefit from suggested interventions arising out of the conclusions and recommendations of a study such as this.

Independent Variables

Caregivers answered questions related to the sample child, family, and household. Where there were two focal children in the household, the caregiver was often the same person for both children, but this was not always the case. Four different family structures were identified in this study. These included traditional two-parent intact families, skipped-generation families with no parent present, co-parented families, and single-parent families, coded by the NSAF from responses to the family roster in Section D of the NSAF questionnaire. In order to identify the four family types used here, participants were categorized as belonging to traditional families if the biological child lived with two parents, while single-parent families were identified if the biological child lived with a single parent. Skipped-generation families were identified if the grandchild lived with no parent present and was cared for solely by the grandparent, and co-parenting families were identified if the grandchild lived with a single grandparent or in a blended family. The final composition of family type, upon which the statistical analyses were performed for this study, is presented in the table below.

The responses of participants of three different ethnicities were studied: White, African American, and Hispanic. Ethnicity was defined in the data set

TABLE 2.1 Family Type Sample Sizes for 1997 and 2002 NSAF Participants

Family Type	1997		2002	
	Original Sample	Random Sample	Original Sample	Random Sample
Traditional	19,412	610	20,776	604
Co-parenting	450	450	446	446
Skipped Generation	802	802	806	806
Single Parent	9,990	587	8,294	591
Total:	29,932	2,449	30,322	2,447

by questions that asked the caregiver to identify whether they were of Spanish or Hispanic origin, in addition to asking them their race. Focal children fell into one of three age categories: 0 to 5 years, 6 to 11 years, or 12 to 17 years. Different well-being-related questions were asked for differing age categories, which depended in part on school-related factors that applied in different ways to the two older groups of children.

Dependent Variables

Caregiver Mental Health

The NSAF questionnaire assesses caregiver mental health by means of a five-item mental health scale, the Mental Health Inventory (MHI-5; Urban Institute, 1999). The five items on the MHI-5 asked caregivers how often in the past month they had (a) been a very nervous person, (b) felt calm and peaceful, (c) felt downhearted and blue, (d) been a happy person, and (e) felt so down in the dumps that nothing could cheer them up. For each item, the caregiver was asked to indicate whether they felt this way *all of the time* (scored 1), *most of the time* (scored 2), *some of the time* (scored 3), or *none of the time* (scored 4). For the purposes of this study, two of the MHI-5 items (b and d) were reverse scored and then scores for all five items were summed to give a final score to represent caregiver mental health, with higher scores indicative of better mental health. The reliability coefficient (alpha) for the 1997 sample on this measure was .81, while the alpha for the 2002 sample was .83.

Caregiver Parental Aggravation

The NSAF questionnaire incorporated a four-item parental aggravation scale—addressing the negative impact of the child's behavior on the caregiver—that was adapted from a component of the National Evaluation of Welfare-to-Work Strategies (NEWWS; Urban Institute, 1999). The four items asked caregivers how often in the past month they had felt their child was much harder to care for than most, that their child did things that really bothered them a lot, that they were giving up more of their lives to meet their child's needs than ever expected, and that they were angry with their child. For each item, the caregiver was asked to indicate whether they felt this way *all of the time, most of the time, some of the time,* or *none of the time.* Respondents' scores were summed to create a scaled score ranging from 4 to 16, with lower scores indicative of a greater negative impact. The reliability for the 1997 sample was .67, while the alpha value for the 2002 sample was .65.

Child's Behavior Problems

The items on the NSAF questionnaire that addressed the behavioral and emotional problems of children were developed for the National Health Interview Survey (NHIS; Urban Institute, 1999). The caregiver of each child aged 6 and up was asked to indicate the extent to which, during the past month, the child did not get along with other kids, could not concentrate or pay attention for long, and had been unhappy, sad, or depressed. These items were scored as *often true* (score of 1), *sometimes true* (score of 2), or *never true* (score of 3). In addition to these questions, the caregivers of children aged 6 to 11 years were asked to indicate whether the child felt worthless or inferior, had been nervous, high strung, or tense, or acted too young for his or her age. The most knowledgeable adults (MKAs) for children aged 12 to 17 years were asked whether the child had trouble sleeping, lied or cheated, or did poorly at schoolwork. All the responses were summed for each child, with a lower score indicating greater behavioral and emotional problems. Alpha values for the measure for children aged 6 to 11 years were .75 for the 1997 sample and .76 for the 2002 sample. Alpha values for the measure for children aged 12 to 17 years were .77 for the 1997 sample and .73 for the 2002 sample.

Child's School Engagement

Four items on the NSAF questionnaire addressed the focal child's school engagement. Respondents of children aged from 6 to 17 years were asked to describe whether the child cared about doing well in school, only worked on schoolwork when forced to, did just enough schoolwork to get by, and always did homework, using the response categories *all of the time*, *most of the time*, *some of the time*, or *none of the time*. Responses were summed to create scale scores that ranged from 4 to 16, where higher scores indicated greater school engagement (Urban Institute, 1999). The reliability coefficient for this measure was .74 for the 1997 sample and .71 for the 2002 sample.

RESULTS

Caregiver Mental Health

Main Effect for Family Type on Caregiver Mental Health

A one-way analysis of covariance (ANCOVA), with family income and caregiver education as covariates, was carried out for the 1997 sample. There was a significant main effect for family type on caregiver mental health

$F(3, 2356) = 6.91$, $p < .05$. Traditional families ($M_{adj} = 15.92$; $SD = 2.46$) were found to have significantly better mental heath scores than those of co-parenting families ($M_{adj} = 15.38$; $SD = 2.86$), skipped-generation families ($M_{adj} = 15.36$; $SD = 3.02$), and single-parent families ($M_{adj} = 15.17$; $SD = 2.90$). The three remaining family types did not differ from one another. A similar main effect for family type on caregiver mental health was found for the 2002 sample $F(3, 2375) = 12.27$, $p < .05$. For this sample, traditional families ($M_{adj} = 16.09$; $SD = 2.33$) were found to have significantly better mental heath scores than those of co-parenting families ($M_{adj} = 15.65$; $SD = 2.82$), skipped-generation families ($M_{adj} = 15.61$; $SD = 3.07$), and single-parent families ($M_{adj} = 15.04$; $SD = 3.07$). Further, co-parenting and skipped-generation family caregivers (while not significantly different from each other) reported better mental health scores than the single parents.

Interaction of Family Type and Ethnicity on Caregiver Mental Health

There was an interaction in the 1997 sample for family type and ethnicity on caregiver mental health $F(6, 2271) = 2.45$, $p < .05$ (see Figure 2.1).

Post hoc analysis indicated that an effect was found for the White families $F(3, 1184) = 3.55$, $p < .05$, with caregiver mental health being better in White traditional families than White single-parent families. White skipped-generation families also reported better caregiver mental health than the White single-parent families. No differences between White co-parenting families and other family types emerged, and no other differences between the White family types were found. For African American families, all caregiver mental health scores were similar across family type. For Hispanic families $F(3, 363) = 7.25$, $p < .05$, post hoc tests indicated

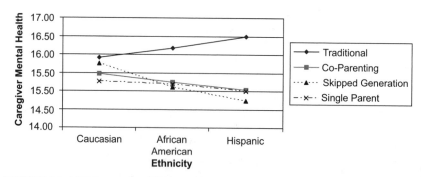

FIGURE 2.1 1997 interaction of family type and ethnicity on caregiver mental health.

that Hispanic traditional families had higher well-being than Hispanic co-parenting families, Hispanic skipped-generation families, and Hispanic single-parent families. The latter three groups were similar in this respect.

Interaction of Family Type and Caregiver Gender on Caregiver Mental Health

There was an interaction for the 1997 sample for caregiver gender and family type on caregiver mental health $F(3, 2352) = 4.05$, $p < .05$ (see Figure 2.2).

Post hoc analyses indicated that an effect for family type was found for female caregivers $F(3, 2063) = 7.57$, $p < .05$ but not for male caregivers, wherein caregiver mental health was better for the female caregivers in traditional families as compared to female caregivers in co-parenting families, skipped-generation families, or single-parent families. No other differences in caregiver mental health between family types emerged.

There was also an interaction for the 2002 sample for family type and caregiver gender on caregiver mental health $F(3, 2371) = 3.46$, $p < .05$ (see Figure 2.3).

Post hoc tests indicated that an effect for family type was found for both female caregivers $F(3, 2049) = 11.33$, $p < .05$ and male caregivers $F(3, 320) = 2.926$, $p < .05$, with caregiver mental health being better for the 2002 female caregivers in traditional families as compared to female caregivers in

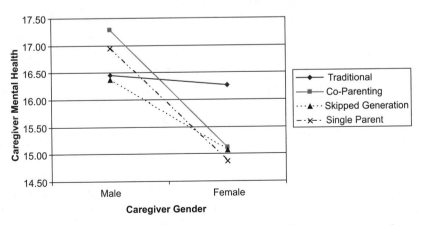

FIGURE 2.2 1997 interaction of family type and caregiver gender on caregiver mental health

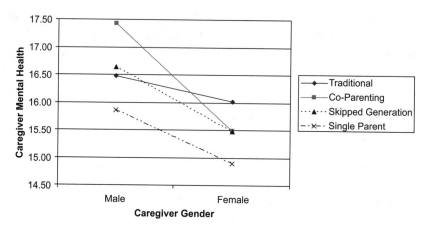

FIGURE 2.3 2002 interaction of family type and caregiver gender on caregiver mental health.

co-parenting families, skipped-generation families, or single-parent families. In addition, female caregivers of co-parenting and skipped-generation families reported better mental health than female single parents. For the 2002 male caregivers, caregiver mental health was better for the male caregivers in co-parenting families as compared to male caregivers in single-parent families.

Caregiver Aggravation

Main Effect for Family Type on Caregiver Aggravation

For the 1997 sample, there was a significant main effect for family type on caregiver aggravation $F(3, 2355) = 8.98$, $p < .05$. Traditional families were found to have less caregiver aggravation than those of co-parenting families, skipped-generation families, and single-parent families. In addition, skipped-generation caregivers reported greater caregiver aggravation than both the co-parenting and single-parent caregivers. There was no difference in reported caregiver aggravation between co-parenting and single-parent caregivers. For the 2002 sample, there was also a main effect for family type on caregiver aggravation $F(3, 2366) = 9.92$, $p < .05$. Traditional families were found to have higher scores, indicating less negative impact of caregiver aggravation, than those of skipped-generation families and single-parent families. In addition, co-parenting families demonstrated less negative impact of caregiver aggravation than the skipped-generation families. The skipped-generation caregivers also reported greater caregiver aggravation than the single-parent caregivers.

Behavior Problems in 6- to 11-Year-Olds

Main Effect for Family Type on Behavior Problems
in 6- to 11-Year-Olds

There was a main effect in the 1997 sample for family type on behavior problems in the 6- to 11-year-old age category $F(3,694) = 5.17$, $p < .05$, wherein traditional families ($M_{adj} = 16.02$; $SD = 1.95$) experienced significantly fewer behavioral problems regarding 6- to 11-year-olds as compared to skipped-generation families ($M_{adj} = 15.15$; $SD = 2.44$). Further, skipped-generation families experienced more behavioral problems in 6- to 11-year-olds than did single-parent families ($M_{adj} = 15.67$; $SD = 2.34$). Co-parenting families ($M_{adj} = 15.53$; $SD = 2.26$) did not differ from the other family types in terms of behavioral problems reported for 6- to 11-year-olds. In the 2002 sample, family type was also found to have a significant main effect on behavioral problems in 6- to 11-year-olds, $F(3, 679) = 2.60$, $p < .05$, wherein caregivers in traditional families reported fewer behavioral difficulties in the 6- to 11-year-olds that they parented ($M_{adj} = 15.91$; $SD = 2.19$) than those of skipped-generation families ($M_{adj} = 15.25$; $SD = 2.50$) and single-parent families ($M_{adj} = 15.40$; $SD = 2.36$), but not when compared to co-parenting families ($M_{adj} = 15.66$; $SD = 2.34$).

Behavior Problems in 12- to 17-Year-Olds

Main Effect for Family Type on Behavior Problems
in 12- to 17-Year-Olds

There was a main effect in the 1997 sample for family type on behavior problems in the 12- to 17-year-old age category $F(3, 574) = 4.50$, $p < .05$, where traditional families ($M_{adj} = 16.21$; $SD = 2.07$) experienced fewer behavioral problems in the 12- to 17-year-old age category as compared to either co-parenting families ($M_{adj} = 14.92$; $SD = 2.60$), skipped-generation families ($M_{adj} = 15.41$; $SD = 2.43$), or single-parent families ($M_{adj} = 15.32$; $SD = 2.59$). In the 2002 sample, family type was also found to be related to behavioral problems in 12- to 17-year-olds $F(3, 655) = 3.917$, $p < .05$, where caregivers in traditional families reported fewer behavioral difficulties in the 12- to 17-year-olds that they parented ($M_{adj} = 15.95$; $SD = 2.16$) than those of skipped-generation families ($M_{adj} = 15.23$; $SD = 2.37$) and single-parent families ($M_{adj} = 15.36$; $SD = 2.19$), but not when compared to co-parenting families ($M_{adj} = 16.10$; $SD = 2.06$). Also, co-parenting families reported fewer behavioral problems in 12- to 17-year-olds than did skipped-generation families.

Interaction of Family Type and Ethnicity on Behavior Problems in 12- to 17-Year-Olds

There was an interaction in the 1997 sample for ethnicity and family type on behavior problems reported by caregivers for the 12- to 17-year-old age group $F(6, 556) = 3.25, p < .05$ (see Figure 2.4).

An effect was found for the White families $F(3, 321) = 4.14, p < .05$, where fewer behavioral problems were reported in White traditional families for children aged 12 to 17 years than in White co-parenting families, White skipped-generation families, or White single-parent families.

Interaction of Family Type and Caregiver Gender on Behavior Problems in 12- to 17-Year-Olds

There was an interaction in the 2002 sample for family type and caregiver gender on behavior problems reported by caregivers for the 12- to 17-year-old age group $F(3, 651) = 3.62, p < .05$ (see Figure 2.5).

An effect for family type was found for female caregivers $F(3, 542) = 4.15$, $p < .05$, where behavioral problems (in 12- to 17-year-olds) were reported to be less serious by female caregivers in traditional families as compared to female caregivers in skipped-generation families.

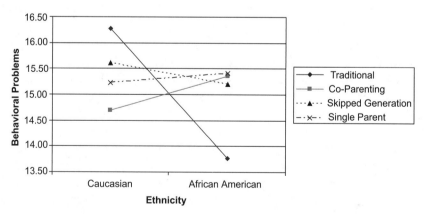

FIGURE 2.4 1997 interaction of family type and ethnicity on behavior problems (12- to 17-year-olds).

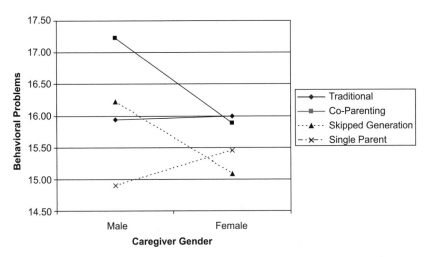

FIGURE 2.5 2002 interaction of family type and caregiver gender on behavior problems (12- to 17-year-olds).

DISCUSSION

Caregiver Mental Health

For both the 1997 and 2002 samples, caregivers in traditional families reported better mental health than did caregivers from the co-parenting, skipped-generation, and single-parent families. For the 1997 sample, no differences were noted between these three latter types of families. In the 2002 sample, however, there were additional differences in that both the co-parenting and skipped-generation caregivers (while not significantly different from each other) reported better mental health than the single-parent caregivers.

This may suggest that there are elements of family structure that appear to favor the mental health of caregivers in traditional families over the other family types and, for the 2002 sample, particularly disadvantage the single parents. One likely explanation may lie in the availability of social support received by the caregivers, which tends to have an impact on one's emotional health (i.e., Antonucci, 2001). The two parents of a traditional family are likely to have a greater convoy of support together than would a single parent. Parents in a traditional family would likely also have each other as a source of support, which would not be the case for single parents. Married co-parenting and skipped-generation caregivers would likely have some of the same advantages of social support as the traditional family caregivers. The co-parenting and skipped-generation households, however, may also have lost some of their support networks during the process of becoming caregivers again, which could explain some of the mental health advantage of traditional parents over the co-parenting and skipped-generation caregivers.

It was noted that differences in caregiver mental health emerged for the 2002 sample that were not evident in the 1997 sample, that is, in 2002, co-parenting and skipped-generation caregivers reported better mental health than single parents. The fact that the 1997 and 2002 family type comparisons were not parallel suggests an historical shift that has magnified the family type differences between single parents and co-parenting or skipped-generation caregivers. It is possible that changes in the environment (i.e., welfare, political and economic changes) may have differentially impacted on caregivers of single-parent families, as compared to grandparent caregivers. Caregivers in co-parenting and skipped-generation families, for example, may have become increasingly aware of or more able to tap into community resources such as support groups or parenting information. Perhaps the custodial grandparent is viewed more normatively. Single parents, on the other hand, may simply not have had the time to explore potential resources in a similar manner to their peers in other family types. In recent years, an increasing number of supports appear to have been developed and directed toward assisting cus-todial grandparents. In November 2000, for example, the National Family Caregiver Support Program (NFCSP) was enacted into law. The NFCSP was designed to provide support to caregivers of those aged 60 and over, as well as to grandparents and older relatives aged 60 and older who raise children (Generations United, 2003a). Moreover, in 2001, the National Center on Grandparents Raising Grandchildren was established in order to support grandparent-headed families and inform service professionals, policy makers, and the general public on the social and health service issues confronted by grandparents (Whitely, n.d.).

Regarding the interaction between family type and ethnicity for the 1997 sample, for White families, parents in traditional families reported better mental health than single parents. White grandparent caregivers in skipped-generation families also reported better mental health than White single par-ents. Whites tend not to view their family of origin as a child-rearing resource. The 1997 White single parents may thus have experienced less support and guidance, which led to poorer mental health than the White skipped-generation grandparent caregivers, who had demonstrated their ability to ex-tend their traditional family boundaries by raising their grandchildren. For African American families, there were no reported differences in caregiver mental health between different family types for either the 1997 or 2002 samples. As expected, these African American families may have adjusted to the more normative role of surrogate parenting (Brown & Mars, 2000). Recent research by Stevenson, Henderson, and Baugh (2007) appears to support this suggestion of adjustment, as they reported that African American grandmothers parenting grandchildren demonstrated resiliency and used a wide range of formal and informal social support resources to address family needs.

For the 1997 sample, Hispanic parents in traditional families reported better mental health than either Hispanic grandparent caregivers (of co-parenting or skipped-generation households) or Hispanic single-parent families. It would appear that *familismo* applied mainly to traditionally structured Hispanic families to assist in maintaining better caregiver mental health. Accordingly, Hispanic caregivers who were not embedded in a traditional family structure may have experienced more stigma or stress in regards to their family differences and thus reported poorer mental health than the caregivers in traditional families. As these results were not replicated in the 2002 sample, a potential historical shift in this respect may suggest that the culturally defined family values such as *familismo* may not always act as a protective factor in the maintenance of mental health for Hispanic families.

In the 1997 sample, an interaction of family type and caregiver gender on caregiver mental health was found in that there were differences for female caregivers, supporting the findings of Burnette (1999) that being female is a risk factor for the health of caregivers. The 1997 female caregivers in traditional families reported better mental health than their counterparts in the co-parenting, skipped-generation, and single-parent families. Since rearing children has historically been regarded as a female role that occurs in the context of a traditionally structured family, the 1997 female caregivers in the nontraditional families may have generally felt less overall support, less competent, and under more pressure from assuming a less normative role than mothers in traditionally structured families.

These findings were partly replicated for the 2002 sample in that the female caregivers of traditional families reported better mental health than female caregivers of co-parenting, skipped-generation, and single-parent families. It may be that social support mitigates some stress for traditional caregivers and to a lesser extent for grandparent caregivers (in both the co-parenting and skipped-generation families) as compared to single parents; this would also apply to female caregivers, where female caregivers of both co-parenting and skipped-generation families reported better mental health than female single parents, suggesting that an historical shift may have occurred in respect to caregiver mental health. Female single parents may not have as much access to community resources and interventions, or not perceive as much support, compared to female caregivers in the other family types.

A further difference emerged for the 2002 sample; male caregivers in co-parenting families reported better mental health than caregivers in skipped-generation families. It may be easier for males to accept their caregiving role in a co-parenting situation, where they have the presence of at least one of the child's parents in the family, as opposed to male caregivers in a skipped-generation household, where they may experience a compounded effect of the nonnormative roles of grandparent caregiver and male caregiver, without the presence of the child's parent. In this respect as well, an historical shift has possibly taken place, in that increased community supports, resources, and interventions are more available for more families, with the exception of single-parent families.

Caregiver Aggravation

Caregiver aggravation was found to be worse for caregivers in skipped-generation families as compared to caregivers in the traditional, co-parenting, or single-parent families. This is consistent with earlier work suggesting that skipped-generation caregivers reported more difficult interactions with their grandchildren than co-parenting caregivers (Musil & Standing, 2005) and that conflict between skipped-generation caregivers and their focal grandchildren was higher than in co-parenting households (Goodman & Silverstein, 2002). Goodman and Silverstein (2002) argue that co-parenting grandparents more often assume care to assist their adult children financially, assist working parents, or as a result of divorce, while skipped-generation grandparents more often assume care due to a parent's drug use, mental or emotional problems, child abuse or neglect, or a grandchild's medical problems. The children of skipped-generation households may thus be harder to care for than most and have difficulties that result in their caregivers feeling they are giving up more of their lives to meet their child's needs than they ever expected.

Further, caregivers in the traditional families were at an advantage in that they reported less caregiver aggravation than single parents for both the 1997 and 2002 samples. Traditional caregivers have the advantage of a partner (the child's other parent) on hand with whom they can share day-to-day parenting challenges and aggravations, unlike many single parents, who may feel more challenged and isolated in their parenting. Some single parents may hold negative feelings toward, or have an adversarial relationship with, their child's other parent, which could spill over into their relationship with their child, particularly if that child reminds them of a former partner. For the 1997 sample, traditional parents also reported less caregiver aggravation than co-parenting families. This effect was not repeated for the 2002 sample. Perhaps there has been a shift in such a manner that co-parenting caregivers in particular feel less aggravated by the children they care for. It is possible that ecological factors in general (such as educational, political, economic, and societal changes) have leveled the playing field in such a manner that traditional parents and co-parenting grandparents are equally impacted negatively by their children's behavior. It may have become more normative over time for traditional families to encourage grandparents to come and live with them to assist with parenting duties. These grandparents, in turn, may view their caregiving duties (and grandchildren) in a more positive light than their skipped-generation peers, who (as discussed above) have come into the role for different and often more adverse reasons.

Behavior Problems in Children Aged 6 to 11 Years

For the 1997 sample, grandparent caregivers in skipped-generation families reported greater behavioral and emotional difficulties in their 6- to 11-year-old focal children as compared to those reported by parents in traditional families or those in single-parent families. The findings for the 2002 sample were similar in that the grandparent caregivers in skipped-generation families reported greater behavioral and emotional difficulties for their 6- to 11-year-old group of children as compared to those reported by parents in traditional families. In the 2002 sample, single parents also reported greater behavioral and emotional difficulties for their 6- to 11-year-old children than were reported by parents in traditional families. When one considers that grandparent caregivers may have a tendency to minimize the extent of their grandchildren's difficulties, this finding underscores the need to identify custodial grandchildren from skipped-generation households as particularly vulnerable to behavioral and emotional difficulties and to offer professional support and services to these skipped-generation families.

Behavior Problems in Children Aged 12 to 17 Years

In the 1997 sample, the parents in the traditional families reported the fewest behavioral and emotional difficulties amongst 12- to 17-year-olds, as compared to all three of the other family types. It is possible that the traditional family structure, particularly since it has likely been long-standing for families with this older group of children, offers greater stability, leading to the lower reported behavioral difficulties in children by their caregivers. For the 1997 sample, there were no other differences in behavioral and emotional difficulties among 12- to 17-year-olds in the other family types. In the 2002 sample, 12- to 17-year-olds were once again reported to have fewer behavioral and emotional difficulties in traditional families as compared to skipped-generation and single-parent families. This supports the findings of the earlier reported study by Goodman and Silverstein (2002), where grandmothers of skipped-generation families reported greater behavioral problems than children in co-parenting households and conflict between grandmother and grandchild was higher in skipped-generation households than co-parenting households. With respect to historical shifts, the presence of one or more additional adults in the house may be becoming more normative or accepted, leading to better behavioral outcomes in 12- to 17-year-olds. Perhaps increased actual or perceived supports for the co-parenting grandparent caregivers have filtered down to the well-being of the children they care for.

School Engagement

The only reported differences between families for school engagement emerged in the 2002 sample for traditional families, whose caregivers reported greater school engagement than did either the grandparent caregivers in skipped-generation families or single parents. It is possible that traditional families, who may have the advantage of greater stability, may also have greater supports, time, and knowledge to support their children in their school-related endeavors. It is also possible that the school environments themselves have been more favorable for children from traditionally structured families than children and caregivers of more nontraditional families, who may feel more stigmatized.

Implications of These Findings for Counseling and Interventions With Grandfamilies

Overall, the findings of this study do appear to provide evidence of a need for greater support for the challenges faced by co-parenting and skipped-generation caregiving grandparents, and in this respect, identifying grandfamilies with the greatest need for help may be especially important. In this respect, while the selection criteria for the NSAF samples biases the findings of this study toward a lower-income group and thus limits their generalizability, low-income groups are less amenable to study and are more vulnerable, which helps to justify the use of the NSAF samples to explore the antecedents of well-being in grandparent-headed families.

Since family structure appears to play a role in determining the well-being of co-parenting and skipped-generation households, counseling psychologists and other mental health professionals should direct greater efforts toward family-focused interventions for these families that might present as struggling. This could take the form of family therapy, with a focus on identifying significant issues and areas of stress salient for that particular family, and encouraging grandparent-headed households to think about how they function and explore ways of resolving their difficulties. In this respect, Goodman (2007) recommends the use of triad analysis (that is, examining representatives from all three family generations and their interactions) to address intergenerational issues for both co-parenting and skipped-generation families. Family therapy may then address any negative histories, blurred boundaries, and conflicts that have arisen within the grandparent-headed household.

A further effective intervention may be to offer parent education to grandparent caregivers. Dolbin-MacNab (2006) reported that grandparent caregivers tend to perceive second-time-around parenting as more difficult due to contemporary social challenges such as the media, drugs and alcohol, peer pressure, more liberal attitudes toward sex, crime and violence, and a lack of prosocial peers. Making parent education more grandparent-friendly might be helpful, and framing it in terms of re-education, or updating one's parenting skills with current research-based knowledge on issues pertinent to child rearing, may be necessary. For example, the University of Wisconsin–Madison offers (via the Web site http://www.uwex.edu/relationships/) parenting information specifically tailored toward the context of custodial grandparenting (Poehlmann, Britnall-Peterson, Shlafer, & Morgan, 2003). For grandparents caring for a younger child, filial therapy, which involves training the grandparent how to use play as a means of communication with their grandchild, may be effective as well.

Individual counseling may also assist grandparents to better cope with the demands of caregiving. For example, Ross and Aday (2006) reported that African American grandparent caregivers who used professional counseling as a resource reported lower levels of stress compared to those grandparent caregivers who did not. Given that many grandparent-headed households are financially challenged, they may benefit from free or sliding-scale professional counseling services.

This study also suggests that family type plays a role in determining the well-being of children who are raised in co-parenting and skipped-generation households, who tend to fare worse than children in traditional families. There has been less emphasis in the custodial grandparent literature on the well-being of the child (versus that of the caregiver); a need for more interventions and resources for this vulnerable group of children is evident.

From a preventive perspective, schools could be encouraged to increase support toward custodial grandchildren (see Mauderer, this volume). While some states are changing their educational enrollment requirements (Generations United, 2002), local school districts that require caregivers to show documentation of legal custody or guardianship in order to enroll children should be made aware that grandparent caregivers often raise their grandchildren informally and should therefore not unjustly prevent grandchildren from attending school or accessing special education services. Edwards (2006) has suggested that children raised by grandparents may experience greater stability if school officials can work toward placing them with the same teachers and classmates in consecutive years. Grandchildren who are perceived to struggle, for example, in terms of poor grades or social skills, should be closely monitored and offered opportunities to join support groups or have access to increased tutoring, mentoring, or counseling services as necessary within the school environment. An example of a school-based program that incorporates a combination of tutoring, mentoring, counseling, advocacy, and resource procurement for children being raised by kin is the Kinship Care Connection, which has been demonstrated to improve caregivers' sense of self-efficacy in addition to benefiting children's self-esteem (Strozier, McGrew, Krisman, & Smith, 2005).

Ross and Aday (2006) found that custodial grandchildren's use of school programs such as tutoring and special education provided a protective effect against the stress perceived by their grandparent caregivers, as well as helped the grandchildren themselves. Administrators may thus have to make a greater effort to educate custodial grandparents as to the services that are available to their grandchildren, given that the school environment may have changed significantly since the grandparents last negotiated the system (or they may not have made the most of the available services the first time around).

Grandparents may be less aware of the services available to them or their grandchildren than both traditional and single parents. Grandparents may benefit from referrals to a wide variety of resources such as support groups (in person, on-line, or telephone groups), respite care (i.e., before- or after-school care or summer camp information for their grandchildren), resources for legal aid, legislative advocacy, parent training, information about any disabilities that their grandchild may be experiencing, transportation assistance, housing assistance, and health insurance information. Many more resources targeting grandparent caregivers have appeared in recent years, for example, the National Family Caregiver Support Program, established in 2000 in partnership with Area Agencies on Aging, offers older caregivers information and assistance to gain access to relevant services. Younger grandparent caregivers may be able to access aging-network services through a number of organizations: Generations United, a national nonprofit organization that assists and trains service providers as well as identifies state-specific caregiver resources; the American Association of Retired Persons Grandparent Information Center, which offers a national database of grandparent support groups; the Brookdale Foundation Relatives as Parents Program, a national network of support groups for relatives raising children informally; the Children's Defense Fund, which provides information on health insurance for children and information on the child welfare system; Eldercare Locator, which provides 24-hour access to community-assistance resources for seniors; the National Association of Child Care Resource and Referral Agencies, which offers information on community-based childcare resources; and the National Council on Aging Benefits Checkup, an internet-based service to help identify state and federal assistance programs (Generations United, 2003b). Practitioners may wish to educate themselves on these resources, as well as the availability of support services for grandparent-headed households specific to their geographical areas.

REFERENCES

Antonucci, T. C. (2001). Social networks, social support, and sense of control. In J. E. Birren & K. W. Schaie (Eds.), *Handbook of the psychology of aging* (5th ed.). New York: Academic Press.

Brown, D. R., & Mars, J. (2000). Profile of contemporary grandparenting in African-American families. In C. Cox (Ed.), *To grandmother's house we go and stay: Perspectives on custodial grandparents* (pp. 203–217). New York: Springer.

Burnette, D. (1999). Physical and emotional well-being of custodial grandparents in Latino families. *American Journal of Orthopsychiatry, 69*, 305–318.

Casper, L. M., & Bryson, K. R. (1998). Co-resident grandparents and their grandchildren: Grandparent maintained families. (Population Division Working Paper No. 26). Washington, DC: U.S. Bureau of the Census.

Dolbin-MacNab, M. L. (2006). Just like raising your own? Grandmothers' perceptions of parenting a second time around. *Family Relations, 55*, 564–575.

Dolbin-MacNab, M. L., & Targ, D. B. (2003). Grandparents raising grandchildren: Guidelines for family life educators and other family professionals. In B. Hayslip, Jr., & J. Hicks Patrick (Eds.), *Working with custodial grandparents* (pp. 213–228). New York: Springer.

Edwards, O. W. (1998). Helping grandkin—Grandchildren raised by grandparents: Expanding psychology in the schools. *Psychology in the Schools, 35*, 173–181.

Edwards, O. W. (2006). Teachers' perceptions of the emotional and behavioral functioning of children raised by grandparents. *Psychology in the Schools, 43*, 565–572.

Fuller-Thomson, E., & Minkler, M. (2000). America's grandparent caregivers: Who are they? In B. Hayslip, Jr., & R. Goldberg-Glen (Eds.), *Grandparents raising grandchildren: Theoretical, empirical, and clinical perspectives* (pp. 3–21). New York: Springer.

Fuller-Thomson, E., Minkler, M., & Driver, D. (1997). A profile of grandparents raising grandchildren in the United States. *The Gerontologist, 37*, 406–411.

Generations United. (2002). *Grandparents and other relatives raising children: Access to education.* Retrieved July 6, 2007, from http://ipath.gu.org/documents/AO/Education_11_05.pdf

Generations United. (2003a). *A guide to the National Family Caregiver Support Program and its inclusion of grandparents and other relatives raising children.* Retrieved July 6, 2007, from http://ipath.gu.org/documents/AO/NFCSP_Guide.pdf

Generations United. (2003b). *Grandparents and other relatives raising children: Information and assistance services.* Retrieved July 6, 2007, from http://ipath.gu.org/documents/AO/Information_and_Assistance_12_5.pdf

Goodman, C. C. (2007). Family dynamics in three-generation families. *Journal of Family Issues, 28,* 355–379.

Goodman, C. C., & Silverstein, M. (2001). Grandmothers who parent their grandchildren: An exploratory study of close relations across three generations. *Journal of Family Issues, 22,* 557–578.

Goodman, C. C., & Silverstein, M. (2002). Grandparents raising grandchildren: Family structure and well-being in culturally diverse families. *The Gerontologist, 42,* 676–689.

Hayslip, B., Jr., & Hicks Patrick, J. (2006). *Custodial grandparents: Individual, cultural, and ethnic diversity.* New York: Springer.

Hayslip, B., Jr., & Kaminski, P. (2006). Custodial grandchildren. In G. Bear & K. Minke (Eds.), *Children's needs III: Understanding and addressing the needs of children* (pp. 771–782). Washington, DC: National Association of School Psychologists.

Hayslip, B., Jr., Shore, R. J., & Henderson, C. E. (2000). Perceptions of grandparents' influence in the lives of their grandchildren. In B. Hayslip & R. Goldberg-Glen (Eds.), *Grandparents raising grandchildren: Theoretical, empirical, and clinical perspectives* (pp. 35–46). New York: Springer.

Jendrek, M. P. (1994). Grandparents who parent their grandchildren: Circumstances and decisions. *The Gerontologist, 34,* 206–216.

Musil, C. M., & Standing, T. (2005). Grandmothers' diaries: A glimpse at daily lives. *International Journal of Aging and Development, 60,* 317–329.

Pinson-Millburn, N. M., Fabian, E. S., Schlossberg, N. K., & Pyle, M. (1996). Grandparents raising grandchildren. *Journal of Counseling and Development, 74,* 548–554.

Poehlmann, J., Britnall-Peterson, M., Shlafer, R., & Morgan, K. (2003). *Grandparents raising grandchildren: Introduction.* Retrieved July 6, 2007, from http://www.uwex.edu/relationships/

Pruchno, R. A., & McKenney, D. (2002). Psychological well-being of black and white grandmothers raising grandchildren: Examination of a two factor model. *The Journals of Gerontology, 57B,* 444–452.

Roe, K. M., & Minkler, M. (1998–1999). Grandparents raising grandchildren: Challenges and responses. *Generations, 22,* 25–32.

Ross, M. E., & Aday, L. A. (2006). Stress and coping in African American grandparents who are raising their grandchildren. *Journal of Family Issues, 27,* 912–932.

Sawyer, R., & Dubowitz, H. (1994). School performance of children in kinship care. *Child Abuse and Neglect, 18,* 587–597.

Silverstein, N. M., & Vehvilainen, L. (2000). Grandparents and schools: Issues and potential challenges. In C. Cox (Ed.), *To grandmother's house we go and stay: Perspectives on custodial grandparents* (pp. 268–282). New York: Springer.

Stevenson, M. L., Henderson, T. L., & Baugh, E. (2007). Vital defenses: Social support appraisals of black grandmothers parenting grandchildren. *Journal of Family Issues, 28,* 182–211.

Strozier, A., McGrew, L., Krisman, K., & Smith, A. (2005). Kinship care connection: A school-based intervention for kinship caregivers and the children in their care. *Children and Youth Services Review, 27,* 1011–1029.

Urban Institute. (1999). *Snapshots of America's families: Appendix.* Retrieved June 10, 2006, from the Urban Institute at http://www.urban.org/url.cfm?ID=900875

Whitley, D. M. (n.d.). *National Center on Grandparents Raising Grandchildren: Home.* Retrieved July 6, 2007, from http://chhs.gsu.edu/nationalcenter/

CHAPTER 3

Mentally Healthy Grandparents' Impact on Their Grandchildren's Behavior

Catherine Chase Goodman and Bert Hayslip, Jr.

Most studies of caregiving grandparents have been cross-sectional, although a few longitudinal studies have attempted to capture the impact of caregiving over time (Hayslip, Emick, Henderson, & Elias, 2002; Minkler, Fuller-Thomson, Miller, & Driver, 1997; Minkler, Fuller-Thomson, Miller, & Driver, 2000; Musil, 2000; Strawbridge, Wallhagen, Sherma, & Kaplan, 1997; Szinovacz, DeViney, & Atkinson, 1999), or have identified caregiving patterns that involved current and past caregiving (Lee, Ensminger, & LaVeist, 2006). A study of grandparent caregivers and noncaregiving peers (Minkler et al., 1997; Minkler et al., 2000) drew on two phases of the National Survey of Families and Households. This study found that grandparents who had begun caregiving during the previous 5 years had higher levels of depression compared to noncaregiving grandparents, even after controlling for pre-caregiving depression and demographic factors. Another study using the same sample found that grandmothers showed increased depression when grandchildren moved into the house, whereas grandfathers had increased depression when grandchildren left the household (Szinovacz et al., 1999). Using a purposive sample of

Acknowledgments: The Grandmother Parenting Project was supported in part by grants from the National Institute on Aging (RO1AG14977), the California Social Work Education Center (CalSWEC), and the Scholarly and Creative Activities Award, California State University, Long Beach.

caregiving grandparents, Musil (2000) found no time effects for depression or anxiety over a 10-month period, although parenting distress showed increases over time for both primary and partial caregivers. Hayslip et al. (2002) also found stability over a 6-month time period; specifically, grandparents caring for grandchildren with problems remained the most distressed at both time periods in terms of role strain and response to grandchild. Some temporal shifts occurred in that all grandparents were less likely to describe positive aspects of their relationship with their grandchild over the 6 months, whether they were custodial or traditional grandparents. These studies suggest that grandmothers new to the role may be most vulnerable to depression, and that parenting stress may actually increase and positive descriptions decrease as grandchildren become older. In another longitudinal study, Strawbridge et al. (1997) found that problems experienced 20 years prior (financial, marital, and health-related) were more common among grandparent than spousal or adult-child caregivers, suggesting past crises were common experiences in their life trajectory. Furthermore, Lee and colleagues (2006) identified types of caregivers based on current, former, or noncaregiving experiences, finding that former caregivers were worse off than other groups, possibly because they had been unable to continue caregiving due to economic or social burdens, or had been depleted by the caregiving itself.

These studies provide a beginning view of factors that impact the well-being of the caregiving grandparent over time. To be sure, grandparent caregivers assume care due to parental crises and often confront transitions in their employment, marital, and financial status as a result. Additional stress arises from grandchildren who may have severe behavior problems as a result of parental neglect or grief over the loss of a normative parent: Many studies have linked a child's problem behaviors to lower grandparent well-being, in terms of lower role satisfaction, greater personal distress, and greater depression (Hayslip, Shore, Henderson, & Lambert, 1998; Hayslip, Temple, Shore, & Henderson, 2006; Young & Dawson, 2003). From the child's perspective, lower self-worth and less social acceptance were related to having a lower-quality relationship with the kinship caregiver (Keller & Stricker, 2003), although grandparent well-being was not examined in this study. While not always confirmed (e.g., Force, Botsford, Pisano, & Holbert, 2000), the relationship between a child's disability or problem behavior and the grandparents' well-being has been remarkably constant and has been descried cross-nationally (Oburu & Palmérus, 2006) as well as in the United States.

The link between grandchildren with behavioral problems and distressed grandparent caregivers has generally been interpreted as evidence of the stress of caring for troubled children, since these children may have been neglected by their parents and their troubled behavior often precedes living with their grandparents. This chapter presents two pilot studies from different samples that address the issue of reciprocal influence between grandparent caregiver and grandchild over time. Specifically the studies attempt to establish the extent to which the grandchild's problem behavior causes a decline in the grandmother's mental health or well-being versus the extent to which the grandmother or grandparent's mental health or well-being contributes to adaptation and change in the grandchild's behaviors.

HAYSLIP LONGITUDINAL PILOT

Considering the nontraditional roles assumed by grandparent caregivers, this pilot addressed short-term changes in satisfaction with the grandparenting role, the relationship with grandchildren, the level of parenting stress, as well as depression and life satisfaction in grandparent caregivers, as these elements are reciprocally impacted by changes in the grandchild's behavior.

Sample and Data Collection. The sample consisted of 36 custodial grandparents raising grandchildren with a range of emotional, physical, or behavioral problems. Grandparents were recruited through media advertisements, presentations at local agencies, and through professionals in school and health settings. They were interviewed in their homes after completing a self-report questionnaire to elicit demographic information and were reassessed after 6 months. They evaluated one selected grandchild in light of the different types of responses possible with different children. The sample, consisting of 6 grandfathers and 30 grandmothers, was primarily middle-aged ($M = 56.50$, $SD = 6.02$) and White (95%). Grandchildren were aged 1–18 ($M = 7.84$), and two out of three were male.

Measures. The grandchild's problems were evaluated by their grandparent caregivers using 10 items on a 5-point scale from 1 (*no problem*) to 5 (*severe problem*). Items tapped hyperactivity, depression, oppositional behavior, learning difficulties, and alcohol use among other problems (see Emick & Hayslip, 1999 for details). The grandparents' role satisfaction was assessed using 15 Likert-type items such as, "life has more meaning for me because of my grandchild." Coefficient alpha was .79 (Thomas, 1988). Also measured were the grandparents' perceptions of their relationship with their grandchild in terms of positive and negative affect. This 20-item measure consists of the Positive Affect Index, which taps mutual understanding, trust, fairness, respect, and affection felt for the grandchild; and the Negative Affect Index, which taps negative response to irritating behaviors (Bence & Thomas, 1988). Additionally, the grandmother's level of depression was measured using the well-known CES-D, a 20-item measure using a 4-point Likert scale, from

1 (*rarely or none of the time*) to 4 (*most or all of the time*). Internal consistency was .85 (Radloff, 1977). Psychological well-being was measured using Liang's (1985) self-report, which consists of 15 items assessing happiness and positive and negative affect. Finally, a 36-item Parenting Stress Index (PSI; Abidin, 1990) elicits parental distress, parent-child dysfunctional interaction, and the child's ability to self-regulate. Coefficient alpha was .91 for the index.

Analyses. Correlational and cross-lagged correlational analyses were used. The cross-lagged correlational analyses (Pearson-Filon Z) test for differences among cross-lagged relationships between grandparent mental health and parental variables and grandchild problems.

Results. Correlations between the grandparent's mental health and relational variables and the grandchild's reported problem behaviors were substantial for Negative Affect, Parental Stress, Depression, and Satisfaction with Role at Time 1, but not at Time 2.

In the cross-lagged correlational analyses, no causal path existed between grandparent and grandchild variables, except for the Parental Stress Index (PSI). For this index, scores trended ($p < .09$) to predict grandchild problem behaviors to a greater extent over time than did grandchild problem behaviors predict PSI scores. Indeed, the relationship between PSI Time 1 scores and the grandchild's problem scores at Time 2 exceeds the relationship between grandchild problem scores themselves over time (see Figure 3.1). Together, these analyses suggest that there may be a bidirectional relationship between grandparent mental health and parenting attitudes and practices and grandchild problem behaviors, especially for PSI scores, positive affect and negative affect. For CES-D scores, there is a suggestion that more problematic grandchild behaviors may predispose some grandparent caregivers to depression.

Limitations. It should be noted that the small sample here undermined the power of the Pearson-Filon test to detect differential changes in relationships over time. Additionally, all data were self-reported and only from the grandparent caregiver's perspective. On the other hand, the longitudinal analysis permits stronger inferences regarding causation than is possible with cross-sectional data.

GOODMAN LONGITUDINAL PILOT

This pilot longitudinal study addressed the mental health of grandmothers raising their grandchildren in relation to their grandchild's behavior problems over a 1- to 2-year period. Grandmothers in the study were not new to the role, and the elapsed time period reflects ongoing rather than initial adjustments.

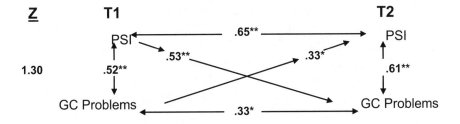

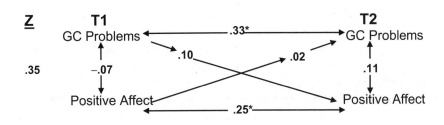

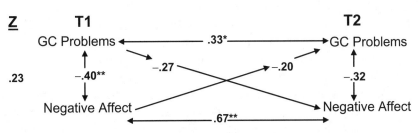

FIGURE 3.1 Cross-lagged analysis for parental stress, relationship, and well-being variables as related to grandchild problem behaviors.

It was hypothesized that the grandchild's behavior problems would contribute to a decline in the grandmother's mental health; and conversely, that the grandmother's mental health would be related to the grandchild's behavior. Demographic and health factors were controlled in the assessment of change in light of their possible contribution to the grandmother or grandchild's well-being.

Sample and Data Collection. This convenience sample consisted of 181 custodial grandmothers, who were interviewed initially during 1998–2000 as part of a larger study of grandparents raising grandchildren. These grandmothers were subsequently reinterviewed over the telephone during 2001. All were raising school-aged grandchildren without a parent in the household, and 55.2% were under the supervision of the formal child welfare system when they were first interviewed. The original sample was recruited through notices sent home with students in 223 schools in the Los Angeles Unified School District and through the media. Of the 181 interviewed a second time, 51.4% had been recruited originally through the schools and 48.6% through media announcements. The original study used a quota sample of African American, Latina, and White grandmothers, resulting in a distribution in this follow-up sample of African American (40.9%), Hispanic (23.2%), and White (35.9%) grandmothers. Therefore, African American and White grandmothers were oversampled for the Los Angeles region. Grandmothers were asked to respond in detail about a targeted grandchild (i.e., the child identified through the school or a randomly selected child).

Recruitment for follow-up was attempted for all grandmothers in this original sample whose grandchild was in the custody of the child welfare system, and a 60% random sample of grandmothers providing care informally, therefore oversampling child welfare families. At the time of follow-up, many of the grandmothers had moved or were no longer eligible. The follow-up sample represented 68% of those who were selected, eligible, and available in the community. In the follow-up study, potential subjects received a letter and phone call from research staff requesting participation. Those participating received $20 for the 1-hour interview conducted between January and June, 2001. On average, the elapsed time between data collections was 16.1 months, and 50% of the grandmothers were interviewed between 11 and 21 months after their initial interview. Spanish-speaking grandmothers were interviewed by a bilingual interviewer.

Measures. The SF-36 (Ware, 1993) was used to assess health and mental health of the grandmothers. This 36-item measure has eight subscales, which are weighted and aggregated to form global scales for physical and mental health. Subscale coefficient alpha for Time 1 ranged from .93 for Physical Functioning to .73 for Bodily Pain, and for Time 2 from .89 for Physical Functioning to .63 for Bodily Pain. The grandchild's well-being was measured using the Behavior Rating Index for Children (BRIC), a 10-item problem list rated on a 5-point scale from 1 (*rarely or never*) to 5 (*most or all of the time*; Stiffman, Orme, Evans, Feldman, & Keeney, 1984). Coefficient alpha was .82 for both Time 1 and Time 2. Demographic descriptors were the grandmother's age, employment, marital status, and per capita family income, and the grandchild's age, time with grandmother, and original-study recruitment method.

Analysis. Analysis consisted of hierarchical regressions to examine predictors of the grandmother's mental health and the grandchild's behavior problems. Initially, significant cross-sectional predictors were sought for Time 1 and Time 2 separately. Subsequently, prediction was addressed to examine change in the grandmother's mental health or the grandchild's behavior problems. To predict the grandmother's mental health at Time 2, her mental health at Time 1 and the grandchild's Time 1 problem behaviors were entered in the model with controls (grandmother's marital status, age, ethnicity, and health; family yearly per capita income; grandchild's age and time living with grandmother). Similarly, to predict the grandchild's behavior problems at Time 2, behavior problems at Time 1 and the Time 1 grandmother's mental health were entered, with demographic and health variables controlled.

Results. Time 1 to Time 2 showed bivariate shifts toward single, unemployed status, although per capita income did not change (see Table 3.1). No differences from Time 1 to Time 2 were evident for mental health, although physical health declined and grandchild's behavior problems increased. Analysis of change in the grandmother's mental health from Time 1 to Time 2 (evaluated by adjusting Time 2 mental health for Time 1 mental health) showed no significance for the child's behavior as a predictor, although this

TABLE 3.1 Time 1 and 2 Demographics: Grandmothers Raising Grandchildren in Skipped-Generation Families

Characteristics		Time 1	Time 2	χ^2 or t	df
Grandmother					
Age	M	57.7	58.8	−6.3***	180
	SD	7.5	7.7		
Married	%	42.0	37.8	134.7***	1, n = 180
Working	%	42.0	32.6	71.0***	1, n = 181
Income	M	9897.8	9330.6	1.6	178
	SD	6976.3	6228.2		
Mental Health	M	52.2	52.6	−.5	178
	SD	10.1	10.5		
Physical Health	M	48.0	45.3	3.9***	178
	SD	11.4	11.4		
Grandchild					
Age	M	9.3	10.4	−10.5***	177
	SD	3.3	3.3		
Time With GM	M	6.6	7.8	−6.9***	179
	SD	3.9	3.7		
Behavior Problems	M	26.2	29.3	−3.4***	180
	SD	17.6	17.9		

* $p \leq .05$; ** $p \leq .01$; *** $p \leq .001$

TABLE 3.2 Prediction of Change in Mental Health and Grandchild's
Behavior Problems

	Time 2 GM Mental Health			Time 2 GC Behavior Problems		
	B	SE B	β	B	SE B	β
Time 2 mental health	.48	.08	.47***	−.30	.11	−.17**
Per capita family income	.00	.00	.08	.00	.00	.03
African American versus other	.47	1.70	.02	2.66	2.47	.07
Hispanic versus other	.95	2.01	−.04	7.31	2.99	.16*
Married grandmother	−1.01	1.50	−.05	−.38	2.18	.01
Age of grandmother	−.04	.10	.03	.24	.15	.10†
Physical health of grandmother	.01	.06	.01	.03	.09	.02
Time 1 grandchild behavior problem	−.07	.04	−.12†	.63	.06	.62***
Time living with grandmother	.53	.21	.20*	.38	.30	.08
Age of grandchild	−.42	.26	−.13	−.16	.38	−.03

Note. Mental health R^2 = .30; $F(10, 169)$ = 7.26, p = .000; Grandchild behavior R^2 = .50; $F(10, 169)$ = 16.93, p = .000. GM = grandmother; GC = grandchild.

† $p < .10$. * $p < .05$. ** $p < .01$. *** $p < .001$.

factor showed an inverse trend ($p ≤ .10$). The length of time the grandchild lived with the grandmother was the only significant predictor (see Table 3.2), suggesting grandmothers who had lived with their grandchildren longer had mental health gains and that an adjustment had occurred.

However, analysis of change in the grandchild's behavior problems from Time 1 to Time 2 (evaluated by adjusting Time 2 behavior problems for Time 1 behavior problems) showed the grandmother's mental health as a significant negative predictor (see Table 3.2). Change in the grandchild's behavior problems was predicted by the grandmother's mental health at Time 1, suggesting mentally healthy grandmothers contributed to their grandchild's adaptation. It should be noted that the effect size was very small (semipartial r^2 = .022), therefore accounting for only about 2% of the variance at Time 2, whereas continuity in the grandchild's behavior from Time 1 to Time 2 was strong, accounting for 44% of the variance at Time 2 (r^2 = .438, with

95% confidence limit from .290 to .517). Among demographic predictors, Hispanic grandmothers perceived an increase in their grandchild's problem behaviors. Overall, change results provide modest support for the hypothesis that the grandchild's improvement in behavior problems is related to their grandmother's mental health. However, there was insufficient support for the alternative hypothesis—that the grandmother's deterioration in mental health was related to having a grandchild with serious behavior problems.

DISCUSSION

Results of these two pilot studies support the association between the grandchild's behavior problems and the grandmother's well-being often found in the cross-sectional literature (e.g., Hayslip et al., 1998; Young & Dawson, 2003). Going a step further through longitudinal analysis, the grandmother's mental health and parenting stress predicted change in the grandchild's behavior, a red flag to professionals interested in protecting children. The grandparents' well-being resulted in their grandchildren's improved or deteriorated behavior—more so than difficult children led to distressed caregivers. On the other hand, many other unknowns contribute to grandchildren's changes in behavior over time, and continuity or a family legacy of depression (Weissman et al., 2005) may be contributing factors. Nevertheless, these studies suggest that protecting the grandparent may, in the long run, protect the child.

Implications for Practice. Results imply that strong caregivers, who manage their stress, may be able to help difficult and disturbed children to develop and adjust. This result is congruent with studies showing a direct link between parenting practices and the behavior of children (Kazdin, 2002). Currently, there are many effective treatments for children that rely on caregiver education, and these interventions may have dual benefit—strengthening the caregiver as well as helping the child. Effective treatments for disruptive children are plentiful (Kazdin, 2002; Weisz, Jensen-Doss, & Hawley, 2006). While outcome evaluations address changes in the child's behavior, intervention may also strengthen the caregiver and reduce their stress by providing greater continuity and consistency of parenting. For example, parent-child interaction therapy has shown positive results of successful discipline, improvement in child behavior, and decreased parenting stress (Schuhmann, Foote, Eyberg, Boggs, & Algina, 1998). Some well-researched approaches with demonstrated effectiveness have manuals for parents or caregivers readily available, and can teach problem-solving-skills training for children (Shure, 2005) and parent management training (Forehand & Long, 2002). These programs help caregivers develop clear rules, mild punishments, and positive reinforcement for prosocial behavior. Caregivers are guided to spend more time with the children, diffuse conflict, and improve communication in the family. Therefore grandparent caregivers can contribute to the well-being of their grandchildren, and at the same time improve their own sense of efficacy and well-being.

Moreover, well-known programs to help grandparents gain stability and confidence in their new role are likely to have a ripple effect, helping to stabilize their grandchildren as well. Grandparent educational programs and support groups (Smith, 2003), conflict resolution, anger management, and training in interpersonal skills (Matthews & Zeidner, 2000) are all program approaches that may contribute to strengthening the grandparents and helping them maintain nurturance under difficult circumstances. When children have been neglected or abused, child welfare social workers need to be mindful of the stresses on kinship caregivers and offer them ongoing support (Sumner-Mayer, 2006) to facilitate their constructive influence and high morale. Society relies on grandparent caregivers to maintain their families. The family system involves reciprocal influence between family members: Difficult relationships and individual family members with problems impact the family unit. Assisting grandchildren and grandparent caregivers will maximize the potential of grandparent families to provide care over time.

REFERENCES

Abidin, R. R. (1990). *Parenting stress index—short form.* Charlottesville, VA: Pediatric Psychology Press.

Bence, S. L., & Thomas, J. L. (1988, November). *Grandparent-parent relationships as predictors of grandparent-grandchild relationships.* Paper presented at the Annual Scientific Meeting of the Gerontological Society of America, San Francisco, CA.

Emick, M. A., & Hayslip, B., Jr. (1999). Custodial grandparenting: Stresses, coping skills, and relationships with grandchildren. *International Journal of Aging and Human Development, 48,* 35–61.

Force, L. T., Botsford, A., Pisano, P. A., & Holbert, A. (2000). Grandparents raising children with and without a developmental disability: Preliminary comparisons. *Journal of Gerontological Social Work, 33*(4), 5–21.

Forehand, R., & Long, N. (2002). *Parenting the strong-willed child: The clinically proven five-week program for parents of two- to six-year-olds.* New York: Contemporary Books.

Hayslip, B., Jr., Emick, M. A., Henderson, C. E., & Elias, K. (2002). Temporal variations in the experience of custodial grandparenting: A short-term longitudinal study. *Journal of Applied Gerontology, 21,* 139–156.

Hayslip, B., Jr., Shore, R. J., Henderson, C. E., & Lambert, P. L. (1998). Custodial grandparenting and the impact of grandchildren with problems on role satisfaction and role meaning. *Journal of Gerontology: Social Sciences, 53B,* S164–S173.

Hayslip, B., Jr., Temple, J. R., Shore, R. J., & Henderson, C. E. (2006). Determinants of role satisfaction among traditional and custodial grandparents. In B. Hayslip, Jr., & J. H. Patrick (Eds.), *Custodial grandparenting: Individual, cultural, and ethnic diversity* (pp. 21–35). New York: Springer.

Kazdin, A. E. (2002). Psychosocial treatments for conduct disorder in children and adolescents. In P. E. Nathan & J. M. Gorman (Eds.), *A guide to treatments that work* (2nd ed., pp. 57–85). New York: Oxford University Press.

Keller, S., & Stricker, G. (2003). Links between custodial grandparents and the psychological adaptation of grandchildren. In B. Hayslip, Jr., & J. H. Patrick (Eds.), *Working with custodial grandparents* (pp. 27–43). New York: Springer.

Lee, R. D., Ensminger, M. E., & LaVeist, T. A. (2006). African American grandmothers: The responsibility continuum. In B. Hayslip, Jr., & J. H. Patrick (Eds.), *Custodial grandparenting: Individual, cultural, and ethnic diversity* (pp. 119–132). New York: Springer.

Liang, J. (1985). A structural integration of the Affect Balance Scale and the Life Satisfaction Index A. *Journal of Gerontology, 40*, 552–561.

Matthews, G., & Zeidner, M. (2000). Emotional intelligence, adaptation to stressful encounters, and health outcomes. In R. Bar-On & J. D. A. Parker (Eds.), *The handbook of emotional intelligence: Theory, development, assessment, and application at home, school, and in the workplace* (pp. 459–489). San Francisco: Jossey-Bass.

Minkler, M., Fuller-Thomson, E., Miller, D., & Driver, D. (1997). Depression in grandparents raising grandchildren: Results of a national longitudinal study. *Archives of Family Medicine, 6*, 445–452.

Minkler, M., Fuller-Thomson, E., Miller, D., & Driver, D. (2000). Grandparent caregiving and depression. In B. Hayslip, Jr., & R. Goldberg-Glen (Eds.), *Grandparents raising grandchildren: Theoretical, empirical, and clinical perspectives* (pp. 207–220). New York: Springer.

Musil, C. M. (2000). Health of grandmothers as caregivers: A 10-month follow-up. *Journal of Women and Aging, 12*, 129–145.

Oburu, P. O., & Palmérus, K. (2006). Stress-related factors among primary and part-time caregiving grandmother of Kenyan grandchildren. In B. Hayslip, Jr., & J. H. Patrick (Eds.), *Custodial grandparenting: Individual, cultural, and ethnic diversity* (pp. 225–234). New York: Springer.

Radloff, L. S. (1977). The CES-D scale: A self-report depression scale for research in the general population. *Applied Psychological Measurement, 1*, 385–401.

Schuhmann, E. M., Foote, R., Eyberg, S. M., Boggs, S., & Algina, J. (1998). Parent-child interaction therapy: Interim report of a randomized trial with short-term maintenance. *Journal of Clinical Child Psychology, 27*, 34–35.

Shure, M. B. (2005). *Thinking parent, thinking child: How to turn your most challenging everyday problems into solutions.* New York: McGraw-Hill.

Smith, G. C. (2003). How caregiving grandparents view support groups: An exploratory study. In B. Hayslip, Jr., & J. H. Patrick (Eds.), *Working with custodial grandparents* (pp. 69–91). New York: Springer.

Stiffman, A. R., Orme, J. G., Evans, D. A., Feldman, R. A., & Keeney, P. A. (1984). A brief measure of children's behavior problems: The Behavior Rating Index for Children. *Measurement and Evaluation in Counseling and Development, 17,* 83–90.

Strawbridge, W. J., Wallhagen, M. I., Shema, S. J., & Kaplan, G. A. (1997). New burdens or more of the same? Comparing grandparent, spouse, and adult-child caregivers. *The Gerontologist, 37,* 505–510.

Sumner-Mayer, K. (2006). Children in foster families. In L. Combrinck-Graham (Ed.), *Children in family contexts: Perspectives on treatment* (2nd ed., pp. 190–220). New York: Guilford.

Szinovacz, M. E., DeViney, S., & Atkinson, M. P. (1999). Effects of surrogate parenting on grandparents' well-being. *Journal of Gerontology: Social Sciences 54B,* S376–S388.

Thomas, J. L. (1988, November). *Relationships with grandchildren as predictors of grandparents' psychological well-being.* Paper presented at the Annual Scientific Meeting of the Gerontological Society of America, San Francisco, CA.

Ware, J. E., Jr. (1993). *SF-36 health survey: Manual and interpretation guide.* Boston, MA: The Health Institute, New England Medical Center.

Weissman, M. M., Wickramaratne, P., Nomura, Y., Warner, V., Verdeli, H., Pilowsky, D. J., et al. (2005). Families at high and low risk for depression: A 3-generation study. *Archives of General Psychiatry, 62,* 29–36.

Weisz, J. R., Jensen-Doss, A., & Hawley, K. M. (2006). Evidence-based youth psychotherapies versus usual clinical care: A meta-analysis of direct comparisons. *American Psychologist, 61,* 671–689.

Young, M. H., & Dawson, T. J. (2003). Perception of child difficulty and levels of depression in caregiving grandmothers. *Journal of Mental Health and Aging, 9,* 111–122.

CHAPTER 4

Grandchildren's Difficulties and Strengths Impact the Mental Health of Their Grandparents

Bert Hayslip, Jr., Jennifer K. King, and Jane L. Jooste

Grandparents are often thrust unexpectedly into a re-parenting role for which they may be ill prepared, leaving them feeling confused and unsure (Cox, 2000). The energy levels and physical demands of raising children, particularly young infants or rebellious teenagers, are taxing for grandparents. If, in addition, the grandparents are in poor health, this may impede their ability to effectively fulfill the demands of their role (Cox, 2000).

Grandparent caregivers face several challenges in becoming active parents once more. One such unique challenge is having to act in both a parental and grandparental role. As the role of the grandparent caregiver becomes closer to that of a parenting role, the original grandparent-grandchild relationship, which may have been highly valued, is sometimes lost (Cox, 2000; Targ & Britnall-Peterson, 2001).

Musil (2000) reported that primary-caregiver grandmothers reported significantly greater parenting stress than the partial caregivers. Grandparent caregivers may be dissatisfied with their original child-rearing outcomes that ultimately led them to assume care of their grandchild, and now hope to improve their parenting (Hayslip & Kaminski, 2005a). Grandparent caregivers themselves have requested direction and information about parenting issues (Kennedy & Keeney, 1987). Grandparent caregivers who have participated in parent training have reported a decrease in negative affect scores related to their grandchild's behavior, in addition to an increase in parental self-efficacy and the quality of their relationship with their grandchild over time (Hayslip, 2003).

While parents themselves are faced with unprecedented parenting stress related to recent cultural changes, it is likely that this may be exacerbated for custodial grandparents. The understanding of several disorders, especially Attention Deficit Hyperactivity Disorder (ADHD), has changed markedly over the past few decades and it is likely that grandparents may have little knowledge of current diagnostic and treatment procedures (Baker, 2000; Hayslip, 2003). Current knowledge that grandparent caregivers may not be fully aware of includes familiarity with STDs, drug use, school violence, or peer influences on their grandchildren (Silverthorne & Durrant, 2000). Since grandparent caregivers may be particularly susceptible to parenting children with disruptive behavior disorders (Baker, 2000; Silverthorn & Durrant, 2000), they are likely to benefit from education and information about such disorders.

Parenting for grandparent caregivers can also be complicated by their grandchild's temporary or permanent loss of a parent. The bereaved grandchild is likely to require more emotional resources than usual (Hayslip & Kaminski, 2006). Since grandparents may be mourning some sort of loss related to their adult child themselves, they may not be in a position to be as emotionally available. When an adult child is in jail or experiencing substance abuse problems, grandparent caregivers may need to deal with their own feelings of sadness, frustration, and disappointment (Chenoweth, 2000).

Complicating such challenges in parenting a grandchild is a lack of both emotional and instrumental support from others, leading to isolation, depression, and poorer health. Indeed, the availability of social support has been shown to have an impact on one's physical (Krause, 2001) and emotional health (i.e., Antonucci, 2001). The availability of adequate social support (or lack thereof) may thus be an important factor in contributing to the success (or difficulties) of grandparent-headed households. Changes in social support are often one of the consequences of becoming a grandparent caregiver. Giarrusso, Silverstein, and Feng (2000) found evidence that social support, in the number of confidants that one has, buffers the negative effects of stress on a grandparent caregiver's psychological well-being.

An important area of difficulty for grandparent caregivers involves changes in their social supports when they assume caregiving responsibilities. Many grandparent caregivers report feeling isolated (Kopera-Frye, Wiscott, & Begovic, 2003) and less satisfied with their social lives than before taking in their grandchildren (Fuller-Thomson & Minkler, 2000; Hayslip, Shore, Henderson, & Lambert, 1998). Wohl, Lahner, and Jooste (2003) noted that the most prominent themes emerging from a group intervention program with custodial grandparents were difficulties involving relationships with others, relationships with the parents of the grandchildren, and relationships with the grandchildren themselves. Grandparents reported losing friends when they took on the caregiving role, mostly because the active parent role was no longer relevant to their friends' lives. In addition, finding support and friendship among active parents may be difficult if the age difference between grandparent caregivers and traditional parents creates barriers to relationships (Wohl, Lahner, & Jooste, 2003), putting grandparent caregivers at risk for social isolation (Cox, 2000).

Family relationships also tend to change, which is likely to impact upon the grandparent's sources of support. An adult child may have become an adversary. Hayslip, Baird, Toledo, Toledo, and Emick's (2006) qualitative study of grandparent caregivers also suggested adversarial relationships with their adult children in their comments advising others to "hire a lawyer" and "get custody to keep the parents away from the grandchildren." Alternatively, the grandparent may have less support after experiencing the death of his or her own child (see Waldrop & Weber, 2001).

GRANDPARENT CAREGIVER STRESS AND COPING

Gatz, Bengtson, and Blum (1990) have provided a framework for understanding grandparent caregiver stress and coping. They identified four elements within the framework. First, stressors were broken down into the health problems of the care recipient and changes in the caregiver's life from meeting the demands of providing care. Relevant to the present study, changes in the caregiver's life include parental role overload and strain, time limitations, and financial difficulties. The second element is the appraisal of the symptoms of the care recipient and the alterations to the caregiver's life. In that light, Haley, Levine, Brown, and Bartolucci (1987) found that subjective appraisals of care-recipient problems and self-efficacy in managing behavioral problems were able to predict levels of depression better than objective measures. The last element of the framework is outcomes or indicators of stress, such as emotional distress, illness, and altered relationships.

As Gatz et al. (1990) described, the stress-and-coping framework "highlights the salience of appraisals and mediators in determining what aspects of caregiving are difficult, it allows for individual differences in interpreting and handling stressors, and it employs multiple indicators of adaptation" (p. 415). For the purposes of this study, the Gatz et al. (1990) conceptual framework of caregiver stress and coping was utilized as a working framework for examining the role of the perception of grandchild strengths and difficulties in predicting caregiver outcomes.

CAREGIVING IN CONTEXT

Emphasizing the interpersonal context of caregiving is consistent with the importance of the relationship between the characteristics of the person being cared for and adjustment among grandparent caregivers. As suggested by Montgomery and Williams (2001), the caregiving context is largely defined by the role relationship, and they described two levels to this relationship: (a) the structural level or norms associated with gender, generation, and culture that influence behaviors; and (b) the dyadic history of interaction level or individual and family histories of the relationship, as well as personality factors of each person. These researchers stated that caregiving dyads adopt general societal norms to the unique realities of their own families, creating individualized sets of expectations for the role of the caregiver. Therefore, the interpersonal context is a dynamic feature that may impact the caregiving experience in a multitude of ways. For grandparent caregivers, impaired parental skills may create problems in their grandchildren, or problems in a grandchild (that may predate or be caused by the new familial arrangement) may undermine parental efficacy and personal adjustment (see Hayslip & Kaminski, 2006).

According to Gatz et al. (1990), impact constitutes a dimension of the stressors to which caregivers respond. In this light, Talkington-Boyer and Snyder (1994) found that higher levels of perceived negative impact were related to higher self-rated levels of depressive symptoms, while less overall impact was associated with higher degrees of problem-solving coping behaviors, self-esteem, and social support. Indeed, the problematic behaviors of grandchildren have been found to exert greater demands on grandparents who are raising these grandchildren (Hayslip, Shore, Henderson, & Lambert, 1998).

PURPOSE OF THE PRESENT STUDY

In the context of a lack of attention to grandchild variables as keys to understanding grandparent caregivers, and in view of the above emphasis upon the role of the interpersonal/dyadic relationship between grandparent and grandchild, the purposes of the present study were to (1) present normative data regarding perceptions of grandchild strengths and difficulties by grandparent caregivers, and (2) to examine the relationship between such perceptions and grandparent caregiver stress and adjustment.

METHOD

Participants

A total of 92 grandparent caregivers who provided full-time care in their home to a child under the age of 18 participated in the study (10 males and 82 females). Volunteers from caregiving support groups within the North Texas area were recruited, as well as friends or relatives of undergraduate students in psychology classes from the University of North Texas.

Table 4.1 presents descriptive data for the grandparent caregiver group. Grandparents raising grandchildren had a mean age of 58.66 (SD = 9.22), and 56.28 (SD = 11.50) respectively, while the parents' mean age was 37.83 (SD = 8.84). Of these grandparents, 54.3% were working outside the home. Of those caregivers who were employed, the majority reported working full time (83.7%). The majority of grandparents (58.7%) reported spending 30 plus

TABLE 4.1 Description of Sample: Grandparents Raising Grandchildren

		n	%
Marital status			
	Single	6	6.5
	Married	56	60.9
	Divorced	18	19.6
	Widowed	11	12.0
Race			
	White	64	69.6
	Hispanic	6	6.5
	African American	18	19.6
	American Indian	1	1.1
	Asian American	1	1.1
	Other	0	0
		M	**SD**
Age		58.66	9.22
Education		13.34	2.74
Number of children		2.90	1.65
Number of grandchildren		4.03	3.61
Number of years providing care		5.33	4.83
Age of person caring for		9.74	7.36

hours a week caring for their grandchild, and the majority of grandparents (53.3%) in the sample indicated that they were caring for a male grandchild.

Measures

Demographic variables. All of the participants were asked to provide basic demographic information including race, gender, age, marital status, religion, education, gender of the child being cared for, and employment status. Specific information concerning the provision of care was also obtained from all participants (e.g., age of care recipient, length of time providing care, number of hours per week spent in providing care, relationship to care recipient, whether the caregiver co-resided with the care recipient, reasons for assuming care, and a single item indicator of the quality of the relationship with the grandchild and burdens linked to it at present).

Impact of caregiving. The impact of caregiving factor of the Caregiving Appraisal Scale (CAS; Lawton, Kleban, Moss, Rovine, & Glicksman, 1989) was utilized as a measure of the negative changes in the caregiver's life (e.g., harmful effect upon relationships with family members). This factor of the CAS includes four items on which participants use a 5-point Likert scale to rate the extent to which a statement is true (*nearly always* to *never*) or the extent to which the caregiver agrees with a statement (*strongly agree* to *strongly disagree*). Lawton et al. (1989) reported a test-retest coefficient over 16 weeks for the institutionalization sample of .75 for caregiving impact. Internal consistency (Cronbach's alpha) for the respite sample was .70 for caregiving impact. For the institutionalization sample, Cronbach's alpha was .65. Higher scores indicated increased changes in the caregiver's life.

Life disruption. To also assess caregiving impact, the extent of life disruption experienced was measured by applying items proposed by Jendrek (1993) in research relative to grandparents raising grandchildren. The scale consists of 20 items addressing the extent to which caring for a relative has affected the caregiver. The items are rated on a 5-point Likert scale ranging from *not at all* to *a great deal.* An internal consistency reliability coefficient of .93 was calculated based on a study of grandparents raising grandchildren (Hayslip, 2003). Participants were asked about such disruptions as the impact of caregiving upon their lives in areas such as recreation time, interactions with friends, and privacy. Higher scores revealed increased disruption.

Behavioral and emotional problems of grandchildren and children. The central focus of the present study—perceived grandchild difficulties—was assessed via the Strengths and Difficulties Questionnaire (SDQ; Goodman, 1997), which provided a measure of the grandchildren and children's symptoms, as well as positive attributes as perceived by the grandparent. The informant-rated version was designed for use with either parents or teachers. The scale consists of 25 items with five items on each of five scales: conduct problems, hyperactivity-inattention, emotional symptoms, peer problems, and prosocial behavior. Items consist of 10 attributes generally identified as strengths (e.g., thoughtful of the feelings of others), 14 generally thought of as difficulties (e.g., fidgets, tearful), and 1 neutral item (e.g., relates better to adults). Items are rated on a 3-point Likert scale from *not true* (0) to *certainly true* (2), with five items being reversed scored. A total score is obtained by adding all the scales together, except the prosocial behavior scale, for a total difficulties score ranging from 0 to 40. Higher scores corresponded to greater difficulties, except on the prosocial scale on which higher scores indicate more prosocial behavior.

An item from the parent-specific impact supplement (Goodman, 1999) was also included but was expanded so that participants provided more specific information. Rather than rating their grandchild or child's overall difficulty in four areas, participants were asked to rate the extent of the child's difficulty in each of the four areas separately, which included emotions, concentration, behavior, and relationships. The ratings ranged from *no difficulties* to *severe difficulties*. Again, higher scores indicated more difficulties.

In detecting conduct and emotional problems, the SDQ has been found to compare to the Child Behavior Checklist and to the Rutter questionnaires, providing evidence of high convergent validity (Goodman, 1997, 1999). The test-retest reliability was calculated with an intraclass correlation of .85 for the total difficulty score and .63 for the impact rating with a 3- to 4-week interval (Goodman, 1999).

Caregiver appraisal. The Caregiving Appraisal Scale (CAS; Lawton et al., 1989) measures three factors: (1) subjective burden (e.g., tired due to caregiving, unpredictable needs of loved one make it difficult to make plans); (2) caregiving satisfaction (e.g., providing care is enjoyable, feel closer to loved one); and (3) impact of caregiving (e.g., harmful effect upon relationships with family members). The impact of caregiving and caregiving satisfaction factor items of the CAS were included in this study. The CAS used here comprises 10 items on which participants use a 5-point Likert scale to rate the extent to which a statement is true (*nearly always* to *never*) or the extent to which the caregiver agrees with a statement (*strongly agree* to *strongly disagree*). Higher scores revealed increased subjective burden or caregiving satisfaction dependent on the factor being examined.

Lawton et al. (1989) reported a test-retest coefficient over 16 weeks for the institutionalization sample of .78 for subjective burden and .76 for caregiving satisfaction. Internal consistencies (Cronbach's alpha) for the respite sample were .85 for subjective burden and .67 for caregiving satisfaction. For the purposes of this study, only the burden and satisfaction components of caregiver appraisal as assessed by Lawton et al. were utilized to reflect appraisal, while the impact component was included as a stressor variable as discussed above.

Caregiver mastery. Pearlin and Schooler (1978) originally developed the Mastery Scale (MS) that was used here to assess the level of caregiving competency and self-efficacy perceived by caregivers. Aneshensel, Pearlin, Mullan, Zarit, and Whitlatch's (1995) study utilized this measure of mastery, reporting an internal consistency reliability of .75. There are seven items on a 4-point Likert scale ranging from 1 (*strongly disagree*) to 4 (*strongly agree*). Items included statements about the caregiver's perceived ability to manage problems and their feelings of helplessness. Higher scores indicated higher perceived mastery.

Positive aspects of caregiving. A scale developed by Tarlow et al. (2004), the Positive Aspects of Caregiving, was used to address the extent to which the caregiver felt that the caregiving experience provided satisfaction and rewards. The measure consists of nine items rated on a 5-point Likert scale from 1 (*disagree a lot*) to 5 (*agree a lot*). The participants responded to statements about whether providing care made them feel better about themselves or life (e.g., useful, appreciated, confident). Higher scores indicated a higher degree of perceived positive rewards from caregiving.

Work and family conflict. The work and family conflict components of measures specifying the caregiver stress process were also included (Gaugler, Kane, & Langlois, 2000; Pearlin, Mullan, Semple, & Skaff, 1990). Work conflict was assessed by five items with a 4-point Likert scale ranging from 1 (*strongly disagree*) to 4 (*strongly agree*). Statements included responses to their level of energy at work and concern about their loved one while at work. Family conflict was measured by 12 items asking participants to estimate the amount of interpersonal tension with family members. Items are rated on a 4-point Likert scale ranging from 1 (*no disagreement*) to 4 (*quite a bit*). Statements included disagreements among the family about a lack of patience with the loved one and family members not providing enough help with caregiving. Internal reliability coefficients of .90 and .75 for family and work conflict, respectively, have been noted. Higher scores suggested higher work and family conflict.

Social support. The Multidimensional Scale of Perceived Social Support (MSPSS), developed by Zimet, Dahlem, Zimet, and Farley (1988), was used to explore the caregiver's perceived social support from family, friends, and significant others. The internal consistency reliability coefficient for the measure is .88. For the significant other, family, and friend subscales, the reliability coefficients were .91, .87, and .85 respectively. With 12 items, the scale employs a 5-point Likert scale from *very strongly disagree* (1) to *very strongly agree* (5). Higher scores indicate more perceived social support. Statements included responses concerning obtaining emotional support from family, having a special person to share both positives and negatives with, and being able to talk with friends about problems (Dahlem, Zimet, & Walker, 1991; Levin, 2000). Higher scores indicate higher levels of social support.

Caregiver burden. The short version of the Zarit Burden Interview (ZBI; Bedard et al., 2001) consists of 12 items addressing aspects of caregiver burden (e.g., not enough time for self, health has suffered, negative effect upon relationships). A 4-point Likert scale ranging from *never* (0) to *nearly always* (4) was used. Internal consistency for the short version was high (Cronbach's alpha = .88), with an alpha of .89 for the personal strain factor and .77 for the role strain factor. Higher scores indicated higher burden.

Depression. The Geriatric Depression Scale–Short Form (GDS–SF; Sheikh & Yesavage, 1986) was included as a measure of depression. The measure consists of 15 items in a *yes* or *no* format, with 10 items indicating the presence of depression when answered positively and the other five indicating depression when answered negatively. Questions included experiences of depressive symptoms such as dissatisfaction with life, feelings of worthlessness, and lack of energy. The short form was shown to successfully differentiate depressed from nondepressed participants. Higher scores suggested more depressive symptoms.

Quality of life. The Medical Outcomes Study 36-Item Short-Form Health Survey (SF–36; Frytak, 2000; McHorney, 1996; Ware & Sherbourne, 1992) was included as a measure of quality of life. The measure consists of an overall health status from the past year, as well as eight health concepts for which participants were asked to consider how they felt in the past 4 weeks: physical functioning, role limitations due to physical problems, social functioning, bodily pain, general mental health, role limitations due to emotional problems, vitality, and general health perceptions. These eight concepts are then divided into a physical and a mental component for scoring purposes. For the eight scales, internal consistency reliability coefficients exceed .75, with most exceeding .80. Higher scores indicated better physical or mental health. The measure has been shown to be associated with longer-health surveys (e.g., Sickness Impact Profile) and is capable of discriminating between types and levels of disease. For this study, good internal consistency reliability was found for the physical component (alpha = .92), as well as the mental component (alpha = .90).

Results and Discussion: Practical Implications of These Findings for Custodial Grandparents

Our findings with respect to the perceived difficulties of grandchildren can be viewed in normative terms, for example, what strengths and difficulties emerge as the most salient in this sample of grandparent caregivers. With reference to the fact that each SDQ item was rated on a scale of 0 = *not true of the grandchild*, 2 = *somewhat true of the grandchild*, and 3 = *certainly true of the grandchild*, Table 4.2 suggests that normatively speaking, the presence of prosocial behavior (e.g., sharing, being considerate of others' feelings, being kind to other children) is the most salient grandchild behavior-related issue in this sample of grandparent caregivers. That such behaviors would be labeled as most characteristic may reflect the importance that this sample of older caregivers places on the quality of one's relationships with others, as well as the negative effects of their grandchildren's observable actions, the absence of which would serve to alienate them from their peers. Indeed, the presence of such behavior is often readily observed by parents and children alike and would likely be characterized as externalized in nature (see Hayslip, Silverthorn, Shore, & Henderson, 2000; Silverthorn & Durant, 2000) to the extent that such problems are likely to create difficulties with other parents, children, or teachers.

This normative finding underscores the importance that grandparent caregivers place on their grandchildren acting altruistically. Indeed, it could reflect the positive manner in which they have chosen to view their grandchildren in the face of the difficulties these children have faced, for example, the death or divorce or their parents. Significantly, as prosocial behavior seems to predict academic achievement in children, the presence of such altruism reflects the additional advantages in grandparents developing communication skills that promote prosocial thinking and behavior in the children under their care (Grusec, 1991; Mills & Grusec, 1989), as well as developing disciplinary techniques (i.e., induction—explaining why a behavior is wrong; Labile & Thompson, 2002). Developing skills that promote altruism is of additional importance in light of the fact that young children (the average age of grandchildren here was 9.74 years, SD = 7.36) are motivated by the approval of others to act prosocially (see Bukatko & Daehler, 2004).

Interestingly, other externalizing behaviors such as hyperactivity or conduct problems were not rated as consistently present in nature as prosocial behaviors. While there is evidence in Table 4.2 that other difficulties such as being scared, anxious, or even having difficulties with other children are viewed as problems, there is a great deal more variability in such perceptions than those associated with prosocial or altruistic behavior. This variability emerges as a source of the difficulties some grandparents and not others face in raising their grandchildren (Hayslip & Hicks Patrick, 2006). Table 4.2 also suggests that the weight given to some problems as characteristic of a grandchild could reflect the fact that such difficulties are indeed remediable, and is consistent with the observation that grandparents often seek help for their

TABLE 4.2 Grandchild Strengths and Difficulties: Normative Data

	M	SD	Range
Considerate of other people's feelings	1.41	.56	0–2
Restless, overactive, cannot stay still for long	.93	.77	0–2
Often complains of headaches, stomachaches, sickness	.54	.70	0–2
Shares readily with other children (treats, toys, pencils)	1.34	.64	0–2
Often has temper tantrums or hot tempers	.57	.67	0–2
Rather solitary, tends to play alone	.44	.65	0–2
Generally obedient, usually does what adults request	1.46	.57	0–2
Many worries, often seems worried	.53	.71	0–2
Helpful if someone is hurt, upset, or feeling ill	1.68	.50	0–2
Constantly fidgeting or squirming	.64	.75	0–2
Has at least one good friend	1.64	.58	0–2
Often fights with other children or bullies them	.16	.43	0–2
Often unhappy, down-hearted, or tearful	.23	.51	0–2
Generally liked by other children	1.61	.54	0–2
Easily distracted, concentration wanders	.96	.70	0–2
Nervous or clingy in new situations, easily loses confidence	.61	.60	0–2
Kind to younger children	1.61	.54	0–2
Often lies or cheats	.39	.60	0–2
Picked on or bullied by other children	.23	.53	0–2
Often volunteers to help others (parents, teachers, other children)	1.45	.64	0–2
Thinks things out before acting	.90	.60	0–2
Steals from home, school, or elsewhere	.20	.51	0–2
Gets on better with adults than with other children	.61	.74	0–2
Many fears, easily scared	.52	.70	0–2
Sees tasks through to the end, good attention span	.95	.63	0–2
Emotional difficulties[a]	.75	.79	0–3
Difficulty in concentration[a]	.99	.89	0–3
Behavioral difficulties[a]	.84	.83	0–3
Difficulties in relationships[a]	.56	.72	0–3
SDQ pro (5 items)[b]	1.50	.42	.20–2
SDQ hyp (5 items)[b]	.91	.54	0–2

(Continued)

TABLE 4.2 (*Continued*)

	M	SD	Range
SDQ emo (5 items)[b]	.46	.45	0–1.60
SDQ con (5 items)[b]	.34	.30	0–1.40
SDQ peer (5 items)[b]	.39	.33	0–1.40
SDQ diff (4 items)[b,c]	.76	.63	0–3

Note. All data presented are with reference to the grandchild's behavior in the previous 6 months. [a] = General perceived difficulties. [b] = Corrected for number of items in each scale. [c] = Overall difficulties (summative across hype, emo, con, and peer).

grandchildren before they seek help for themselves (Hayslip & Shore, 2000). In this sample, this seems to be particularly true for hyperactivity or inattention (see Baker, 2000).

The relative lack of such problem behaviors perceived to be characteristic of one's grandchild may reflect a grandparent's sense that the ultimate parental accomplishment is to raise a grandchild who grows up to be a caring and compassionate human being, reflecting the importance that older caregivers place on such outcomes, especially given the likelihood that many feel that they will not live long enough to see their grandchildren grow into adulthood. This could reflect the sense of generativity (see Erikson, 1963; McAdams, 2001) associated with custodial grandparenting, often at the expense of one's physical or mental health (Hayslip & Kaminski, 2005a). The normative data here regarding prosocial behavior also suggest that grandparents view their primary function as a role model, advisor, and communicator of traditional values, family customs, and beliefs (Kopera-Frye & Wiscott, 2000; Ruiz, 2004).

Of considerable importance here are the relationships between SDQ variables and other dimensions of both grandchild relationship quality and grandparent caregiver functioning. This is important to the extent that such grandchild-specific variables have largely been ignored in recent discussions of custodial grandparenting (Park & Greenberg, 2007). Moreover, grandparent caregivers whose grandchildren display either emotional or behavioral difficulties face qualitatively different challenges in raising them than do those whose do not display such difficulties (see Silverthorn & Durant, 2000; Hayslip & Kaminski, 2006). Given that grandparent caregivers who are raising problematic grandchildren, who are more often than not males, are more severely impacted by such challenges (Hayslip, Shore, Henderson, & Lambert, 1998; Young & Dawson, 2003), uncovering and understanding such relationships can enlighten grandparent caregivers, therapists, school personnel, and social workers to more fully appreciate the role that such influences play in determining the mental, physical, and psychosocial health of grandparent caregivers. Such caregivers are often marginalized by others and report feeling isolated, alone, and "invisible" (Wohl et al., 2003).

Table 4.3 suggests that grandchild difficulties may indeed play a powerful role in influencing the mental and psychosocial adjustment of grandparent caregivers. As these data are correlational, one should be cautious about inferring causality in that such difficulties may reflect ongoing problems (i.e., grief; see Hayslip & Kaminski, 2006) predating the grandchild's placement with the grandparent and stemming from the death, divorce, incarceration of, or abandonment by the child's parents. Alternatively, they may reflect difficulties associated with a problematic relationship with the grandparent, and thus represent dyadic, communicative difficulties between grandchild and grandparent that would need to be addressed in family therapy. In this respect, Goodman and Hayslip (this volume) suggest that better grandparent mental health may influence the grandchild's adjustment, or that the grandchild's problems may undermine grandparent caregiver health. Thus, the relationship between the two may be bidirectional in nature.

With these cautions in mind, it is quite clear (see Table 4.3) that perceived grandchild difficulties are reliably associated with numerous self-reported difficulties among custodial grandparents in this sample. For example, increased prosocial behaviors were associated with less work conflict and with older grandparent caregiver age. In the latter respect, it may be that older grandparent caregivers are more able to promote such characteristics, born of greater life experience, wisdom, or generativity (being committed to the welfare of younger persons who are likely to outlive them). On the other hand, in both a specific and a more general sense, greater perceived difficulties are consistently associated with greater work and family conflict, lower grandchild relationship quality, greater burdens associated with caregiving, less perceived social support from others, greater caregiver depression, less caregiver mastery, greater life disruption, and less role satisfaction and positive thinking.

These findings clearly suggest that the presence of grandchild behavioral or emotional problems may indeed serve to undermine grandparent caregivers' mental health and deprive them of needed emotional and instrumental support from others, leading to their social isolation and perhaps poorer mental health (see Hayslip et al., 1998; Hayslip & Shore, 2000). Such difficulties not only serve to alienate grandparent and grandchild, but also create barriers to maintaining a semblance of a normal life in light of their likely negative impact on the grandparents' acquisition of specific child-care and communication skills when they must cope with emotional problems, hyperactivity or inattention, conflicts with peers and other adults, and behavior that is impulsive or

TABLE 4.3 Relationships Between SDQ and GP/GC Variables

	SDQ pro[a]	SDQ hyp[b]	SDQ mot[c]	SDQ con[d]	SDQ peer[e]	SDQ diff[f]	Emot[g]	Con[h]	Beh[i]	Rel[j]
GC age	-.21*	—	—	—	—	—	.23*	—	—	—
Work conflict	—	.24*	.37**	.27*	—	.31*	—	.22*	.31*	.24*
Home conflict	—	.35**	—	.41**	.28*	.47**	.41**	.41**	.45**	.45**
GC relationship quality	—	.36**	.28*	—	—	.50**	.41**	-.45**	-.49**	-.41**
GC burden	—	—	.41**	—	—	.34**	.42**	—	—	.35**
GP age	.23*	-.25*	—	—	—	—	—	—	—	—
GP education	—	—	-.24*	—	—	—	—	—	—	—
Support	—	-.32**	-.25*	—	.35**	-.28*	-.30**	-.32*	-.21*	-.28*
GP depression	—	—	.24*	—	-.28*	—	—	—	—	—
Caregiver mastery	—	-.26*	-.30**	—	-.28*	-.35**	-.28*	—	—	-.38**
Life disruption	—	—	.26*	.27*	.31*	.39**	.21*	—	—	.45**
CG burden	—	.31**	.33**	.31**	.29*	.51**	.43**	.36**	.37**	.48**
Positive thinking	—	-.39**	—	-.30**	—	-.41**	—	-.45**	-.24*	-.37**
CG imp	—	.51**	.38*	.46**	—	.67**	.52**	.60**	.45**	.60**
CG sat	—	-.26*	-.39**	-.32**	—	-.44**	-.34**	-.30**	-.33**	.42**
QOL physical	—	—	-.24*	—	-.31**	—	—	—	—	—
QOL mental	—	-.38**	-.41**	—	-.39**	-.35**	-.30**	-.33**	—	-.28*

* p < .05; ** p < .01

CGimp = impact of caregiving; CGsat = satisfaction with caregiving.

Note. [a] = prosocial behavior (5 items). [b] = hyperactivity-inattention (5 items). [c] = emotional problems (5 items). [d] = conduct problems (5 items). [e] = peer difficulties (5 items). [f] = total difficulties (4 items). [g] = emotional difficulty—single rating. [h] = difficulties in concentration—single rating. [i] = behavioral difficulties—single rating. [j] = difficulties in relationships—single rating.

destructive. The processes that explain such relationships are many. It may be, for example, that poor grandparent mental health predisposes the caregiver to be preoccupied with their own unhappiness and the impact of raising a grandchild on their mental and physical health, their relationships with others, or on the quality of their marriages. Thus, they may fail to pick up on cues from the grandchild that he or she is distressed. Difficulties in relationships created by a grandchild's problems may exacerbate the situation further, and underscore the timely provision of social, emotional, or instrumental support from friends, family, or service providers.

It is also certainly possible that the difficulties children bring to their relationship with a grandparent (or those that predate the move from the child's family of origin) cause grandparents to delay seeking help for themselves because of the stigma of either raising an adult child who failed as a parent (see Wohl et al., 2003), or having to now raise a grandchild who is manifesting emotional or behavioral difficulties. Indeed, there is some evidence to suggest that seeking help for mental health issues is viewed negatively by older persons (Currin, Hayslip, Schnieder, & Kooken, 1998; Knight, Kaskie, Shurgot, & Dave, 2006), who must interact with numerous barriers to seeking professional help (e.g., access to and knowledge of services, cost, service provider attitudes and biases).

In this respect, being consumed with one's own emotional or physical problems may not be a priority in the context of mustering the energy to actively parent a child on a daily basis, having to deal with conflicts about caregiving demands involving family members (e.g., one's spouse or adult child) or one's employer, adjusting to a newly defined lifestyle, giving up time for oneself or with one's spouse, or changing future plans (i.e., retirement), to say nothing of needing to understand and seek help for a grandchild's depression, school difficulties, conflicts with age peers, or hyperactivity or inattention. Grandparents therefore may be treading water emotionally, leaving them little time and resources to tend to their own grief, sadness, disappointment, or depression as a reaction to raising a grandchild in midlife or late adulthood. That grandparent caregivers in the United States would see such responsibilities as an impediment or a requirement thrust upon them, versus seeing them (as is the case among Mexican-born grandparent caregivers) as an extension of an ongoing relationship with a grandchild or adult child in the context of "family first," as has been demonstrated elsewhere (Hayslip, Baird, Toledo, Toledo, & Emick, 2006; Toledo, Hayslip, Emick, Toledo, & Hendson, 2000).

Interestingly, we found that there were no grandchild gender differences in SDQ scores. This is inconsistent with previous work (Hayslip et al., 1998) suggesting that problematic grandchildren (who were more often than not males) are associated with impaired grandparent caregiver functioning and role satisfaction. Moreover, they are inconsistent with a larger scale ($n = 733$) study by Smith and Palmieri (2007), who found higher SDQ scores among male versus female custodial grandchildren. Perhaps sampling differences between the present study and those of Hayslip et al. and Smith and Palmieri might account for these discrepancies, though the grandchildren in the Smith and Palmieri sample were similarly aged, relative to the present sample of grandchildren about whom grandparents reported.

These data are not only consistent with the additional burdens that grandparents raising problematic grandchildren face in raising them (see Hayslip et al., 1998), but also suggest that in light of the sometimes problematic child-rearing attitudes that custodial grandparents may hold (see Kaminski, Hayslip, Wilson, & Casto, in press), parental training to impact child-rearing skills should be encouraged. This might take the form of training grandparents in productive ways of communicating with a grandchild, positive discipline (explaining why a child is being disciplined), maintaining one's cool in the face of conflicts, being emotionally and physically present for the child, encouraging emotional intimacy and openness, encouraging responsible behavior, and fostering positive views of oneself (Hayslip & Kaminski, 2006; Kern, 2003). Such skills are consistent with an authoritative parenting style (Baumrind, 1991).

These findings also suggest that support and respite are critical to custodial grandparents who are raising problematic grandchildren. This might come in the form of helping the grandparent gain access to support groups (see Smith, 2003), making it possible for the grandparent to access mental health care, or encouraging more contact with age peers (i.e., grandparents who are not raising their grandchildren), who might provide a needed break from the everyday demands of child rearing. Likewise, bringing custodial grandparents into contact with professionals who might assist them in developing new parenting skills or honing old ones, strengthen their sense of efficacy as a parent, or educate them about such issues as ADHD, drug use, antisocial behavior, learning difficulties, depression, grief, and suicide, are all viable alternatives in targeting stressed and distressed custodial grandparents. Likewise, grandparent caregivers' well-being might be enhanced by helping them to (1) develop techniques to minimize or stabilize the influence of a "sometimes here, sometimes not here" parent in the grandchild's life (see Dannison & Smith, 2003) by setting clearly defined visiting hours, or otherwise setting boundaries with an adult child; (2) gain confidence in their ability to help a grandchild adjust to new routines at school, perhaps by immersing themselves in the child's interpersonal network of friends and teachers; or (3) even assist grandchildren with their homework.

As these findings suggest that problematic grandchildren's impact on family functioning or work performance may be substantial (though bidirectional in nature), family therapy can be very helpful in this respect (see Brown-Standridge & Floyd, 2000). Moreover, encouraging proactive discussions with a spouse or close friends about the necessity of reallocating the time one spends working, or asking for redefined work responsibilities when difficult times demand more parental involvement, might be quite helpful for many custodial grandparents. As with persons who are grieving the loss of a family member through death (see Corr, Nabe, & Corr, 2006), grandparents should be encouraged to talk about their own losses, for example, friendships, career or retirement aspirations, good health, time alone with a spouse, so that they can not only avoid the sense of feeling isolated and "invisible" (Wohl et al., 2003), but also be more emotionally available to a troubled grandchild. Indeed, grief is a central dimension of raising a grandchild (Baird, 2003) and is often underrecognized by others, leading to its disenfranchisement among grandparent caregivers (Miltenberger, Hayslip, Harris, & Kaminski, 2003–2004).

These findings reflect needed attention to the role of a grandchild's strengths and difficulties as a dimension of the adjustments grandparent caregivers face in dealing with their newly acquired roles as parents, as well as in influencing family system processes (see Goodman, 2003). That such factors have been largely ignored in the custodial grandparenting literature to date should alert us to the active role that grandchildren play in defining the experience of custodial grandparenting, growing out of the mutually interactive and influential role that such grandparents and their grandchildren play in one another's lives.

REFERENCES

Aneshensel, C. S., Pearlin, L. I., Mullan J. T., Zarit, S. H., & Whitlatch, C. J. (1995). *Profiles in caregiving: The unexpected career.* New York: Academic Press.

Antonucci, T. C. (2001). Social networks, social support, and sense of control. In J. E. Birren & K. W. Schaie (Eds.), *Handbook of the psychology of aging* (5th ed.). New York: Academic Press.

Baird, A. (2003). Through my eyes: Service needs of grandparents who raise their grandchildren, from the perspective of a custodial grandmother. In B. Hayslip, Jr., & J. Patrick (Eds.), *Working with custodial grandparents* (pp. 59–68). New York: Springer.

Baker, D. (2000). Custodial grandparenting and ADHD. In B. Hayslip, Jr., & R. Goldberg-Glen (Eds.), *Grandparents raising grandchildren: Theoretical, empirical, and clinical perspectives* (pp. 145–160). New York: Springer.

Baumrind, D. (1991). Parenting styles and adolescent development. In R. M. Lerner, A. C. Petersen, & J. Brooks-Gunn (Eds.), *Encyclopedia of adolescence.* New York: Garland Publishing.

Bedard, M., Molloy, D. W., Squire, L., Dubois, S., Lever, J. A., & O'Donnell, M. (2001). The Zarit burden interview: A new short version and screening version. *The Gerontologist, 41,* 652–657.

Brown-Standridge, M., & Floyd, C. (2000). Healing bittersweet legacies: Revisiting contextual family therapy for grandparents raising grandchildren. *Journal of Marital and Family Therapy, 26,* 185–197.

Bukatko, D., & Daehler, M. (2004). *Child development: A thematic approach.* Boston: Houghlin Mifflin.

Chenoweth, L. (2000). *Grandparent education.* In B. Hayslip, Jr. & R. Goldberg-Glen (Eds.), *Grandparents raising grandchildren: Theoretical, empirical, and clinical perspectives* (pp. 307–326). New York: Springer.

Corr, C., Nabe, P., & Corr, D. (2006). *Death and dying: Life and living.* Pacific Grove, CA: Wadsworth.

Cox, C. (2000). Empowering grandparents raising grandchildren. In C. Cox (Ed.), *To grandmother's house we go and stay: Perspectives on custodial grandparents* (pp. 253–267). New York: Springer.

Currin, J., Hayslip, B., Jr., Schneider, L., & Kooken, R. (1998). Cohort differences in attitudes toward mental health services among older persons. *Psychotherapy, 35,* 506–518.

Dahlem, N. W., Zimet, G. D., & Walker, R. R. (1991). The multidimensional scale of perceived social support: A confirmation study. *Journal of Clinical Psychology, 47,* 756–761.

Dannison, C., & Smith, A. (2003). Custodial grandparents' community support program: Lessons learned. *Children & Schools, 25,* 87–95.

Erikson, E. (1963). *Childhood and society.* New York: Norton.

Frytak, J. R. (2000). Assessment of quality of life in older adults. In R. L. Kane & R. A. Kane (Eds.), *Assessing older persons: Measures, meaning, and practical applications* (pp. 200–236). New York: Oxford University Press.

Fuller-Thomson, E., & Minkler, M. (2000). America's grandparent caregivers: Who are they? In B. Hayslip, Jr., & R. Goldberg-Glen (Eds.), *Grandparents raising grandchildren: Theoretical, empirical, and clinical perspectives* (pp. 3–21). New York: Springer.

Gatz, M., Bengtson, V. L., & Blum, M. J. (1990). Caregiving families. In J. E. Birren & K. W. Schaie (Eds.), *Handbook of the psychology of aging* (3rd ed., pp. 404–426). New York: Academic Press.

Gaugler, J. E., Kane, R. A., & Langlois, J. (2000). Assessment of family caregivers of older adults. In R. L. Kane & R. A. Kane (Eds.), *Assessing older persons: Measures, meaning, and practical applications* (pp. 320–359). New York: Oxford University Press.

Giarrusso, R., Silverstein, M., & Feng, D. (2000). Psychological costs and benefits of raising grandchildren: Evidence from a national survey. In C. Cox (Ed.), *To grandmother's house we go and stay: Perspectives on custodial grandparents* (pp. 71–90). New York: Springer.

Goodman, C. (2003). Intergenerational triads in grandparent-headed families. *The Gerontologist, 42,* 676–689.

Goodman, R. (1997). The strengths and difficulties questionnaire: A research note. *Journal of Child Psychology and Psychiatry, 38,* 581–586.

Goodman, R. (1999). The extended version of the strengths and difficulties questionnaire as a guide to child psychiatric caseness and consequent burden. *Journal of Child Psychology and Psychiatry, 40,* 791–799.

Grusec, J. (1991). Socializing concern for others in the home. *Developmental Psychology, 27,* 338–342.

Haley, W. E., Levine, E. G., Brown, S. L., & Bartolucci, A. A. (1987). Stress, appraisal, coping, and social support as predictors of adaptational outcome among dementia caregivers. *Psychology and Aging, 2,* 323–330.

Hayslip, B., Jr. (2003). The impact of a psychosocial intervention on parental efficacy, grandchild relationship quality, and well-being among grandparents raising grandchildren. In B. Hayslip, Jr., & J. H. Patrick (Eds.), *Working with custodial grandparents* (pp. 163–176). New York: Springer.

Hayslip, B., Jr., Baird, A., Toledo, R., Toledo, C., & Emick, M. (2006). Cross cultural differences in traditional and custodial grandparenting: A qualitative approach. In B. Hayslip, Jr., & J. Hicks Patrick (Eds.), *Custodial grandparents: Individual, cultural, and ethnic diversity.* (pp. 169–182). New York: Springer.

Hayslip, B., Jr., & Hicks Patrick, J. (2006). Epilogue. In B. Hayslip, Jr., & J. Hicks Patrick (Eds.), *Custodial grandparents: Individual, cultural, and ethnic diversity* (pp. 321–330). New York: Springer.

Hayslip, B., Jr., & Kaminski, P. L. (2005a). Grandparents raising their grandchildren. *Marriage and Family Review, 37,* 147–169.

Hayslip, B., Jr., & Kaminski, P. L. (2005b). Grandparents raising their grandchildren: A review of the literature and suggestions for practice. *The Gerontologist, 45,* 262–269.

Hayslip, B., Jr., & Kaminski, P. L. (2006). Custodial grandchildren. In G. G. Bear & K. Minke (Eds.), *Children's needs III: Development, prevention, and intervention* (pp. 771–782). Washington, DC: National Association of School Psychologists.

Hayslip, B., Jr., & Shore, R. J. (2000). Custodial grandparenting and mental health services. *Journal of Mental Health and Aging, 6,* 367–384.

Hayslip, B., Jr., Shore, R. J., Henderson, C., & Lambert, P. (1998). Custodial grandparenting and the impact of grandchildren with problems on role meaning. *Journals of Gerontology, 53B,* S164–S174.

Hayslip, B., Jr., Silverthorn, P., Shore, R. J., & Henderson, C. (2000). Determinants of custodial grandparents' perceptions of problem behavior in their grandchildren. In B. Hayslip, Jr., & R. Goldberg-Glen (Eds.), *Grandparents raising grandchildren: Theoretical, empirical, and clinical perspectives* (pp. 225–268). New York: Springer.

Jendrek, M. (1993). Grandparents who parent their grandchildren: Effects in lifestyle. *Journal of Marriage and the Family, 55,* 609–621.

Kaminski, P., Hayslip, B., Jr., Wilson, J., & Casto, L. (in press). Parenting attitudes and adjustment among custodial grandparents. *Journal of Intergenerational Relationships.*

Kennedy, J., & Keeney, V. (1987). Group psychotherapy with grandparents raising their emotionally disturbed grandchildren. *GROUP, 11,* 15–25.

Kern, C. W. (2003). Grandparents who are parenting again: Building parenting skills. In B. Hayslip, Jr., & J. H. Patrick (Eds.), *Working with custodial grandparents* (pp. 179–193). New York: Springer.

Knight, B., Kaskie, B., Shurgot, G., & Dave, J. (2006). Improving the mental health care of older adults. In J. E. Birren & K. W. Shaie (Eds.), *Handbook of the psychology of aging* (pp. 407–424). San Diego, CA: Academic Press.

Kopera-Frye, K., & Wiscott, R. (2000). Intergenerational continuity: Transmission of beliefs and culture. In B. Hayslip, Jr., & R. Goldberg-Glen (Eds.), *Grandparents raising grandchildren: Theoretical, empirical and clinical perspectives* (pp. 65–84). New York: Springer

Kopera-Frye, K., Wiscott, R. C., & Begovic, A. (2003). Lessons learned from custodial grandparents involved in a community support group. In B. Hayslip, Jr., & J. Hicks Patrick (Eds.), *Working with custodial grandparents* (pp. 243–256). New York: Springer

Krause, N. (2001). Social support. In R. H. Binstock & L. K. George (Eds.), *Handbook of aging and the social sciences* (5th ed., pp. 273–294). San Diego, CA: Academic Press.

Labile, D., & Thompson, R. (2002). Mother-child discourse, attachment security, shared positive affects, and early conscience development. *Child Development, 73,* 1187–1203.

Lawton, M. P., Kleban, M. H., Moss, M., Rovine, M., & Glicksman, A. (1989). Measuring caregiving appraisal. *Journal of Gerontology, 44,* P61–P71.

Levin, C. (2000). Social functioning. In R. L. Kane & R. A. Kane (Eds.), *Assessing older persons: Measures, meaning, and practical applications* (pp. 170–199). New York: Oxford University Press.

McAdams, D. (2001). Generativity in midlife. In M. Lachman (Ed.), *Handbook of midlife development* (pp. 395–446). New York: Wiley.

McHorney, C. A. (1996). Measuring and monitoring general health status in elderly persons: Practical and methodological issues in using the SF-36 Health Survey. *The Gerontologist, 36,* 571–583.

Mills, R., & Grusec, J. (1989). Cognitive, affective, and behavioral consequences of praising altruism. *Merrill-Palmer Quarterly, 35,* 299–326.

Miltenberger, P., Hayslip, B., Jr., Harris, B., & Kaminski, P. (2003–2004). Perceptions of the losses experienced by custodial grandmothers. *Omega: Journal of Death and Dying, 48,* 245–262.

Montgomery, R. J., & Williams, K. N. (2001). Implications of differential impacts of care-giving for future research on Alzheimer care. *Aging & Mental Health, 5*(Supplement 1), S23–S34.

Musil, C. (2000). Health of grandmothers as caregivers: A 10-month follow-up. *Journal of Women and Aging, 12,* 129–145.

Park, H. H., & Greenberg, J. S. (2007). Parenting grandchildren. In J. Blackburn & C. Dulumus (Eds.), *Handbook of gerontology: Evidence based approaches to theory, research, and policy* (pp. 397–425). New York: Wiley.

Pearlin, L. I., Mullan, J. T., Semple, S. J., & Skaff, M. M. (1990). Caregiving and the stress process: An overview of concepts and their measures. *The Gerontologist, 30*, 583–594.

Pearlin, L. I., & Schooler, C. (1978). The structure of coping. *Journal of Health and Social Behavior, 19*, 2–21.

Ruiz, D. (2004). *Amazing grace: African American grandmothers as caregivers and conveyors of traditional values.* New York: Praeger.

Sheikh, J. I., & Yesavage, J. A. (1986). Geriatric depression scale (GDS): Recent evidence and development of a shorter version. In T. L. Brink (Ed.), *Clinical gerontology: A guide to assessment and intervention* (pp. 165–173). New York: Haworth Press.

Silverthorn, P., & Durrant, S. (2000). Custodial grandparenting and the difficult child: Learning from the parenting literature. In B. Hayslip, Jr., & R. Goldberg-Glen (Eds.), *Grandparents raising grandchildren: Theoretical, empirical, and clinical perspectives* (pp. 47–64). New York: Springer.

Smith, G. C., & Palmieri, P. A. (2007). Risk for psychological difficulties in children raised by custodial grandparents. *Psychiatric Service, 58*, 1303–1310.

Smith, G. S. (2003). How caregiving grandparents view support groups: An exploratory study. In B. Hayslip, Jr., & J. Hicks Patrick (Eds.), *Working with custodial grandparents* (pp. 69–91). New York: Springer.

Talkington-Boyer, S., & Snyder, D. K. (1994). Assessing impact on family caregivers to Alzheimer's disease patients. *The American Journal of Family Therapy, 22*, 57–66.

Targ, D. B., & Britnall-Peterson, M. (2001). Grandparents raising grandchildren: Impact of national satellite video program. *Journal of Family Issues, 22*, 579–593.

Tarlow, B. J., Wisniewski, S. R., Belle, S. H., Rubert, M., Ory, M. G., & Gallagher-Thompson, D. (2004). Positive aspects of caregiving: Contributions of the REACH project to the development of new measures for Alzheimer's caregiving. *Research on Aging, 26*, 429–453.

Toledo, J. R., Hayslip, B., Jr., Emick, M. A., Toledo, C., & Henderson, C. (2000). Cross-cultural differences in custodial grandparenting. In B. Hayslip, Jr., & R. Goldberg-Glen (Eds.), *Grandparents raising grandchildren: Theoretical, empirical, and clinical perspectives* (pp. 107–123). New York: Springer.

Waldrop, D. P., & Weber, J. A. (2001). From grandparent to caregiver: The stress and satisfaction of raising grandchildren. *Families in Society, 82*, 461–472.

Ware, J. E., & Sherbourne, C. D. (1992). The MOS 36-item Short-Form Health Survey (SF-36): I. Conceptual framework and item selection. *Medical Care, 30*, 473–483.

Wohl, E., Lahner, J., & Jooste, J. (2003). Group processes among grandparents raising grandchildren. In B. Hayslip, Jr., & J. Hicks Patrick (Eds.), *Working with custodial grandparents* (pp. 195–221). New York: Springer.

Young, M., & Dawson, T. (2003). Perception of child difficulty and levels of depression in caregiving grandmothers. *Journal of Mental Health and Aging, 9*, 111–122.

Zimet, G. D., Dahlem, N. Q., Zimet, S. G., & Farley, G. K. (1988). The multidimensional scale of perceived social support. *Journal of Personality Assessment, 52*, 30–41.

CHAPTER 5

Promoting Health for Grandmothers Parenting Young Children

Karen A. Roberto, Megan L. Dolbin-MacNab,
and Jack W. Finney

Grandparents parenting their grandchildren experience changes in lifestyles, relationships, and social roles that may directly and indirectly influence their ability to attend to their own physical and mental health needs (Szinovacz, DeViney, & Atkinson, 1999). Time demands, as well as the physical strain and emotional stress of caring for children at a time in the grandparents' lives when they did not expect to be in a full-time parenting role, leave less time and energy for self-care activities (Pruchno, 1999; Roe, Minkler, Saunders, & Thomson, 1996) and may even promote less than optimal health behaviors such as increased smoking and alcohol consumption and decreased exercise (Burton, 1992; Hughes, Waite, LaPierre, & Luo, 2007; Waldrop & Weber, 2001; Whitley, Kelley, & Sipe, 2001). There also is a tendency among grandparents with parenting responsibilities to delay seeking help for their own health problems (Burnette, 1999; Joslin & Harrison, 1998), which may exacerbate acute and chronic illnesses. Risky health behaviors and physical vulnerabilities may compromise grandparents' functional ability and their ability to parent their grandchildren effectively.

Research on the physical and mental health of grandparents parenting their grandchildren suggests that some grandparents view their health as not affected or even improved as a result of a more active lifestyle and involvement with their grandchild, whereas others report increased physical and mental health problems (Grinstead, Leder, Jensen, & Bond, 2003). Sample size and selection methods, as well as the depth and breadth of the investigations, contribute to these contradictory findings. As noted in a recent review of the literature on the health of grandparents assuming the parental role, the associations between caregiving and health may reflect initially poorer health among grandparents who care for grandchildren, either from increased risk behaviors that place grandparents at greater likelihood of health decline, as a causal effect of caregiving on health, or some combination of these factors (Hughes et al., 2007).

Most empirical investigations of grandparents raising grandchildren have included an assessment of grandparents' mental or emotional health. Results of both small-scale studies and analyses of national data suggest that, when compared to grandparents in more traditional roles, grandparents raising their grandchildren are more likely to report greater stress (Jendrek, 1994; Minkler, Roe, & Price, 1993; Musil & Ahmad, 2002), symptoms of depression (Szinovacz et al., 1999), or clinical depression (Kelley, 1993; Minkler, Fuller-Thomson, Miller, & Driver, 1997). Few researchers include physical health as a primary focus of their studies. When physical health is assessed, researchers tend to use general measures of overall health and note the existence of chronic health conditions such as arthritis and heart disease (Minkler & Fuller-Thomson, 1999; Solomon & Marx, 1999; Strawbridge, Walhagen, Shema, & Kaplan, 1997). Consistently, the findings from these studies suggest that grandparents who serve as primary caregivers for their grandchildren reported significantly worse overall health and more specific health problems than noncaregiving grandparents. Other aspects of health, including engagement in preventive and risky health behaviors, have received little attention in the literature of grandparents raising grandchildren.

Investigators examining patterns of health care use by older adults frequently cite Andersen's (1968, 1995; Andersen & Newman, 1972) Social Behavioral Model (SBM) as their theoretical framework. This model proposes that health care use is a function of predisposing characteristics (e.g., age, education, ethnicity, beliefs or attitudes about health care), enabling factors that either facilitate or impede the use of services (e.g., income, insurance coverage, access to transportation, awareness and availability of health services, family support), and the perceived or evaluated need for services. The SBM is thought to be sequential; that is, need alone does not prompt the use of health care services. Rather, health service use depends upon need, the person's predisposition to seek health care services, and the availability of necessary resources required to use health care services. Although this model is not explicitly referenced in studies of grandparents parenting their grandchildren, findings from the available literature suggest that several predisposing and enabling variables may influence these grandparents' health care practices and behaviors.

For example, the amount of attention grandparents are able to give to their own physical and mental health may be associated with the substantial financial burdens incurred when grandparents assume the parental role (Bachman & Chase-Lansdale, 2005). Having insufficient funds to meet their own needs has been found to contribute to the emotional stress experienced by caregiving grandparents (Burnette, 1999; Dowdell, 1995; Kelley, 1993). Data from a nationally representative household survey of persons living in the United States revealed that grandmothers raising their grandchildren alone (i.e., parents of the grandchildren were absent from the home) were the most likely to be poor and rely on public assistance, while two-grandparent households with no parents present were most likely to be without health insurance (Casper & Bryson, 1998). Together, these findings support the premise that grandparent-headed families, particularly those with fewer economic resources, may be at risk for engaging in less than optimal health practices and experiencing more negative health outcomes.

Family structure, including the age of the grandparents, ages of the grandchildren, the length of time caregiving, the health and behavioral issues of the grandchildren, as well as perceptions of family functioning, also may influence grandparents' health practices and perceptions of physical and mental health. Normative health changes experienced as grandparents age may be exacerbated by the daily activities associated with raising grandchildren. As grandparents get older, they may experience decreasing physical abilities and energy levels that prohibit them from participating fully as a parent. Such age-related declines have been associated with negative expressions of grandparent well-being (Goodman, 2006) and less role satisfaction (Hayslip, Shore, & Emick, 2006). In addition, given their often-complicated histories, children being raised by their grandparents are likely to pose particular parenting challenges, especially during difficult developmental transitions such as adolescence. Grandparents raising grandchildren with physical health or behavior problems reported greater anxiety (Sands & Goldberg-Glen, 2000), more depressive symptoms (Burnette, 1999), more parental stress, and less relationship satisfaction (Bowers & Myers, 1999; Emick & Hayslip, 1999) than those raising healthy grandchildren.

As more grandparents assume the parental role, they will need greater support from educators, practitioners, and clinicians to help them maintain and manage their physical and emotional health in light of the challenges of their altered family life. In this chapter we explore the health status, practices, and behaviors of 40 grandmothers parenting their preadolescent grandchildren. First, we describe the health perceptions of the women and their use of preventive health practices as well as behaviors that may negatively influence their overall health and well-being. Next, we examine the relationships between aspects of the grandmothers' health and their perceptions of their grandchildren's health and behavior, financial and parental stress, and family functioning. We end the chapter with specific recommendations for addressing health risks and behaviors among this growing segment of the population.

OVERVIEW OF THE STUDY

Sample

The participants in this study were 40 grandmothers, ranging in age from 44 to 79 years (M = 56.4; SD = 7.77), who self- identified as the primary caregiver for a grandchild younger than 13 years of age. If the grandmother was caring for more than one grandchild, we randomly selected a grandchild about whom to answer the survey questions. The 24 female and 16 male focal grandchildren ranged in age from 2 to 13 years (M = 8.54; SD = 2.95). Table 5.1 summarizes the demographic characteristics of the grandmothers and their grandchildren.

Procedure

This research was approved by the Institutional Review Board of Virginia Polytechnic Institute and State University. We recruited grandmothers from throughout the Commonwealth of Virginia using a variety of methods including e-mail notices posted on listservs for older adults and those associated with agencies serving older adults, and flyers distributed to civic and community groups, medical practices, churches, school counselors, day care centers, grandparent raising grandchildren support groups, and selected other Virginia entities where the investigators had contacts with community individuals. We also published study notices in newspapers and in several grandparent support group newsletters and made presentations about the study to a statewide task force on kinship care and other relevant community groups. Grandmothers contacted the researchers via telephone or e-mail for more information. If they were interested in participating, we scheduled either an interview or mailed the grandmother a survey, depending on the grandmother's preference and geographic location. Doctoral-level graduate students conducted the interviews. Completion of the survey took approximately 60 minutes. All data was entered into SPSS for statistical analyses.

TABLE 5.1 Characteristics of the Grandmothers and Their Grandchildren

Grandmothers		M (SD) or %	Grand-children	M (SD) or %
Age	Range = 25–89	56.43 (7.77)	Range = 2–13	8.45 (2.95)
Sex	Female	100		60
Race/Ethnicity	White/not Hispanic	80.0		72.5
	Black	15.0		15.0
	Hispanic	2.5		2.5
	Other	2.5		10.0
Education	Less than high school	7.5		
	High school or less	32.5		
	Some training/college	20.0		
	Tech school/college degree	7.5		
	Post-grad education			
Marital status	Married	55.0		
Annual house-hold income	Under $15,000	30.0		
	$15,001 –$25,000	27.5		
	$25,001– $50,000	27.5		
	Over $50,000 or more	15.0		
Relationship to grandchild	Son's/stepson's child	25.0		
	Daughter/stepdaughter's child	72.5		
	Not specified	2.5		
Years grandchild has lived with grandmother	Less than one year	12.5		
	1–2 years	22.5		
	3–4 years	17.5		
	5–6 years	15.0		
	8–9 years	22.5		
	10 or more years	10.0		
Guardianship or legal custody of grandchild	Yes	82.5		

Measures

Demographic information collected included grandparent age, race, and marital status, grandchild age and race, number of adults and children in the household, the grandparent's relationship to the grandchild (paternal vs. maternal), and the length of the caregiving arrangement. We used the two summary measures of the General Health Index of the Medical Outcomes Study 36-Item Short-Form Health Survey (SF–36; Ware & Sherbourne, 1992) to assess the grandmothers' overall physical and mental health. The physical health measure included items assessing physical functioning, limitation on physical roles, experiences of pain, and general perceptions of physical health. The mental health items included perceptions of vitality, social functioning, limitation on emotional roles, and general perceptions of mental health. The SF–36 measure has been widely used and has acceptable reliability and validity. In addition, we obtained self-reported assessments of grandmother health care use (i.e., physician visits), their use of preventive health care practices in the last 2 years (i.e., flu shots, blood pressure checks, cholesterol screening, colonoscopies, skin cancer screening, diabetes screening, osteoporosis screening, vision exams, hearing exams, dental exams, mammograms, pap smears, routine physicals) and health risk behaviors (i.e., weight, exercise, smoking, alcohol use, seatbelt use, sunscreen use).

The total problem scale of the Child Behavior Checklist (CBCL; Achenbach & Rescorla, 2000; Achenbach & Rescorla, 2001) was used to assess the focal grandchild's overall functioning including behavioral, social, and emotional functioning. Grandmothers completed the CBCL, indicating the degree to which each item was true of their grandchild in the last 6 months. Higher scores indicate greater amounts of dysfunctional or problematic behavior. The CBCL is widely used in research and clinical settings and has strong evidence of reliability and validity. In the present study, reliability was very high (α = 1.00 for both the preschool and school-age versions).

Two measures were used to assess grandmothers' perceptions of the stress related to parenting. To assess financial stress related to parenting we developed a 22-item measure that required the grandmothers to indicate if they had experienced a particular situation (e.g., increased household costs such as buying toys, games, or hobby supplies for your grandchild; lost time at work or income after grandchild joined the household) and if so, to rate how stressful it was for them on a scale from 1 (*no stress*) to 5 (*much stress*). The internal reliability of this measure was acceptable at .82. General parenting stress was assessed using an adapted version of the Parental Stress Scale (Berry & Jones, 1995). Grandmothers completed this 18-item measure by indicating how strongly they agreed or disagreed with each statement (e.g., I feel close to my grandchild; Caring for my grandchild sometimes takes more time and energy than I have to give; If I had it to do over again, I might decide not to raise my grandchild). The Parental Stress Scale has demonstrated satisfactory reliability and convergent and discriminatory validity. In the present study, α = .85.

Family functioning was measured using the General Functioning Scale of the Family Assessment Device (FAD; Miller, Epstein, Bishop, & Keitner, 1985), which addresses six dimensions of family interaction: problem solving, communication, roles, affective responsiveness, affective involvement, and behavior control. The General Functioning Scale contains 12 Likert-style items from these six dimensions and measures the overall health and pathology of the family; higher scores reflect better family functioning. It has been widely used in research and demonstrates acceptable reliability and validity. In the present study, α = .91.

RESULTS[1]

Health Perceptions, Practices, and Behaviors

When asked to rate their overall health, 25% of the grandmothers indicated that their health was very good or excellent, 37.5% said their health was good, 25% rated their health as fair, and 12.5% indicated that their health was poor. Their SF–36 physical health scores ranged from 8.33 to 100 (M = 59.0; SD = 29.05) and their mental health scores ranged from 32.1 to 75.0 (M = 58.4; SD = 11.67), indicating that the grandmothers' mean physical and mental health scores were slightly above the average (M = 50; SD = 10). Seventy-five percent of the grandmothers had a regular source of health care and 85% had health insurance. During the 2 years prior to the interview, the grandmothers reported an average of 11.1 (SD = 12.88) total health care visits, with approximately 2 (SD = 1.99) of the visits for regular health checkups. They also indicated that they had seen a doctor an average of 1.9 times (SD = 3.66) for a specific chronic illness and 1.7 times (SD = 3.99) for emotional or behavioral problems.

In the 2 years preceding the interviews, the grandmothers actively engaged in an average of 8 (SD = 3.05; Range = 0–13) preventive health care behaviors. In those 2 years, approximately two-thirds or more of grandmothers had their blood pressure checked, had been screened for cholesterol and diabetes, had a mammogram, and had a vision exam (Table 5.2). Less than one-third had a colonoscopy and less than one-fifth had participated in skin cancer screening.

Although the majority of the grandmothers had engaged in at least a few preventive health care behaviors, many also engaged in behaviors that could negatively impact their health. The grandmothers reported an average of 2.3 (SD = 3.05; Range = 0–4) risky behaviors often associated with poor health outcomes (Table 5.3). Based on their reported body weight and height, over three-fourths of the women were overweight or obese. One-half of the women were past or current smokers. A little more than one-third of the women did not engage in any physical exercise and approximately another third exercised only 1 or 2 days a week. One-fourth of the grandmothers currently drank alcohol.

TABLE 5.2 Grandmothers' Preventive Health Practices

Preventive Practices	# of Yes Responses	% of Yes Responses
Blood pressure check	38	95.0
Cholesterol screen	35	87.5
Vision exam	31	77.5
Diabetes check	28	70.0
Mammogram	28	70.0
PAP smear	26	65.0
Dental exam	26	65.0
Flu shot	22	55.5
Hearing exam	17	42.5
Osteoporosis screen	17	42.5
Colonoscopy	11	27.5
Skin cancer screening	7	17.5

TABLE 5.3 Grandmothers' Health Behaviors

Health Behaviors	# of Yes Responses	% of Yes Responses
Weight		
Healthy	7	17.5
Overweight	7	17.5
Obese	26	65.0
Exercise		
No	15	37.5
Once a week	5	12.5
Twice a week	9	22.5
Three or more times a week	11	27.5
Smoke cigarettes		
Currently	9	22.5
In the past	11	27.5
Drink alcohol		
Currently	10	25.0
In the past	9	22.5
Wear seatbelt		
Never	2	5.0
Sometimes	7	17.5
Always	31	77.5

TABLE 5.3 (*Continued*)

Health Behaviors	# of Yes Responses	% of Yes Responses
Wear sunscreen		
Never	11	27.5
Sometimes	16	40.0
Always	13	32.5

Family Structure and Functioning

Because the literature suggests that family structure and functioning might be associated with grandparent well-being, we examined relationships among the various health measures and the grandmother's age, the grandchild's age, and the number of behavior problems the grandchild exhibited, as well as the grandmother's perceptions of financial and parenting stress and overall family functioning. The grandmothers' age and the length of time in the parenting role were associated with their use of preventive health practices. The older the grandmothers, the more preventive health practices they engaged in ($r = .27$, $p < .10$). However, the longer the grandmothers were in the parenting role, the fewer preventive health practices they reported ($r = -.28$, $p < .10$). Caring for older grandchildren ($r = .34$, $p < .05$) and parenting for a longer period of time ($r = .28$, $p < .10$) were associated with participating in more risky health behaviors. Caring for younger grandchildren was associated with the grand-mothers' more negative assessment of their overall mental health ($r = -.29$, $p < .10$). Grandmothers parenting grandchildren with more problem behaviors also reported poorer mental health ($r = -.29$, $p < .10$).

Perceived financial and parental stress also was associated with grandmothers' reports of their health. Grandmothers reporting more financial stress participated in a greater number of risky health behaviors ($r = .28$, $p < .10$) and reported poorer mental health ($r = -.51$, $p < .001$). Similarly, higher parental stress was associated with engaging in more risky health behaviors ($r = .28$, $p < .10$). Unexpectedly, grandmothers reporting higher parental stress reported more positive mental health ($r = .38$, $p < .05$).

Grandmothers' perceptions of family functioning were associated with both their use of health services and their assessment of their mental health. Grandmothers who reported poorer family functioning used more health care services ($r = -.33$, $p < .05$) whereas grandmothers reporting more positive family functioning also reported more positive mental health ($r = .39$, $p < .05$).

Predictors of Health Practices and Behaviors

To examine predictors of grandmothers' health practices and behaviors, we conducted a series of multiple regression analyses. We first examined predictors of grandmothers' preventive health care practices and risk behaviors. Results of the regression analysis ($F(2, 38) = 2.46, p < .10$) indicated that the number of risk behaviors was a significant predictor of preventive health care practices in that high numbers of risk behaviors predicted fewer preventive health care practices ($\beta = -.27, p < .09$). No other health or family-functioning variables were significant. Next, we examined predictors of grandmothers' health care use. The model was significant ($F(4, 34) = 4.47, p < .006$). Grandmothers' physical health was a significant predictor of health care use ($\beta = -.55, p < .01$). That is, better physical health predicted fewer health care visits. No other health or family-functioning variables were significant.

SUMMARY OF FINDINGS

The current sample of grandmothers raising grandchildren varied on several demographic characteristics, including educational attainment, marital status, annual household income, and duration of parenting their grandchildren. Their self-reported health status (25% in excellent or very good health) was comparable to other women of similar age, but their overall use of health care services was considerably lower (11.1 visits in the past 2 years) than that of a national sample of women (7.6 visits in the past year; Henderson & Weisman, 2005). Higher use of health care was associated with poorer physical health and poorer family functioning.

Many preventive health care practices were common in this group (e.g., blood pressure checks, cholesterol screening, diabetes checks, mammograms), whereas other practices important for women this age were uncommon (e.g., osteoporosis screening, colonoscopies, skin cancer screening). Most grandmothers reported that they wore seatbelts and sunscreen sometimes or always. Older grandmothers reported greater use of preventive health practices, but a longer duration of parenting grandchildren was associated with lower use of preventive health practices.

Risky health behaviors were also common: High percentages of the grandmothers were obese and seldom exercised, and approximately one-fourth of them smoked or used alcohol. Higher risky behaviors were associated with duration of parenting, greater financial stress, and higher parental stress.

IMPLICATIONS FOR PRACTICE

A range of practitioners can help grandparents parenting grandchildren maintain and manage their physical and emotional health, promote family functioning, and enable access to health care and other supportive services. As suggested by the Social Behavioral Model (SBM; Anderson, 1968, 1995), grandparents may not recognize the need for health care services for themselves or their grandchildren, or they may be unaware of the availability of services. Practitioners can reduce barriers to service use (e.g., cost, accessibility) by making referrals to affordable services that may be available. Predisposing characteristics may also need to be addressed, including health beliefs and attitudes of grandparents that are inconsistent with the use of services as well as racial, ethnic, or cultural beliefs and practices that may impact grandparents' attitudes toward and ability to locate appropriate services. Thus, the SBM provides a useful framework for practitioners when implementing strategies designed to influence grandparents' health care practices and behaviors.

Teachers, counselors, and nurses working in the schools need to be cognizant that they are very likely to be interacting with students who are being raised by their grandparents. Child behavior problems present at school may also be present at home, and raising a child with behavior problems involves heightened parenting stress (Sands & Goldberg-Glen, 2000) and challenges to optimal family functioning. School conferences provide an opportunity for teachers and school counselors to establish a supportive relationship with grandparents, to provide referrals to counseling and psychological services when problems are serious enough to warrant referral, and to work cooperatively to implement behavior-management strategies to improve the grandchild's behavior. School nurses may provide health education to influence health beliefs and promote appropriate health care practices and to encourage regular preventive care for both grandparents and grandchildren (Champion, 1999). With the support of teachers, counselors, and nurses, the stress associated with school and home-based behavior problems may be reduced and child and family functioning may be improved. These improvements, in turn, may help mitigate the health impacts for grandparents.

Social workers and other mental health professionals who have contact with grandparents raising grandchildren also have an important role to play in promoting optimal grandparent health and family functioning. These professionals often have effective problem-solving skills to deal with a number of predisposing and enabling factors related to health service use. Access to physical and mental health services can be severely curtailed by a lack of health insurance; the problem is most acute for low-income families. Grandparents who do not yet qualify for Medicare may be at special risk for limited access to health care and referral to low- or no-cost clinics may provide needed services for these individuals. Lower educational attainment, which is often closely associated with lower socioeconomic status, is also a predictor of several health risk behaviors, including smoking, binge drinking, obesity, and limited physical activity (Harper & Lynch, 2007). Grandparents may need referral for services to reduce these risky health behaviors and social workers may either provide individual counseling or make referrals with special consideration for the financial burden that such services may place on low-income families. Social workers may also be well positioned to educate grandparents about the importance of proper health care and match grandparents with support services and support groups that can aid in addressing the challenges of raising grandchildren. The matching of grandparents with services should take into consideration beliefs and attitudes that may be associated with age, education, and racial, ethnic, and cultural factors.

Health care providers too must be attentive to the special challenges faced by grandparents who are raising their grandchildren. Promoting regular health checkups—for the grandparent and for the grandchild—should be emphasized at each health care visit. It is especially important that grandparents seek the appropriate health screenings such as osteoporosis screenings, colonoscopies, and skin cancer screenings that allow for the detection and treatment of potentially serious long-term health problems. If emergency-care providers detect that grandparents do not have a regular source of health care, they need to discourage the use of emergency services for non-urgent care needs and facilitate linking grandparents with regular providers. Further targeted referrals for health-promotion services to address risky health behaviors such as obesity, smoking, and alcohol use, as well as the promotion of physical activity and other preventive health behaviors, may be necessary as well.

In conclusion, professionals from all service sectors are more likely than ever before to interact with grandmothers parenting grandchildren. Regardless of their specific role—teacher, counselor, health care worker, or service provider—they need to take advantage of their positions to encourage grandmothers to take care of themselves and not delay seeking help for their own physical and emotional health problems. Addressing predisposing and enabling factors that promote the use of health care services, and ensuring that grandparents recognize and respond to their own and their grandchildren's physical and mental health needs, can influence service use and health outcomes. Diligent community outreach efforts are necessary to reach grandmothers whose health status, practices, and behaviors place them at greatest risk for poor physical and psychological outcomes that ultimately will interfere with their ability to effectively meet the needs of their grandchildren.

REFERENCES

Achenbach, T. M., & Rescorla, L. A. (2000). *Manual for the ASEBA preschool forms & profiles.* Burlington, VT: University of Vermont, Research Center for Children, Youth, & Families.

Achenbach, T. M., & Rescorla, L. A. (2001). *Manual for the ASEBA school-age forms & profiles.* Burlington, VT: University of Vermont, Research Center for Children, Youth, & Families.

Andersen, R. (1968). *A behavioral model of families' use of health services.* (Research Series No. 25, Center for Health Administration Studies). Chicago: University of Chicago.

Anderson, R. (1995). Revisiting the behavioral model and access to medical care: Does it matter? *Journal of Health and Social Behavior, 36,* 1–10.

Andersen, R., & Newman, J. (1972). Societal and individual determinants of medical care utilization in the United States. *Milbank Memorial Fund Quarterly, 51,* 95–124.

Bachman, H. J., & Chase-Lansdale, P. L. (2005). Custodial grandmothers' physical, mental, and economic well-being: Comparisons of primary caregivers from low-income neighborhoods. *Family Relations, 54,* 475–487.

Berry, J. O., & Jones, W. H. (1995). The Parental Stress Scale: Initial psychometric evidence. *Journal of Social and Personal Relationships, 12,* 463–472.

Bowers, B. F., & Myers, B. J. (1999). Grandmothers providing care for grandchildren: Consequences of various levels of caregiving. *Family Relations, 48,* 303–311.

Burnette, D. (1999). Custodial grandparents in Latino families: Patterns of service use and predictors of unmet needs. *Social Work, 44*(1), 22–34.

Burton, L. M. (1992). Black grandparents rearing children of drug-addicted parents: Stressors, outcomes, and social service needs. *The Gerontologist, 32,* 744–751.

Casper, L. M., & Bryson, K. R. (1998). *Co-resident grandparents and their grandchildren: Grandparent-maintained families.* (U.S. Census Bureau, Population Division Working Paper No. 26). Retrieved April 7, 2007, from http://www.census.gov/population/www/documentation/twps0026/twps0026.html

Champion, V. L. (1999). Revised susceptibility, benefits, and barriers scale for mammography screening. *Research in Nursing and Health, 22,* 341–348.

Dowdell, E. B. (1995). Caregiver burden: Grandparents raising their high risk children. *Journal of Psychosocial Nursing, 33*(3), 27–30.

Emick, M. A., & Hayslip, B., Jr. (1999). Custodial grandparenting: Stresses, coping skills, and relationships with grandchildren. *International Journal of Aging and Human Development, 48,* 35–61.

Goodman, C. C. (2006). Grandmothers raising grandchildren: The vulnerability of advancing age. In B. Hayslip, Jr., & J. Hicks Patrick (Eds.), *Custodial grandparenting: Individual, cultural, and ethnic diversity* (pp. 133–150). New York: Springer.

Grinstead, L., Leder, S., Jensen, S., & Bond, L. (2003). Review of the research on the health of caregiving grandparents. *Journal of Advanced Nursing, 44,* 318–326.

Harper, S., & Lynch, J. (2007). Trends in socioeconomic inequalities in adult health behaviors among U.S. states, 1990–2004. *Public Health Reports, 122,* 177–189.

Hayslip, B., Jr., Shore, R. J., & Emick, M. A. (2006). Age, health, and custodial grandparenting. In B. Hayslip, Jr., & J. Hicks Patrick (Eds.), *Custodial grandparenting: Individual, cultural, and ethnic diversity* (pp. 75–88). New York: Springer.

Henderson, J. T., & Weisman, C. S. (2005). Women's patterns of provider use across the lifespan and satisfaction with primary care coordination and comprehensiveness. *Medical Care, 43,* 826–833.

Hughes, M. E., Waite, L. J., LaPierre, T. A., & Luo, Y. (2007). All in the family: The impact of caring for grandchildren on grandparents' health. *Journal of Gerontology: Social Sciences, 62B,* S108–S119.

Jendrek, M. (1994). Grandparents who parent their grandchildren: Circumstances and decisions. *The Gerontologist, 34,* 206–216.

Joslin, D., & Harrison, R. (1998). The "hidden patient": Older relatives raising children orphaned by AIDS. *Journal of the American Women's Medical Association, 53*(2), 65–71.

Kelley, S. (1993). Caregiver stress in grandparents raising grandchildren. *IMAGE: Journal of Nursing Scholarship, 25,* 331–337.

Miller, I. W., Epstein, N. B., Bishop, D. S., & Keitner, G. I. (1985). The McMaster Family Assessment Device: Reliability and validity. *Journal of Marital and Family Therapy, 11,* 345–356.

Minkler, M., & Fuller-Thomson, E. (1999). The health of grandparents raising grandchildren: Results of a national study. *American Journal of Public Health, 89*(9), 1384–1389.

Minkler, M., Fuller-Thomson, E., Miller, D., & Driver, D. (1997). Depression in grandparents raising grandchildren: Results of a national longitudinal study. *Archives of Family Medicine, 6,* 445–452.

Minkler, M., Roe, K. M., & Price, M. (1992). The physical and emotional health of grandmothers raising grandchildren in the crack cocaine epidemic. *The Gerontologist, 32,* 752–761.

Musil, C. M., & Ahmad, M. (2002). Health of grandmothers: A comparison by caregiver status. *Journal of Aging and Health, 14,* 96–121.

Pruchno, R. A. (1999). Raising grandchildren: The experiences of Black and White grandmothers. *The Gerontologist, 39,* 209–221.

Roe, K. M., Minkler, M., Saunders, F., & Thomson, G. E. (1996). Health of grandmothers raising children of the crack cocaine epidemic. *Medical Care, 34,* 1072–1084.

Sands, R. G., & Goldberg-Glen, R. S. (2000). Factors associated with stress among grandparents raising their grandchildren. *Family Relations, 49,* 97–105.

Solomon, J., & Marx, J. (1999). Who cares? Grandparent/grandchild households. *Journal of Women & Aging, 11*(1), 3–25.

Strawbridge, W., Wallhagen, M., Shema, S., & Kaplan, G. (1997). New burdens or more of the same? Comparing adult grandparent, spouse and adult-child caregivers. *The Gerontologist, 37,* 505–510.

Szinovacz, M. E., DeViney, S., & Atkinson, M. P. (1999). Effects of surrogate parenting on grandparents' well-being. *Journal of Gerontology: Social Sciences, 54,* S376–S388.

Waldrop, D. P., & Weber, J. A. (2001). From grandparent to caregiver: The stress and satisfaction of raising grandchildren. *Families in Society, 82,* 461–472.

Ware, J. E., Jr., & Sherbourne, C. D. (1992). The MOS 36-item short-form health survey (SF-36): I. Conceptual framework and item selection. *Medical Care, 30,* 473–483.

Whitley, D. M., Kelley, S. J., & Sipe, T. A. (2001). Grandmothers raising grandchildren: Are they at increased risk of health problems? *Health and Social Work, 26,* 105–114.

NOTE

1. Given the exploratory nature of our research, we set the probability level for all analyses at .10. We report only those significant findings; however, the complete results are available upon request from the authors.

SECTION 2

Parenting Grandchildren

This section deals with the essence of raising grandchildren—parenting them effectively. In light of their newly reacquired roles as parents, these chapters address such questions as: What are grandparents' concerns about their parenting skills and their relationships with their grandchildren? What are the personal and social issues faced by custodial grandparents? How are grandparents' parenting skills seen by age peers, who may be an important source of social support to them? Are the parenting practices of custodial grandparents effective or not? How do such skills impact the social and personal adjustment of their grandchildren? How might helping efforts to assist grandparents in taking better care of themselves be best carried out?

CHAPTER 6

Raising a Granddaughter: Sharing Our Experience

Lee Hipple and John Hipple

We have had custody of our now 2-year-old granddaughter for a year. At this point in time it looks like we will have her for another 3 to 6 months. Sophia came to us when the Texas Department of Family and Protective Services (CPS) removed her and her half sister from their parents' home, because of their parents' drug abuse. At our ages of 67 and 62, it was not in our plans to again become primary parents of an infant, or any youngster for that matter. John still works full time as a college counselor and Lee is a retired social worker. Both of us enjoyed our active lives before this dramatic change took place. We recognize there are many reasons why grandparents assume the full responsibility for raising grandchildren. Consequently the issues faced by grandparents will vary from situation to situation. And of course the length of time this type of parenting goes on is also highly variable. With this said, we will get on with our story.

OUR STORY

Our son David, Sophia's father, has struggled with problems surrounding his use of drugs and alcohol for the last 15 years. Consequently we are very familiar with the problems drug use can bring to a family. All of us, including our younger son, have been involved in one sort of treatment or another over these years. For David, there have been periods of relative calmness during times of sobriety and then terribly chaotic downhill slides into use. For the rest of us, there have been periods of hope when he enters treatment or moves into sobriety on his own and then times of great sadness and despair when he begins to use or drink again. It has been a struggle to maintain a level life at home and at work during these intense roller-coaster rides.

One of the decisions we made early on in this addiction ride was that it would not tear us apart. There is often much guilt and many *what ifs* for parents of an addicted child. It becomes easy to blame yourself and also to blame your spouse. We realized at some point that those feelings were getting in the way of us being able to work together in making decisions about what was best for our son as well as for our family. We also realized that so much of our energy was focused on him that we tended to almost forget about the needs of our younger child or ourselves. Lee once described it as feeling that when David walked into a room, he sucked all of the air out and all she could do was fight to continue breathing. Our way of handling all of this was to commit to ourselves that David and his actions would not tear our marriage or our family apart. We find that this decision, made long ago, has also helped us as we have moved back into a full-time parenting role.

So, on one level, we were not shocked and were perhaps even a bit prepared when the girls were removed by CPS. At the time of the removal, Sophia's mother was in jail and Sophia was being cared for by her father, with us taking care of her during the day when he was at work. David seemed to be doing a fairly good job with her and it has always been clear that he loved her and had a great deal of patience with her. We had to leave town for a short period of time and although we had a wonderful child-care situation in place for Sophia, David quickly fell apart with us not there and began to use heavily; this frightened the child-care person we had hired and she quit. We do not know who notified CPS that Sophia was at risk, but we are thankful for their caring and willingness to take action.

The investigative worker took Sophia into custody and placed her in a foster home for the 10 days it took for a study of our home to be completed. At the first court hearing 2 weeks after her removal, we were given physical custody of Sophia with CPS having conservatorship. It was established that we would have physical custody of our granddaughter for at least 12 months.

The complexity of the legal and CPS system can be overwhelming. We found there was considerable stress associated with being interviewed by the CPS investigator, the ongoing CPS worker, and by the guardian ad litem, who was appointed by the Court to represent Sophia. It has been a challenge to keep this stress from interfering with our parenting efforts.

From the very beginning there were glitches in the legal system that were problematic for us. Sophia became eligible for Medicaid as soon as CPS took conservatorship. However, either the investigative worker (who left the agency and thus perhaps became an easy person to blame) or the ongoing worker made a computer error and so after 2 months Sophia's Medicaid eligibility was rejected. This happened at a time when she was having chronic ear infections and needed to see the pediatrician as well as have medication. CPS, represented by the ongoing worker, made it clear this was a mistake made by the investigative worker and that it was now our problem and we were expected to fix it ourselves. Lee spent considerable time and energy trying to resolve the problem until she was confronted by a former colleague, who asked her when she had ever heard of an individual client being able to rectify an error made by a state agency.

Lee was a social worker for 38 years and certainly knew how to help a client deal with a situation such as the one described above. But in this situation Lee realized she had been functioning totally as a grandma, not as a social worker. Once her colleague helped set her on the right path, she was able to use her social-work skills to get Sophia the services she needed. The guardian ad litem was asked to help but she seemed to believe there was nothing she could do. The next step we took was to write a letter to the court with copies to the worker, her supervisor, the program director of the agency, and the guardian ad litem. What had been proclaimed as unfixable by the ongoing worker was "magically" fixed within 48 hours of the letters being received. The original worker was suddenly transferred to a different caseload and a new worker was assigned to us. This change of caseworker has proven to be very positive for us, as she has been unfailingly responsive and helpful.

This was an important learning experience for us and taught us that, as the ones who loved and cared the most for Sophia, we were the ones most focused on her best interest. We learned we could not fully trust any of the professionals involved to always focus on what was best for her. Once we understood that fully, we were better able to move into what might be termed an advocacy role and firmly stick to our guns about a variety of issues.

It is our opinion that those having physical custody of a child, who CPS has in conservatorship, must be assertive to get the full benefit of CPS services. It is essential to have a good working relationship with the ongoing worker and her or his supervisor. This is not always easy as sometimes problems are based on personality differences, sometimes on philosophical differences, and sometimes on the letter of the law that CPS must follow. The reality is that CPS workers have a tremendously difficult job and the burnout rate is very high. Thus, there are times when grandparents may have to work with a caseworker who is burned out and either angry at all clients or indifferent to them. This can be stressful and at times seem like one is negotiating a minefield. But this is a minefield that must be negotiated.

To return to the subject of Medicaid, it is important to note that many physicians do not take Medicaid patients or severely limit the numbers of these patients. Thus it can be very difficult to find a Medicaid provider. At one point we searched for a dermatologist to treat a skin condition that Sophia developed, and in that search learned there were no dermatologists accepting Medicaid in the 50-mile area surrounding our home. We did find several offices receptive to our circumstances and learned to swallow our pride and simply ask if there might be a possibility of a reduced fee. We paid a full fee on the first office visit, but the physician reduced his charges dramatically for future visits. This helped us understand the importance of asking about what help might be available in a variety of different situations.

The official policy of CPS is to work toward family reunification, so there are funds available for all types of counseling for parents and children: individual, couple, family, and drug and alcohol. Sophia's parents have benefited from this assistance in a variety of ways. Her mother has gotten a positive handle on her addiction and is doing relatively well at this point in time. She has clearly benefited from parenting classes, individual and group counseling, and substance abuse education. Our son recently went through a serious relapse and it is unclear right now whether or not he will have his parental rights terminated or if they will instead be severely restricted. The one-day-at-a-time philosophy of addiction treatment is something we learned years ago, and we find it is an important key to maintaining our sanity when alcohol and drugs are involved.

One agency that we have found to be tremendously helpful is the Infant and Toddler Intervention Program (ECI). They are available to provide services to any child, age 0 to 3, who is under the conservatorship of CPS. We found the entire ECI team to be very receptive to our concerns, evaluating Sophia and planning services based on what was found in the evaluations. A social worker coordinates a wide variety of professional services such as occupational and physical therapy, speech-language therapy, psychological services, nutritional services, and nursing services that are designed to meet children's needs. We had concerns about the fact that Sophia seemed very slow in her speech development and was an extremely restless sleeper, often crying out and throwing herself around in bed. Evaluations were carried out and many suggestions made that have proved to be helpful. It was also a tremendous relief to us to be reassured that she was normal in her development. One of the things we had earlier learned, after the CPS removal, was that her mother had used drugs up until the day before she delivered. Both of us had been concerned about the possibility of neurological or other damage.

Helping Sophia understand that she has a mom and a dad as well as a grandpa and grandma has been a constant challenge. Her parents' contacts with her are tightly regulated by CPS and initially they were limited to an hour a week in the CPS playroom and always under the supervision of a worker. That was of tremendous concern to us as Sophia had already suffered several different losses and seemed to be losing her feelings of attachment to her parents. Although we certainly are not suggesting that anyone should break with what CPS has set as the rules, we do believe that grandparents may have the best interest of their grandchild as a more central component in their decision making. We began pushing CPS to allow the parents to come to our home for a few hours a week to see their daughter in a more natural environment and also to do some of the child-care jobs of parents such as feeding, changing diapers, and putting down for a nap. Now, 12 months into the custody, Sophia gets to be with her mother in her home for 4 hours a week and we are beginning to look toward longer visits and eventually toward overnight visits. We are not sure that this process would have moved as it has without pushing from us. It appears to us that children are frequently returned to their parents without a long enough transition period of slowly increasing visits.

Concerns with CPS's way of doing things have been an ongoing dilemma for us. We want what is best for Sophia and it has been our experience that CPS and the courts, while giving lip service to wanting what is best for a child, at times in reality seem more intent on punishing parents or, at least, on putting up a great many hoops for them to jump through. We do not see there is anything wrong with that in and of itself, as it seems as good a screening device as any to determine how committed to parenthood a parent might be. However, by severely limiting the time and circumstances under which a parent may see a child, we believe that children may end up being inadvertently punished as the bond they feel toward their parents is stretched. We are both fairly rule-bound individuals, and it is hard to know if we would have reached the decision to advocate loudly for the kind of visitation we thought Sophia needed if it had not been for our experience with the agency in regard to the Medicaid issue.

From a psychological perspective, Sophia could be described as having abandonment issues. She is quite insecure when it comes to having changes in her life and her daily routine. We do see that she has made great strides in her ability to deal with new situations. We now have her in an in-home day care situation that has helped with her sense of security and her socialization skills. This has been at our expense but there is financial help available for day care for those families who qualify.

CHANGES IN OUR LIVES

Having a baby 24–7 requires so many changes. We both find we have more patience than we had when we were raising our two boys and we don't seem to sweat the small stuff like we probably did years ago. On the other hand we have had worries about our granddaughter that we never had with our boys. Because of her early life experiences she becomes extremely upset at unexpected loud noises and even with voices that are raised. We have had to work with her on that. Our boys had only the experience of one of us always coming to pick them up when they had been left with a day care provider or sitter. Sophia has not had that experience, as those she loved and depended on have one by one suddenly disappeared from her life. She was extremely clingy when she first came to live with us and terrified of new situations. It has been a long haul to get her to feel safe and understand that we will always come back for her.

We don't have the physical energy that is needed to parent an active young child. Small things, like getting on our knees to bathe her in the tub, are so much more difficult than they used to be. Both of us are in fairly good physical shape, and we have no major illnesses or disabilities, but we simply do not have the energy that we once had. Being tired much of the time is not what we had expected during our golden years. We had also forgotten how stressful it can be to take a little one to a restaurant or how much advanced preparation is involved in a simple day trip. Keeping a reasonable sense of good humor is not always easy but we have found it to be one of our salvations.

Of course there are also many important and often touching events that come from having a little person in the house again. Naturally there are many things that bring us a sense of excitement, satisfaction, love, affection, and reward as we spend our days and nights with Sophia. We saw her first step, heard her first word, "Papa" (grandpa), and we are the recipients of her many hugs and kisses. John was the only male and the only grandparent in an infant and parent swim class.

Some things we have experienced that have definitely not been helpful or joyous are the platitudes we have encountered. We can't tell you how many times someone has said to us, "I know she keeps you young." We aren't sure why people believe they have the right to make this assumption since we generally feel tired and sometimes overwhelmed. It is not dissimilar to what has been said to us in relation to our son's addictions: "God does not give us more than we can carry." Those kinds of statements have seemed insensitive and even trite to us. On the other hand, the things that have been particularly helpful and nourishing to us have been those people who have really listened with a caring ear. People who see that we are, at times, overwhelmed and who acknowledge the reality of how difficult our situation can be are appreciated. It is also a wonderful and reassuring experience to hear from others as they provide compliments and support for the efforts we make as we carry out our full-time parenting. So many of those we know have been quick to offer helpful words and actions. It has also amazed us to find out how common it is for grandparents to be the primary parents of their grandchildren. We had no idea of the extent of this situation. It has certainly helped us to not feel that we are alone.

As we face the future, we find there are a myriad of worries and concerns that amble in and out of our minds. During visitations in our home, it has become clear to us that some of the ideas we have about child care, discipline, and reward are different from those held by Sophia's mother and father. We believe that consistency is critical for her and yet the differences in parenting do not always allow for that. We try to keep Sophia's parents apprised of our reasons for doing what we do. Having faith that it will work out when Sophia is returned to her mother's care is not always easy. We have worked hard to remain on good terms with Sophia's mother so that we can remain in her life as a constant.

Both of Sophia's parents have criminal records that made it difficult for them to find good jobs. They are both working full time now, but at low wages, and we worry about how they will be able to make ends meet when custody is restored. An additional dilemma is what our responsibility will be as far as subsidizing things we know Sophia needs.

A further complicating issue is that Sophia has a half sister who is being parented by her paternal grandparents. This compounds the complexity of parenting styles. The sisters have not been able to spend as much time together as we would wish, and obviously there will be another period of adjustment when everyone is reunited. To us a gradual reunification of the family seems the best way to go, but that has not always been the path CPS wants to take. We try to maintain a good working relationship with the other custodial grandparents, and we frequently touch base with them so some coordination is in place. We have found that if we approach CPS together we often have a louder voice and are more clearly heard.

RECOMMENDATIONS FOR PROFESSIONALS

Perhaps the primary word of caution would be *don't assume*. Most likely every grandparent you work with will have at least some sadness and loss that they are dealing with, but beyond that they are each uniquely different. Every professional has learned a language of jargon and everyone has been educated in particular theories, which is important in that it gives a framework for the work you do; however, those perspectives can also create horribly restrictive blinders. The grandparents you work with probably don't need any of that. If ours is a family with drug and alcohol problems we have already had enough lay and professional people assume that ours is a dysfunctional family. We had an experience many years ago, when our son's drug problems were only beginning, of being at a party and talking with another professional who knew nothing of our personal family life. She made the comment that she loved working with families of kids who were drug addicted, because they were "always so screwed up." She is a perfectly nice woman who happened to have a set of blinders on that gave her preconceived ideas about why adolescents became involved in drugs. What she said was obviously hurtful to us but it was also frightening, showing us what we already knew but did not like thinking about—that many of the people we were looking to for help might have the very same preconceived ideas.

When grandparents assume the role of being the primary parents of grandchildren, the potential for emotional, intellectual, and physical stress becomes very high. Successfully dealing with this stress is not an easy task. There are so many invested players in this endeavor that consistent resolution and progress is very difficult.

From our perspective, grandparents, parents, and children who are involved with a legal system, such as CPS, must be especially patient, persistent, assertive, and willing to compromise. We have found that hope and a high tolerance for ambiguity and changing rules also helps. Having strangers rule your life is no fun. It is our opinion that custodial grandparents should make good use of all aspects of the helping system within their community. Personal pride and family independence can become obstacles to finding the most constructive path or getting the services that you or your grandchild needs. Involved professionals can be the most helpful in these situations if they are aware of how the legal systems really work and if they are willing to coach or teach grandparents how to deal and cope with the various systems that are in play.

We find there is no easy way to summarize this chapter since the final act in the drama has not ended and realistically may not end during our lifetime. So we ask that you wish us well and know that it is our hope that our few words will be of help to others.

CHAPTER 7

Parenting Concerns of Grandparents Raising Grandchildren: An Insider's Picture

Carol M. Musil, Camille B. Warner, Mary McNamara, Stacey Rokoff, and Dawn Turek

What are the main concerns and worries of grandmothers raising grandchildren? This chapter draws on the experiences of custodial grandmothers to help us understand the issues they face on a daily basis. We present the concerns they shared about their role as grandmothers raising grandchildren, and then follow each concern with a brief discussion of background information and support strategies.

As part of our ongoing study of grandmothers (The Grandmother Study NR05067), we asked grandmothers raising grandchildren to share with us the main sources of family concern, worry, or conflict they experience in their roles as primary caregivers to their grandchildren. These 141 grandmothers were participating in a larger, longitudinal study and shared their concerns at 2 time points 12 months apart. Grandmothers, who were recruited using random-digit dialing and supplemental convenience sampling, completed mailed surveys that included the question: What is the greatest source of concern, worry, and conflict in your family at this time? We used a content analysis and grouped their responses by themes. Additional information about the study and other results are available (Musil, Warner, Jeanblanc, Zauszniewski, & Kercher, 2006; Standing, Musil, & Warner, 2007).

The grandmothers who provided responses ranged in age from 37–82 years, with an average age of 56 years. Over half of the grandmother respondents were White (59%), and 41% were women of color; 53% were married, and 60% were unemployed while 40% worked either full or part time. In terms of education, 49% had at least some technical school or college, 31% had a high school diploma or equivalent, and 20% did not complete high school. The grandmothers represented 71 of 88 counties in the state of Ohio, and thus reflect the parenting concerns of Midwest urban, rural, and suburban grandmothers raising grandchildren.

The worries, concerns, and conflicts that grandmothers reported covered a range of parenting issues and situations. Their responses included financial problems, dealing with teens and adolescents, education, grandchild and grandmother health problems, grandchildren's relationships with their parents, custody issues, dealing with adult children, child care, and other family conflicts. We present each concern using the grandmothers' written quotes and examples, and then we provide addition background information about the issues the grandmothers raised. The worries and concerns are presented based on the number of grandmothers who reported each concern.

FINANCIAL CONCERNS

Nearly 35% of grandmothers in our study ($n = 49$) reported financial problems. Many of these grandmothers indicated that there was not enough money to make ends meet and that paying bills was difficult. One grandmother was worried about possible eviction from her home, while another was unable to afford to move and worried about her family's safety in their current neighborhood. Cutbacks in government funding contributed to fears that the grandmothers' financial problems might escalate further. One grandmother noted that when her grandson turned 18 years old, they lost monetary support for him, even though he still had another year of high school to complete.

A number of grandmothers indicated that they lacked medical insurance for themselves or their grandchildren, and that they often did not have money for prescription medications. Several noted that they or their spouses had been hospitalized, and the related loss of income and medical bills posed a financial burden. One wrote, "No medical insurance for me and spouse, not enough money, prescriptions out of reach. No money for things like movies, going to the zoo, swimming passes. . . ." Grandmothers with high school–aged grandchildren were uncertain how they would be able to pay for college, and several others worried about their own or their spouse's retirement and the effects of a fixed income on their lifestyle. "We have adopted our grand-kids and are trying to prepare and plan for retirement."

DISCUSSION: FINANCIAL CONCERNS

Grandparents living on a fixed income with primary parenting responsibilities face challenges in supporting their families, but these caregivers and their families often qualify for services and resources that they may not be aware of or realize they are eligible to receive. Several federal and national programs and foundations have directed part of their monies for services to kin caregivers, primarily for child-related services. The passage of the National Family Caregiver Support Program in 2000 was the first federal policy that directed monies and services toward caregivers, and 10% of each state's funds to Area Agencies on Aging are allocated to support programs for kinship caregivers, usually grandparents age 60 and over. The Child Welfare League and the Children's Defense Fund have been at the forefront in promoting legislation that supports relative caregivers and their children. The financial resources for grandparent and other kin caregivers can include foster care monies, Temporary Assistance for Needy Families (TANF) funds, and food stamps, but also might include low-cost lunches and tuition and activity scholarships. Moreover, grandparent-headed families often need assistance with health care (e.g., medical, mental health, and dental care). Many states have resources in place that are staffed with individuals who help relative caregivers address and access resources such as children's and older adult services, legal and financial services, and mental health care.

Grandparent caregivers consider legal options a high priority (AARP, 2003). Legal services can be expensive, as well as confusing and disruptive to already strained family dynamics. At the same time, formalizing a legal relationship between the grandparent and grandchild can provide the stability that children need and makes navigating the school and medical systems much smoother. For kinship caregivers, declaring their legal relationship—whether that is no legal status, custody, or adoption—is essential for determining eligibility for the receipt of social services. Custody procedures vary from state to state but to be eligible for benefits it is necessary for the relative caregiver to prove that he or she is the primary custodian of the child.

Several national resources are available to support kin caregivers and the local programs that may support them. The AARP Grandparent Information Center maintains a national database of 600 support groups and other programs for caregivers. Generations United is a national membership group dedicated to intergenerational programming with a primary focus on grandparent-headed families and advocacy. The Brookdale Foundation's Relatives as Parents Program offers seed monies to innovative programs and start-up programs for caregivers.

DEALING WITH TEENS AND ADOLESCENTS

In the study, 32 grandmothers (23%) worried about "being able to deal with teenager problems" such as setting limits and maintaining discipline, dealing with dating and sexuality, and peer pressure. Grandmothers with grandchildren as young as age 11 remarked about their grandchild's attitude and their own apprehensions about the teen years: "Will I be able to deal with my grandchild when he becomes a teenager with all the issues and problems that arise in today's world?" (such as the prevalence of alcohol and drug use, teenage sexuality, and violence in and out of school).

Discipline. Several grandmothers reported that young teens did not want to follow rules. One grandmother reported conflict with her grandchild, who she felt did not respect her or her decisions, and the grandmother worried because they were unable to resolve some of their problems. Two other grandmothers reported difficulty establishing or enforcing limits, often related to the intrusion of a third person: one grandmother noted disagreements between her husband and herself about rules, and another grandmother reported problems "making one set of rules stick for the children as primary caregiver rather than what the grandchild's [absent] mother said." Another grandmother worried about her grandchild's aggressive behavior toward family members. Two grandmothers reported that the teenage grandchildren they were raising were currently out of the grandmother's house (one ran away and another was in a detention facility) and they were worried about the children's return to the home.

Relationships, sex, and dating. Some grandmothers were anxious about boy-girl relationships, sex, and dating. One stated, I worry "when my granddaughter is out and I don't know where she is. She is 14 years old. . . ." One year later, her concerns had not abated: "I worry about my 15-year-old granddaughter and my 11-year-old grandson keeping the right company." One grandmother was worried that her teen granddaughter was pregnant.

Even in the best of situations, grandmothers worry about the children's exposure to "external influences." One grandmother wrote, "Raising teenagers. Drugs. Peer pressure," but a year later felt more comfortable with her granddaughter's development and wrote, "My 15-year-old getting adjusted with comfort and dignity to being a teenager. This is a stage of life where we let go and let God. But it can be a hard adjustment for her, new responsibilities, earning and keeping trust." Several grandmothers mentioned that they hoped that the way they had raised their grandchildren would lead to relatively few problems with them in the teen years.

DISCUSSION: DEALING WITH TEENS AND ADOLESCENTS

The middle school and high school years are often the most challenging for grandparents and parents alike. While younger children require physical attention that is exhausting, adolescents and teens require ongoing support, monitoring, and vigilance. Many grandparents raising grandchildren also recalled this as a difficult time with the parent of their grandchild, and were concerned about doing it better this time.

Relationships with peers are paramount for most middle school and high school children. Friends have a significant influence on behavior, especially whether an adolescent engages in risky behaviors. Grandparents' worries for grandchildren include sexual activity, sexually transmitted diseases, and pregnancy. It is important to talk with teens about sexuality and male-female relationship issues and to encourage safe sex practices and the use of birth control for sexually active teens of either gender. For older adolescents, alcohol and substance use becomes an increasing worry to grandparents, especially if the grandchild's parents have problems with addictions. Grandparents often do not know how to link their grandchild with the appropriate help to prevent the negative effects these at-risk behaviors can have on their grandchild. The child's primary health provider can discuss, at routine physicals, the dangers of drug and alcohol abuse and reinforce what the child may have already heard from others. If it is evident that the child has already begun using drugs or alcohol, then prompt intervention should be initiated, which includes counseling, rehabilitation programs, or psychiatric involvement as appropriate.

ADULT CHILDREN

A total of 25 (18%) grandmothers reported concerns with their adult children that impact how the grandparents raise their grandchildren. These issues include their adult children's health and legal problems, the grandchild's relationship with their parents, and custody issues. Of these, 11 grandmothers (8%) reported that the grandchildren's parents were their major source of stress: "My granddaughter's mother . . . she won't get herself together to get her children back. She is not trying to conform to what the court has ordered." In another situation, an adult child had become violent and a court restraining order was obtained to keep the parent away from the grandchild and family.

Adult children with physical and mental illnesses, alcoholism, drug addiction, or impending release from jail or prison made grandmothers feel apprehensive about the stability of their family situation and had ramifications for their parenting of the grandchild.

Grandchildren's relationship with their parent(s). Nine grandmothers (6%) identified that their grandchildren's relationship with their parents was a concern. One grandmother noted that the grandchild had lost respect for the parent. In several cases, visitation with the parent was an impending problem, especially if he or she was to be released from prison in the near future. "Children's parent (father) in jail. We filed for custody." One year later that grandmother wrote, "We received legal custody of grandchild. Father in jail, due out in September. Visitation will be different for him. Don't know how that will be resolved."

Many of the custodial families face complex relationship and visitation issues that can be emotionally charged. "My grandson's mom (my daughter) wants to come in and out of his life and now is getting married to an abusive man and they are on drugs." Sometimes the grandchild wants to live with the parent, but it is not possible to do so. As one grandmother wrote, "my daughter is trying to get custody back from me after I had him his whole life." One year later, the grandmother wrote, "Parents had another baby, and [grand]daughter wants to live with them but parents can't support her." Other grandmothers relayed similar stories: my "grandchild wants a closer relationship with parents than with [me]" or "the children think they are going back to their mother," even though the parent(s) are not planning to take the child out of the grandmother's home. In such situations, the grandmother must deal with the child's disappointment and her own ambivalent feelings.

Custody issues. Five grandmothers (3.5%) indicated that the parents wanted to have the grandchild back. One grandmother wrote, "Will my son take them and raise them?" Another wondered "whether we will get legal custody of the kids or will the kids' dad separate them and get custody?" Sometimes the situations resolved in favor of the grandparents. In other families, the family composition changed and the grandmother was no longer the primary caregiver, for example, if the adult child was now living with her in a multigenerational home, while at other times the grandmother and grandchild no longer lived together.

DISCUSSION: RELATIONSHIPS WITH ADULT CHILDREN

Most custodial grandchildren try to maintain contact with their biological mother to varying degrees. Some children express a longing to be with their mother rather than their grandparents, even if they feel their grandparent provides adequate care for them (Turek, 2005). In turn, many grandmothers are disturbed by the effects of the biological mother's inconsistent involvement with their grandchildren, as they unpredictably come in and out of their lives. Custodial grandmothers are also frustrated by the parent's inability to "get their lives together" to care for their children. Despite this, if it is possible for grandchildren to have contact with their mother, they try to do so, even if visits are sporadic. Importantly, however, most grandchildren do feel cared for by their grandparents (Turek, 2005).

Some grandparents have discussed the negative effects of the grandchild's contact with his or her mother. They note behavior changes in the grandchild; for example, an older child may not want to see his mother when she comes to visit, while other children have emotional outbursts or express anger after the mother has visited. One grandmother discussed her grandson's loss of motivation in school and anger management problems, which seemed to stem from his anger toward his mother. Many children in grandparent homes have long-standing anger towards birth parents, grandparents, or other kinship parents about their loss. Children and teens need constructive and safe ways to express their anger as well as to learn to recognize triggers and to manage and channel their anger more appropriately. Children who are demonstrating anger management problems can benefit from counseling, and school counselors also can assist the child to find classes or activities that might complement their interests. As more school counselors are encountering grandparents raising grandchildren, some are developing school-based support groups for them (Hayslip and Glover, in this volume). Other examples of therapeutic activities for custodial grandchildren include creating memory books, participating in drama activities, and using poetry and music to tell their stories in their own words. Summer day or overnight camps, especially if they are geared to grandchildren living with grandparents (e.g., the Fairhill Center's Kinship Kids' Camp and Kinship Teens' Summer Leadership Program) provide respite for caregivers and help normalize the experience of living with a custodial grandparent.

Children and their grandparent caregivers cope differently with the stresses of the family situation. Sometimes it is difficult for caregivers to understand their grandchildren's behaviors as being related to trauma, loss, and disappointment, while simultaneously mourning their own losses when raising grandchildren. The availability of culturally sensitive programs and qualified professionals who are aware of how families grieve and cope with these unique dynamics can be an effective support strategy often found in grandparent-support communities.

EDUCATION

The main concern of 19 grandmothers (13.5%) was about their grandchild starting school, doing well in school, or continuing their education long enough to complete high school. Some urban grandmothers thought, "The educational choices are not the best" and wondered, "Is there something better?" They did not have the resources for other educational options for their grandchildren. While some grandmothers were getting their grandchildren ready for kindergarten or dealing with preschool, others were preparing to send children to college. Other grandmothers worried about their grandchildren's behavior in school and their receiving detentions and suspensions.

DISCUSSION: EDUCATION

There has been national emphasis on helping children to succeed in school, as well as increased resources for children with special needs, whether they are cognitively, physically, or emotionally challenged, or gifted. This additional help can begin in the preschool years through local preschool and day care programs offered through school systems. If a grandparent is concerned about the grandchild's readiness for school, their local kindergarten or preschool assessment clinic can help with assessment and placement in an appropriate preschool or kindergarten class. As children get older, many grandparents report incidents of truancy, suspension, and fighting, which can lead to the grandchild doing poorly in school. Lack of motivation for completing school is a common problem reported by grandmothers about their older grandchildren. Helping students to recognize their talents and begin to make plans for their future is an important strategy for helping students stay focused while in school. For boys and girls alike, gangs and exposure to violence in schools are an increasingly common reality. Helping teens to identify positive role models and participating in community action programs are ways for grandparents to convey their values to their grandchildren and to make a positive difference in their community. Grandparents are encouraged to participate in their grandchild's school and parent-teacher organizations as these build ties to other parents, which may help in reducing at-risk behavior.

GRANDCHILD HEALTH PROBLEMS

In the study, 17 (12%) grandmothers identified grandchildren's health problems as the main source of concern or worry. The grandchild health problems reported by the sample include asthma, HIV infection, full-blown AIDS, autism, communication disorders, muscular dystrophy, and other chronic disorders. Several grandmothers identified that their grandchild's ADHD (Attention Deficit Hyperactivity Disorder) was a main concern, and noted the impact of this condition on family life and school. Another grandmother reported that she was home schooling her granddaughter to "help her get back to grade level, [but she] now struggles in social [development]; has ADD (Attention Deficit Disorder); sending her for tutoring." Another wrote, "My grandchild's emotional problems—bipolar [disorder] and ADHD; [she has] problems with behavior at home and in school." Depending on the severity of the health problems, grandmothers also may provide physical care to grandchildren in addition to try to set limits and structure the environment.

Many grandmothers were troubled by the mental health problems of their grandchildren, including reactive attachment disorder (characterized by inability to form bonds with or to trust others) and alcohol and drug syndromes. Another wrote, my "grand[child] is also oppositional defiant [and has] depression; how to live with all this can be emotionally draining." Another summed up her hope for her grandchild as "being able to teach granddaughter to control her anger and to not be so mean to people, to be beautiful on the outside as well as on the inside."

DISCUSSION OF GRANDCHILD HEALTH PROBLEMS

At-risk children. Good health and normal developmental progress in a child are concerns for all parents, but grandparents who are raising infants or very young children may be uncertain about the state of the child's health, especially if the child was premature, spent time in the intensive care nursery, or was exposed to drugs or alcohol before birth (Delaney-Black et al., 2000). At-risk infants and their grandparents can benefit from referrals to state or local early-intervention services, such as the Ohio Help-Me-Grow programs for children up to age 3, or the Easter Seals Foundation. These programs provide evaluation, referral, and service coordination for children with developmental delays and disabilities. Grandparents with concerns should talk with their primary health provider or social worker, investigate resources online, or call the United Way First Call for Help for information and referral if they suspect developmental delays or other disorders. By monitoring grandchild developmental progress and seeking help when needed, grandparents can provide the highest quality of care to their grandchildren, and the evidence suggests that the quality of the home environment is crucial for children of all abilities (Singer et al., 2004).

Child with complex medical and health needs. Many grandchildren being raised by grandparents have chronic health problems, such as asthma, that require medication and monitoring but often can be effectively managed. Other children being raised by grandparents have more complex medical problems and health care needs. Children born with birth defects or genetic conditions, fetal alcohol syndrome, cerebral palsy, sickle cell disease, or mental retardation all present intensive and often long-term health care needs. Grandparents often require assistance with obtaining ongoing medical care and the appropriate therapies (speech, hearing, physical, or occupational) and equipment (wheelchairs, beds, and assistive devices, such as bath chairs, feeding chairs, or orthopedic devices) for the child. When children are of preschool and school age, finding school programs that adequately support children with special needs is important, and some grandparents may consider moving to a school district with better services for children who have disabilities and developmental delays. As children with special needs get older, grandparents often find it more difficult to handle day-to-day care, and they will need to plan for the long-term care of the grandchildren. In addition, children with physical and emotional problems or other special health care needs may place a strain on family functioning and relationships, and some grandparents may seek counseling for themselves or their families.

Mental health. Nearly 5% of children are reported to have an emotional or behavioral disorder that affects their daily functioning, their ability to learn, or to make and keep friends (National Institutes of Mental Health, 2007a). From the time of puberty into mid-adolescence, children are at increased risk of emotional and mental health problems, especially anxiety, depression, and attention and eating disorders. Frequently, the symptoms of mental health problems manifest as behavior problems. According to the National Institutes of Health, 15%–20% of U.S. teens have experienced a serious depressive episode, with girls twice as likely as boys to become depressed (National Institutes of Mental Health, 2007a). Children's worries about school achievement, relationships, and family conflicts contribute to emotional distress. Teens with symptoms of depression or mental health problems should be evaluated by the primary care provider or be referred to a children's mental health specialist for further intervention. Conduct disorders (acting out and behavior problems with illegal activity) and violence are major problems for teens that have escalated in recent years and are often processed through the court system, even when there is an underlying psychiatric disorder requiring intervention. The National Institute of Mental Health's Child and Adolescent Mental Health Web site contains additional reading materials on child, adolescent, and adult mental health, as well as useful links, including the surgeon general's report on the mental health of the nation.

Attention disorders. One of the most common mental health problems reported by grandmothers raising grandchildren is ADHD, which is more common in boys than in girls (National Institutes of Mental Health, 2007b). During the preschool years, grandparents sometimes mistake their grandchild's nonstop activity or difficulty sitting still with attention disorders. Although signs of ADHD can become apparent in the preschool years, it is difficult to diagnose at this age because the active nature and restlessness of preschoolers is normal (Behrman, Kliegman, & Jenson, 2004). If grandparents share their observations with their grandchild's health provider, they can decide whether to evaluate the child and consider ways to manage the child's restlessness. As learning disabilities, such as ADHD, and behavior problems are more apparent in grade school and middle school, when symptoms interfere with school performance, grandparents may receive calls from school personnel regarding the child's behavior or the child may be failing. This is a critical time for the child to be evaluated by the school psychologist or counselor for behavioral strategies to help the child focus on their work, and if necessary, receive medication.

CHILD CARE AND CHILD WELFARE

A total of 16 grandmothers (11%) noted child care and child welfare as a concern. Child care was noted by five grandmothers (3.5%) as a problem, especially during the summer. "Keeping the kids busy for summer; so far their 4H activities have helped." For others, time off from child care is lacking. "We do not get many breaks. [There is] no family around to help, and finances do not allow for respite."

Grandmother's health and child's welfare. An additional 11 (8%) grandmothers expressed worries about their health and its effect on their ability to care for the grandchildren both now and over time. As one grandmother wrote, "Since I'm not feeling well, how much longer will I be able or choose to take care of the girls . . . ?" Several grandmothers wrote that they had undergone recent surgery or were dealing with chronic conditions, such as cancer, which pose immediate and potentially long-term consequences for the family's stability.

DISCUSSION: CHILD CARE AND WELFARE

Many grandparents comment on the responsibility of daily child care in conversation or anecdotally in their questionnaires, but do not identify it as their main source of concern or worry. Nevertheless, questions about raising children are present and usually reflect the age of the children and sometimes the state of the grandmother's own health. Respite care is one of the services most desired by caregivers and yet one of the most unavailable and underfunded (Minkler, 2002). Respite care provides caregivers with temporary relief from their caregiving responsibilities. Some respite programs offered on a local basis include opportunities for children to go to summer camp, spring break activities, mentoring programs, and child care respite during workshops and meetings (AARP, 2003).

Young children. Parenting young children is a demanding task, and many grandparents report that having enough patience can be difficult to maintain. Not uncommonly, many grandparents are uncertain about their toddler's behavior and need to be reminded that young children have yet to develop abilities such as delay of gratification or understanding another's point of view. The toddlers require consistent and firm limits in a supportive environment to reinforce the child's ability to maintain self-control. Attending parenting classes, reading books and online resources, and talking with the child's primary care provider are ways for grandparents to have up-to-date information and guidance about age-appropriate developmental expectations.

Children between 2 ½ and 5 years benefit from the education and socialization of preschool. Opportunities to be with other children of the same age group are increasingly important so that the grandchild can develop and practice social skills, especially if the grandchild has limited exposure to other young children. Preschool also allows grandmothers a needed break. Most children, even those with disabilities or developmental delays, can participate in public or private preschool programs, whether through Head Start programs or other initiatives, and grandparents may be eligible to obtain vouchers for some preschool programs.

School-age children. Grandparents often find that children in elementary and middle school are concerned with their school performance and want to participate in and be successful at outside activities, such as sports, scouts, or 4H clubs. Activities may pose a strain for grandparents if finances are limited and there are no fee reductions, or if there is difficulty in arranging transportation. In addition, grandparents are often challenged by the new methods of teaching familiar subjects and the homework requirements of their grandchildren. Grandparents can help their grandchildren by accessing tutors through school systems, and encouraging grandchildren to keep up with their work. Another big concern about grandchildren of these ages is safety, especially when children walk or bicycle to school, friends' homes, or other activities by themselves; many grandparents and parents share neighborhood and block watches or coordinate supervising children on the way to school. Offsetting the benefits of activity, sports injuries, especially bicycle accidents, are common among children and early teens, and motor vehicle accidents and unintended injuries are the leading causes of death for 10–24 year olds (National Center for Chronic Disease Prevention and Health Promotion, 2006).

FAMILY CONFLICT

A total of 4 grandmothers (2.8%) noted conflicts between family members as concerns. In one case, the conflict was between the grandmother and her spouse; in another case it was between the grandfather and the grandchild. Two grandmothers noted that other teenage or adult children were jealous of the custodial grandchild.

DISCUSSION: FAMILY CONFLICT

All families of grandparents raising grandchildren experience some loss and stress. It may be tangible, such as the death of the grandchild's parent, or intangible, such as the loss of hopes and expectations for them. Many custodial grandparent families have had multiple and complex losses that can affect the caregivers and the children. Grandmother caregivers in particular may be raising a grandchild (or children) while also providing care to another family member or friend, and the balancing act of multiple caregiver roles can amplify their stress. A critical time of intervention is early in any caregiving transition, when the stress and mental health consequences may be more pronounced (Minkler, Fuller-Thomson, Miller, & Driver, 2002; Standing et al., 2007). Depression risk for grandparent caregivers may wax and wane, decreasing as the grandparents begin to adjust to their roles and come to terms with the situation of their adult child, or as younger grandchildren become more self-sufficient. Support groups create environments where grandparent caregivers can learn new parenting skills, practice communication skills, and build their overall competence in their role. Sometimes, engaging the entire family in brief counseling may be a valuable intervention with enduring benefits.

SUMMARY

Grandparents share many of the same concerns for their grandchildren as parents who are raising their own children, often with additional challenges, such as custody issues, age-related health problems, difficulties with the grandchild's parent, and additional financial strains. Grandmothers raising grandchildren have had a powerful and influential voice in generating support for themselves and their families. Armed with current information about child health and development, skills in managing children and teens, and a network of supportive others, grandparents should feel confident about parenting their grandchildren.

REFERENCES

AARP. (2003). *Lean on me: Support and minority outreach for grandparents raising grand-children.* Retrieved on May 8, 2007, at http://www.aarp.org/research/family/grandparenting/aresearch-import-483.html

Berhman, R. E., Kliegman, R. M., & Jenson, H. B. (2004). *Nelson's textbook of pediatrics* (17th ed.). Philadelphia: Saunders.

Delaney-Black, V., Covington, C., Templin, J. A., Nordstrom-Klee, B., Martier, S., Leddick, L., Czerwinski, H., & Sokol, R. J. (2000). Teacher-assessed behavior of children prenatally exposed to cocaine. *Pediatrics, 106*(4), 782–791.

Minkler, M. (2002). Grandparents and other relatives raising children: characteristics, needs, best practices, and implications for the aging network. *Monograph of the Administration on Aging.*

Minkler, M., Fuller-Thomson, E., Miller, D., & Driver, D. (2002). Grandparent caregiving and depression. In B. Hayslip, Jr., & R. Goldberg-Glen (Eds.), *Grandparents raising grandchildren: Theoretical, empirical, and clinical perspectives* (pp. 207–219). New York: Springer.

Musil, C., Warner, C., Jeanblanc, A., Zauszniewski, J., & Kercher, K. (2006). Grandmothers, caregiving, and family functioning, *Journal of Gerontology, Social Sciences, 61B*(2), S89–S98.

National Center for Chronic Disease Prevention and Health Promotion. (2006). *Injury and violence.* Retrieved September 15, 2007, from http://www.cdc.gov/healthyyouth/injury

National Institutes of Mental Health. (2007a). *Child and adolescent mental health.* Retrieved September 15, 2007, from http://www.nimh.nih.gov/healthinformation/childmenu.cfm

National Institutes of Mental Health. (2007b). *Attention Deficit Hyperactivity Disorder.* Retrieved September 15, 2007, from http://www.nimh.nih.gov/publicat/adhd.cfm#intro

Scannapieco, M., & Hegar, R. L. (2002). Kinship care providers: Designing an array of supportive services. *Child and Adolescent Social Work Journal, 19*(4), 315–327.

Singer, L. T., Minnes, S., Short, E., Arendt, R., Farkas, K., Lewis, B., Klein, N., Russ, S., Min, M. O., & Kirchner, H. L. (2004). Cognitive outcomes of preschool children with prenatal exposure. *Journal of the American Medical Association, 291*(20), 2448–2456.

Standing, T., Musil, C., & Warner, C. (2007). Grandmothers' transitions in caregiving to grandchildren. *Western Journal of Nursing Research, 13*(1), 613–631.

Turek, D. (2005). *Adolescents in custodial grandparent care: A qualitative analysis.* Unpublished doctoral thesis, Case Western Reserve University.

CHAPTER 8

Implementing Parenting Programs for Custodial Grandparents

Lenora Campbell and Margaret Shandor Miles

Children being raised by grandparents are one of the fastest growing groups of children in the United States. Since the mid 1980s, the number of children being raised by relatives in what is known as kinship care has grown exponentially and most of the caregivers are grandparents. Grandparents are responsible for most of the basic needs of their grandchildren in more than 2.4 million homes. Moreover, ethnic and racial differences exist; census data from 2000 indicate that 4.2% of all White children are living in grandparent-headed homes, while 13.2% of African American children live with their grandparents. For many grandparents, raising one's grandchild can be a long commitment (Coles, 2006; Minkler, 1999). Custodial grandparents often have responsibility for their grandchildren for 5 years or more (U.S. Census Bureau, 2000). In addition, grandparent caregivers, on average, provide care to two grandchildren (Landry-Myers, 2000). Most custodial

Acknowledgments: The authors wish to acknowledge the assistance of Catherine Joyner, Currissa Townsend, and Kelcy A. Eady with this project. The Grandparenting Program was supported by a grant from the Kellogg Foundation and the State of North Carolina. Support was provided by grants from the National Institute of Nursing Research and National Center on Minority Health and Health Disparities, P20 NR 8369 and P20 NR 8366.

grandparenting is done by grandmothers or other female kin (Ruiz, Zhu, & Crowther, 2003).

The circumstances that result in raising grandchildren are born out of life experiences that place grandparents and their grandchildren at risk. These include parental illness, especially HIV and mental illness, or early death; divorce or teen pregnancy resulting in reduced economic and emotional resources for parenting; and, of most concern, incarceration, child abuse, abandonment, or neglect (Bryson & Casper, 1999; Woodworth, 1996). Short-term reasons may include financial and emotional overload of the parents or transitional situations such as a parent on a military assignment.

In most instances, grandparents are thrust unexpectedly into this challenging new role, disallowing the time necessary to progress through experiences and adjustments critical to the parenting role. With little opportunity to plan, they are confronted with a myriad of problems and encounter many stresses associated with parenting their grandchildren. Even when the experience does not occur abruptly, raising infants, young children, and adolescents changes everything about the grandparents' lives including leisure, friendships, work, health, and finances (Pinson-Millburn, Fabian, Schlossberg, & Pyle, 1996). With low-income grandparents, the parental responsibilities assumed must be viewed within the context of issues such as poverty, inadequate housing, and chronic illness (Coles, 2006). In addition, challenges with the adult child and behavioral and emotional problems with the grandchildren have the potential to make parenting difficult. All of these factors can compromise the grandparent-child relationship and impact both the child and the grandparent. Therefore, while grandparents may constitute a good safety net that diverts children from the child welfare and foster care system, there is clearly a need for interventions aimed at helping grandparents become competent in providing responsive and effective parenting, while also reducing their stress and effectively integrating this new role into their lives.

This chapter presents an overview of some of the challenges faced by these custodial grandparents, and identifies key issues important in developing parenting interventions that meet the needs of grandparents. We also describe our experiences with a community-based grandparenting program.

SPECIFIC CHALLENGES OF CUSTODIAL GRANDPARENTS

Three specific challenges of custodial grandparents must be considered in the development of programs. These include challenges related to the actual parenting, those related to family conflict, especially the relationship with their adult child, and those related to the grandparents' own needs.

Parenting Challenges

The complex needs of grandchildren are a critical factor that may compromise a grandparent's ability to parent effectively and be a source of ongoing stress. This includes health, developmental, cognitive, behavioral, and emotional problems (Brown et al., 2000; Smith & Palmieri, 2007). Some of the children's needs relate to prior health problems including high-risk neonatal histories, prenatal exposure to drugs and alcohol, premature birth or low birth weight, and related health problems (McNichol & Tash, 2001). Many have physical disabilities, neurological problems, delayed development, and other special developmental needs (Dowell, 1995; Minkler, 1999; Shore & Hayslip, 1994). Studies have also found that many children in grandparent-headed households have cognitive delays and experience academic difficulties, thus placing them at risk for school dropout, delinquency behaviors, teen pregnancy, and a host of other adverse behaviors and outcomes. Several studies have found that many children in foster or nonfoster kinship care have serious behavioral and emotional problems (Billing, Ehrle, & Kortenkamp, 2002) and problems with attention-demanding behaviors, hyperactivity, and aggression (Dubowitz & Sawyer, 1994). None of this is surprising considering the large number of children being reared by grandparents as a result of a disruption in the primary parenting relationship. This may include abuse or neglect by their own parent or exposure to violence in the family.

The behavioral and emotional problems of the children also may arise from their ambivalence or confusion about their level of commitment and loyalty towards their own parent and the custodial grandparent (Hayslip & Patrick, 2003). If the parent maintains some level of contact with the child, they may experience repeated rejection and conflict in that relationship. It is not uncommon for parents to make unfulfilled promises to the child or reject the child by direct or indirect communication. Children may question their placement, experience loss and bereavement, feel isolated or stigmatized, and view their families as different and perhaps inferior to other families (Kropf & Burnette, 2003).

Even if the children have few, if any, of these health and behavioral problems, parenting children of various ages can also be stressful, especially for grandparents who are elderly. Young children are highly dependent on adults, requiring more effort and time, while older children are often a behavioral challenge. Grandparents have particularly voiced concerns about rearing teenagers, and boys may be particularly difficult (Hayslip, Shore, Henderson, & Lambert, 1998; Smith & Palmieri, 2007). Of utmost concern are behavioral acting out, sexuality and sexual behavior, suspected or actual drug use, and exposure to violence in the community (Brown et al., 2000). Too, grandparents can be unrealistic in their discipline practices, especially for older children.

They often do not understand the strong peer influence on teenagers and may discipline them in the presence of their peers. They also might not appreciate that, developmentally, teens are less accepting of requests without understanding the reasons, which is consistent with their level of cognitive development. Similarly, grandparents need to understand when children are not reaching developmental milestones and seek appropriate referrals.

Thus, grandparents are challenged to learn a parenting style that works for both them and the grandchildren. Elderly grandparents come from an era when expectations of children were clearly defined and children displayed less resistance to these expectations. They are not accustomed to some of the behaviors the children exhibit, such as lack of respect and resistance to authority. Indeed, youth today are exposed to a variety of information, behaviors, and experiences that are both foreign and unacceptable to many of their grandparents. The parenting styles of the grandparent may also differ greatly from that of the parents of the child, creating parenting stress and difficulties for the children that could lead to negative child outcomes.

One factor that makes parenting difficult is that grandparents may be unclear about the permanency of their parenting role. Lack of permanency has the potential to make them reluctant to provide expectations and discipline to grandchildren. This can further erode the parental role, increase grandparenting stress, and cause behavioral and academic problems among grandchildren. Thus, some grandparents seek more permanent arrangements with their grandchildren through custody and adoption. However, the processes are complicated, costly, and slow.

Finally, as custodial parents, these grandparents also are expected to be advocates for the grandchildren in a variety of settings, but lack of permanency can make their advocacy role even more difficult. Their advocacy role includes being informed about school needs and communicating with teachers, standing up for the needs of the children, and keeping the children safe. Since poor communities have limited recreational resources and high levels of violence and crime, grandparents are often caught in a dilemma regarding how to keep children safe, give them positive peer influences, and at the same time provide for their social and recreational needs. Another advocacy role, finding resources for the mental health and behavioral needs of the children, can be very complex in resource-poor areas. When resources are identified, transportation to access those resources is often a challenge.

Family Conflict

Family conflict, especially with the parent of the custodial grandchildren (usually the mother), can impact on the response of grandparents and on their parenting. The relationship between the parent and grandparent is often strained at best and can often be hostile or estranged. One source of conflict is the anger and resentment felt when the parent continues to engage in the risk-taking behaviors (e.g., substance abuse) that led to them forfeiting their parental responsibility. This resentment can interfere with grandparents' ability to provide nurturing and responsive parenting to the grandchildren and can create strife in the grandparent-grandchild relationship. At the same time, grandparents are often grappling with the perceived failure of their own parenting role with their adult children and how to meet the needs of their children while also meeting the needs of their grandchildren.

Many parents maintain a presence in their children's lives and provide some parenting. While this can be helpful to grandparents, it is not uncommon for adult children to request, and even demand, that the children spend time with them, even when their living circumstances are not conducive for child rearing. Grandparents who are challenged by the intrusiveness of adult children in the lives of their grandchildren worry about the toxic influence parents have on them, and feel helpless in these situations.

Informal and open-ended custody arrangements can lead to conflict between the grandparent and parent. While many grandparents are hopeful that their children will reclaim their parental status with their own children, they also may be concerned about the children returning to an inadequate and even unsafe home environment. This is particularly difficult when the children are moved back and forth between their custody and that of the parent.

The decision to rear grandchildren has the potential to cause conflict among other family members and even friends. In some instances, other adult children, their children, and other family members may resent grandparents assuming the custodial role. Consequently, many custodial caregivers do not have an opportunity to receive support, relief, or respite from their caregiving role from other family members.

Personal Needs of Grandparents

A major source of stress for grandparents is the loss of time and energy to meet their own physical, emotional, and social needs. In addition to their caregiving role, many work, leaving little time for self-care, social life with friends, and attention to health needs. This may reduce the availability of social support and place them at risk for emotional and physical health problems (Kelley, Yorker, & Whitley, 1997; Musil, 1998).

Financial stresses and inadequate resources are also a strain (Rodgers-Farmer & Jones, 1999). Almost one-half of grandparent-headed households live in poverty and, if the grandparents work, they often have low-paying jobs without benefits. Since grandparents often provide the caretaking responsibilities to their grandchildren in an informal arrangement, they may not be eligible for the additional resources that might be available to them if they were made custodians to their grandchildren through the state child welfare system. Moreover, community resources such as mental health counseling, parenting classes, and respite help are limited for persons living in impoverished circumstances.

Further compromising the parenting role of grandparents is the fact that many custodial grandparents are elderly, with chronic health problems and limitations in the activities of daily living (Minkler & Fuller-Thompson, 1999, 2001). Thus grandparents' functional status, particularly fatigue, may make it difficult to provide effective parenting. Because caregiving demands a great deal of time and chronic illness generally requires careful management, including obtaining regular health care, the health problems for some custodial caregivers are poorly managed. Too, the stresses associated with custodial parenting may place them at risk for additional health problems such as cardiovascular disease (Grinstead, Leder, Jenson, & Bond, 2003; Lee, Colditz, Berkman, & Kawachi, 2003; Minkler & Fuller-Thompson, 1999). Poor health is further compromised by the number of grandparents who are reluctant to acknowledge health-related problems, possibly due to lack of time or health insurance (Joslin & Harrison, 1998). When health problems are not well managed, grandparents are not able to fully engage in the activities of daily living, including parenting.

In addition, it is well documented that grandparents who assume care for grandchildren are at risk for emotional distress, depressive symptoms, and other mental health problems (Grinstead et al., 2003; Minkler & Fuller-Thompson, 2001). Further, grandparents' ties to the grandchild's parent (particularly in the case of incarceration, addiction, death, and unresolved issues) all increase emotional stress for grandparents (sJanicki, McCallion, Grant-Griffin, & Kolomer, 2000). This distress can seriously impact on parenting and child outcomes. We know that a clinically depressed parent (mother) is hindered in her ability to provide parenting that is responsive to the interests and needs of her children (Hoffman, Crnic, & Baker, 2006). Children of women with depression or elevated depressive symptoms are at increased risk for difficulties in emotion regulation, less optimal interactions, insecure attachment, problem behaviors, and delays in the acquisition of competencies (Murray & Copper, 1997; Radke-Yarrow, 1999).

One's degree of resilience is also thought to have considerable effect on determining whether or not risks lead to adverse outcomes—in this case ineffective parenting and grandparent and grandchild negative outcomes. The presence of protective factors, defined as "influences that modify, ameliorate, or alter a person's response to some environmental hazard that predisposes to a maladaptive outcome" (Rutter, 1985, p. 600), may moderate the effects of risks, and prevent negative parenting and the development of negative behaviors by grandchildren. One such protective factor is the meaning placed on custodial grandparenting by the grandparent. Some perceive taking on a parental role as a blessing or a second chance, and feel renewed meaning for their lives (Kelley & Damato, 1995). They also may feel rewarded by the presence of youth in their lives and the related companionship (Rodgers-Farmer & Jones, 1999). In addition, grandparents who have been in the parenting role for a longer period of time may have accepted their parenting role and have adjusted. These grandparents may be less likely to perceive their role as stressful and they may demonstrate greater parenting competencies. Thus, the length of time in the parenting role may moderate the relationship between assuming the custodial role, parenting stress, and parental competence by increasing one's resilience.

DEVELOPING PARENTING PROGRAMS FOR CUSTODIAL GRANDPARENTS

It is clear that programs aimed at helping custodial grandparents must address the three major concerns discussed above. Thus, programs need to focus on parenting and parenting skills in the context of possible family conflicts and the impact of parenting on the personal life of the grandparents. In addition, a focus on the needs of the children under their care must be included in such programs.

We present specific ideas for developing parenting programs for grandparent caregivers based on our experience in developing and implementing the Grandparenting Program in Winston-Salem, North Carolina. This is a family-centered, strength- and empowerment-based program designed to enhance the well-being and successful functioning of custodial grandparents and their grandchildren.

The overall program encompasses a case-management approach based on Project Healthy Grandparents (Kelley, Yorker, Whitley, & Sipe, 2001). Individual families (grandparents and grandchildren) are followed individually by a case management team comprised of a nurse and a social worker. The goals of case management are to conjointly assess the issues and needs of the family, identify the key issues for which the family wants help, problem solve with the family, help them connect to resources, and provide individualized parenting skills. We also have a parenting group intervention. This program, which meets weekly, focuses on (a) enhancing parenting skills for effective parenting; (b) navigating the school system; (c) advocating and accessing services; and (d) assisting grandparents to meet their own personal needs. The program also encompasses self-development and academic enhancement for the children in their care.

Enhancing Parenting Skills for Effective Parenting

To address the parenting needs of custodial grandparents, we provide a supportive and evidence-based parenting program. Evidence supports the benefits of parent-training interventions to empower custodial grandparents, improve parenting skills, and enhance child functioning. A number of parenting curricula are available; some provide evidence to support improved outcomes such as increased knowledge and skill. Among these are the Nurturing Parenting Program (Bavelok, 2000), Incredible Years (Webster-Stratton, 1998, 2000), the Positive Parenting Program, (Sanders, Cann, & Markie-Dadds, 2003), and the Strengthening Families Program (Spoth, Guyll, Chao, & Molgaard, 2002). None of these were designed for grandparents. The only program designed specifically for grandparents was that of Cox (2002), which emphasizes the empowerment of grandparent caregivers.

We use an adaptation of the Incredible Years program, which was designed to foster positive and effective parenting practices leading to positive improvements in parent-child interactions and a reduction in children's problem behaviors (Webster-Stratton, 2000). In this program, there are two types of training curricula that are targeted at parents rearing children up to 12 years of age. The BASIC parent program reinforces the use of play, praise and reward, effective limit setting, logical consequences, monitoring, helping children learn to problem solve, and family problem solving. These parenting behaviors are directly targeted at enhancing the parent-child relationship through engaging in pleasurable interactions and activities, providing encouragement and support for desired behaviors, matching expectations with the developmental level of the child, thus reducing the need for controlling attitudes, and eliminating negative behaviors through the use of discipline. It was found to be successful in promoting positive improvements in parent-child interactions and in reducing children's problem behavior. We supplemented the BASIC program with additional content from the ADVANCE parent program, which emphasizes parents' interpersonal skills, such as effective communication, anger management, problem solving between adults, and methods of giving and receiving support. Enhancing these skills also impacts the communication between grandparents and their adult children and reduces family conflict. The Incredible Years program has been successfully used to assist parents to learn positive and noncoercive discipline, improve parent-child relationships, and reduce mental health problems among children (Patterson, Mockford, & Stewart-Brown, 2005; Webster-Stratton, 1998). We adapted the program to fit the African American cultural background of the grandparents, their generational issues related to parenting, the issues they faced in rearing teenagers, and the special needs of the custodial grandchildren.

Parenting sessions encompass a number of strategies. Grandparents are expected to read assignments from the Incredible Years parent manual. The key principle from the assignment is highlighted by the leader. Participants are then encouraged to discuss the principle and give examples from their own parenting. Videotapes of parents using effective and ineffective parenting techniques are used to help reinforce parenting skills, especially for visual learners. Then the sessions use role-playing and rehearsal of skills, techniques found to be effective in producing behavioral changes (Cox, 2002; Webster-Stratton, 1998). Scenarios for role-play are created by grandparents based on some of their personal experiences. Allowing grandparents to discuss and role-play some of their own experiences helps to personalize the parent training, allows them to try out new and unfamiliar parenting behaviors, and lets them become more at ease with challenging and sensitive parenting situations. It also allows them to incorporate effective parenting practices for children beyond the middle school years.

Homework assignments are given at each session. These usually involve asking grandparents to observe and record behaviors at home or practice a particular strategy, such as giving the child verbal praise. Grandparents are also asked to read specific content in preparation for the next week's topic.

Because grandparents often have inappropriate expectations of their grandchildren and lack an understanding of developmental issues, our parenting program also incorporates content on developmental stages. We also added sessions to help grandparents deal with the emotional and behavioral needs of grandchildren. These included discussions on child mental health issues (including specific conditions such as Attention Deficit Hyperactivity Disorder), treatment modalities, and mental health resources. Professionals from university-based child mental health clinics, school counseling departments, or local mental health and counseling centers are invited to talk with the grandparents and provide needed information and resources.

Navigating the School System

Our program also incorporates a 5-week series on navigating the school system. Custodial grandparents are often called upon to deal with numerous academic and behavioral problems of the children within the school system. Thus, an important component of our parenting program is enhancing grandparents' knowledge of the school system, including policies, procedures, expectations, and resources. We developed a manual for grandparents that incorporates critical information needed to assist their children with school readiness and academic success. We invite school personnel to talk with grandparents about academic and school requirements and students' and parents' expectations. Grandparents are assisted in such activities as reading and understanding academic records, what to expect at parent-teacher conferences, and how to obtain available resources to enhance their grandchild's academic performance.

Advocating and Accessing Resources

Assisting custodial grandparents to effectively advocate for the needs of their children gives them another important caregiving skill. Custodial grandparents must learn how to deal with organizations and institutions to obtain the support they need. Many of them interact with agencies that historically have policies and procedures that reflect a lack of familiarity with and sensitivity to their circumstances. We provide information on resources as well as include skill-building activities aimed at accessing desired outcomes. Grandparents often lack the skills involved in setting up appointments, preparing for meetings, using effective communication, and engaging in appropriate follow-up. We bring in representatives from schools, child welfare agencies, and financial, housing, and legal institutions to share available resources with grandparents. We also engage in role-play to enhance their advocacy skills. An important area of advocacy for grandparents is around custody issues. We invite speakers from the child welfare and legal communities who are familiar with custody issues to help grandparents understand the various types of legal authority (custody, guardianship, adoption) and determine which is appropriate for their circumstances and will best meet the needs of their grandchildren. Grandparents are helped to understand that the lack of legal recognition of their caregiving status might make it difficult, if not impossible, to access social support systems or medical, educational, or financial services. This knowledge also prevents their adult children from removing the grandchildren from their homes prematurely.

Assisting Grandparents to Meet Their Personal Needs

Effective parenting is in part regulated by the parents' own emotional and physical health. It is clear that the stress on grandparents affects their well-being and the well-being of their grandchildren. Our program incorporates a 6-week series on effective self-care. We begin the series by encouraging the grandparents to explore and discuss how their lives have been interrupted by this new caretaking responsibility, their actual caretaking experiences, and their perceived benefits and challenges associated with rearing grandchildren. This activity gives the grandparents an opportunity to express thoughts that might not have been previously expressed and that might hinder them from exploring their parenting role and being receptive to learning new parenting strategies. Also, hearing about the experiences of others can facilitate their reframing of their custodial role into one that is more helpful to them and their grandchildren.

The relationship with the adult child is especially problematic for many grandparents and can compromise effective parenting. Grandparents are often angry at their adult child for their behavioral and social problems and resentful that they have to assume their parenting responsibilities. Many of these relationships are estranged or fraught with conflict and poor communication. Using the components of the Incredible Years parenting curriculum, we provide content and skills training on effective communication, problem solving, and conflict resolution. In some instances, we have invited mental health consultants to assist the grandparents in processing some of their emotional responses to the conflict with their adult children and other family members.

Evidence clearly shows that the stressful demands of child rearing can have negative effects on the physical heath of grandparents. An effective parenting program for custodial grandparents should address their health needs. We devote 6 weeks to providing a health series designed to assist grandparents in better understanding the need to engage in health promotion and disease prevention, and, when appropriate, to manage their chronic illnesses. We solicit experts in health care to discuss various health-related topics. Because at least one-third of custodial grandparents do not have health insurance, we also provide grandparents with a list of health-care resources in the community to address their health needs.

Arguably, the most pressing concern of grandparents and other kinship caregivers is the need for respite. The lack of informal support is in part associated with grandparents' insufficient time to engage in social and recreational activities and to take care of their personal needs. Grandparents need periodic relief from their child-rearing responsibilities. We devote one session to discussing the need for respite and identifying both formal and informal resources that are available to grandparents. The parenting classes also provide respite since grandchildren are being cared for in the children's program while grandparents are attending the parenting program. We also use the parenting classes to encourage grandparents to participate in enrichment activities. A number of community-based agencies provide personal development and enrichment classes and seminars free of charge, including seminars on computer literacy, financial management, and arts and crafts.

Finally, we target stress reductions for these grandparents, who are dealing with a multitude of experiences that challenge their emotional well-being. The ability to effectively deal with the stress of rearing one's grandchild and the corresponding family conflicts is critical to grandparents' ability to effectively parent their grandchildren. Grandparents are assisted in recognizing key stressors and their response and identifying their personal stress-reduction strategies. Many of the strategies they identify as effective are incorporated into the remainder of the parenting classes. For example, many grandparents in our parenting classes use spiritual interventions to reduce stress, including prayer, scripture reading, and reciting favorite bible verses. To integrate those strategies into the parenting program, we begin and end our parenting sessions with a spiritual reading or prayer. We also teach grandparents more mainstream stress-reduction strategies, including guided imagery, deep breathing, and progressive muscle relaxation. Grandparents are taught to use a "feeling thermometer" to identify their feelings and to understand how emotions influence one's parenting behaviors.

Cultural Considerations

Parenting practices may differ based on the beliefs and values of the caregiver. This is often associated with the age and ethnicity of the grandparent. Consequently, parenting programs should consider the cultural beliefs and practices of the population being served. Our work with a group of primarily low-income, predominately older African American grandmothers revealed important cultural considerations. The use of language is an important cultural consideration. For example, the grandparents participating in our parenting program had difficulty with the concept of "play," an important concept in the Incredible Years parenting curriculum. With further discussion, the grandparents revealed that they indeed spent time engaging in "fun" activities with their grandchildren. However, it was not acceptable to them to call this activity "play." Similarly, grandparents were opposed to the idea of "praising" their grandchildren. Many of them considered the concept of praise in religious terms and were opposed to using the term to refer to encouraging remarks provided to their grandchildren.

The age of the grandparent is another important consideration. There is evidence to suggest that younger grandparents are depressed more often than older grandparents. This might be related to the fact that younger grandparents come to the grandparenting role with different developmental needs, life experiences, and expectations than their older counterparts. They are more likely to have greater demands on their time related to employment, family, and personal interests. They also might perceive the parenting role to be more intrusive in their lives. All of this might cause younger grandparents to respond differently to the parenting role. Too, younger grandparents' parenting styles might reflect those of a different generation. They might have fewer language barriers as well as more recent experiences with children of ages similar to their grandchildren. Parenting programs need to consider the cultural characteristics of the grandparents they serve.

Evaluation

It is important to evaluate the effectiveness and acceptability of the parenting program. This might be done through formal and informal evaluations. Informally, facilitators can spend the last 15 minutes of the groups asking the grandparents to comment on aspects of the session that were helpful and those they found unhelpful. Focus groups can be held after the parenting program ends to gather grandparents' overall impression of the program. In these groups, grandparents can be asked to reflect on the program and to identify the relevance (or lack of relevance) it has for their lives. They can be asked to identify what they liked and disliked about the program and what they would change to make it more meaningful and helpful to them. To evaluate the impact of the parenting program on the health and well-being of grandparents and the outcomes of grandchildren, pre- and post-assessments of the grandparents' physical and emotional health, parenting stress, and parenting competency can be collected. To determine the impact of the program on grandchildren outcomes, pre- and post-assessments of grandchildren's social, emotional, and cognitive well-being may be gathered. All of these data can be used to refine the program to better meet the needs of the grandparents.

Conclusion

Custodial grandparents have a long history of parenting. Many of their needs are different than first-generation parents. Because of the complexity of their circumstances, they need parenting programs that are multifaceted and that address needs, issues, and challenges, both in common with other parents and unique to them. The program must be placed in the context of their stressful lives, with sensitivity to the complexities of their experiences in taking on the role of parenting again. Parenting programs and techniques need to be sensitive to the values and cultural beliefs of grandparents who are from a different generation. Parenting programs also need to fit with the cultural values and beliefs of the population being served, while also providing insights into alternative approaches. Ultimately, the parenting program should improve the lives of the grandparents and the children under their care.

REFERENCES

Bavolek, S. J. (2000). *The Nurturing Parenting Programs.* Washington, DC: U.S. Department of Justice, Office of Justice Programs, Office of Juvenile Justice and Delinquency Prevention.

Billing, A., Ehrle, J., & Kortenkamp, K. (2002). Children cared for by relatives: What do we know about their well-being? *Children and Youth Services Review, 26,* 287–305

Brown, E. J., Jemmont, L. S., Outlaw, F. H., Wilson, G., Howard, M., & Curtis, S. (2000). African American grandmothers' perceptions of caregiver concerns associated with rearing adolescent grandchildren. *Psychiatric Nursing, 14,* 73–80.

Bryson, K., & Casper, L. M. (1999). *Coresident grandparents and grandchildren.* U.S. Bureau of the Census, Population Division Working Paper No. 26. Washington, DC: U.S. Bureau of the Census.

Coles, R. L. (2006). *Race and family: A structural approach.* Thousand Oaks, CA: Sage.

Cox, C. B. (2002). Empowering African American custodial grandparents. *Social Work, 47,* 337–352.

Dowell, E. N. (1995). Caregiver burden: Grandmothers raising their high risk grandchildren. *Journal of Psychosocial Nursing, 33,* 27–30.

Dubowitz, H., & Sawyer, R. J. (1994). School behavior of children in kinship care. *Child Abuse & Neglect, 18,* 899–911.

Grinstead, L. N., Leder, S., Jensen, S., & Bond, L. (2003). Review of research on the health of caregiving grandparents. *Journal of Advanced Nursing, 44,* 318–326.

Hayslip, B., Jr., & Patrick, J. (2003). Custodial grandparenting viewed from within a life-span perspective. In B. Hayslip, Jr., and J. Patrick (Eds.), *Working with custodial grandparents* (pp. 1–13). New York: Springer.

Hayslip, B., Shore, J., Henderson, C. E., & Lambert, P. L. (1998). Custodial grandparenting and the impact of grandchildren with problems on role satisfaction and role meaning. *Journals of Gerontology: Psychological Sciences and Social Sciences, 53B,* S164–S173.

Hoffman, C., Crnic, K. A., & Baker, J. K. (2006). Maternal depression and parenting: Implications for children's emergent emotion regulation and behavioral functioning. *Parenting: Science and Practice, 6,* 271–295.

Janicki, M., McCallion, P., Grant-Griffin, L., & Kolomer, S. (2000). Grandparent caregivers I: Characteristics of the grandparents and the children with disabilities for whom they care. *Journal of Gerontological Social Work, 33,* 35–55.

Joslin, D., & Harrison, R. (1998). The hidden patient: Older relatives raising children orphaned by AIDS. *Journal of the American Medical Women's Association, 53,* 65–71.

Kelley, S. J., & Damato, E. (1995). Grandparents as primary caregivers. *American Journal of Maternal-Child Nursing, 20,* 326–332.

Kelley, S. J., Yorker, B., & Whitley, D. (1997). To grandmother's house we go and stay: Children raised in intergenerational families. *Journal of Gerontological Nursing, 23,* 12–20.

Kelley, S. J., Yorker, W. C., Whitley, D. M., & Sipe, T. A. (2001). A multimodal intervention for grandparents raising grandchildren: Results of an exploratory study. *Child Welfare of America, 1*, 27–50.

Kropf, P., & Burnette, D. (2003). Grandparents as family caregivers: Lessons for intergenerational education. *Educational Gerontology, 29*, 361–372.

Landry-Myers, L. (2000). Grandparents as parents: What they need to be successful. *Family Focus, 45*, F9–F10.

Lee, S., Colditz, G. A., Berkman, L. F., & Kawachi, I. (2003). Caregiving and risk of coronary heart disease in U.S. women. *American Journal of Preventive Medicine, 24*, 113–119.

McNichol, T., & Tash, C. (2001). Parental substance abuse and the development of children in family foster care. *Child Welfare, 80*, 239–242.

Minkler, M. (1999). Intergenerational households headed by grandparents: Context, realities, and implications for policy. *Journal of Aging Studies, 13*, 199–218.

Minkler, M., & Fuller-Thompson, D. E. (1999). The health of grandparents raising grandchildren: Results of a national study. *American Journal of Public Health, 89*, 1384–1389.

Minkler, M., & Fuller-Thompson, D. E. (2001). Physical and mental health status of American grandparents providing extensive child care to their grandchildren. *Journal of the American Medical Women's Association, 56*, 199–205.

Murray, C., & Cooper, P. J. (1997). Prediction, detection, and treatment of postnatal depression. *Archives of Disorders in Children, 77*, 97–99.

Musil, C. (1998). Health, stress, coping, and social support in grandmothers caregivers. *Health Care for Women International, 19*, 441–455.

Patterson, J., Mockford, C., & Stewart-Brown, S. (2005). Parents' perceptions of the value of the Webster-Stratton Parenting Programme: A qualitative study of a general practice based initiative. *Child: Care, Health & Development, 31*, 53–64.

Pinson-Millburn, N. M., Fabian, E. S., Schlossberg, N. K., & Pyle, M. (1996). Grandparents raising grandchildren. *Journal of Counseling & Development, 74*, 548–554.

Radke-Yarrow, M. (1999). *Children of depressed mothers: From early childhood to maturity.* Cambridge: Cambridge University Press.

Rodgers-Farmer, A. Y., & Jones, R. L. (1999). Grandmothers who are caregivers: An overlooked population. *Child and Adolescent Social Work Journal, 16*, 455–466.

Ruiz, D. S., Zhu, C. W., & Crowther, M. R. (2003). Not on their own again: Psychological, social, and health characteristics of custodial African American grandmothers. *Journal of Women and Aging, 15*, 167–184.

Rutter, M. (1985). Resilience in the face of adversity: Protective factors and resistance to psychiatric disorders. *British Journal of Psychiatry, 47*, 598–611.

Sanders, M. R., Cann, W., & Markie-Dadds, C. (2003). The Triple P—Positive Parenting Program: A universal population-level approach to the prevention of child abuse. *Child Abuse Review, 12*, 155–171.

Shore, R. J., & Hayslip, B., Jr. (1994). Custodial grandparenting: Implications for children's development. In A. E. Gottfried & A. W. Gottfried (Eds.), *Redefining families: Implications for children's development* (pp. 171–218). New York: Plenum Press.

Smith, G. C., & Palmieri, P. A. (2007). Risk of psychological difficulties among children raised by custodial grandparents. *Psychiatric Services, 58,* 1301–1310.

Spoth, R., Guyll, M., Chao, W., & Molgaard, V. (2003). Exploratory study of preventive intervention with general population African American families. *Journal of Early Adolescence, 23,* 435–468.

U.S. Census Bureau. (2000). Grandparents living in the home of their grandparents, (1970–2000). *World almanac & book of facts, 00841382.*

Webster-Stratton, C. (1998). Parent training with low-income families: Promoting parental engagement through a collaborative approach. In J. Lutzker (Ed.), *Handbook of child abuse and treatment* (pp. 183–210). New York: Plenum.

Webster-Stratton, C. (2000). *Bulletin: The Incredible Years training series.* Washington, DC: U.S. Department of Justice, Office of Juvenile Justice and Delinquency Prevention.

Woodworth, R. S. (1996). You're not alone . . . you're one in a million. *Child Welfare, 75,* 619–635.

CHAPTER 9

Understanding the Parenting Practices of Custodial Grandmothers: Overcompensating, Underserving, or Overwhelmed?

Gregory C. Smith and Rhonda A. Richardson

Although numerous studies have examined the socioemotional and physical well-being of custodial grandparents (see, for review, Hayslip & Kaminski, 2005), scant attention has been paid to how these caregivers function as surrogate parents. In this chapter, we examine parenting practices used by custodial grandmothers and then consider interrelationships between these parenting practices, grandmothers' psychological distress, and grandchildren's adjustment. The implications of our findings for practice with this target population are also discussed.

Research on custodial grandparents' parenting is warranted on several grounds. First, custodial grandchildren often have emotional, behavioral, and physical problems stemming from substance abuse and other dysfunctions within their biological families that add to the complexities of parenting them (Ghuman, Weist, & Shafer, 1999; Smith & Palmieri, 2007; Williamson, Softas-Nell, & Miller, 2003). In particular, some problems experienced by custodial grandchildren, such as Reactive Attachment Disorder and Conduct or Behavioral Disorder, require grandparents to develop highly effective parenting skills (Edwards, 2003). Second, the parenting ability of custodial grandparents is further challenged by the heightened psychological distress and many contextual stressors (e.g., inadequate social support, social stigma and isolation, undesired lifestyle changes, financial strain, the grandparent's own aging and declining health) experienced by these caregivers (Kelley, Whitley, Sipe, & Yorker, 2000). A consistent finding in the parenting literature is that both psychological distress and high exposure to stress are associated with the risk of dysfunctional parenting (Downey & Coyne, 1990). Third, the common belief that biological mothers have the sole or greatest effect on children's development is questionable, especially when other relatives become centrally engaged in parenting (Cowan, Powell, & Cowan, 1997). Finally, there is evidence that sound parenting, exemplified by warmth and effective discipline, can lessen the mental health problems of children who were previously exposed to major stressors (Sandler, Wolchik, Davis, Haine, & Ayers, 2003).

Despite the above reasons why parenting may be especially challenging for custodial grandparents, there has been little systematic research on the actual parenting behaviors of these caregivers. Yet, concerns have been expressed over the ability of custodial grandparents to perform in the role of parent. For example, there is speculation that a possible intergenerational transmission of poor parenting may exist, whereby custodial grandparents who previously did an inadequate job of raising their own children may be even less competent in raising a grandchild (Berrick, 1997; Gibson, 2005). In fact, custodial grandparents themselves often report guilt over how their offspring have fared while questioning their own parenting competency (Edwards, 2003; Glass, 2002; Pinson-Milburn, Fabian, Schlossberg, & Pyle, 1996; Williamson et al., 2003). These caregivers also worry about their ability to parent their grandchildren as they reach old age (Berrick, 1997; Landry-Meyer & Newman, 2004). In addition, some professionals are concerned that custodial grandparents' parenting skills and knowledge of child rearing may be outdated (Bratton, Ray, & Moffit, 1998; Glass, 2002; Strom & Strom, 1993; Williamson et al., 2003).

There have also been conflicting accounts regarding the ability of custodial grandparents to apply effective discipline. For example, Bratton et al. (1998) found that custodial grandparents participating in play therapy showed difficulty in disciplining and setting limits with grandchildren due to the conflicting nature of their dual roles as traditional grandparent (favoring unconditional love, indulgence, and fun) and surrogate parent (requiring authority and limit setting). In contrast, Dannison and Smith (2003) argued that custodial grandparents view corporal punishment as an essential part of parenting their grandchildren due to their belief that insufficient physical punishment had contributed to their offspring's inability to parent effectively. Similarly, Williamson et al. (2003) reported that custodial grandmothers did not understand why they could not spank their grandchildren and craved better ways to deal with their discipline problems.

An important caveat is that the information presented above is based primarily on clinical and anecdotal observations, while virtually no in-depth investigations of custodial grandparents' parenting behaviors have been reported to date. One exception, however, is a study by Rodgers-Farmer (1999), who examined the relationships between stress, depression, and the self-reported parenting practices of custodial grandmothers. Consistent with the general parenting literature, she hypothesized that higher levels of parenting stress reported by grandmothers would be associated with both increased depression and greater use of dysfunctional parenting practices (i.e., inconsistent discipline, harsh punishment, and rejection-oriented behaviors). The overall findings supported these expectations. Higher parenting stress was significantly related to depression, and increased depression was associated with more inconsistent discipline. Unexpectedly, however, neither parenting stress nor depression predicted the use of harsh punishment, leading Rodgers-Farmer to speculate that custodial grandmothers avoid harsh discipline due to their grandchildren's history of physical abuse.

In this chapter, we extend Rodgers-Farmer's pioneering research on custodial grandmothers' parenting practices in three important ways. First, because one cannot assume that parenting constructs (and their corresponding measures) developed for use with young biological parents are germane to custodial grandparents, a major aim of our investigation is to determine if a model of parenting practices derived from the literature on parenting children with emotional and behavioral problems is applicable with custodial grandmothers.

As shown in Figure 9.1, this parenting-practices model encompasses five distinct categories of parenting behaviors known to be associated with behavioral outcomes of at-risk children (Perepletchikova & Kazdin, 2004; Rubin & Burgess, 2002; Webster-Stratton, Reid, & Hammond, 2001): Inconsistent Discipline, Harsh Discipline, Appropriate Discipline, Monitoring, and Positive Parenting. We use the terms effective and ineffective respectively to refer to parenting behaviors that either do or do not successfully discourage inappropriate behavior and gain child compliance (Locke & Prinz, 2002). In this model, inconsistent and harsh discipline represent ineffective methods of parenting.

Second, while Rodgers-Farmer (1999) focused only on ineffective parenting behaviors, we broaden the scope of parenting to also encompass those regarded as more effective (i.e., monitoring, appropriate discipline, and positive parenting). Our use of the terms effective and ineffective is in line with the contemporary view that some parenting practices encourage appropriate

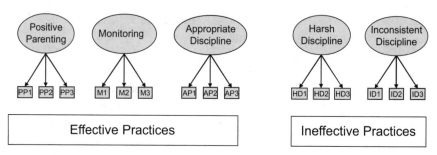

FIGURE 9.1 Proposed model of parenting practices.

child behavior and prevent misbehavior, while others are ineffective because they reinforce child misbehavior or model inappropriate behavior such as poor temper control (Locke & Prinz, 2002; Prevatt, 2003). We hypothesize that the elements of effective parenting will be positively correlated with each other, but inversely related to elements of ineffective parenting. The ineffective parenting components are expected to be positively correlated with one another.

A third way in which this chapter extends what is known about custodial grandmothers' parenting practices is by examining the associations between each category of parenting behaviors and indices of both grandmothers' mental health and grandchildren's adjustment. We hypothesize that higher levels of depression and anxiety among custodial grandmothers will be positively related to the use of ineffective disciplinary strategies such as harsh and inconsistent discipline, and inversely related to the use of effective strategies such as monitoring, appropriate discipline, and positive parenting. These hypotheses are based on the consensus in the general parenting literature that negative affect like depression and anxiety is associated with such problematic parenting as decreased warmth and sensitivity, withdrawal, inconsistent responding, and lack of guidance and limit setting (Conley, Caldwell, Flynn, Dupre, & Rudolph, 2004; Lovejoy, Graczyk, O'Hare, & Neuman, 2000).

We also hypothesize that greater externalizing behavioral difficulties in custodial grandchildren will be associated with less frequent use of effective parenting practices and more frequent use of ineffective practices. Although it has not been examined in the custodial grandparenting literature, there is strong evidence in the parenting literature that such disciplinary tactics as low monitoring, lack of warmth, failure to use positive change strategies, inconsistent discipline, and harsh discipline are correlated with children's maladjustment (Rubin & Burgess, 2002; Smith, Sprengelmeyer, & Moore, 2004). We conversely hypothesize that higher levels of grandchildren's prosocial behavior will be positively associated with grandmothers' use of effective parenting and inversely related to their use of ineffective practices. These predictions are consistent with evidence in the parenting literature that positive parenting accounts for most variance in child adaptive behaviors (Prevatt, 2003), whereas negative parenting is more predictive of behavior problems in children (Locke & Prinz, 2002; Prevatt, 2003; Shelton, Frick, & Wooton, 1996).

The present study involves data obtained in a large-scale national study of stress and coping from 733 custodial grandmothers (average age of 56.2 years). All of the grandmothers in our sample had been providing full-time care to a grandchild in absence of the child's parents for at least 3 months (average length of caregiving was 6.4 years, with a range from 3 months to 16 years). The reasons for providing care mostly concerned crisis or tragedy within the parent generation, such as substance abuse or incarceration. By study design, the sample was half African American (n = 366) and half White (n = 367), and nearly half (47.8%) of the grandmothers resided in urban areas, while 32.5% had rural and 19.2% had suburban residences. Other demographic information about the sample is shown in Table 9.1.

When describing their parenting practices and their grandchildren's behavior, grandmothers were instructed to refer to just one target grandchild (TG) between the ages of 4 and 17. If a grandmother was caring for multiple grandchildren in this age range, the TG was then designated as the one with the most recent birthday. The TG for the 733 grandmothers was 391 girls and 342 boys with an average age of 9.8 years. The majority of these grandchildren (65.8%) had been born to daughters of the grandmothers.

During a telephone interview, grandmothers described their parenting practices by responding to 15 items adapted from the Parenting Practices Interview (PPI) that was originally developed by Webster-Stratton et al. (2001) for use with caregivers of young children (see appendix). Grandmothers rated each item along a 5-point scale (see appendix for specifics) to describe how often they used Inconsistent Discipline, Harsh Discipline, Appropriate Discipline, Monitoring, and Positive Parenting. Grandmothers also completed the prosocial scale from the Strengths and Difficulties Questionnaire to measure positive adjustment as well as the conduct problems and hyperactivity-inattention scales as measures of externalizing behavior (Goodman, 2001; Palmieri & Smith, 2007). Grandmothers' depression was assessed by the Center for Epidemiologic Studies Depression Scale (CES-D; Radloff, 1977), a 20-item self-report measure of depressive symptoms with an emphasis on depressed mood. Anxiety was assessed by the 3-item anxiety scale from the Mental Health Inventory II (Stewart, Ware, Sherbourne, & Wells, 1992). Grandmothers rated how much during the past month they had been very nervous, tense, or restless on a scale from 1 (*all of the time*) to 6 (*none of the time*).

TABLE 9.1 Descriptive Demographic Statistics of Grandmothers and Target Grandchildren ($N = 733$)

Variable	n	%		n	%
Marital Status					
Married	352	48.0	Divorced	159	21.7
Widowed	102	13.9	Single, never married	66	9.0
Separated	49	6.7	Living with partner (not married)	5	0.7
Education					
Less than 5 years	5	0.7	Some college	260	35.5
5–8 years	19	2.6	College graduate	95	13.0
Some high school	99	13.5	Graduate/professional training	50	6.8
High school graduate	205	28.0			
Work Status					
Not working	202	27.6	Retired	144	19.6
Working full or part-time	329	44.9	Full-time homemaker	41	5.6
Seeking employment	17	2.3			
Income					
Under $10,000	123	16.8	$36,000–$50,000	99	13.5
$10,000–$15,000	109	14.9	$51,000–$75,000	59	8.0
$16,000–$20,000	85	11.6	$76,000–$100,000	19	2.6
$21,000–$25,000	90	12.3	$101,000–$125,000	4	0.5
$26,000–$35,000	112	15.3	More than $125,000	5	0.7
			Not reported	28	3.8
Formal Legal Arrangements					
Formal custody	271	37.0	Foster parent	16	2.2
Adoption	90	12.3	Currently seeking legal custody	69	9.4
Guardianship	215	29.3			
			None	72	9.8
Reasons for Care[a]					
Child abandonment	205	28.0	Parental substance abuse	406	55.4
Physical or emotional abuse	201	27.4	Parents' incarceration	312	42.6
			Parents' HIV-AIDS	11	1.5
Removed from parental custody	225	30.7	Other (not AIDS) health problems	114	15.6
Parents' mental health problems	218	29.7	One of the parents deceased	47	6.4
Parents' teen pregnancy	133	18.1			

[a] Respondents were asked to report all reasons for assuming care of the target grandchild that applied to their situation.

To determine whether or not the items included on our adaptation of the Parenting Practices Interview measured the five parenting constructs as hypothesized in Figure 9.1, we first conducted a confirmatory factor analysis using a randomly selected half of the sample and then replicated the results with the entire sample. The overall results showed that each item uniquely assessed the respective parenting construct (i.e., Positive Parenting, Monitoring, Appropriate Discipline, Harsh Discipline, and Inconsistent Discipline) that it was originally intended to measure, thus matching what is found in research on traditional parents.

Table 9.2 reports the frequency by which custodial grandmothers reported using the various parenting strategies included on our adaptation of the Parenting Practices Interview. The findings reveal that both effective and ineffective parenting practices are evident among custodial grandmothers. In terms of effective practices, positive parenting and monitoring are most widely used. Over 80% of the custodial grandmothers in our sample reported using these strategies often or very often. Rewarding a grandchild with praise, hugs, or material rewards appears to come easily to these custodial grandmothers, perhaps because these sorts of behaviors are consistent with the traditional grandparent role. Keeping track of a grandchild's activities and whereabouts also is a highly frequent component of parenting by custodial grandmothers. Perhaps custodial grandmothers are extra vigilant about monitoring because they do not want their grandchildren to be exposed to the same types of environmental risks that contributed to their own children's problems. In comparison to positive parenting and monitoring, appropriate discipline such as grounding, removing privileges, or generally responding to a grandchild's misbehavior with punishment is not quite as frequent. While over three-fourths of custodial grandmothers reported using these strategies at least sometimes, only about half use them often or very often.

While not as apparent as the effective practices, our findings do point to some evidence of ineffective parenting strategies among the custodial grandmothers in this study. For example, under the construct of harsh discipline, two-thirds of the grandmothers reported raising their voice and yelling at their grandchild at least sometimes, and almost one-fourth described this as something they did often or very often. Almost half show anger when administering discipline, with one out of eight doing so often or very often. Additionally, one out of four custodial grandmothers reported that they at least sometimes let arguments escalate to a point where they say or do things they don't mean. Inconsistent discipline is another aspect of ineffective parenting reported by custodial grandmothers in our sample. About half of them reported that at least sometimes they are inconsistent or have difficulty following through

TABLE 9.2 Self-Reported Frequency of Selected Parenting Practices by Custodial Grandmothers

Parenting Practices	Response Alternatives (in percentages)				
	Never	Seldom	Sometimes	Often	Very Often
Harsh Discipline					
Raise your voice, scold, or yell	11	22	44	14	19
Show anger when you discipline (TGN)	26	27	35	9	3
Let arguments with (TGN) build up and do or say things you do not mean	54	25	14	3	5
Inconsistent Discipline					
Threaten to punish (TGN) but not really punish him/her	25	25	33	11	5
(TGN) gets away with things that you feel s/he should have been disciplined for	21	30	34	10	5
(TGN) is successful in getting around the rules that you have set	23	20	31	15	11
Appropriate Discipline					
Ground or give (TGN) a time out	6	12	29	34	18
Take away privileges like TV, playing with friends	10	12	31	31	16
Punish (TGN) if s/he misbehaves	3	12	35	34	16
Positive Parenting					
Praise or compliment (TGN)	.5	2	10	35	53
Give (TGN) a hug, kiss, pat, handshake, or "high five"	1	3	6	28	62

TABLE 9.2 (*Continued*)

Parenting Practices	Response Alternatives (in percentages)				
	Never	Seldom	Sometimes	Often	Very Often
In an average week, how often do you praise or reward (TGN) for doing a good job at home or school?	5	12	29	29	24
Monitoring					
How often do you know where (TGN) is when s/he is away from your direct supervision?	.5	2	4	18	76
How often do you know what (TGN) is doing when s/he is away from you?	1	5	13	35	46
How much effort do you put into knowing exactly what (TGN) is doing when s/he is away from you?[a]	1	2	8	26	64

[a] Response alternatives for this item: 1 = *None*, 2 = *A little bit*, 3 = *Moderate*, 4 = *Quite a bit*, and 5 = *Very much*.

with discipline, with as many as one-fourth of the grandmothers reporting they do this often or very often.

To examine the correspondence between effective and ineffective parenting practices, the three items comprising each of the five parenting construct scales (i.e., Positive Parenting, Monitoring, Appropriate Discipline, Harsh Discipline, Inconsistent Discipline) were summed to yield an overall score on each of the respective constructs. Zero order correlations between each pair of scales were then performed. (Note: due to skewness of some variables, appropriate transformations were performed.) We found that all of the hypothesized relationships among the parenting constructs were statistically significant and in the expected direction, except for those involving appropriate discipline. Grandmothers who used positive parenting more frequently also reported more frequent use of monitoring ($r = .32$, $p < .01$) and less frequent use of harsh discipline ($r = -.26$, $p < .01$) and inconsistent discipline ($r = -.12$, $p < .01$). While we expected that appropriate discipline would be associated with positive parenting and monitoring that was not the case ($PP\ r = .06$; $M\ r = .01$). Rather it was most strongly linked to the use of harsh discipline ($r = .34$, $p < .01$).

HOW PARENTING PRACTICES RELATE
TO GRANDMOTHERS' MENTAL HEALTH
AND GRANDCHILDREN'S BEHAVIOR

As hypothesized, higher frequency of both harsh and inconsistent discipline were associated with greater depression (HD r = .22, p < .01, ID r = .20, p < .01) and anxiety (HD r = .22, p < .01, ID r = .20, p < .01) in grandmothers and greater hyperactivity (HD r = .24, p < .01; ID r = .23, p < .01) and conduct problems (HD r = .32, p < .01; ID r = .30, p < .01) in their grandchildren. Conversely, higher frequencies of positive parenting and monitoring were associated with less psychological distress in grandmothers and more adaptive behaviors in grandchildren (PP with depression r = −.20, p < .01; PP with anxiety r = −.13, p < .01; M with depression r = −.20, p < .01; M with anxiety, r = −.15, p < .01; PP with conduct problems r = −.18, p < .01; PP with prosocial behavior r = .23, p < .01; M with conduct problems r = −.13, p < .01; M with prosocial behavior r = .17, p < .01).

These findings expand knowledge of custodial grandparents' parenting practices beyond the initial work of Rodgers-Farmer (1999) in several important ways. First, because we looked at both anxiety and depression as indices of grandmothers' psychological distress, our findings reinforce the emerging belief that negative affect *in general* as opposed to depression *per se* is detrimental to good parenting (Lovejoy et al., 2000). Second, our findings clearly indicate that the parenting practices used by custodial grandmothers are related not just to their own psychological well-being but also to that of their grandchildren. Third, the present findings underscore the need to shift from a narrow deficit model of parenting to a broader view that encompasses both the strengths and difficulties of custodial grandparents and the grandchildren in their care. Better mental health status of both custodial grandparents and their grandchildren in our sample was associated with less ineffective parenting as well as greater use of effective parenting practices.

IMPLICATIONS FOR WORKING WITH
CUSTODIAL GRANDMOTHERS AND THEIR
GRANDCHILDREN

Our findings suggest that that several key parenting constructs from the literature on young biological parents are useful in examining parenting among custodial grandparents. Specifically, inconsistent discipline, harsh discipline, monitoring, appropriate discipline, and positive parenting were confirmed as distinct dimensions of parenting behavior in our national sample of custodial grandmothers. Despite the special challenges encountered by grandparents raising grandchildren, it is important that practitioners avoid adopting a deficit view of these families and be attuned to not just potential problem areas in parenting, but also areas of strength. We found that custodial grandmothers report many instances of positive parenting and monitoring. Furthermore, these components of effective parenting are associated with more positive adjustment for grandchildren and grandmothers alike. Conversely, harsh and inconsistent discipline are related to caregiver psychological distress and to behavioral difficulties in custodial grandchildren.

While it does not provide a comprehensive assessment of parenting, our adaptation of the Parenting Practices Inventory (Appendix A) may be used by practitioners to conduct a preliminary appraisal of the parenting strategies of custodial grandmothers. Grandmothers' responses to the inventory may point to areas where in-depth follow-up assessment might be warranted, such as in cases where grandmothers report frequent use of harsh or inconsistent discipline or limited use of positive parenting or monitoring. The inventory as written taps only responses to grandchildren's misbehavior in general, yet it is likely that the parenting practices of custodial grandmothers may vary as a function of the particular characteristics of a given grandchild or the particular types of behavior demonstrated by that grandchild. Therefore, we recommend that practitioners follow up by asking the grandparent to describe specific examples of how they would respond to a particular transgression (e.g., fighting, not listening), including attention to whether the reported response is appropriate to the age of the grandchild.

Practitioners should also bear in mind that although we categorized parenting practices as either effective or ineffective, there is no agreed-upon standard for discipline practices in terms of lesser or greater effectiveness (Locke & Prinz, 2002). To conclude that some parenting practices are more or less effective than others for custodial grandmother families, practitioners would need to track changes in custodial grandchildren's behaviors over time as a function of specific discipline strategies. It is possible that some parenting behaviors that conceptually would be labeled as effective may not always be so. For example, positive parenting and monitoring, if used excessively and indiscriminately, can become ineffective. Practitioners working with custodial grandmother families may want to remind grandmothers that not every single behavior merits a praise or reward and watch for signs of overindulgence in the grandchildren. As children get older, they need opportunities to take more responsibility for their own actions, so custodial grandmothers will need help in distinguishing when and how to monitor their grandchildren's behavior and whereabouts in ways that are age appropriate.

Among custodial grandmothers, appropriate discipline does not appear to fit into a model of effective parenting. This unanticipated finding in our study points out the importance of recognizing that parenting involves distinct behavioral and affective components (Jacob, Moser, Windle, Loeber, & Stouthamer-Loeber, 2000). Often referred to as parenting practices, the behavioral component encompasses *what* parents do, whereas the affective component includes the style or *how* parents do what they do (Locke & Prinz, 2002). Although the items comprising our appropriate discipline scale reflect intent to discipline, they do not specify the affective element of that discipline (see appendix). For example, the item stating "you punish your grandchild when he or she misbehaves" does not distinguish punishment rendered in a harsh or threatening tone from that rendered in a warm and caring manner. The positive relationship we found between appropriate discipline and both harsh discipline and inconsistent discipline suggests that discipline techniques that are typically regarded as appropriate (e.g., punishment, time outs, taking away privileges) may be carried out by custodial grandmothers in a harsh or inconsistent manner (i.e., with yelling, anger, and idle threats). Similarly, the lack of relation between appropriate discipline and both positive parenting and monitoring suggests that practices such as grounding, punishing, and denying privileges are not balanced with such positive affective displays as praising the grandchild or expressing physical affection. In order to accurately evaluate parenting practices of custodial grandmothers, practitioners are advised to include an observational component in order to evaluate the affective tone of the parenting behaviors.

Based on our findings, we also recommend that interventions designed to improve behavioral outcomes for custodial grandchildren should involve a combination of modalities including parent training, engaging grandparents in positive interactions with their grandchildren, stress reduction, and counseling for grandparents' psychological distress (Conley et al., 2004; Webster-Stratton & Hammond, 1998). In parent training, practitioners need to encourage custodial grandmothers to continue monitoring and praising within reason, but also need to provide instruction in how to discipline with consistency and without anger. Grandmothers may need coaching in specific methods for following through with appropriate punishments like time out and removal of privileges. Teaching grandmothers how to recognize when they are feeling angry or frustrated with their grandchild and how to implement simple relaxation or stress-reduction practices such as deep breathing may be useful in reducing harsh and inconsistent discipline.

Nurturance is just as important as discipline when rearing children (Locke & Prinz, 2002), and our findings clearly show that children benefit from positive expressions of affection. Practitioners can encourage custodial grandmothers to spend time with their grandchildren in relaxing, recreational activities. This is relatively easy when children are young, but as they approach the preadolescent years it can be more difficult. Having a family movie night is one strategy practitioners can suggest to grandparents. Richardson and Pevec (2007) have identified particular movies that are appropriate for grandparents and children ages 10–14 to watch together. These authors also provide guidelines for engaging in meaningful conversation based on the movies.

Our findings support the conjecture that "a grandmother's adjustment difficulties could influence the way in which she interacts with her grandchild, which, in turn, might contribute to the development and maintenance of her grandchild's behavior problem" (Daly & Glenwick, 2000, p. 116). The statistically significant relationships we found between grandmothers' psychological distress and ineffective parenting are especially noteworthy given that the data are from a nonclinical sample of custodial grandmothers. This suggests that the amount of stress experienced by custodial grandparents does not have to be severe for it to be associated with grandchildren's adjustment. In light of this it is important for practitioners to assess grandmothers' psychological distress in addition to parenting practices, as their distress may be serving to reinforce parenting difficulties (Forehand & McCombs, 1998). Moreover, intervention studies with biological parents have also shown that parents with high psychological distress are likely to show less improvement in child behavior and drop out of parent-training programs if the caregiver's psychological well-being is overlooked (Forehand & McCombs, 1988; Webster-Stratton & Hammond, 1998). Based on our findings, we recommend that when assessing and counseling for grandparents' psychological distress, practitioners should focus not just on depressive symptoms but anxiety-related symptoms as well.

In summary, the results of our study shed new light on an important topic that has been virtually ignored in the literature on custodial grandparents. These grandparents may be some of the best caregivers for their grandchildren when the children's parents are unable to care for them because of their close biological linkages (Edwards, 2003). However, our findings suggest that, like foster care parents, custodial grandparents are likely to benefit from training in appropriate disciplinary techniques for parenting abused and neglected children, ongoing support, and monitoring by social service agencies (Berrick, 1997). Custodial grandparents have already demonstrated their emotional attachment to their grandchildren by giving them a home and care; providing these caregivers with effective parenting tools will help to strengthen the existing bond between custodial grandparents and their grandchildren (Bratton et al., 1993).

REFERENCES

Berrick, J. D. (1997). Assessing quality of care in kinship and foster family care. *Family Relations, 46*, 273–280.

Bratton, S., Ray, D., & Moffit, K. (1998). Filial/family play therapy: An intervention for custodial grandparents and their grandchildren. *Educational Gerontology, 24*, 391–406.

Conley, S., Caldwell, M. S., Flynn, M., Dupre, A. J., & Rudolph, K. D. (2004). Parenting and mental health. In M. Hoghughi & N. Long (Eds.), *Handbook of parenting: Theory and research for practice* (pp. 276–295). Thousand Oaks, CA: Sage.

Cowan, P. A., Powell, D., & Cowan, C. P. (1997). Parenting interventions: A family systems perspective. In W. Damon, I. Sigel, & K. A. Renninger (Eds.), *Handbook of child psychology: Child psychology in practice* (5th ed., pp. 3–72). New York: Wiley.

Daly, S. L., & Glenwick, D. S. (2000). Personal adjustment and perceptions of grandchild behavior in custodial grandmothers. *Journal of Clinical Child Psychology, 29*, 108–118.

Dannison, L. L., & Smith, A. B. (2003). Custodial grandparents community support program: Lessons learned. *Children & Schools, 25*, 87–95.

Downey, G., & Coyne, J. C. (1990). Children of depressed parents: An integrative review. *Psychological Bulletin, 108*, 50–76.

Edwards, O. W. (2003). Living with grandma: A grandfamily study. *School Psychology International, 24*, 204–217.

Forehand, R., & McCombs, A. (1988). Unraveling the antecedent-consequence conditions in maternal depression and adolescent functioning. *Behavior Research and Therapy, 26*, 399–405.

Ghuman, H. S., Weist, M. D., & Shafer, M. E. (1999). Demographic and clinical characteristics of emotionally disturbed children being raised by grandparents. *Psychiatric Services, 50*, 1496–1498.

Glass, J. C. (2002). Grandparents parenting grandchildren: Extent of situation, issues involved, and educational implications. *Educational Gerontology, 28*, 139–161.

Goodman, R. (2001). Psychometric properties of the Strengths and Difficulties Questionnaire. *Journal of the American Academy of Adolescent Psychiatry, 40*, 1337–1345.

Hayslip, B., Jr., & Kaminski, P. L. (2005). Grandparents raising their grandchildren: A review of the literature and suggestions for practice. *The Gerontologist, 45*, 262–269.

Jacob, T., Moser, R. P., Windle, M., Loeber, R., & Stouthamer-Loeber, M. (2000). A new measure of parenting practices involving preadolescent and adolescent-aged children. *Behavior Modification, 24*(5), 611–634.

Kelley, S. J., Whitley, D., Sipe, T. A., & Yorker, B. C. (2000). Psychological distress in grandmother kinship care providers: The role of resources, social support, and physical health. *Child Abuse & Neglect, 24*, 311–321.

Landry-Meyer, L., & Newman, B. M. (2004). An exploration of the grandparent caregiver role. *Journal of Family Issues, 25*, 1005–1025.

Locke, L. M., & Prinz, R. J. (2002). Measurement of parental discipline and nurturance. *Clinical Psychology Review, 22,* 895–929.

Lovejoy, C., Graczyk, P. A., O'Hare, E., & Neuman, G. (2000). Maternal depression and parenting behavior: A meta-analytic review. *Clinical Psychology Review, 20,* 561–592.

Palmieri, P., & Smith, G. C. (2007). Examining the structural validity of the Strengths and Difficulties Questionnaire (SDQ) in a U.S. sample of custodial grandmothers. *Psychological Assessment, 19,* 189–198.

Perepletchikova, F., & Kazdin, A. E. (2004). Assessment of parenting practices related to conduct problems: Development and validation of the management of children's behavior scale. *Journal of Child & Family Studies, 13,* 385–403.

Pinson-Milburn, N. M., Fabian, E. S., Schlossberg, N. K., & Pyle, M. (1996). Grandparents raising grandchildren. *Journal of Counseling and Development, 74,* 548–554.

Prevatt, F. F. (2003). The contribution of parenting practices in a risk and resiliency model of children's adjustment. *British Journal of Developmental Psychology, 21,* 469–480.

Radloff, L. S. (1977). The CES-D scale: A self-report depression scale for research in the general population. *Applied Psychological Measurement, 1,* 385–401.

Richardson, R. A., & Pevec, A. M. (2007). *What kids REALLY want to ask: Using movies to start meaningful conversations.* Acton, MA: VanderWyk & Burnham.

Rodgers-Farmer, A. Y. (1999). Parenting stress, depression, and parenting in grandmothers raising their grandchildren. *Children and Youth Services Review, 21,* 377–388.

Rubin, K. H., & Burgess, K. B. (2002). Parents of aggressive and withdrawn children. In M. N. Bornstein (Ed.), *Handbook of parenting* (2nd ed., pp. 383–418). Mahwah, NJ: Erlbaum.

Sandler, I., Wolchik, S., Davis, C., Haine, R., & Ayers, T. (2003). Correlational and experimental study of resilience in children of divorce and parentally bereaved children. In S. S. Luthar (Ed.), *Resilience and vulnerability: Adaptation in the context of childhood adversities* (pp. 213–242). New York: Cambridge University Press.

Shelton, K., Frick, P. J., & Wooton, J. (1996). Assessment of parenting practices in families of elementary school-age children. *Journal of Clinical Child Psychology, 25,* 317–329.

Smith, G. C., & Palmieri, P. A. (in press). Risk for psychological difficulties in children raised by custodial grandparents. *Psychiatric Services.*

Smith, D. K., Sprengelmeyer, P. G., & Moore, K. J. (2004). Parenting and antisocial behavior. In M. Hoghughi & N. Long (Eds.), *Handbook of parenting: Theory and research for practice* (pp. 237–255). Thousand Oaks, CA: Sage.

Stewart, A. L., Ware, J. E., Sherbourne, C. D., & Wells, K. B. (1992). Psychological distress/well-being and cognitive functioning measures. In A. L. Stewart & J. E. Ware (Eds.), *Measuring functioning and well-being: The medical outcomes study approach* (pp. 102–142). Durham, NC: Duke University Press.

Strom, R. D., & Strom, S. K. (1993). Grandparents raising grandchildren: Goals and support groups. *Educational Gerontology, 19,* 705–715.

Webster-Stratton, C., & Hammond, M. (1998). Maternal depression and its relationship to life stress, perceptions of child behavior problems, parenting behaviors, and child conduct problems. *Journal of Abnormal Child Psychology, 16,* 299–315.

Webster-Stratton, C., Reid, M. J., & Hammond, M. (2001). Preventing conduct problems, promoting social competence: A parent and teacher training partnership in Head Start. *Journal of Clinical Child Psychology, 30,* 283–302.

Williamson, J., Softas-Nall, B., & Miller, J. (2003). Grandchildren: An exploration of their experiences and emotions. *The Family Journal: Counseling and Therapy for Couples and Families, 11,* 23–32.

APPENDIX A

Interview Protocol for Adapted Version of Parenting Practice Inventory

The following are things that grandparents might do when their grandchild misbehaves. In general how often do you do each of the following when (TGN) misbehaves?

Harsh Discipline Items:
HD1—Raise your voice, scold, or yell.
HD2—Show anger when you discipline (TGN).
HD3—Let arguments with (TGN) build up and you do or say things you do not mean.

Inconsistent Discipline Items:
ID1—Threaten to punish (TGN) but not really punish him/her.
ID2—(TGN) gets away with things that you feel s/he should have been disciplined for.
ID3—(TGN) is successful in getting around the rules that you have set.

Appropriate Discipline Items:
AP1—Ground or give (TGN) a time out.
AP2—Take away privileges like TV, playing with friends.
AP3—You punish (TGN) if s/he misbehaves.

Here's a list of things that caregiving grandparents might do when their grandchild behaves well or does a good job at something. In general, how often do you do each of the following when (TGN) behaves or does a good job?

Positive Parenting Items:

PP1—Praise or complement (TGN).

PP2—Give (TGN) a hug, kiss, pat, handshake, or "high five."

PP3—In an average week, how often do you praise or reward (TGN) for doing a good job at home or school?

Monitoring Items:

M1—How often do you know where (TGN) is when s/he is away from your direct supervision?

M2—How often do you know what (TGN) is doing when s/he is away from you?

M3—How much effort do you put into knowing exactly what (TGN) is doing when s/he is away from you?

NOTE

TGN indicates where interviewers inserted the Target Grandchild's name into the item. All items except for M3 contained the following response choices: 1 (*Never*), 2 (*Seldom*), 3 (*Sometimes*), 4 (*Often*), and 5 (*Very often*). Response choices for M3 were 1 (*None*), 2 (*A little bit*), 3 (*Moderate*), 4 (*Quite a bit*), and 5 (*Very much*).

CHAPTER 10

Traditional Grandparents' Views of Their Caregiving Peers' Parenting Skills: Complimentary or Critical?

Bert Hayslip, Jr., and Rebecca J. Glover

In today's society, primarily due to increases in longevity, becoming a grandparent can occur at virtually any age (Lemme, 2002), creating a relationship that may extend well into a grandchild's adult life. This has the potential to be significant for both generations (Hodgson, 1988) in terms of the bidirectional positive effect each person has upon the other (Tomlin, 1998). In this context, grandparents play an important role in a grandchild's emotional, cognitive, and social development (Tomlin, 1998). Emotionally, grandchildren who benefit from a positive relationship with a grandparent may be better equipped to handle psychosocial conflicts throughout their lifetime (Kivnick, 1982), and by providing unconditional love, grandparents can aid in the grandchild's development of self-esteem (McAdoo & McWright, 1994). Moreover, through the transmission of values and by serving as a support system in times of crisis, grandparents can exert a powerful stabilizing effect on the lives of their grandchildren (Hodgson, 1988; Ruiz, 2003).

One can safely assume (except in cases where the grandparent assumes parental responsibility at or shortly after the grandchild's birth) that custodial grandparents began as grandparents whose relationship with their grandchild was a more traditional one—for example, one that did not require extensive amounts of time and energy devoted to child care, and where such activities, if present, were not imposed upon them by virtue of a parent's divorce, death, incarceration, or drug abuse (see Hayslip & Kaminski, 2005). Moreover, anecdotal evidence suggests that grandparents may feel stigmatized by their traditional grandparent peers as having failed as parents by raising children who became incompetent or irresponsible parents (Baird, 2003; Wohl, Lahner, & Jooste, 2003).

From an interpersonal perspective, traditional grandparent peers may be an important source of social support and serve as an implicit benchmark for grandparent caregivers' evaluations of changes in their lifestyle, mental and physical health, and interpersonal relationships as a function of becoming full-time caregivers to their grandchildren. As the availability of social support has been shown to have an impact on one's physical (Krause, 2001) and emotional health (Antonucci, 2001), its availability may be an important factor in contributing to the success (or difficulties) of grandparent-headed households.

Wohl, Lahner, and Jooste (2003) noted that the most prominent themes emerging from a group intervention program with custodial grandparents were difficulties involving relationships with others, relationships with the parents of their grandchildren, and relationships with the grandchildren themselves. Since the grandparents' peers generally do not have caregiving responsibilities for children, grandparent caregivers commonly perceive themselves as outcasts, whereby they neither belong with their former friends nor the younger parents of their grandchildren's friends (Wohl et al., 2003). Grandparents report losing friends when they take on the caregiving role, mostly because the active parent role is no longer relevant to their friends' lives. This puts grandparent caregivers at risk for social isolation (Cox, 2000).

Some grandparent caregivers report feeling alienated from social networks such as churches and other mediating structures that had previously acted as sources of support (Fuller-Thomson & Minkler, 2000; Minkler & Roe, 1993). As their social networks may be disrupted by such feelings (Emick & Hayslip, 1999; Fuller-Thomson & Minkler 2000; Solomon & Marx, 2000), the physical and mental health of custodial grandparents, as well as their ability to parent, may be undermined.

From a broader social perspective, the prejudices and perceptions of society are likely to have an impact on grandparent-headed households. Joslin (2000), for example, points out that for grandparent caregivers who are taking care of grandchildren orphaned and affected by HIV or AIDS, there is an additional social stigma that can threaten self-esteem and social support. In this context, Miltenberger, Hayslip, Harris, and Kaminski (2003–2004) explored the perceptions others have of losses experienced by grandparent caregiers. They reported that the depth and intensity of sensitivity to the losses experienced by grandparent caregivers are influenced by feelings regarding the diverse circumstances surrounding role assumption and feelings evoked by the level of adjustment problems experienced by the grandchild. There appears to be a greater sensitivity to loss due to death, abandonment, child abuse, drug abuse, and incarceration than there is relative to loss due to divorce or job loss. This suggests that others might underestimate grandparents' disappointments in their adult children's marriages or lack of career success, presumably because they assume grandparent caregivers implicitly contributed to such difficulties via poor parenting practices or failure to model marital or vocational success. There was also a greater sensitivity to loss where there was knowledge that the grandchild was experiencing problems relative to those grandchildren not experiencing problems. Particularly important in this respect are needs for emotional support from one's age peers, wherein some custodial grandparents appear to be more overwhelmed and isolated, expressing the need for greater emotional support in terms of support groups, mentoring, or counseling services (King, Hayslip, & Kaminski, 2006).

The aforementioned perspectives reinforce the mutually interactive nature of the connection between traditional and custodial grandparents, as they underscore the importance of viewing grandparenting, and specifically custodial grandparenting, within the larger framework of relationships with others, best understood in terms of the interpersonal context that impacts and is impacted by how such persons define such relationships (Hayslip & Patrick, 2003).

Many custodial grandparents also report numerous psychological and physical difficulties that stem, in part, from the grandparents' perceptions of their responsibilities as parents. For example, "good" parents, whether they are grandparents or not, must work hard to raise children in concert with what society deems proper (Strom, Griswold, Collinsworth, & Strom, 1991, p. 188). According to Gettinger and Guetschow (1998), proper parenting requires meeting the emotional and medical needs of the child as well as assuring the child's success in school. Custodial grandparents may have more difficulty meeting these expectations or the needs of the grandchildren they are raising due to the circumstances surrounding their role acquisition (e.g., parental divorce, drug abuse, incarceration) and the often-unforeseen nature of the responsibilities they assume.

Raising a grandchild requires numerous adjustments, and grandparents newly returned to the parenting role must fulfill these roles to an adequate degree: "the good mother must be physically present and available to meet her child's every need, . . . [and] the good father is the good provider who works full-time to support the family" (Etaugh & Folger, 1998, p. 222). Importantly, a parent's belief that he or she has the power to benefit the child (i.e., a parent's sense of efficacy) is always a prerequisite to good parenting

(Gettinger & Guetschow, 1998). Good parenting is likely to require a great deal of effort, and in this respect, custodial grandparents may face more barriers than the average parent, in that many custodial grandparents are divorced or widowed and have neither the energy they had when younger, the time, nor the monetary resources of a household led by two employed persons (Hayslip & Kaminiski, 2005). It is not surprising then that their own views of their efficacy to parent might be seen as poor at best (Gettinger & Guetschow, 1998). However, while grandparents may struggle with becoming surrogate parents, this second chance at parenting often leads to an effort to perform better in their parenting role with a grandchild versus that accomplished with their own children (Emick & Hayslip, 1999).

Two distinct groups of custodial grandparents exist: (1) those grandparents whose difficulties primarily stem from the demands of the parenting role, and (2) those grandparents whose difficulties relate to a grandchild with developmental, emotional, or behavioral difficulties, the majority of which are male (Emick & Hayslip, 1999; Hayslip & Shore, 2000; Hayslip, Shore, Henderson, & Lambert, 1998). Among this latter group, such difficulties are likely to exacerbate the challenges such grandparents face beyond those described above (Kolomer, McCallion, & Overeynder, 2003; McKinney, McGrew, & Nelson, 2003), placing many at increased risk for depression often to the detriment of their own physical health (Hayslip & Kaminski, 2005). Such difficulties might include Attention Deficit Hyperactivity Disorder (Baker, 2000), substance abuse (Hirshorn, Van Meter, & Brown, 2000) or HIV disease (Joslin, 2002). In this respect, Hayslip and Shore (2000) found that custodial grandparents who reported greater degrees of problem behaviors in their grandchildren experienced more psychosocial distress. At present, it is unclear whether the negative perceptions of others (traditional grandparents) contribute to this picture. In addition, those custodial grandparents who had sought mental health care assistance were the most psychosocially impaired and had the most negative and conflicted relationships with their grandchildren. Clearly, however, for some custodial grandparents, the effects of the demands of assuming a parental role in midlife or beyond are distinct from those that are exacerbated by raising a grandchild who is experiencing physical, emotional, or behavioral difficulties (Emick & Hayslip, 1999; Hayslip et al., 1998).

RATIONALE FOR THE PRESENT STUDY

Traditional grandparents often define the reference group against which custodial grandparents define themselves in terms of personal adjustment, grandchild outcomes, and parental success. Indeed, as most were traditional grandparents before they became caregivers for their grandchildren, such expectations and self-appraisals regarding one's parenting skills are likely. At the same time, the social interpersonal context and associated stigma of having failed as a parent may contribute to such perceptions. Understanding the views of older adult age peers regarding custodial grandparenting may also help to more clearly understand the impact of a grandparent's assumption of the parental role on other grandchildren for whom he or she is not providing care (see Shore & Hayslip, 1994). From a social support perspective, these grandparent peers who were once friends, coworkers, or neighbors may also constitute an important dimension of the custodial grandparent's convoy of support (Antonucci, 2001) and, therefore, directly or indirectly influence (a) the grandparent's access to social or educational services, (b) the availability of instrumental or emotional support to them, or (c) the affirmation of a caregiving grandparent's values as a competent parent in the face of chronic health difficulties, social isolation, lessened income, depression, or the stigma associated with raising a grandchild.

The parameters chosen here to operationalize young adults' perceptions of custodial grandparents reflect several important themes that have defined the literature regarding concerns custodial grandparents have of their own parental abilities as well as concerns they perceive others to have about them, for example, parental efficacy, the impact of custodial grandparenting on one's physical and psychological well-being, the importance of social support for such grandparents, and their need for a variety of social services (see Hayslip & Kaminiski, 2005; Hayslip & Patrick, 2003).

As discussed above, grandparent peers often serve as members of the convoy of support for older adults raising grandchildren. Consequently, of additional relevance to the present study is the manner in which young adults' perceptions of these custodial grandparents might be impacted by particular developmental, emotional, or behavioral difficulties of the grandchild in their care, either in response to the new caregiving arrangement or as a function of difficulties that predate the grandchild's new relationship with the grandparent (see Emick & Hayslip, 1999; Hayslip et al., 1998; Hayslip & Kaminski, 2005; Young & Dawson, 2003). Indeed, individuals who hold more problematic parental attitudes or who feel less efficacious as parents might also experience more parental stress, in part due to the bidirectional relationship between parental attitudes and child behaviors (Holden & Buck, 2002; Melamed, 2002).

Gettinger and Guetschow (1998) argue that the involvement of any parent in a child's life requires a clear "understanding of role expectations" by both society and the parent, and therefore, if grandparents are to be successful parents, the role they play must be well understood. However, it could be argued that in many custodial grandparent homes, the clarity with which they define their parental role is marginal, their sense of parental efficacy is poor, and the barriers to meaningful involvement in their grandchild's life are often seen as insurmountable. An understanding of the basis for the perceptions of custodial grandparents by others might therefore greatly help in understanding influences on parental efficacy among custodial grandparents and, thus, may benefit both these grandparents and their grandchildren.

As the majority of custodial grandparents are women (see Hayslip & Kaminiski, 2005), the present study focused on factors influencing perceptions of custodial grandmothers' parenting skills utilizing multiple measures of such views. Indeed, this suggests that we can learn a great deal about custodial grandparenting by viewing it from the outside, in that others' perceptions, biases, and attitudes can have a powerful influence on the well-being of custodial grandparents themselves. Over and above their value in understanding the interpersonal context defining custodial grandparenting, these data also provide a baseline against which grandparents' views about what others think of them as parents can be validated. The feelings and attitudes of grandparent caregivers have been well documented, and they in part may reflect how others might feel toward them (i.e., feelings of isolation, alienation, and shame, as well as depression). It becomes important that the bases for views that others might hold about custodial grandparents and their grandchildren be explored. Such feelings may be related to the perceived stigma attached to the reasons for the assumption of the caregiving role.

METHOD

Participants

Participants were 610 traditional grandparents (143 males, 437 females, 30 cases missing gender information) living in the community who did not have primary caregiving responsibility for their grandchildren, who were being raised by their parent(s). They ranged in age from 40 to 94 (M age = 63.46, SD = 11.4), and on average, had completed at least 1 year of college. Most (74%) rated their health as at least "good" both in absolute terms and relative to others of their age. Of the participants, 88% had never had full-time responsibility for their grandchildren, and among those who had such responsibility, it had been at least a year since such responsibilities had ceased. Reported ethnicity was 82% White, 10% African American, 4% Hispanic, 1% Asian American, and 2.8% "other–not specified." Seventy percent of the sample married, while the remainder was single, divorced, or widowed.

Procedure

Participants were randomly assigned to one of two orders of administration, wherein half first completed a demographic survey and then were randomly assigned to read a particular scenario depicting a relationship between a custodial grandmother and her grandchild (see Appendix A); participants then responded to a series of questions as they applied to the scenario. The remaining half first read the scenario to which they had been randomly assigned and responded to the questions pertaining to it, and then answered the demographic questions. Cell sizes (complete data) ranged from 14 to 25, with the average cell size being 15.

Demographic Questionnaire

The questionnaire included sociodemographic items regarding age, gender, ethnicity, marital status, and level of education. Items assessing relationships with one's grandparents asked the participant if he or she lived or had lived with the grandparent and if the grandparent had helped in raising the participant. Specific questions about participants' grandparents were also asked (e.g., if they were living, the extent of their contact with participants).

Grandparent Perception Questionnaire

Selected items pertaining to parenting were derived from a 69-item questionnaire, developed to measure participants' perceptions of the profiled custodial grandmother. Its content was based on the first author's experience in workshops with custodial grandparents (see Hayslip, 2003; Wohl et al., 2003) and upon a review of the grandparent caregiving literature. Such questions were designed to measure perceptions of the custodial grandparent as a parent in the scenario along the following parameters: (1) Parenting Efficacy (24 items), where higher scores indicated greater perceived efficacy of the grandparent as a parent to the grandchild she was raising (alpha = .83; e.g., This grandparent is a better parent than the child's natural parent; This grandparent is a loving parent; This grandparent will be able to communicate effectively with this grandchild); and (2) Efficacy as Adult Parent (6 items), where higher scores indicated perceptions of the grandparent as having been a more adequate parent to her adult child, the grandchild's parent (alpha = .51; e.g., This grandparent was a poor parent; This grandparent should have been a better parent to her children). As an indirect measure of the grandparent's impact on the grandchild, the following dependent variables were also utilized here: (3) Grandchild Adjustment (4 items), where higher scores indicated better perceived emotional adjustment in the grandchild being cared for (alpha = .92; e.g., The grandchild will experience problems in school; The grandchild will experience emotional problems); and (4) Grandchild Openness (4 items), where higher scores indicated greater comfort and security in the grandchild being cared for in expressing his or her feelings toward the grandparent (alpha = .81; e.g., This grandchild feels close to this grandparent; This grandchild trusts the grandparent).

Independent Variables

The independent variables were defined with regard to those which were manipulated via the construction of the scenario: gender of the grandchild, the presence or absence of a problem in the grandchild (i.e., behavioral/learning problems), and the reason for role acquisition (e.g., abandonment, child abuse, death of a parent, a parent's drug abuse, imprisonment of a parent, loss of employment, divorce). Participants were randomly assigned to read a scenario that varied according to the above-mentioned variables.

RESULTS

Perceptions of custodial grandmothers were analyzed via a MANOVA manipulating grandchild problem (2 levels), grandchild gender (2 levels), and reason for role assumption (7 levels), followed by univariate tests and post hoc comparisons as appropriate. The above perceptual dimensions served as dependent variables. As no main effects for ethnicity had been found in previous work with young adults (see Hayslip et al., under review), and due to the likelihood of not being about to recruit an ethnically heterogeneous sample (requiring at least 1300 traditional grandparents), the impact of ethnicity was not explored here. This MANOVA yielded multivariate main effects for Grandchild Gender, $F(8, 461) = 2.04$, $p < .04$, $eta^2 = .034$; Grandchild Problem, $F(8.461) = 43.85$, $p < .01$; and Reason for Role Assumption, $F(48, 2796) = 2.21$, $p < .01$, $eta^2 = .037$. There were no multivariate interaction effects.

Subsequent univariate tests revealed the main effect for grandchild gender to be particular to grandchild adjustment, with boys being seen as better adjusted ($M = 15.97$, $SD = 5.15$) than girls ($M = 14.95$, $SD = 4.95$).

The impact of grandchild problem was substantial for all dependent variables (all $Fs(1, 496) > 13.94$, $p < .01$, all $eta^2 > .03$). In each case, in the presence of a problem grandchild, grandparents were seen as raising grandchildren who were less well adjusted ($M = 13.07$ vs. $M = 18.04$) and less emotionally available to such grandparents ($M = 14.09$ vs. $M = 18.23$). In addition, when the grandchild was described as problematic, grandparents were seen as less efficacious parents to their grandchildren ($M = 85.88$ vs. $M = 96.09$) as well as with regard to having parented their adult children ($M = 18.37$ vs. $M = 19.43$).

The effect of reason for role assumption was specific to efficacy as a parent to the grandchild ($F(6, 536) = 6.40$, $p < .01$, $eta^2 = .068$) as well as to efficacy as a parent to the adult child ($F(6, 536) = 6.56$, $p < .01$, $eta^2 = .067$). For parental efficacy for the grandchild, means were highest for child abuse ($M = 96.09$), followed by parental abandonment ($M = 91.52$), death ($M = 91.49$), and parental drug use ($M = 91.30$), and least high for job loss ($M = 84.38$), divorce ($M = 89.69$), and imprisonment ($M = 88.76$). For parental efficacy to the adult child, scores were again highest for child abuse ($M = 20.16$), parental abandonment ($M = 19.59$), death ($M = 19.02$), and parental drug abuse ($M = 19.01$), relative to job loss, where scores were lowest ($M = 17.56$), with the remaining causes of role assumption falling in between these extremes (Ms being 18.05 and 18.60).

Discussion and Implications for Grandfamilies

Perhaps most strongly and indeed somewhat surprisingly, these data clearly suggest that there may indeed be a basis for grandparent caregivers' feelings of being harshly judged or stigmatized by their traditional grandparent age peers, leading to feelings of isolation and poorer mental and physical health among such persons (see Baird, 2003; Wohl et al., 2003). Indeed, these findings reflect them as parental failures to their grandchildren, wherein traditional grandparents viewed grandparent caregivers, if they were raising troubled grandchildren, as raising grandchildren who were more emotionally damaged, less able to express their feelings to the grandparent, and less well adjusted. Moreover, the presence of grandchild problems was associated with poorer parental efficacy in not having done an effective job of raising the adult child. In contrast, grandmothers raising grandchildren who were not experiencing behavioral or emotional problems were perceived as providing significantly more adequate parenting to their grandchildren and having been more effective parents to their own adult children. In this respect, while the fact that grandchildren were viewed as less well adjusted and less emotionally open could also be attributed to the harsh familial circumstances under which they came to be under the care of their grandparents, the lack of similarly negative impact of reason for role assumption (see below) on these grandchild variables renders this explanation unlikely.

It should be noted here that such perceived difficulties in parenting may also be responses to the demands made on grandparents by a problem grandchild

(Kaminski & Hayslip, 2004), or reflect difficulties in their grandchildren's adjustment that predate the assumption of the parental role by the grandparent. Clearly, under these circumstances, such influences are likely to undermine perceptions of a grandparent's parental efficacy as others unfairly blame the grandparent for the grandchild's problems. In this respect, previous research has indicated that grandparents raising grandchildren *in general* tend to see themselves as less adequate in their parenting role to the grandchild and very much in need of support from others (see Hayslip & Shore, 2000).

Interestingly, when the reason for role assumption is considered, perceptions of parental efficacy (both with regard to the grandchild and to the adult child) were highest for child abuse, parental abandonment, death, and parental drug abuse. This may indicate that noncaregiving grandparents do not hold grandparent caregivers directly responsible for their adult children's problems, many of which are out of the grandparent caregiver's control or beyond his or her direct influence (e.g., death, abandonment, child/drug abuse). Indeed, in the face of such difficulties, they are viewed as persevering in being efficacious parents to their grandchildren. In contrast, for job loss, divorce, and imprisonment, outcomes where the grandparent may be viewed as more influential in serving as a role model for the adult child (i.e., in remaining married, in continuing to hold a job, in not committing a crime that would lead to imprisonment), grandparent caregivers are judged more harshly.

Surprisingly, but yet consistent with the above regarding the reason for role assumption, and in contrast to previous findings suggesting that boys tend to be more problematic to raise among grandparent caregivers (Hayslip et al., 1998), these data indicate otherwise. They suggest that grandparent caregivers are indeed viewed as up to the task of raising boys.

The apparent contradiction between the fact that grandparent caregivers are viewed more negatively as parents when their grandchildren manifest behavioral, emotional, or school-related difficulties and the fact that some, but not all, reasons for role assumption are also associated with harsher views of grandparents' parental skills, can be understood in terms of the fact that such difficulties in grandchildren might be classified as externalized in nature (see Silverthorn & Durant, 2000). Thus, the presence of problems that are more easily observed by others (e.g., school personnel, other grandparents) can more powerfully influence others' judgments regarding the *apparent* connection between the grandparent caregiver's efficacy as a parent in dealing with such difficulties and grandchild outcomes. On the other hand, the reason for a grandparent's assuming care, not readily observable by others, would only come to light in the context of additional information (e.g., a conversation with the grandparent caregiver). Moreover, the more negative in nature or the more the circumstances are seen as beyond the grandparent's control and influence, the more positively she is viewed in being able to assume full-time responsibility for the grandchild, mirroring grandparent's reports that in many cases they take on responsibility for a grandchild in light of concern for the grandchild's well-being. At the same time, such grandparents are, in effect, being admonished for their inability to model appropriate behaviors critical to being gainfully employed, happily married, or avoiding run-ins with the law.

Importantly, it is worth noting that such biases and preconceptions may covary with one's own caregiving experiences, wherein scores for each of the above four parental dimensions were higher for traditional grandparents who reported that at some time in the past, they had parental responsibility for their grandchildren ($p < .01$ in each case). This suggests that traditional grandparents who have not had such experiences may be the most prone to differentially evaluate custodial grandparents' parental skills.

Implications for Health Professionals and Other Helpers

At the minimum, these findings are important for school professionals, counselors, and especially other grandparents who could aid the grandparent caregivers by providing a needed physical and emotional respite for the demands of caregiving; these findings should encourage them to look beyond what they see with regard to the obvious difficulties they observe in grandchildren who are being raised by such grandparents, as well as aid them in more compassionately understanding the nature of the difficulties such grandparents face in raising a problematic grandchild.

In the context of grandparent caregivers' feelings of being stigmatized, invisible to, or isolated from others (especially those feelings about personal responsibility for the circumstances creating the necessity for caregiving), from a cognitive behavioral perspective emphasizing the reframing of one's experiences (see Ellis & Velton, 1998), it is critical that grandparents understand that their adult children indeed make their own choices and decisions, often leading to less than desirable outcomes for themselves and their own children.

That such guilt and presumed responsibility may explain why grandparent caregivers allow themselves to suffer is consistent with older persons' views about elder abuse, for example, that their previous failures as parents legitimize the fact that they are now being abused physically and psychologically by an adult son or daughter (Childs, Hayslip, & Radika, 2000). Such self-persecutory thinking is likely to be exacerbated by social isolation (even from other grandparent caregivers), born as it is from the lack of feedback about the quality of one's thinking and the validity of the interpretation that the explanation for one's present situation (caring for a grandchild) lies within oneself rather than to circumstances and events outside oneself.

This study is unique in that its focus is not on the grandparent caregiver's perspective, but on that maintained by the age peers with whom one can easily identify (grandparents), and against whom one may compare one's own life situation, physical health, and emotional well-being. It therefore helps to define and understand more clearly the social interpersonal context in which custodial grandparenting occurs. Indeed, these data clearly suggest custodial grandparents' interactions with other grandparents are likely to be colored by others' knowledge of and attitudes toward them as potential failures as parents, as persons who helped create the necessity for their newly acquired roles, as persons who are victims of circumstances over which they may or may not have control, and by implication, as persons in need of both formal and informal support and help from others. That these perceptions would co-vary with the presence of behavioral or emotional problems in the grandchild and the reason for role assumption suggests that some grandparent caregivers might be more differentially affected by such biases than others. Not only do grandparents themselves report that they feel isolated from others and have difficulty obtaining needed social services (see Hayslip & Kaminski, 2005), but they also state that their lives have been considerably disrupted by their caregiving responsibilities (see Jendrek, 1994), often to the detriment of their personal and marital well-being, plans for the future, and relationships with both their children and grandchildren (see Cox, 2000). Such factors interfere with their roles as grandparents, parents, spouses, workers, and their friendships and relationships with age peers (see Hayslip et al., 1998).

In this respect, not only might grandparent caregivers be victimized by others' views about them, but traditional grandparents may also be impacted by expectations others might hold about them in the event that they too might be asked to raise their grandchildren, and they may feel fearful about this occurring. Not surprisingly, as grandparents report uncertainty about how to raise their grandchildren (see Chenoweth, 2000, for a discussion), others' views about custodial grandparents' effectiveness as parents are quite relevant to the present findings. Internalizing others' views about what it might be like to be a custodial grandparent could easily undermine one's own efforts in getting needed information about social services, seeking professional mental health assistance, joining a support group, or availing oneself of respite care (see Roberto & Qualls, 2003). Likewise, as problems in their grandchildren may bring caregiving grandparents into conflict with other adults (e.g., as teachers, social service providers) and demand immediate intervention (see Hayslip, Silverthorn, Shore, & Henderson, 2000; Silverthorn & Durant, 2000), traditional grandparents' views about the extent of, and basis for, such problems are likely to impact their willingness to provide needed support to friends, neighbors, or coworkers who are now raising a grandchild, or influence their own efforts to recommend professional help for a troubled grandchild (Daly & Glenwick, 2000; Hayslip & Shore, 2000; Young & Dawson, 2003). Such biases about custodial grandparents may also limit information available to them regarding likely resources for help available in the community (Minkler, Drive, Roe, & Bedeian, 1993), as well as interfere with traditional grandparents making timely referrals to professionals who can help grandparent caregivers deal with the parenting demands of raising a grandchild.

REFERENCES

Antonucci, T. C. (2001). Social relations: An examination of social networks, social support, and sense of control. In J. Beiren & K. W. Schaie (Eds.), *Handbook of the psychology of aging* (5th ed., pp. 427–453). San Diego, CA: Academic Press.

Baird, A. (2003). Through my eyes: Service needs of grandparents who raise their grandchildren, from the perspective of a custodial grandmother. In B. Hayslip, Jr., & J. Patrick (Eds.), *Working with custodial grandparents* (pp. 59–68). New York: Springer.

Baker, D. (2000). Custodial grandparenting and ADHD. In B. Hayslip, Jr., & R. Goldberg-Glen (Eds.), *Grandparents raising grandchildren: Theoretical, empirical, and clinical perspectives* (pp. 145–160). New York: Springer.

Chenoweth, L. (2000). Grandparent education. In B. Hayslip, Jr., & R. Goldberg-Glen (Eds.), *Grandparents raising grandchildren: Theoretical, empirical, and clinical perspectives* (pp. 307–326). New York: Springer.

Childs, H., Hayslip, B., Jr., & Radika, L. (2000). Young and middle aged adults' perceptions of elder abuse. *The Gerontologist, 40,* 75–85.

Cox, C. (2000). Empowering grandparents raising grandchildren. In C. Cox (Ed.), *To grandmother's house we go and stay: Perspectives on custodial grandparents* (pp. 253–267). New York: Springer.

Daly, S. L., & Glenwick, D. S. (2000). Personal adjustment and perceptions of grandchild behavior in custodial grandmothers. *Journal of Clinical Child Psychology, 1,* 108–118.

Ellis, A., & Velton, E. (1998). *Optimal aging: Getting over getting older.* Chicago: Open Court.

Emick, M. A., & Hayslip, B., Jr. (1999). Custodial grandparenting: Stresses, coping skills, and relationships with grandchildren. *International Journal of Aging and Human Development, 1,* 35–61.

Etaugh, C., & Folger, D. (1998). Perceptions of parents whose work and parenting behaviors deviate from role expectations. *Sex Roles, 39,* 215–223.

Fuller-Thomson, E., & Minkler, M. (2000). America's grandparent caregivers: Who are they? In B. Hayslip, Jr., & R. Goldberg-Glen (Eds.), *Grandparents raising grandchildren* (pp. 3–21). New York: Springer.

Gettinger, M., & Guetschow, K. W. (1998). Parental involvement in schools: Parent and teacher perceptions of roles, efficacy, and opportunities. *Journal of Research and Development in Education, 32,* 38–52.

Hayslip, B., Jr., & Kaminski, P. (2005). Grandparents raising their grandchildren: A review of literature and suggestions for practice. *The Gerontologist, 45,* 262–269.

Hayslip, B., Jr., & Patrick, J. (2003). Custodial grandparenting viewed from a life span perspective. In B. Hayslip, Jr., & J. Patrick (Eds.), *Working with custodial grandparents* (pp. 3–12). New York: Springer.

Hayslip, B., Jr., & Shore, R. J. (2000). Custodial grandparenting and mental health services. *Journal of Mental Health and Aging, 6,* 367–384.

Hayslip, B., Jr., Shore, R. J., Henderson, C. E., & Lambert, P. L. (1998). Custodial grandparenting and the impact of grandchildren with problems on role satisfaction and role meaning. *Journal of Gerontology: SOCIAL SCIENCES, 3,* S164–S173.

Hayslip, B., Jr., Silverthorn, P., Shore, R. J., & Henderson, C. (2000). Determinants of custodial grandparents' perceptions of problem behavior in their grandchildren. In B. Hayslip, Jr., & R. Goldberg-Glen (Eds.), *Grandparents raising grandchildren: Theoretical, empirical, and clinical perspectives* (pp. 225–268). New York: Springer.

Hirshorn, B., M. Van Meter, M., & Brown, D. R. (2000). When grandparents raise grandchildren due to substance abuse: Responding to a uniquely destabilizing factor. In B. Hayslip, Jr., & R. Goldberg-Glen (Eds.), *Grandparents raising grandchildren: Theoretical, empirical, and clinical perspectives* (pp. 269–288). New York: Springer.

Hodgson, L. G. (1988). Grandparents and older grandchildren. In M. E. Szinovacz (Ed.), *Handbook on grandparenthood* (pp. 171–183). Westport, CT: Greenwood Press.

Holden, G. W., & Buck, M. J. (2002). Parental attitudes toward childrearing. In M. Bornstein (Ed.), *Handbook of parenting: Vol. 3. Being and becoming a parent* (2nd ed., pp. 537–562). Mahwah, NJ: Lawrence Erlbaum Associates Publishers.

Jendrek, M. P. (1994). Grandparents who parent their grandchildren: Circumstances and decisions. *The Gerontologist, 34,* 206–216.

Joslin, D. (2000). Grandparents raising children orphaned and affected by HIV/AIDS. In C. Cox (Ed.), *To grandmother's house we go and stay: Perspectives on custodial grandparents* (pp. 167–183). New York: Springer.

Joslin, D. (2002). *Invisible caregivers: Older adults raising children in the wake of HIV/AIDS.* Columbia, NY: Columbia University Press.

Kaminski, P., & Hayslip, B., Jr. (2004, August). *Parenting attitudes of custodial grandparents.* Paper presented at the Annual Convention of the American Psychological Association, Honolulu, HI (refereed).

King, J., Hayslip, B., Jr., & Kaminski, P. L. (2006). Variability in the need for formal and informal social support among grandparent caregivers: A pilot study. In B. Hayslip, Jr., & J. Hicks Patrick (Eds.), *Custodial grandparenting: Individual, cultural, and ethnic diversity* (pp. 407–424). San Diego, CA: Academic Press.

Kivnick, H. Q. (1982). Grandparenthood: An overview of meaning and mental health. *The Gerontologist, 22,* 59–71.

Kolomer, S., McCallion, P., & Overynder, J. (2003). Why support groups help: Successful interventions for grandparent caregivers of children with developmental disabilities. In B. Hayslip, Jr., & J. Patrick (Eds.), *Working with custodial grandparents* (pp. 111–126). New York: Springer.

Krause, N. (2001). Social support. In R. H. Binstock & L. K. George (Eds.), *Handbook of aging and the social sciences* (5th ed., pp. 273–294). San Diego, CA: Academic Press.

Lemme, B. H. (2002). Family ties, transitions, and challenge. In C. Merrill & T. Pauken (Eds.), *Development in adulthood* (pp. 243–301). Boston, MA: Allyson & Bacon.

McAdoo, H. P., & McWright, L. A. (1994). The roles of grandparents: The use of proverbs in value transmission. *Activities, Adaptation, & Aging, 19,* 27–38.

McKinney, J., McGrew, K., & Nelson, I. (2003). Grandparent caregivers to children with developmental disabilities: Added challenges. In B. Hayslip, Jr., & J. Patrick (Eds.), *Working with custodial grandparents* (pp. 93–110). New York: Springer.

Melamed, B. G. (2002). Parenting the ill child. In M. Bornstein (Ed.), *Handbook of parenting: Vol. 5. Practical issues in parenting* (2nd ed., pp. 329–348). Mahwah, NJ: Lawrence Erlbaum Associates Publishers.

Miltenberger, P., Hayslip, B., Jr., Harris, B., & Kaminski, P. (2003–2004). Perceptions of the losses experienced by custodial grandmothers. *Omega: Journal of Death and Dying, 48,* 245–262.

Minkler, M., Drive, D., Roe, K. M., & Bedeian, K. (1993). Community interventions to support grandparent caregivers. *The Gerontologist, 6,* 807–811.

Minkler, M., & Roe, K. M. (1993). Support networks and social support. In *Grandmothers as caregivers* (pp. 99–115). London: Sage Publications.

Roberto, K., & Qualls, S. (2003). Intervention strategies for grandparents raising grandchildren: Lessons learned from the caregiving literature. In B. Hayslip, Jr., & J. Patrick (Eds.), *Working with custodial grandparents* (pp. 13–26). New York: Springer.

Ruiz, D. (2003). *Amazing grace: African American grandmothers as caregivers and conveyors of traditional values.* New York: Praeger.

Shore, R. J., & Hayslip, B., Jr. (1994). Custodial grandparenting: Implications for children's development. In A. Gottfried & A. Gottfried (Eds.), *Redefining families: Implications for children's development* (pp. 171–218). New York: Plenum.

Silverthorn, P., & Durant, S. (2000). Custodial grandparenting and the difficult child: Learning from the parenting literature. In B. Hayslip, Jr., & R. Goldberg-Glen (Eds.), *Grandparents raising grandchildren: Theoretical, empirical, and clinical perspectives* (pp. 47–64). New York: Springer.

Solomon, J. C., & Marx, J. (2000). The physical, mental, and social health of custodial grandparents. In B. Hayslip, Jr., & R. Goldberg-Glen (Eds.), *Grandparents raising grandchildren* (pp. 183–205). New York: Springer.

Strom, R., Griswold, D., Collinsworth, P., & Strom, S. (1991). An inside view of parent success in Black families. *Journal of Instructional Psychology, 18,* 187–197.

Tomlin, A. M. (1998). Grandparents' influences on grandchildren. In M. E. Szinovacz (Ed.), *Handbook on grandparenthood* (pp. 159–170). Westport, CT: Greenwood Press.

Wohl, E., Lahner, J., & Jooste, J. (2003). Group processes among grandparents raising grandchildren. In B. Hayslip, Jr., & J. Patrick (Eds.), *Working with custodial grandparents* (pp. 195–212). New York: Springer.

Young, M. H., & Dawson, T. J. (2003). Perception of child difficulty and levels of depression in caregiving grandmothers. *Journal of Mental Health and Aging, 9*(2), 111–122.

APPENDIX A

Mrs. Smith, a Hispanic woman, is a married grandparent and has several adult children. She has recently become a full-time grandparent caregiver to one of her grandchildren. Mrs. Smith has been caring for her elementary school–aged granddaughter for 1 year and her good health has allowed her to provide for the grandchild. Her granddaughter has exhibited some behavior and learning problems in school and has been involved in fights with friends. Also her grandchild has begun to experience some symptoms of depression such as not eating and trouble sleeping at night. Mrs. Smith became the primary caregiver of her granddaughter when the child's parents abandoned the child. Due to these circumstances, Mrs. Smith will remain the primary caregiver of her grandchild for an indefinite period of time.

CHAPTER 11

Social Support and Parenting Behaviors Influence Grandchildren's Social Competence

Vidya Ramaswamy, Navaz Bhavnagri, and Elizabeth Barton

SOCIAL SUPPORT, AGING, AND STRESS

Grandmothers report that they benefit from receiving support from church, community, and governmental agencies (Burton, 1992). African American grandmothers report that social support is one of the primary influences on their parenting (Stevenson, Henderson, & Baugh, 2007). Social support is particularly crucial in an aging population because grandmothers identify health challenges and limited energy as one of their main concerns (Dolbin-MacNab, 2006). Within the context of aging, African American grandparents may have problems with their emotional and physical health (Burton, 1992; Emick & Hayslip, 1999; Minkler & Roe, 1996) and report negative emotions such as fatigue (Waldrop, 2003).

In this context, aging morale may be a factor in how social support is viewed in its relationship to different stressors in a grandmother's life (Stevenson et al., 2007) such as drug abuse, teen pregnancy, incarceration of the adult child (Bryson & Casper, 1999), divorce, abandonment of children, parental abuse (Burton, 1992; Shore & Hayslip, 1994), disturbed family relationships (Waldrop, 2003), work responsibilities, and financial stress (Rodgers & Jones, 1999).

In addition to these stressors, grandmothers may experience stress as a parent. Grandparents of emotionally and behaviorally disturbed children express bewilderment, fear, and guilt at having to interact with children (Seligman, 1991), and this problem may be compounded if the grandchild resides with them (Emick & Hayslip, 1999). Furthermore, lack of adequate knowledge about child development and current parenting strategies can exacerbate the level of parenting stress in an environment perceived to be difficult for parenting, especially if grandparents are thrust into the parent role with little preparation (Dolbin-MacNab, 2006). Undoubtedly, the combined impact of these different stressors can lead to serious problems for grandparent caregivers. In one study involving African American grandmothers, 94% reported a clinically significant level of stress (Ross & Aday, 2006), wherein the impact of such stress on the experience of parenting may be negative. In a study of parents of children attending Head Start, parenting stress was significantly related to different aspects of parenting behavior as well as social competence and internalizing problems in young children attending Head Start (Anthony et al., 2005). Indeed, many children who are raised by grandparents exhibit behavioral and emotional symptoms and are treated in mental health settings (Shore & Hayslip, 1994), and this may be related to parenting stress and its impact on the grandchild's social competence.

Although research on the impact of parenting stress on specific parenting behaviors is lacking, we know that specific parenting behaviors such as warmth, control, and consistent discipline are related to healthy child development (Baumrind, 1971), and parenting strategies may even impact a child's peer relationships (Bhavnagri & Parke, 1991). Brody, Flor, and Gibson (1999) found that competence-promoting parenting practices and parenting-efficacy beliefs were related to social competence in children. Although research on the value of parenting is strongly in its favor, there is a need to clarify how parenting variables are related to children's social competence in African American families (Fagan, 2000; Hill, 2001), particularly with respect to the potential for intervention.

While grandmothers express some concern about parenting strategies, in one study of grandparents, 80% reported that they had never been to parenting classes (Emick & Hayslip, 1999). In a qualitative study of 17 African American grandmothers concerning parenting, major themes of concern included maintaining positive communication with grandchildren and taking a lead role in children's learning (Gibson, 2005). In the case of African American grandmothers raising grandchildren, exploring the value derived from parenting may be useful because being able to take satisfaction in parenting their grandchildren may lessen the stress of raising them (Burton, 1992; Minkler & Roe, 1996). It seems that caring for a grandchild can give rise to an inner strength and a feeling of happiness (Waldrop, 2003). A similar finding is reported by Rodgers and Jones (1999), who found that African American grandmothers reported rewards from their parenting role because it made them feel useful and younger. Consequently, the benefits of a high-quality interaction between the grandmother and the grandchild can serve as a family resource for the entire family system.

Parenting intervention with grandmothers raising grandchildren needs to incorporate findings about social support (Stevenson et al., 2007), aging (Dolbin-MacNab, 2006), parenting stress (Anthony et al., 2005; Ross & Aday, 2006), and parenting behaviors in grandmothers (Rodgers & Jones, 1999). Information about how specific discipline practices and communication strategies influence grandchildren's social competence will also help in constructing appropriate interventions strategies (Dolbin-MacNab, 2006) and increase parental efficacy (Hayslip, 2003).

The current study explores the impact of social support, aging morale, parenting stress, and parenting behaviors of grandmothers on grandchildren's social competence. The relationship between specific parenting behaviors of the grandmother and the grandchild's negative and prosocial behaviors will also be examined.

METHOD

Participants

Grandmothers. The mean age of grandmothers ($n = 101$) was 55.85 ($SD = 9.73$). Five caregiving great-grandmothers also participated in this study. The mean number of years the focal child lived with the grandmothers was 4.80 ($SD = 2.29$). More than a third (39.6%) of the grandmothers had legal custody of their grandchild and more than half (54.1%) were part of grandparenting programs. About a third (31.7%) of the grandmothers were married, and 18.8% were never married. The remainder were divorced or widowed. About a third (34.7%) were unemployed or retired and about three-quarters (73.3%) had an annual income of less than $20,000. More than half (59.4%) had a high school diploma or less. The majority of grandmothers (87.1%) were African American.

Grandchildren. The mean age of the grandchild being cared for was 6.16 ($SD = 1.95$). The percentage of boys and girls was 49.5 and 50.5 respectively.

Procedure

Grandmothers ($n = 101$) were recruited through social service agencies in the state of Michigan. Typically these grandmothers were part of service programs that were conducted in schools and churches. Most grandmothers lived in the Detroit area. Data was collected from the fall of 2005 until the spring of 2007, and each grandmother was paid $30 for her participation. Grandmothers completed self-report measures and were asked to respond after selecting a (focal) grandchild between the ages of 3 and 9.

Measures

Demographic Questionnaire. This instrument asked grandmothers for the following information: name, age, number of years caring for the focal child at the time of the study, age of the focal grandchild, total number of grandchildren, ages of the youngest and oldest grandchild, and who else lived with the grandmother at the time of the interview. Grandmothers indicated if they had legal custody of the grandchild and indicated whether or not they had participated in grandparenting programs. Grandmothers also rated their physical and emotional health on a 4-point Likert rating scale ranging from poor to excellent.

Social Support Questionnaire (SSQ). This measure focuses on who is available for support and how satisfactory the support is (Sarason, Sarason, Shearin, & Price, 1987). There are 12 items, each with two parts: Part A requires the respondent to list up to nine persons who provide support, and Part B asks how satisfactory the support provided by persons listed in Part A is, utilizing a scale of 1 to 6, ranging from *very dissatisfied* to *very satisfied*. For purposes of the present study, two items (Part B) assessed satisfaction with social support, whose internal consistency reliability was .65 in this study.

Philadelphia Geriatric Center Morale Scale (PGCMS). This measure assesses agitation, attitudes towards aging, and lonely dissatisfaction (Lawton, 2003), and is composed of 17 statements that can be responded to in terms of *yes* or *no*. Mean scores were used to represent aging morale in the present study; its reliability was .85.

Parenting Stress (PSI-SF). This measure focuses on parental distress, parent-child dysfunctional interaction, and interactions with a difficult child (Abidin, 1995). The Parental Distress subscale indicates level of distress resulting from personal factors such as depression and restrictions because of child rearing. The Parent-Child Dysfunctional Interaction subscale measures satisfaction of the parent with interactions with the child. The Difficult Child subscale measures parents' perceptions of their child's self-regulatory abilities. There are 36 items with 12 items in each of the subscales that are rated by parents on a 5-point scale ranging from *strongly agree* to *strongly disagree*, wherein higher scores represent more parenting stress. The mean score (36 items) was used to represent parenting stress in the present study. The internal consistency for this measure was .92.

Parents as a Teacher Inventory (PAAT). This measure focuses on five different aspects of the parent-child interaction: Creativity, Frustration, Control, Play, and Teaching/Learning (Strom, 1986). The Creativity subscale measures parental acceptance and encouragement of creativity. The Parental Frustration subscale measures parental tolerance of frustration in daily interactions with the child. The Parental Control subscale measures the extent to which parents relinquish control. The Play subscale measures the parent's knowledge and acceptance of play, and the Teaching–Learning subscale measures the parent's ability to encourage the teaching-learning process with their children. The PAAT has 50 statements with four possible answers ranging from *strong yes* to *strong no*. The mean scores for the Play subscale were used in the present study to represent parental support of play in the present study; its internal consistency was .76.

Parenting Sense of Competence (PSOC). This measure focuses on a parent's sense of satisfaction and self-efficacy (Gilbaud-Wallston & Wandersman, 1978). It has 17 statements that respondents rate on a 7-point scale ranging from *strongly agree* to *strongly disagree*. It has two subscales: the Skill/Knowledge subscale and the Valuing/Comfort Subscale. Scoring was changed from the original version so that higher scores reflect a higher sense of competence. The mean score for the total scale was used to represent parental self-efficacy in the present study, and the internal consistency of the PSOC was .75.

Parenting Dimensions Inventory-S (PDI-S). This measure focuses on six dimensions of parenting: Nurturance, Inconsistency, Following Through on Discipline, Organization, Amount of Control, and Type of Control, which includes Letting Situation Go, Physical Punishment, Material/Social Consequences, Reasoning, Scolding, and Reminding (Slater, 1987). Part one of the measure has 13 statements that respondents rate on a 6-point scale ranging from *not at all like me* to *exactly like me* and measures Nurturance, Inconsistency, and Following Through on Discipline. Part 2 has four statements about dinner schedules and organization in household activities that parents rate on a 6-point scale ranging from *never* to *always* and measures Organization. Part 3 has five pairs of statements in a forced-choice format and measures Amount of Control. Part 4 requires parents to respond to five scenarios by rating different ways of responding, ranging from *very likely to do* to *very unlikely to do* and measures the six different types of control listed earlier. A mean score for Organization was calculated on the basis of three of the four items because one item showed little relationship to the other items; this represented parental organization in the present study. A mean score for the Letting Situation Go subscale represented parental permissiveness in the present study. The internal consistency for the Organization subscale and the Letting Situation Go (permissiveness) subscale was .71 and .72 respectively.

Strengths and Difficulties Inventory (SDQ). This measure reflects a total difficulties score (based on an emotional symptoms score, a conduct problems score, a hyperactivity score, a peer problem score) and a prosocial behavior score (Goodman, 1997). The total score for negative behavior of grandchild was computed by summing the scores for emotional symptoms, conduct problems, hyperactivity, and peer problems. Three items were omitted from the negative behavior score so that this version could be used with 3-year-old children. The internal consistency for the items measuring negative behavior of grandchild and the items measuring prosocial behavior of grandchild was .84 and .60 respectively.

Hypotheses

A preliminary model was developed (see Figure 11.1), which proposed that parenting behaviors mediate the influence of social support, aging morale, and parenting stress on the grandchild's social competence (negative behaviors and prosocial behaviors). In the final model, only those parenting behaviors that had a significant association with the negative or prosocial behavior of the grandchild were retained.

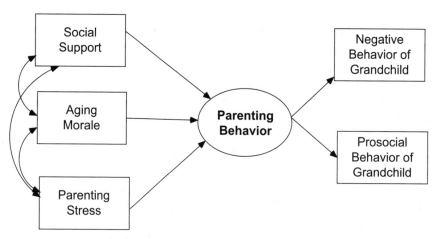

FIGURE 11.1 Conceptual model.

RESULTS

Mean Scores on the Variables

Table 11.1 displays the means, standard deviations, and maximum possible scores for all the variables in this study. These scores suggest that grandparents seem to have a high amount of social support and aging morale and may be performing well as parents. Similarly, grandchildren were perceived by grandmothers to display positive social development as reflected in the scores of prosocial and negative behavior.

Correlations Among the Variables

Table 11.2 displays the correlations among the variables in the study. Scores for social support were positively related to scores for aging morale. Scores for aging morale were negatively related to those for parenting stress. Parenting stress was negatively related to scores reflecting three parenting behaviors (parental organization, parental support of play, and parental self-efficacy). Both parental organization and parental support of play were negatively related to a grandchild's negative behavior. There was a positive relationship between permissiveness and negative behavior of grandchild, and between parental self-efficacy and prosocial behavior of the grandchild.

TABLE 11.1 Mean Score and Standard Deviations for all Variables ($n = 101$)

Variable	Mean (SD)	Maximum Possible Score
1. Social support	5.60 (.82)	6
2. Aging morale	.75 (.22)	1
3. Parenting stress	2.16 (.58)	5
4. Parental support of play	2.20 (.14)	4
5. Parental organization	4.51 (.92)	6
6. Parental permissiveness	.41 (.59)	1
7. Parenting self-efficacy	4.37 (.67)	6
8. Negative behavior of grandchild	1.54 (.36)	3
9. Prosocial behavior of grandchild	2.55 (.38)	3

TABLE 11.2 Correlations Among All the Variables in the Study ($n = 101$)

Variable	1	2	3	4	5	6	7	8	9
1. Social support		.28**	-.21*	.07	.12	.14	.08	-.16	.09
2. Aging morale			-.64**	.22*	.28**	-.04	.25*	-.40**	.07
3. Parenting stress				-.26**	-.25*	-.01	-.23*	.36**	-.08
4. Parental support of play					.02	.04	.19	-.29**	.08
5. Parental organization						.14	.14	-.36**	.20*
6. Parental permissiveness							-.13	.25*	-.09
7. Parenting self-efficacy								-.19	.34**
8. Negative behavior of grandchild									-.39**
9. Prosocial behavior of grandchild									

* $p < .05$ ** $p < .01$

Path Analysis

A path analysis was conducted using Analysis of Moment Structures Version 7 (AMOS-7). The initial model (see Figure 11.1) did not have an acceptable fit to the data (χ^2 = 32.35, df = 13, p = .002; CFI = .86; RMSEA = .12). On this basis, the initial model was changed in several ways; in the final model, aging morale mediated social support and parenting stress. A new path from parenting stress to negative behaviors in grandchildren was added based on modification indices estimates. Errors for negative behavior and prosocial behaviors were correlated. The changed model (see Figure 11.2) showed a good fit (χ^2 = 21.33, df = 20, p = .38; CFI = .99, RMSEA = .03) to the data.

An examination of the path coefficients in the final model suggests that there was a significant effect of social support on aging morale and of aging morale on parenting stress. Parenting stress had a significant effect on three of the four parenting behaviors: parental organization, parental support of play, and parenting self-efficacy, but had no relationship to parental permissiveness. Parenting stress also had a significant positive relationship with negative behavior in the grandchild.

There was a significant positive effect of parental organization and parental support of play on negative behaviors of the grandchild, and a significant

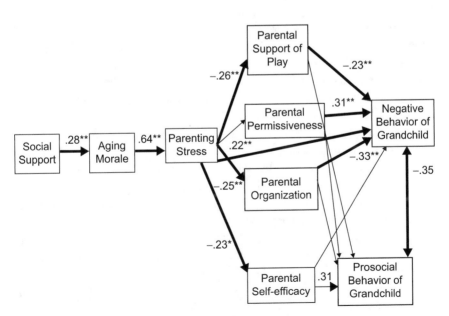

FIGURE 11.2 Final model showing significant paths in bold.

positive effect of parental permissiveness on negative behaviors of grandchild. Parental self-efficacy had no relationship with negative behaviors of grandchildren but had a significant positive effect on grandchildren's prosocial behaviors. Thus, parental behaviors of organization, support of play, and permissiveness were related to negative behaviors of the grandchild, and parental self-efficacy was related to prosocial behaviors of the grandchild. This model accounted for 38% of the variance in negative behaviors of the grandchild and 14% of the variance in prosocial behaviors of the grandchild.

DISCUSSION

Four significant findings with respect to social support, aging morale, parenting stress, and parenting behaviors as they influence grandchildren's social behavior emerged from the present study. Each finding will be discussed with respect to its implications for intervention. The first significant finding was that social support has a significant impact on aging morale. This is supported by research that indicates social support to be a resource that is of great value to grandparents (Waldrop, 2003), wherein social support is viewed by grandparents as supportive of their parenting role (Stevenson et al., 2007). However, the very role of being a caregiver grandparent may cause grandparents to run the risk of losing social support (Hayslip & Kaminski, 2005), and this may impact aging morale negatively as suggested by the current study. Undoubtedly, parenting interventions with grandmothers need to focus on enhancing social support at both community and policy levels (Musil, 1998). Counselors, social workers, and others who work with grandparents need to help grandparents identify social support both through informal networks such as grandparent support groups and formal networks that work through schools and agencies.

The second significant finding here was that aging morale mediates the influence of social support on parenting stress. This suggests that grandmothers may need practical help dealing with issues related to aging such as declining physical and emotional health (Burton, 1992; Emick & Hayslip, 1999; Minkler & Roe, 1996; Waldrop, 2003). Indeed, they may need help that can sustain positive views about growing older by preventing problems in caregiving caused by fatigue and limited energy (Waldrop, 2003). In this respect, social support can be helpful in assisting grandparents so that they can access resources that mitigate problems caused by declining physical and mental health (see Roberto et al., this volume). This may require grandparent groups to set up health camps for themselves that deal with topics such as access to better medical care or awareness of depression. Strategies that promote health in grandparents will most likely support their ability to carry out the parenting role in caring for their grandchildren.

The third significant finding in the present study was that parenting stress negatively impacts specific parenting behaviors related to parental support of play, parental organization in family-related activities, and parental self-efficacy. Many grandparents face problems in caregiving associated with depression and anxiety (Musil, 1998). Indeed, 92% of African American grandparent caregivers in one study were highly stressed as defined by clinical criteria (Ross & Aday, 2006); this may be in part due to problems related to managing the stresses associated with parenting. For example, parenting stress may result from a lack of knowledge about child development and the perception of the current social environment as less supportive of their efforts at parenting (Dolbin-MacNab, 2006). Moreover, appropriate models of child rearing may not exist for grandparents (Hayslip & Kaminski, 2005), causing confusion about how to be an efficacious parent. For instance, grandparents may find some parenting behaviors such as disciplining a child difficult to carry out (Weber & Waldrop, 2000). Thus, interventions with grandparents need to focus on strategies that help deal with such stresses (Seligman, 1991), possibly through the development of problem-focused coping skills such as seeking social support (Ross & Aday, 2006). The use of school programs that focus on educational assistance (Ross & Aday, 2006) and the dissemination of information about, for example, drug abuse and sexual activity can also be helpful (Dolbin-MacNab, 2006) in dealing with potential problems in contemporary society that can contribute to caregiving stress among grandparents. Participating in programs that teach parenting skills such as discipline may also be helpful in mitigating the stresses of parenting a grandchild.

It is important to note that grandparenting is not necessarily a stressful experience. In fact, as studies have suggested, grandparenting can be enjoyable (Hayslip & Kaminski, 2005; Weber & Waldrop, 2000) and many grandparents find inner strength to deal with the challenges of grandparenting (Waldrop, 2003). The grandparent-grandchild relationship is a family resource (Barranti, 1985) that can contribute to grandchildren's development in the context of other problems such as those caused by biological parents. In support of this view, grandmothers in the present study appeared to be functioning well as parents of young children between the ages of 3 and 9 and the grandchildren appeared to be socially competent. This suggests that a strength-based perspective that focuses on parenting capacities at younger ages can help prevent potential problems (such as drug abuse and delinquency) associated with the adolescent years. Recognizing that grandparents have tremendous value in stabilizing the family system needs to be an inherent message of any intervention and can help the spontaneous participation of grandparents in any intervention.

The fourth significant finding that is perhaps unique to this study was the differential relationship between specific parental behaviors and negative and prosocial behavior in young grandchildren. In this study, parental support of play, parental organization, and parental permissiveness impacted negative behavior of the grandchild, whereas only parental self-efficacy influenced prosocial behavior of the grandchild. Thus, grandparenting interventions need to identify different paths to decreasing negative behavior and increasing prosocial behavior in the grandchild. Interventions that can help grandparents by providing knowledge of child development and strategies that enhance the value of play in young grandchildren can not only help caregivers develop plans for being more organized, but also provide strategies for positive disciplinary practices that both reduce permissiveness and foster parental self-efficacy. Such strategies can be very effective in fostering social competence in grandchildren.

CONTRIBUTIONS AND LIMITATIONS OF THE PRESENT STUDY, AND SUGGESTIONS FOR FUTURE RESEARCH AND PRACTICE

A unique contribution of this study is that it has identified relationships between specific parental practices and children's positive and negative behaviors. The examination of social support, aging morale, and parenting stress as they influence parenting and consequently the grandchild's social behavior offers a more comprehensive examination of family functioning in grandmothers raising grandchildren.

It is to be noted that a limitation of the present study is that it focused on self-report data obtained from a modestly sized, convenience sample of grandmothers in a specific geographical region. The use of self-report data may reflect socially desirable responses on the part of grandmothers. Another limitation here is that focal children may be self-selected in a positively biased manner based upon their prosocial characteristics. A third limitation to be noted is the lack of observational data of grandchildren's social behaviors in different settings such as the school. This study was also restricted to grandmothers, and did not take into consideration the role of biological parents as a factor in grandparents' impact on their grandchildren.

Future studies on grandparents raising grandchildren need to include grandfathers as well as other foster parents who are caring for a much younger generation of children. The different pathways between specific parenting behaviors and positive and negative social behaviors in children found here needs to be replicated on larger, more diverse samples of grandparent caregivers. From an applied perspective, these findings suggest that there is indeed a need for interventions that incorporate multiple components (e.g., developing effective parenting skills, engaging in self-care behaviors, treating emotional and behavioral difficulties in grandchildren, effectively utilizing available social support for grandfamilies, and increasing knowledge of normal child development; see Hayslip, 2003). In this context, taking a strengths-based approach may be as effective as one which focuses upon the ameliorating difficulties grandfamilies are experiencing.

REFERENCES

Abidin, R. R. (1995). *Parenting Stress Index.* Odessa, FL: Psychological Assessment Resources. Available from http://www.parinc.com

Anthony, L. G., Anthony, B. J., Glanville, D. N., Naiman, D. Q., Waanders, C., & Barranti, C. C. R. (1985). The grandparent/grandchild relationship: Family resource in an era of voluntary bonds. *Family Relations, 34,* 343–352.

Baumrind, D. (1971). Current patterns of parental authority. *Developmental Psychology,* 4(1, pt. 2), 1–103.

Bhavnagri, N. P., & Parke, R. D. (1991). Parents as direct facilitators of children's peer relationships: Effects of age of child and sex of parent. *Journal of Social and Personal Relationships, 8,* 423–440.

Brody, G. H., Flor, D. L., & Gibson, N. (1999). Linking maternal efficacy beliefs, developmental goals, parenting practices, and child competence in rural single-parent African American families. *Child Development, 70*(5), 1197–1208.

Bryson, K., & Casper, L. M. (1999). *Co-resident grandparents and grandchildren. Current population reports: Special studies.* Census Bureau, P23–198, U.S. Department of Commerce.

Burton, L. M. (1992). Black grandparents rearing children of drug-addicted parents: Stressors, outcomes, and social services needs. *The Gerontologist, 32*(6), 744–751.

Dolbin-MacNab, M. L. (2006). Just like raising your own? Grandmothers' perceptions of parenting a second time around. *Family Relations, 55,* 564–575.

Emick. M. A., & Hayslip, B., Jr. (1999). Custodial grandparenting: Stresses, coping skills, and relationships with grandchildren. *International Journal of Aging and Development, 48*(1), 35–61.

Fagan, J. (2000). African American and Puerto Rican parenting styles, paternal involvement, and Head Start children's social competence. *Merrill-Palmer Quarterly, 46*(4), 592–612.

Gibson, P. A. (2005). Intergenerational parenting from the perspective of African American grandmothers. *Family Relations, 54,* 280–297.

Gilbaud-Wallston, J., & Wandersman, L. P. (1978). *Development and utility of the Parenting Sense of Competence Scale.* Paper presented at the Annual Convention of the American Psychological Association, Toronto, Canada.

Goodman, R. (1997). The strengths and difficulties questionnaire: A research note. *Journal of Child Psychology and Psychiatry, 38*, 581–586.

Hayslip, B., Jr. (2003). The impact of a psychosocial intervention on parental efficacy, grandchild relationship quality, and well-being among grandparents raising grandchildren. In B. Hayslip, Jr. & J. Patrick (Eds.), *Working with custodial grandparents* (pp. 163–178). New York: Springer.

Hayslip, B., Jr., & Kaminski, P. (2005). Grandparents raising grandchildren. *Marriage and Family Review, 37*(1/2), 147–169.

Hill, S. A. (2001). Class, race, and gender discrimination of child rearing in African American families. *Journal of Black Studies, 31*(4), 494–508.

Lawton, M. P. (2003). *Lawton's PGC Morale Scale.* Polisher Research Institute, Abramson Center for Jewish Life. Horsham, PA. Retrieved April 2005, from http://www.Abramsoncenter.org/PRI/

Minkler, M., & Roe, K. M. (1996). Grandparents as surrogate parents. *Generations, 20*, 34–38.

Musil, C. M. (1998). Health, stress, coping, and social supporting grandmother caregivers. *Health Care for Women International, 19*, 441–455.

Rodgers, A. Y., & Jones, R. L. (1999). Grandmothers who are caregivers: An overlooked population. *Child and Adolescent Social Work Journal, 16*(6), 455–466.

Ross, M. E. T., & Aday, L. A. (2006). Stress and coping in African American grandparents who are raising grandchildren. *Journal of Family Issues, 27*(7), 912–932.

Sarason, I. G., Sarason, B. R., Shearin, E. N., & Pierce, G. R. (1987). A brief measure of social support: Practical and theoretical implications. *Journal of Social and Personal Relationships, 4*, 497–510.

Seligman, M. (1991). Grandparents of disabled grandchildren: Hopes, fears, and adaptation. *Families in Society: The Journal of Contemporary Human Services, 72*, 147–152.

Shore, R. J., & Hayslip, B., Jr. (1994). Custodial grandparenting: Implications for children's development. In A. Gottfried (Eds.), *Redefining families: Implications for children's development* (pp. 171–218). New York: Plenum.

Slater, M. A. (1987). The structure of parenting: A psychometric evaluation of the Parenting Dimensions Inventory. *Dissertation Abstracts International, 47*(7-B), 3127.

Stevenson, M. L., Henderson, T. L., & Baugh, E. (2007). Vital defenses: Social support appraisals of Black grandmothers parenting grandchildren. *Journal of Family Issues, 28*(2), 182–211.

Strom, R. (1986). *Parent as a teacher inventory and manual.* Bensenville, IL: Scholastic Testing Service.

Waldrop, D. P. (2003). Caregiving issues for grandmothers raising their grandchildren. *Journal of Human Behavior in the Social Environment, 7*(3/4), 201–223.

Weber, J. A., & Waldrop, D. P. (2000). Grandparents raising grandchildren: Families in transition. *Journal of Gerontological Social Work, 33*(20), 27–46.

SECTION 3

Intervention

This section focuses on clinicians' experiences with a variety of intervention techniques targeting the adjustment and well-being of both grandparents and grandchildren. Using both case study and family systems approaches, the chapters in this section address such questions as: In what terms should we view the experience of parenting a grandchild? What guidelines should one follow in counseling grandfamilies? What are the unique difficulties faced by such grandchildren, and how are they best resolved by the clinician? What strengths do grandfamilies bring to caregiving, and how can these be best utilized? In the context of the grandchild's experiences in school, how can clinicians and counselors effectively help grandparents and grandchildren?

CHAPTER 12

Examining the Losses and Gains Experienced by Grandparents Raising Grandchildren: A Practical Framework for Assessment and Intervention

Heather L. Servaty-Seib and Michael A. Wilkins

Yvonne is a 47-year-old single African American woman who has been caring for her 6-year-old granddaughter, Cassandra, and 3-year-old grandson, Leon, off and on since each was born. Her daughter Sheila, the mother of the children, struggles with drug addiction and has recently tested positive for HIV. Although Sheila has been in treatment a number of times and has made intermittent progress, she is an unpredictable and unreliable caregiver for her two young children. Yvonne works as a clerk at a convenience store, receives minimal government assistance, and is actively involved in her church.

Will and Sue, both married for the second time, are an upper–middle class White couple. They have been married for 10 years and had planned to retire at this point in their lives from their work as small business owners and move to their vacation home in Alaska. Both are in their mid-60s. Sue's oldest male child from her previous marriage, Sam, has a 3-year-old son, Austin. Two years ago, Will and Sue became legal guardians of Austin following their discovery that he was being neglected. Neither Sam nor Austin's biological mother was adequately providing for Austin's needs; he was medically ill (e.g., rashes, malnutrition) and also exhibited signs of social and emotional delays.

Will and Sue are both relatively healthy, but their relationship has been drastically and negatively affected by their role as custodial grandparents.

As the cases of Yvonne and Will and Sue illustrate, the specific experiences of custodial grandparents vary widely. Attempts to categorize this ever growing and diverse group of adults are quite challenging (Pinson-Millburn, Fabian, Schlossberg, & Pyle, 1996). Although research suggests that single, African American, low-income women are disproportionately represented as custodial grandparents in the United States, examining the group as a whole indicates that over half of all custodial grandparents are married, the majority are non-Hispanic Whites, and more than half have completed high school (Fuller-Thomson, Minkler, & Driver, 1997). Custodial grandparent situations also differ based on additional factors including (among others) age of the grandparents, duration of caregiving responsibilities, whether the biological parent lives in the home, the reasons for grandparent caregiving (e.g., death, drug abuse, divorce, AIDS/HIV, teen pregnancy, incarceration), quality of the relationship with the biological parent, legal custody status of the grandchildren, the physical and psychological functioning of the grandchildren, and geography.

In addition to this factual and situational variability is the variability that exists with regard to how custodial grandparents *perceive* their experience as caregivers. The perception of a life event is fundamental in determining whether the event is considered benign or threatening (Lazarus & Folkman, 1984). With regard to custodial grandparents, the research suggests such contrasting perspectives as:

- assuming the caregiver role as expected (Landry-Meyer & Newman, 2004) versus ambivalence about assuming the caregiver role (Essex, Newsome, & Moses, 2004).
- having a second chance at parenting (Hayslip & Kaminski, 2005a) versus missing the chance to be a traditional grandparent (Kolomer & McCallion, 2005).
- feeling a greater sense of meaning and purpose in life (Hayslip & Kaminski, 2005b) versus the decreased meaning and purpose in life associated with the non-occurrence of anticipated life cycle events (Landry-Meyer & Newman, 2004).

Such disparate perceptions can lead custodial grandparents to have distinct experiences during the transition to caregiving for their grandchildren. The power of perception is further emphasized by a recent study on the well-being of grandparents caring for their grandchildren. Sands, Goldberg-Glen, and Thornton (2005) found that cognitions and feelings of apprehension about one's grandparent role were negatively associated with well-being.

WHY A GAIN/LOSS FRAMEWORK?

We argue that using a gain/loss framework when assessing and counseling custodial grandparents allows practitioners to capture and address the multidimensional and unique perceptions and, therefore, the impact of this life event. Understanding the impact of life events is a complex task (Brown, 1989). One continuing challenge is the recognition and assessment of the variability in how individuals who experience similar life events perceive the importance or impact of those life events. In this chapter, we describe our conceptualization of a gain/loss perspective in understanding the impact of life events, address why this conceptualization fits well in the case of custodial grandparents, and directly apply this gain/loss perspective to the experience of custodial grandparents.

The gain/loss framework to conceptualizing life events is based on four core assumptions. First, all significant life events result in perceptions of gains and losses in a variety of life domains (cf. Baltes, 1997; Schlossberg, Waters, & Goodman, 1995). Second, the impact of any significant life event can be determined by assessing the perception of the gains and losses the individual attributes to that life event (Schlossberg et al., 1995). Third, the impact of a life event is malleable such that impact will vary as a result of factors such as time and engagement in counseling. Finally, the relative level of perceived loss associated with a significant life event will be positively associated with adjustment difficulties (cf. Cook & Oltjenbruns, 1998).

The literature on grandparents raising their grandchildren contains some reference to the non-death related losses (Miltenberger, Hayslip, Harris, & Kaminski, 2003–2004; Pinson-Millburn et al., 1996) and the corresponding grief (Lever & Wilson, 2005) experienced by custodial grandparents. In addition, multiple references are made to the cost/benefits (Hayslip & Kaminski, 2005b), advantages/disadvantages (Bullock, 2004), positive/negative outcomes (Dellman-Jenkins, Blankemeyer, & Olesh, 2002), and stressors/satisfactions (Waldrop & Weber, 2001) experienced by this population. However, the possible advantages of using a gain/loss framework for conceptualizing this life transition and counseling individuals who are in the midst of this transition have not been fully explored. The two primary advantages of this approach are the acknowledgement of the complexity of this life experience and the emphasis on the non-pathological nature of the transition.

A gain/loss framework allows practitioners to capture the complexity of the experience of custodial grandparents. An inclusive rather than one-dimensional approach (Pinson-Millburn et al., 1996) is required as these caregiving grandparents are facing multiple issues (e.g., legal, financial, parenting, coping; Dolbin-MacNab & Targ, 2003) and have multifaceted needs

(Wallace, 2001). The life domains where gains/losses can be assessed include the areas of roles, routines, relationships, assumptions about the self and the world, economic conditions, and psychobiological faculties (cf. Schlossberg et al., 1995; Goodman, Schlossberg, & Anderson, 2006). Not only can the gain/loss perceptions in all of these areas vary over time, but individuals are quite capable of perceiving gains in some areas and simultaneous losses in others (Hayslip, Emick, Henderson, & Elias, 2002; Hayslip, Shore, Henderson, & Lambert, 1998). Hayslip et al. (2002) found that "custodial grandparents raising problem grandchildren can separate the positive aspects of being a grandparent from specific arenas regarding the caregiving role in which they experience more distress" (p. 150). In addition, research suggests that grand-mothers and grandfathers may differentially perceive the experience of raising their grandchildren (Hayslip et al., 1998), an idea that can lead to marital disruption and conflict. This was definitely true in the case of Will and Sue. Will had limited commitment to Sam, Sue's son, but was completely committed to their grandson, Austin. Sue was stressed about trying to balance her commitment to her grandson and her concerns about the welfare of her son (Essex et al., 2004; Waldrop & Weber, 2001). Assessing and working with their unique perceptions of the gains/losses associated with their transition to becoming parents to their grandchild was a primary and necessary focus of treatment.

The emphasis on the non-pathological nature of the experience of being a custodial grandparent is a particularly important issue. The gain/loss framework has the potential to reduce rather than increase stigma, normalize the diversity of the experience including both positive and negative aspects, and may even allow for an enhanced connection between custodial grandparents and their potential counselors or service providers. In addition, the gain/loss framework is easily understood by most individuals and is often intuitively appealing, palatable, and may even bring feelings of immediate relief. Many grandparents who are caring for their grandchildren have a high level of concern about how others perceive their role as caregivers (Janicki, McCallion, Grant-Griffin, & Kolomer, 2000), often fearing that others will judge them as incapable of caring for their grandchildren. In fact, research indicates that some custodial grandparents are reluctant to seek or accept help from service organizations (Gerard, Landry-Meyer, & Roe, 2006). These individuals may doubt the value of such services, have reservations about depending on outside help, or even hold negative attitudes about relying on professional help. Custodial grandparents may feel less judged or stigmatized by a gain/loss perspective than they would by approaches that are more focused on deficits or problems (Landry-Meyer, 1999). In general, people are drawn to ways to organize their experience, particularly when it is complex, and the gain/loss framework we are presenting can serve as an organizing structure for grandparent caregivers. Through the acknowledgement of the gains and losses grandparents are experiencing, practitioners will likely find an avenue for connection. They can work to normalize both the negative and positive aspects of the transition and in the process address some of the disenfranchised aspects of the experience (Miltenberger et al., 2003–2004). For example, Yvonne was hesitant to seek services for herself, but did bring Cassandra in for treatment at the recommendation of her granddaughter's teacher. Through the course of the granddaughter's treatment, the counselor "planted seeds" with Yvonne by respectfully acknowledging the gains and losses she was clearly experiencing in connection with caring for her grandchildren. Over time, Yvonne was more open and candid with the counselor and was eventually willing to be seen for a few individual sessions, where the gains and losses she was experiencing could be explored more fully.

DEFINITIONS, ASSESSMENT, AND INTERVENTION

Prior to directly applying the gain/loss framework to the experience of custodial grandparents, we would like to offer more specifics regarding the definitions we are using of the terms loss and gain. Building upon the work done by scholars in the area of loss (e.g., Goodman et al., 2006; Harvey, 2001; Harvey & Weber, 1998; Humphrey & Zimpfer, 1996), we define loss as the state of being deprived of or failing to acquire something (e.g., relationship, object, aspect of self) to which one has been or anticipated being attached. Counterbalanced to this definition is our definition of gain as the state of acquiring or failing to be deprived of (when deprivation was expected) something to which one has been or anticipated being attached. The nuances of these definitions become even clearer when we revisit our cases. In the domain of relationships, Will and Sue are coping with losses of the present/now-absent fashion (e.g., free time with each other), whereas Yvonne is coping with losses of an expected/now-not-occurring fashion (e.g., having time to date and find a new partner). Although the nature of their losses is different, the impact is significant in both cases. Assessment using the gain/loss framework can be done through open-ended questions or through a pen and paper instrument. We conceptualize gains and losses in seven primary life domains (roles, routines, relationships, assumptions about the self, assumptions about the world, economic conditions, and psychobiological faculties). Open-ended questions related to each of these domains could be used to assess gains and losses in each. More specifically, questions such as the following can be used to assess the domains of roles, routines, and relationships, respectively: How have the expectations others have of your behavior or the roles you play in their life shifted? What aspects of your daily life do you miss and/or treasure now that are caring for your grandchildren? How have your relationships changed for the better and/or worse since you began caring for your grandchildren?

If a more expedited approach is appropriate for any number of reasons (e.g., limited contact, time constraints, group assessment), a pen and paper instrument entitled the Perceived Impact of Life Events Scale (PILES) has been developed to assess the seven domains of the gain/loss framework. The PILES contains 42 items in the seven life domains noted above and respondents are asked to rate the level of gain/loss (attributable to their life event) that they experienced with regard to each item. The left anchor of the rating scale is 7 (*gain*) and the right anchor is 1 (*loss*), with 4 indicating neither loss nor gain associated with the item. Example items in each domain include: roles—family roles, roles as productive members of society; routines—participation in activities, lifestyle; relationships—quality of friendships, feeling understood by others; assumptions about the self—control over life, life satisfaction; assumptions about the world—personal values, appreciation for life; economic conditions—financial security, income; and psychobiological faculties—sleep, energy. The items can then be averaged within each domain and practitioners can get a sense of the relative gains and losses experienced by their clients. It is quite likely that some clients will experience overall gains in some domains and losses in other domains and that some clients will experience gains in some domains where other clients will experience losses and vice versa. The PILES is not a copyrighted instrument and is available from the first author.

The assessment process connected with the gain/loss framework allows for an immediate and targeted focus for treatment. Research suggests that clients are likely to make the most progress when their treatment makes sense to them and when treatment is aligned with the client's attitudes, values, and culture (Wampold, 2000). The gain/loss assessment process fits well with the collaborative approach that is desirable when working with custodial grandparents (Dolbin-MacNab & Targ, 2003). Through active involvement in the assessment process, they are already engaged in the treatment process and buying in to the approach upon which treatment will be based.

The primary goal of treatment when using the gain/loss framework is to increase the perception of gains while decreasing the perception of losses. Therapeutic objectives associated with this primary goal include directly and concretely normalizing grandparents' unique constellation of gains/losses, capitalizing upon particular gain domains such as assumptions about the self (e.g., greater purpose in life) to enhance particular loss domain such as psychobiological faculties (e.g., physical health problems), and enhancing gain perceptions within each domain (e.g., positive relationships within support group vs. negative relationship with offspring).

The gain/loss framework is not bound to any one theoretical approach to therapy. In fact, it intersects with a number of elements of various clinical orientations. Practitioners from all perspectives are encouraged to incorporate the gain/loss framework into their ongoing work with clients. Although not inclusive, the following are examples of intersections between primary theoretical orientations and the gain/loss framework: Person-centered—importance of subjective experience, self-actualization; Gestalt—best understood through exploring the individual's interpretation, concept of polarities; and Cognitive—importance of conscious subjective experience, focus on shifting from dysfunctional to functional thought patterns (Fall, Holden, & Marquis, 2004).

GAIN/LOSS FRAMEWORK AND GRANDPARENTS RAISING THEIR GRANDCHILDREN

We will now apply the gain/loss framework to the experience of custodial grandparents and organize the existing literature based on the seven gain/loss domains. We begin with a definition of each life domain, followed by information from the literature relevant to that domain, and end with connections between each life domain and the gains and losses experienced by Yvonne and Will and Sue. It is important to note that there are likely a number of other gains and losses that custodial grandparents experience than those noted here. However, it will likely be helpful to practitioners to have some sense of what gains and losses they may hear from their clients.

Roles. Roles are sets of expectations and behaviors associated with a particular status. Overall, the literature suggests that custodial grandparents experience a good deal of "role overload and role confusion" (Hayslip & Kaminski, 2005b, p. 262) connected to the often-ambiguous circumstance of holding roles of both parent and grandparent (Landry-Meyer & Newman, 2004; Weber & Waldrop, 2000), and also connected to the vast changes in family dynamics that frequently occur (Sands & Goldberg-Glen, 2000). Some may experience the need to expand their personalities to incorporate new roles, while others experience resentment when faced with role restriction (i.e., decreased engagement in roles such as employee or church leader due to parenting responsibilities; Bullock, 2004).

Custodial grandparents take on the parental rather than solely grandparental role in the lives of their grandchildren. Many indicate a gain in the sense that they have a "second chance at parenting; they can learn from their previous experiences and improve their parenting skills" (Hayslip & Kaminski, 2005b, p. 363). Grandfathers in particular may report having played a relatively minor role in caring for their own children and indicate an appreciation for the opportunity to parent their grandchildren (Kolomer & McCallion, 2005). Custodial grandparents often view their role as keeper of familial and cultural history (Landry-Meyer & Newman, 2004), especially when they keep their grandchildren out of foster care and tangibly assist in their grandchildren's growth and development (Waldrop & Weber, 2001). Gains in the area of roles appear to be enhanced when grandparents are able to secure legal custody of their grandchildren (Landry-Meyer & Newman, 2004). Specifically, recognition of their role brings "inferred structure, a feeling of legitimacy, and a sense of control" (Landry-Meyer & Newman, 2004, p. 1016) as well as enhanced feelings of security and stability (Waldrop & Weber, 2001). In addition, gains may also be affected by culture in that African American grandparents may perceive the parent role as more expected and on time than their White counterparts (Landry-Meyer & Newman, 2004). This perspective may lend itself to a greater ease in perceiving role gains versus role losses.

With regard to role losses, custodial grandparents often experience a sense of loss associated with their inability to be traditional grandparents—who enforce fewer rules and even, at times, spoil their grandchildren (Kolomer & McCallion, 2005; Strom & Strom, 2000; Weber & Waldrop, 2000). The role losses they experience can often not be separated from the situations that led them to be in the position of caring for their grandchildren. These situations are frequently traumatic family crises (e.g., death, incarceration, drug addiction, HIV/AIDS) that lead to a sudden shift in child-care responsibilities (Bachman & Chase-Lansdale, 2005; Bullock, 2004; Essex et al., 2004). They can struggle between their role as parent to their offspring and caregiver for their grandchildren and may even feel that they are "turning on their own" (Waldrop & Weber, 2001, p. 466). Custodial grandparents are often faced with the need to give up working outside of the home, ending their societal status as an employed individual (Hayslip & Kaminski, 2005a; Smith, Beltran, Butts, & Kingson, 2000). In addition, grandparents caring for their grandchildren experience losses associated with anticipated life roles that do *not* occur, such as the empty nest phase of life (Essex et al., 2004; Landry-Meyer & Newman, 2004), and without legal custody, grandparents can experience greater levels of anxiety and obstacles related to tasks as basic as enrolling their grandchildren for school (Smith et al., 2000; Waldrop & Weber, 2001). Although African American grandparents may view their role as more on time than their White counterparts do, taking over the care of their grandchildren with "no definite end in sight" may be quite distinct from cultural experiences of the past (Essex et al., 2004, p. 4). Therefore, it is important that practitioners not underestimate the role-related losses African American custodial grandparents may experience.

In contrast to Will and Sue, Yvonne has played at least some parental role in her grandchildren's life since they were born. Sheila and her children have lived with her more than they have not. Although not an abrupt role shift, as it was for Will and Sue, Yvonne grieves the roles that she desires but has not been able to take on as midlife approaches (e.g., returning to school, becoming a leader in her church women's group), even though she also values the difference she is making in her grandchildren's lives. Will and Sue were suddenly faced with the additional role of parenting—a role that they were not expecting and one that led them to grieve over the loss of the traditional role of grandparents. However, they too see the drastic improvement in their grandson's development and how their engagement in the role of parents has contributed to his growth.

Routines. Routines are regularly occurring tasks or activities of daily life that are ordered, predictable, and familiar. The literature contains fewer references to gains and losses in the area of routines than may be expected. This is perhaps because the changes in this life domain are so clear and directly tied to shifting roles. Custodial grandparents report liking to have another person living in their homes (Bullock, 2004) and describe gains related to daily time spent with grandchildren in school, sports, and extracurricular activities (Waldrop & Weber, 2001). In contrast, they struggle with their lack of quiet time and cramped living conditions (Bullock, 2004). They also experience losses with regard to the expected end of daily parenting responsibilities such as basic supervision, assisting with homework, and ensuring proper nutrition (Landry-Meyer & Newman, 2004). In addition, hobbies and plans for travel may be set aside (Kolomer & McCallion, 2005).

Yvonne's daily routines changed the day that Cassandra was born. She secured discounted day care services for Cassandra and Leon through her church and, therefore, has been able to keep her job. However, she changed her work hours and explained to her employer that she will need to leave or miss work if one of the children is ill. Will and Sue were required to suddenly and drastically adjust their daily schedules to take on the care of their grandson (e.g., arranging for day care, relearning how to potty train a child). They struggle between their commitment to his care and the frequent compromises they make with regard to their business.

Relationships. Relationships are dialectical connections between two or more persons that vary with regard to depth, emotionality, dependency, and level of interaction. Custodial grandparents appreciate the relationship gains they experience through the close bond they build with their grandchildren (Hayslip & Kaminski, 2005b). These gains include "feeling appreciated and loved, having companionship, sharing mutually enjoyable activities, and experiencing the sheer pleasure that children can bring" (Essex et al., 2004, p. 6).

Along with these gains in their relationships with their grandchildren, custodial grandparents also perceive relationship losses with regard to their adult offspring and their friends, peers, and spouses. Conflict, strain, and power struggles in the grandparent–adult child relationship are positively associated with perceived stress for custodial grandparents (Sands & Goldberg-Glen, 2000). These difficult relationships can be marked by blame, hostility, and unpredictable behavior on the part of adult offspring and can even include incidents involving criminal behavior, such as stealing from the grandparents (Weber & Waldrop, 2000). In general, grandparents raising their grandchildren have fewer and lower quality relationships than their peers who are not raising grandchildren (Solomon & Marx, 2000). They are often socially isolated from their peers and friends (Hayslip & Kaminski, 2005b; Smith et al., 2000) who are not experiencing similar circumstances (Bullock, 2004; Essex et al., 2004; Strom & Strom, 2000). Some custodial grandparents report having lost friendships after bringing their grandchildren to social events (Giarrusso, Feng, Silverstein, & Marenco, 2000). As compared to their noncustodial peers, grandparents raising their grandchildren do not receive as much emotional support from friends and family members (Emick & Hayslip, 1999; Robinson, Kropf, & Meyers, 2000; Solomon & Marx, 2000). In addition, raising grandchildren can also strain grandparents' marital relationships (Hayslip & Kaminski, 2005a).

Both Yvonne and Sue have conflicts with their adult offspring. These conflicts are difficult in both cases, and these women share the struggle of caring for the well-being of their adult children (e.g., providing money, connecting them to services) while prioritizing the needs of their grandchildren. For Will and Sue, the primary purpose for seeking services was to address the conflicts in their own relationship that have arisen since they became custodial grandparents. Yvonne is thankful for the support group she has found within her church, but Sue feels quite isolated in her experience, even from her husband. However, all three of these grandparents freely discuss the joys they experience in their close relationships with their grandchildren.

Assumptions about the self. Assumptions about the self are an individual's subjective beliefs and views of his or her personal identity. Research suggests that grandparents who raise their grandchildren may experience gains in their sense of self-worth, self-esteem, competence, achievement, self-rated performance, morale, life satisfaction, and control over the future (Dellman-Jenkins et al., 2002; Essex et al., 2004; Giarrusso et al., 2000; Waldrop & Weber, 2001; Weber & Waldrop, 2000). They may perceive the experience as an opportunity to engage and utilize the wisdom and knowledge they have acquired (Essex et al., 2004); moreover, instilling a sense of culture and family history in their grandchildren may strengthen their identity. Related to self-losses, Strom and Strom (2000) found that custodial grandparents who were not open to revising their personal goals (as is likely necessary when entering the caregiving role) were more likely to perceive a loss of their freedom associated with becoming custodial grandparents. The self-related losses that custodial grandparents experience may also be closely connected with their relationship with their adult offspring. More specifically, custodial grandparents whose adult children reported addictive or legal problems scored lower on "positive affect, self-esteem, best possible life, and self-rated performance as a grandparent than caregiving grandparents who do not cite this type of primary stressor" (pp. 302–303, Giarrusso et al.).

Will and Sue found it difficult to perceive gains in the area of assumptions about the self. They had such a firm grasp on who they were as individuals and as a couple prior to taking on the caregiving role for Austin that they had trouble revising these assumptions. They also questioned their abilities to be good parents. In contrast, Yvonne was barely out of the parental role when she became a caregiver for her grandchildren, and her sense of self was and is more aligned with caring for her extended family. Yvonne felt enhanced in the area of assumptions about the self in that she gained a sense of competence and self-esteem through her caregiving responsibilities.

Assumptions about the world. Assumptions about the world are an individual's subjective beliefs and views of how the world operates and what can be expected based on such modes of operation. Research suggests that taking on a caretaking role for grandchildren can enhance grandparents' purpose and meaning in life (Essex et al., 2004; Hayslip & Kaminski, 2005b; Kolomer & McCallion, 2005). Some may believe that they are enacting their love for their adult offspring by caring for their grandchildren (Baird, John, & Hayslip, 2000), while others may be driven by their desire to contribute to the continuity of their family identity (Hayslip & Kaminski, 2005b). Custodial grandparents may also exhibit increases in hope for the future, love and companionship, and high levels of satisfaction related to their experience of helping others (Kolomer & McCallion, 2005).

The losses grandparents experience in the area of assumptions about the world are frequently connected with their attempts to make sense of the family crises that led them to take on the caregiver role for their grandchildren. As parents, custodial grandparents commonly face harsh realities related to their adult child's death, mental or physical illness (including substance dependence), or undesirable behavior (including illegal or criminal activities; Bachman & Chase-Lansdale, 2005). Facing such realities can lead them to question existing assumptions about a benevolent, just, and meaningful world.

Custodial grandparents may also experience challenges and losses associated with seeking anticipated support for themselves and their grandchildren. Societal expectations for grandparents are not aligned with the experience of custodial grandparents (Landry-Meyer & Newman, 2004), which means that anticipated support is often not available. Grandparents who received government assistance while raising their own children may not be eligible for such support when faced with the prospect of raising their grandchildren (Smith et al., 2000). In addition, if they do qualify for government assistance, such benefits are often limited in time or conditionally based on the grandparent working outside of the home.

Much as with assumptions about the self, Yvonne perceived many gains in the area of assumptions about the world. In connection with her strong faith, she viewed her care for her grandchildren as part of her personal ministry to her family and to the world. However, she did seek support from her friends at church when she, at times, questioned God's plan for her family. She also felt discouraged about receiving relatively less government assistance for parenting her two grandchildren than she had received for parenting Sheila. Will and Sue lost much with regard to assumptions about the world. They had their future planned and all of those plans were changed when Austin came to live in their home. Will and Sue were no longer in a position to retire and in many ways felt cheated by a world that they now viewed as unfair, unpredictable, and chaotic. They had a difficult time reconnecting on a shared vision for their future, and Sue had difficulty reconciling what she perceived as the world's expectations of her as a mother to her adult child and as a custodial grandmother to her grandson.

Economic conditions. Economic conditions are aspects of an individual's actual or perceived financial situation. The literature does not indicate any clear economic gains for custodial grandparents, although some type of governmental support may be commonly received (Roe et al., 1996). Instead, financial difficulties and strains are commonly reported by grandparents who are raising their grandchildren (Bullock, 2004; Dellman-Jenkins et al., 2002; Kolomer & McCallion, 2005; Roe, Minkler, Saunders, & Thomson, 1996). Waldrop and Weber (2001) found that custody battles and legal fees contributed to these difficulties for 22% of their sample, while paying for an adult offspring's living expenses was the cause in 24% of cases. It is important to keep in mind, however, that many grandparents were living in poverty prior to taking on caretaking responsibilities for their grandchildren (Essex et al., 2004; Sands & Goldberg-Glen, 2000; Smith et al., 2000).

Yvonne's financial situation actually improved during times when Sheila, her adult child, was not in the home. When Sheila was attempting to care for the children, Yvonne was often in a position of trying to pay for two households, as Sheila was not able to maintain employment. When Sheila was out of touch with the family, she was actually unreachable and, therefore, did not request financial assistance from Yvonne. Finances were not a key area of loss or gain for Will and Sue as custodial grandparents, but it was an issue that they discussed in relationship to Sue's son, who like Sheila struggled with keeping a job. They eventually decided to stop providing him with financial assistance, which was an excruciating decision for Sue, but one she realized the couple needed to make. Sue eventually came to believe that their monetary support of Sam was actually fostering his irresponsibility.

Psychobiological faculties. Psychological and biological faculties are an individual's mental, emotional, and physiological functions or states of being. Although research suggests caring for grandchildren does not negatively affect the health of all grandparents (Bachman & Chase-Lansdale, 2005; Giarrusso et al., 2000; Robinson et al., 2000; Roe et al., 1996; Waldrop & Weber, 2001), it appears that most grandparents are at risk for losses related to physical and mental health including depression, fatigue, and chronic conditions (Dellman-Jenkins et al., 2002; Essex et al., 2004; Hayslip & Kaminski, 2005b; Kolomer & McCallion, 2005; Solomon & Marx, 2000; Waldrop & Weber, 2001). It may be easier for some custodial grandparents to deny their own health problems when their singular focus is on their grandchildren (Bullock, 2004; Strom & Strom, 2000). Other custodial grandparents may try to hide their health problems out of a fear of losing custody of their grandchildren if their failing health is discovered (Kolomer & McCallion, 2005). The physical and emotional health of caregiving grandparents has been found to be negatively associated with an adult child's drug addiction (Giarrusso et al., 2000; Solomon & Marx, 2000), problematic functioning of the grandchildren (Hayslip et al., 1998), unemployment, single status, and lack of government assistance (Bachman & Chase-Lansdale, 2005). In addition, the health of custodial grandparents is positively associated with educational attainment, social support, and age (Bachman & Chase-Lansdale, 2005).

As noted earlier, Yvonne was not mindful of her own emotional and physical needs. She was slow to warm to the idea of focusing on her own well-being, but was more open to the idea when it was presented as needing to care for herself in order to provide the best care for her grandchildren. Through the course of counseling, she attended a local free clinic for a checkup, where she was diagnosed with high blood pressure, placed on medication, and soon experienced improvement in her daily energy level. Will and Sue were relatively healthy. They had health insurance through their work and were fortunate to have had consistent access to quality health care throughout their lives. They did both experience somatic complaints (e.g., headaches, stomachaches), but these appeared to decrease as their relationship improved.

CONCLUSION

The gain/loss framework for conceptualizing life events offers a practical means through which to assess and intervene with grandparents who are raising their grandchildren. It is flexible in that it can be integrated into a variety of theoretical orientations. The framework allows for recognition of the complexity and uniqueness of this life transition and it offers a non-pathological approach to discussing a wide range of feelings and events with grandparents who are raising their grandchildren.

REFERENCES

Bachman, H. J., & Chase-Lansdale, P. L. (2005). Custodial grandmothers' physical, mental, and economic well-being: Comparisons of primary caregivers from low-income neighborhoods. *Family Relations, 54,* 475–487.

Baird, A., John, R., & Hayslip, B. (2000). Custodial grandparenting among African Americans: A focus group perspective. In B. Hayslip & R. Goldberg-Glen (Eds.), *Grandparents raising grandchildren: Theoretical, empirical, and clinical perspectives* (pp. 125–144). New York: Springer.

Baltes, P. B. (1997). On the incomplete architecture of human ontogeny. *American Psychologist, 52,* 366–379.

Bullock, K. (2004). The changing role of grandparents in rural families: The results of an exploratory study in southeastern North Carolina. *Families in Society, 85*(1), 45–54.

Cook, A., & Oltjenbruns, K. (1998). *Dying and grieving: Life-span and family perspectives.* New York: Holt, Reinhart, & Winston.

Dellman-Jenkins, M., Blankemeyer, M., & Olesh, M. (2002). Adults in expanded grandparent roles: Considerations for practice, policy, and research. *Educational Gerontology, 28,* 219–235.

Dolbin-MacNab, M. L., & Targ, D. B. (2003). Grandparents raising grandchildren: Guidelines for family life educators and other family professionals. In B. Hayslip, Jr., & J. H. Patrick (Eds.), *Working with grandparents: Guidelines for family educators and professionals* (pp. 213–228). New York: Springer.

Emick, M. A., & Hayslip, B., Jr. (1999). Custodial grandparenting: Stresses, coping skills, and relationships with grandchildren. *International Journal of Aging and Human Development, 48*(1), 35–61.

Essex, E. L., Newsome, W. S., & Moses, H. (2004). Caring for grandparent-headed families: Challenges and opportunities for school social workers. *School Social Work Journal, 28*(2), 1–19.

Fall, K. A., Holden, J. M., & Marquis, A. (2004). *Theoretical models of counseling and psychotherapy.* New York: Brunner-Routlege.

Fuller-Thomson, W., Minkler, M., & Driver, D. (1997). A profile of grandparents raising grandchildren in the United States. *The Gerontologist 37*(3), 406–411.

Gerard, J. M., Landry-Meyer, L., & Roe, J. G. (2006). Grandparents raising grandchildren: The role of social support in coping with caregiving challenges. *International Journal on Aging and Human Development, 62*(4), 359–383.

Giarrusso, R., Feng, D., Silverstein, M., & Marenco, A. (2000). Primary and secondary stressors of grandparents raising grandchildren: Evidence from a national survey. *Journal of Mental Health and Aging, 6*(4), 291–383.

Goodman, J., Schlossberg, N. K., & Anderson, M. L. (2006). *Counseling adults in transition: Linking practice with theory.* New York: Springer.

Harvey, J. H. (2001). The psychology of loss as a lens to a positive psychology. *American Behavioral Scientist, 44,* 838–853.

Harvey, J. H., & Weber, A. L. (1998). There must be a psychology of loss. In J. H. Harvey (Ed.), *Perspective on loss: A sourcebook* (pp. 319–329). New York: Routledge.

Hayslip, B., Jr., Emick, M. A., Henderson, C. E., & Elias, K. (2002). Temporal variations in the experience of custodial grandparenting: A short-term longitudinal study. *The Journal of Applied Gerontology, 21*(2), 139–156.

Hayslip, B., Jr., & Kaminski, P. L. (2005a). Grandparents raising their grandchildren. *The Hayworth Press, Inc., 37,* 147–169.

Hayslip, B., Jr., & Kaminski, P. L. (2005b). Grandparents raising their grandchildren: A review of the literature and suggestions for practice. *The Gerontologist, 45*(2), 262–269.

Hayslip, B., Jr., Shore, R. J., Henderson, C. E., & Lambert, P. L. (1998). Custodial grandparenting and the impact of grandchildren with problems on role satisfaction and role meaning. *Journal of Gerontology: Social Sciences, 53*(3), 164–173.

Humphrey, G. M., & Zimpfer, D. G. (1996). *Counselling for grief and bereavement.* London: Sage.

Janicki, M. P., McCallion, P., Grant-Griffin, L., & Kolomer, S. R. (2000). Grandparent Caregivers I: Characteristics of the grandparents and the children with disabilities for whom they care. *The Hayworth Press, Inc., 33*(3), 35–55.

Kolomer, S. R., & McCallion, P. (2005). Depression and caregiver mastery in grandfathers caring for their grandchildren. *International Journal of Aging and Human Development, 60*(4), 283–294.

Landry-Meyer, L. (1999). Research into action: Recommended intervention strategies for grandparent caregivers. *Family Relations, 48*(4), 381–389.

Landry-Meyer, L., & Newman, B. M. (2004). An exploration of the grandparent caregiver role. *Journal of Family Issues, 25*(8), 1005–1025.

Lazarus, R. S., & Folkman, S. (1984). *Stress, appraisal, and coping.* New York: Springer.

Lever, K., & Wilson, J. J. (2005). Encore parenting: When grandparents fill the role of primary caregiver. *The Family Journal: Counseling and Therapy for Couples and Families, 13*(2), 167–171.

Miltenberger, P. B., Hayslip, B., Jr., Harris, B., & Kaminski, P. L. (2003–2004). Perceptions of the losses experienced by custodial grandmothers. *Omega, 48*(3), 245–261.

Pinson-Milburn, N. M., Fabian, E. S., Schlossberg, N. K., & Pyle, M. (1996). Grandparents raising grandchildren. *Journal of Counseling & Development, 74,* 548–554.

Robinson, M. M., Kropf, N. P., & Myers, L. L. (2000). Grandparents raising grandchildren in rural communities. *Journal of Mental Health and Aging, 6*(4), 353–365.

Roe, K. M., Minkler, M., Saunders, F., & Thomson, G. E. (1996). Health of grand-mothers raising children of the crack cocaine epidemic. *Medical Care, 34*(11), 1072–1084.

Sands, R. G., & Goldberg-Glen, R. S. (2000). Grandparent caregivers' perception of the stress of surrogate parenting. *Journal of Social Service research, 26*(3), 77–95.

Sands, R. G., Goldberg-Glen, R., & Thornton, P. L. (2005). Factors associated with the positive well-being of grandparents caring for their grandchildren. *Journal of Gerontological Social Work, 45*(4), 65–82.

Schlossberg, N. K., Waters, E. B., & Goodman, J. (1995). *Counseling adults in transition: Linking practice with theory.* New York: Springer.

Smith, C. J., Beltran, A., Butts, D. M., & Kingson, E. R. (2000). Grandparents raising grandchildren: Emerging program and policy issues for the 21st century. *Journal of Gerontological Social Work, 34*(1), 81–94.

Solomon, J. C., & Marx, J. (2000). The physical, mental, and social health of custo-dial grandparents. In B. Hayslip & R. Goldberg-Glen (Eds.), *Grandparents raising grandchildren: Theoretical, empirical, and clinic al perspectives* (pp. 183–206). New York: Springer.

Strom, R. D., & Strom, S. K. (2000). Meeting the challenge of raising grandchildren. *International Journal of Aging and Human Development, 51*(3), 183–198.

Waldrop, D. P., & Weber, J. A. (2001). From grandparent to caregiver: The stress and satisfaction of raising grandchildren. *Families in Society: The Journal of Contempo-rary Human Services, 82*(5), 461–472.

Wallace, G. (2001). Grandparent caregivers: Emerging issues in elder law and social work practice. *Journal of Gerontological Social Work, 34*(3), 127–136.

Wampold, B. E. (2000). Outcomes of individual counseling and psychotherapy: Em-pirical evidence addressing two fundamental questions. In S. D. Brown & R. W. Lent (Eds.), *Handbook of counseling psychology* (pp. 711–739). New York: Wiley.

Weber, J. A., & Waldrop, D. P. (2000). Grandparents raising grandchildren: Families in transition. *Journal of Gerontological Social Work, 33*(2), 27–46.

CHAPTER 13

Counseling Grandparents Parenting Their Children's Children: Case Studies

Robert J. Maiden and Craig Zuckerman

People in the United States today live longer than at any other time in our history, which has produced a new phenomenon—the emergence of three- and four-generational families (Denham & Smith, 1989). At the turn of the twentieth century, people lived to be approximately 47 years old. Today, at the turn of the twenty-first century, people live to be approximately 78 years old and their life expectancy continues to increase steadily each year. Thus, grandparents are available to enjoy time with their grandchildren in greater numbers for longer periods than ever before in history (Aldous, 1995; Barranti-Ramirez, 1985; Glass & Huneycutt, 2002; Uhlenberg, 1996). Most grandparents are younger than age 70, with nearly half of all grandparents under age 60 (Aldous, 1995).

Source of protection. These grandparents often form a safety net that when called upon acts as the family "watchdog," "safety shield," or "second line of defense" (Jendrek, 1993; Minkler, Roe, & Price, 1992; Tinsley & Parke, 1984; Troll, 1985). As their children encounter devastating problems in their personal lives and are unable to parent their children, grandparents have increasingly taken on the challenge of surrogate parenting either for the short or long term. They provide resources such as emotional support, financial assistance, stability, and shelter for their grandchildren, as well as provide assistance for their adult children (Ghuman, Weist, & Shafer, 1999).

The impulse to protect. The grandparents assume that they can ameliorate the negative impact of family crises when they consent to parent their grandchildren. Johnson (1998) also reports that "most grandparents rise to the occasion" (p. 186) to extend assistance to their children and grandchildren during times of crisis, but they prefer these periods to be short lived. However, grandparents become more resistant and ambivalent when they are forced to provide surrogate parenting for longer periods.

The reality of long-term custodianship. Yet, despite their hesitation, many grandparents assist their adult children for longer periods than anticipated. For example, Minkler, Fuller-Thomson, Miller, and Driver (1997) discovered that as many as 10% of all grandparents acted as surrogate parents for their grandchildren for a period of 2 years or more. In many cases, these children have a plethora of mental health problems often related to, if not directly caused by, their own parents' difficulties. These interconnected mental health problems place tremendous stress on the mutigenerational family (Glass & Huneycutt, 2002; Hayslip, Shore, Henderson, & Lambert, 1998). To cope with family and intergenerational stressors, the grandparents, their adult children (if they are available), and their grandchildren often require extensive or prolonged intensive psychotherapy (Glass & Huneycutt, 2002). Yet there is scant published research or information about how to counsel these families (O'Reilly & Morrison, 1993).

Goals of this chapter. Thus, the purpose of this chapter is to provide guidelines on how to counsel multigenerational families. In this process, we examine specific case histories to illustrate how mental health specialists can work with multigenerational families in achieving effective solutions and symptom relief. Moreover, we explore the impact of grandparents as surrogate parents on the quality of mental health and level of stress that these families experience and offer specific suggestions to reduce intergenerational conflict and to promote increased well-being and life satisfaction for both the grandchild and grandparent. Our guidelines suggest an integrative counseling approach utilizing different counseling techniques depending upon the phase of counseling or the specific situation, although a family systems approach, we believe, is most desirable (Elgar, McGrath, Waschbusch, Stewart, & Curtis, 2004; Goodman, 2003). Through our case studies, we will illustrate the basic rules, the best practices, and sine qua non in understanding how to counsel families in which grandparents are raising their grandchildren. This practical hands-on information is acutely needed by mental health professionals today as they are increasingly being called upon by the family court system, child protective services, other social service agencies, and the grandparents themselves to provide evaluation, assessment, and counseling to such families (Hayslip et al., 1998; Ooms, 1990).

In the presentation of our case studies, we are mindful that psychotherapy ultimately remains an art. As such, an ongoing interactive and dynamic dialogue among the therapist, the patients, and the unique circumstances that lace each particular family system provides the basis for one's psychotherapeutic approach. Despite the uniqueness each case study brings, there are broad commonalities that relate to most multigenerational families. Yet, this chapter ultimately does not pretend to impart a "cookbook" or how-to representation, but rather offers general principles and the basic steps employed in practicing psychotherapy with extremely complex and often dysfunctional multigenerational families.

Therapeutic intervention: family systems approach. In terms of selecting an overall psychotherapeutic strategy, family systems therapy seems the most appropriate, since we are dealing with family units rather than individual clients (Weber & Waldrop, 2000). Family systems theory has several therapeutic assumptions that we need to be aware of (Hackney & Cormier, 2005). One assumption is that the therapists must deal with the system as a whole and that any change in the properties of any part or subunit of the system changes the properties of the entire system. Families have rules that define acceptable and unacceptable behavior. Sometimes these rules are open and clear to all family members; sometimes these rules are hidden and below the conscious awareness of the members of a particular family. Some families maintain rigid and closed boundaries, and contrastingly some families have few or wide-open boundaries. Family therapists generally view changes as positive because any change in the system creates a disequilibrium, which ripples through the entire structure, creating a new configuration based on a new equilibrium (Okum & Rappaport, 1980).

Communication problems. One of the main axioms within the family systems approach is that dysfunctional families must change their style of communication with one another. It is critical for grandparents and their adult children to communicate honestly, openly, and positively with each other.

One of the most common communication problems found in dysfunctional multigenerational families is the tendency for the grandparent or the adult child to say belittling remarks about the other. This is particularly a problem when they put down the other person in front of the grandchildren (Clarke, Preston, Raksin, & Bengtson, 1999; Glass & Huneycutt, 2002; Weber & Waldrop, 2000). These comments may be well intended and even accurate, but the therapist should inform the offending person that they are inappropriate because these negative comments alienate the child's love for his parent or grandparent.

For example, a grandparent might say, in a negative and belittling tone, that the grandchildren "all have their mother's personality." Alternatively, they might say, regarding an adult son's situation because of his wife's behavior, "I warned him many times not to marry her." These comments are hurtful even when the offending party states them in a subtle and indirect manner. Comments spoken in front of the children that are more directly inappropriate are of the following type: "She drinks all the time and has men over at all hours of the night and lets him [the grandchild] do whatever he wants unsupervised." Therapists should not let these comments go by unchallenged. They should immediately convey to the client, if possible, that these comments are intolerable (no matter how accurate they might be).

Sometimes grandparents stubbornly maintain their right to speak their mind truthfully. They say, in effect, "I refuse to lie to my grandchild." The best practice here is to separate the grandparent from the child so one can explore this issue outside of the child's hearing, to avoid further alienating the child or embarrassing the grandparent. For the most part, we as family therapists try to be supportive of the grandparents and their authority when the child is in the room.

Therapists can concomitantly treat these communication conflicts multidimensionally, as they often cut across several communication levels (Clarke et al., 1999). For example, grandparents and their adult children tend to blame each other for their negative communication. In effect, they believe they are in the right and the other person is in the wrong. Therefore, it is important for the clinician, when reviewing a communication dialogue between the dyad of the grandparent and the adult child, to direct the reporting person to describe in their account the specific words and context of the recalled event (Fraenkel & Markham, 2003). Frequently, one discovers that, for example, the grandparent said something judgmental about the lifestyle of the adult child, sparking an angry retort, which frequently degenerates into open warfare as underlying power conflicts or hidden agendas become exposed, and each person tries to one-up the other (Weber & Waldrop, 2000). For example, the grandmother may complain that her daughter is rude and obnoxious. Yet, when the therapist asks exactly what the grandmother said to her daughter, aloud word for word, the grandmother oftentimes will hear for the first time the harshness of her statement or its metamessage. Thus, the negative connotation of one's communication pattern, in this case that of the grandmother, becomes clearer as the interpersonal communication dialogue is unpacked and scrutinized word by word. Grandparents and adult children must learn the skill of conveying critical comments, if they need to say them at all, in a more diplomatic or softer style. They ought to make a conscious effort not to communicate negative feelings toward each other (Weber & Waldrop, 2000) for the sake of the grandchildren and the integrity of the family.

The clinician may desire to "normalize" the negative communication (in effect, taking the sting out of the admonishments) by informing the family members that "conflict seems to be both pervasive and a natural part of family interactions" (Clarke et al., 1999, p. 269). Nevertheless, clinicians must be mindful that the key therapeutic intervention here is not to reframe, but to encourage the grandparent or adult child to acknowledge and change the way their own faulty communication style contributes to the family conflict. Helping family members attain these sorts of insights about their communication style is very challenging, as family systems (even more so when they are patently dysfunctional) persistently and stubbornly resist change (Nichols & Schwartz, 1995).

Yet, on the positive side of the ledger, there is a counterforce that motivates change: Most, if not all, grandparents and their adult children (underneath it all) love one another (Goldenberg & Goldenberg, 1985) and desire to be on good terms. The adroit therapist can build on this underlying force to encourage positive shifts in attitudes and behaviors. Nonetheless, managing the ambivalence, surface bitterness, and conflictual communication among family members renders multigenerational counseling extremely demanding, daunting, and exhausting.

The therapist's initial questions and assumptions. In engaging in multigenerational counseling, a therapist is faced with some initial questions such as: Who is the real client? What is my role? To whom do I owe my allegiance? How do I handle confidentiality? How do I extricate the presumed triangulated child? What steps should my plan of action or agenda entail? In psychotherapy, practitioners have few, if any, fixed fundamental assumptions, guidelines, or agendas. Generally, there are only a few rules of thumb available to the clinician when practicing the art of psychotherapy.

Be that as it may, the therapist's primary objectives are to act in the best interest of the child and do no harm. Thus, the first items on our therapeutic agenda are to identify the presenting problems and secure the safety of the child (Hackney & Cormier, 2005; Ooms, 1990). Next, we focus on preserving the family unit (Ooms, 1990). To accomplish these goals we need to develop good rapport and trust with the family members. In line with this, we ask the grandparent, when they are the custodial parent, to allow us to maintain the confidentiality of the child. Yet, we caution the grandparent that we will breach the child's confidentiality if, for example, we become aware of any dangerous activity the grandchild might be engaged in, such as illegal drug use, suicidal ideation, or self-harm behaviors. We will first try to discuss these issues with the grandchild in an attempt to secure his or her permission to discuss our concerns with their surrogate parent or to mention something that we think is important on behalf of the grandchild to the grandparent.

An illustrative case history. Below is a multilayered and complex case history in which the solutions are difficult, if not seemingly out of reach. The family is very dysfunctional and appears to have much more going against it than for it. This case involves a paternal grandmother who has temporary custody of her grandchild.

The grandmother referred Jim, a 15-year-old tall, dark, and lanky but well-built adolescent, for counseling. Social services had removed Jim along with his four siblings (two of whom were the products of the mother and her husbands at the time, while the other three were the products of her affairs with different men) from their mother's residence because she and her current husband (her fourth) engaged in a violent and drunken brawl in the presence of their children. In the fray, Jim's stepfather brutally broke his wife's jaw. Someone called the police. The police contacted Child Protective Services (CPS). CPS ordered the stepfather out of the home and offered Jim's mother the option of keeping her children upon the condition she did not allow her husband to return to the house. Despite CPS's order, the mother allowed her husband back into the home. When CPS discovered what she had done, it removed the children and placed them with their paternal grandparents. (In each case, the grandmother had remarried. Thus, all the grandfathers were step-grandparents.) CPS did not place Jim with his maternal grandmother because she was currently serving time in another state for the possession and sale of drugs. At first, Jim saw his mother along with his four siblings for supervised visitation for a few hours every Saturday. However, these visitations came to an abrupt halt when the police arrested his mother for stealing a doctor's prescription pad and prescribing herself OxyContin—a very strong painkiller. Actually, she had prescribed the painkiller for her husband, who was addicted to it. When confronted by the police, the mother first denied she had purchased the drugs, but the police produced a videotape showing her picking up the prescription at the pharmacy. The judge, at the request of the county's district attorney, remanded her to the county jail for trial. Jim was devastated and withdrew deeper into himself. Jim believed everything his mother had told him when she said she was innocent of the charges. He was depressed, oppositional, resented his grandmother very much, and oddly blamed her for his plight. He believed that he would betray his mother if he cooperated or even offhandedly communicated with anyone whom he saw as thwarting his chances of returning home to his mother.

Because of Jim's depression, anger, and low grades in school, the grandmother, a rugged, well-scrubbed woman whose appearance belied her basic gentleness, brought him in for counseling. When I (Robert, first co-author) initially saw this family, I was overwhelmed by its complexity and the degree of its dysfunction, and, momentarily, I was flummoxed as to what to do. (Nevertheless, I told myself that I along with this family would resolve the issues successfully. I just needed to roll up my sleeves, be confident, and utilize my clinical knowledge and experience.) One of my first objectives was to stabilize this family, which was currently in a crisis. To assist this goal, I focused on developing rapport and trust with the grandson and his grandmother, which are the quintessential elements of a successful outcome in therapy (Hackney & Cormier, 2005). I met with them together first, then, to give them the opportunity to speak more openly and freely with me, I met with them individually (I contracted with the grandmother so that I can maintain Jim's confidentiality). In my counseling sessions with Jim, I affirmed the grandparent's home as a safe harbor. Since I implemented a systems approach, I was aware that even small changes in the family system could lead to major changes in the identified patient and other family members over the long run. My therapeutic objectives, beyond stabilization and rapport, were to promote family harmony, decrease Jim's depression and anger, increase Jim's engagement in the family, and promote Jim's well-being and life satisfaction.

In the next phase of therapy, I considered the following question: What behaviors or attitudes were interfering with or hindering the attainment of the therapeutic objectives of stability and a more harmonious relationship between Jim and his grandmother? One problem stood out: that although the grandmother was on board with the plan, Jim was not. He was very resistant to and distant from his grandmother and distrusted most adults in authority positions, especially me, since I was associated with the system that stole him away from his mother. On the other hand, he discerned that I was a caring and objective psychologist. I was someone (perhaps the only one) to whom he could talk about his misery and anger about his separation from his mother. Jim, at first testing the waters, tentatively and gingerly spoke to me about his feelings.

As is not unusual in these cases, Jim was performing poorly in his schoolwork. Thus, I also focused on improving Jim's academic performance at the school district where his grandmother lived. I considered conducting an assessment on Jim to evaluate his level of cognitive ability and academic skills, which I usually do in cases of academic difficulty. However, given the tenuousness of our relationship and his suspicions regarding counseling with me, I decided to forestall testing for a while, as he might find it threatening, and continued to target developing rapport and attacking Jim's most pressing problem—acclimating to his grandmother's home and accepting her authority over him. In the interim, I advised the grandmother how to target Jim's schoolwork and get him to do his homework without becoming an ogre in his eyes. At the same time, I addressed with Jim in our individual sessions how to change his academic attitude and habits to improve his grades. In addition, I met with Jim and his grandmother jointly to gently reinforce and validate any positive gains toward our therapeutic objectives of stabilization, concord, and improved academic performance.

As our interventions took hold Jim's grades improved, but he continued to be somewhat oppositional, withdrawn, and untrusting. As I noted from the very beginning of our sessions, Jim displayed some, albeit reluctant, willingness to disclose to me his feelings concerning the most stressful issues on his mind. This was positive. On the negative side, he would mumble only a few words and cut our conversation short, and his self-disclosures were quite limited. Yet, these disclosures epitomized the beginning of a trusting relationship. In my therapeutic sessions with Jim, I stayed far away from his traumatic issues surrounding his separation from his mother, as they were too threatening and he was not ready to discuss them. Forcing the issue would have only risked irreparably rupturing our nascent therapeutic relationship. Yet, Jim continued to maintain his psychological distance from me, although he continued to vent his feelings of anger and emotional unrest to a limited degree.

Reaching out to the extended family. Looking for other avenues of help, as my interventions were only minimally taking hold, I reached out into Jim's extensive family system. Aware that Jim trusted and respected his natural grandfather who lives in Florida and who communicated with him occasionally by phone, I urged his grandmother to contact Jim's grandfather and ask him to call his grandchild. I directed that in his phone call, the grandfather should be supportive, but also should encourage Jim to respect his grandmother and to make the best of his current situation. I also reached out to another member of the family: the child's father. He frequently visited his mother, but because of his work (he traveled extensively during the week as a laborer digging ditches to put gas pipelines into the ground) he saw his son only briefly on the weekends. I invited him to come to one of Jim's counseling sessions. When he came to our counseling session, I directed him to spend more time with Jim (who was lonely and sorely missed his mother). Although I realized that, for Jim, his natural father could not replace his mother, his spending quality time with Jim would aid in diminishing Jim's feelings of isolation and abandonment. In addition, the ability to spend time with his father may induce Jim to feel better about living with his grandmother, as getting to spend time with his father was one of the perks of living with her. I recognize that these interventions represented baby steps, yet they transpired to important behavioral changes. For example, Jim's attitude improved; he became less angry and hostile and began to feel comfortable living under his grandmother's roof.

To add to the above advancements, another event occurred. Jim's mother decided to tell Jim the truth about why she was incarcerated. This admission went a long way to moderating Jim's anger toward his paternal grandmother, who he had irrationally blamed for all his and his immediate family's hardships. This admission on the part of Jim's mother freed Jim from the previously unacknowledged family rule: his mother could do no wrong. We clearly made gains in our therapy, and I became more confident in Jim's long-term prognosis.

Implementing behavioral strategies. As in the above case, assisting the grandchild to perform well academically is challenging and like the proverbial pulling of teeth. Many such grandchildren have difficulty concentrating and paying attention in school and elsewhere and may be suffering from a form of Attention Deficit Disorder. These children strongly resist doing their homework assignments (and if they complete their homework, they fail to turn it in!). The teacher, frustrated with the child's behavior, often only wants the child medicated. The grandparents, also frustrated, are at a loss as to how to get their grandchild to behave at home or at school. In some cases, the grandparents in desperation use overly punitive measures, or, alternatively, may become overly indulgent and lenient.

The Premack principle. Consequently, practitioners must teach grandparents how to employ behavioral interventions that successfully reward the child for his or her good behavior. One technique that we find very useful in this regard is Premack's (1959) principle. Premack defines his principle by the following rule: any behavior or activity emitted by a child is reinforced by a behavior or activity that occurs more frequently in the child's repertoire. We find that most grandparents are generally well intentioned and believe they are practicing solid behavioral techniques when they take away toys, the computer, TV, or playtime to punish the grandchild for failing to do what the grandparents want the grandchild to do. Grandparents soon find that they have run out things to take away from their grandchild, yet the child is still misbehaving and is worse than ever. They throw up their hands in frustration and exclaim loudly that punishing (and rewarding) the child doesn't work!

In these situations, we suggest to the grandparents that they implement the Premack principle. For example, we might suggest they can increase a specific activity of their grandchild, such as getting dressed for school, without going through a war, by making his behavior contingent on another more frequently occurring behavior or activity such as eating breakfast or getting on the school bus. One of the benefits of Premack's principle is that it matters little whether the reinforcing activity (such as getting on the boring bus) is undesirable to the grandchild. The activity simply must occur more frequently to reinforce the targeted behavior. Moreover, we encourage grandparents to reverse the direction of conditioning their grandchild: Instead of punishing their grandchild by taking away objects and toys, we direct them to structure the context so that the desired behavior is contingent upon the reward (Premack, 1962). For example, we suggest that they make their grandchild's request to go to the movies, to play a video game, or simply to go outside contingent upon cleaning up the bedroom, or doing the dishes, or completing their homework. We recommend that the grandparent divide the task into small graduated steps such as setting the table, removing plates from the table, putting the dishes in the dishwasher, and so on. We find that generally the grandchild is not up to the task of doing all the dishes or cleaning up an entire bedroom. Requiring the grandchild to bite off more than he or she can chew ultimately defeats the purpose. Of course, these techniques do not work 100% of the time, but they are effective if applied conscientiously and consistently.

The inclusion of all family members. In treating the family system, the clinician should try to interview everyone that is active in the family, especially the surrogate parent's partner, to assess their possible role in parenting the grandchild even if the person appears to be uninvolved, such as the step-grandparent (generally a male).

Clinicians who do not assess the parenting role of the noncustodial step-grandparent do so at their peril. For example, I was interviewing a step-grandfather when he talked about his grandson's misdeeds and he voiced his concern that his significant other was too soft and inconsistent in disciplining her grandchild. This comment immediately raised a red flag for me. Moreover, the step-grandfather, a tall, strong, well-built farmer in his sixties with huge calloused hands, said that all six of his own children were alienated from him with the possible exception of his youngest son who phoned him from time to time. When I inquired as to why, he said that his former wife "had poisoned them against him." Then, he told me she was so unhappy and bitter in the marriage she told him that when the last child graduated from high school she was going to leave him, and she did.

Redirecting the interview session into a therapeutic one, I focused on his relationship with his children and the possible explanations for his estrangement from his erstwhile family. As we plunged into further discussion, he revealed that he had inherited his parents' farm. To make a go of it, he worked all the time from morning until night, 7 days a week, and was not able to spend quality time with his children or wife. Furthermore, he spent little or no money on them. He fed all his income into the farm. In our discussion, I could sense rigidity and inflexibility in his attitudes, and it was very difficult for him to acknowledge his responsibility for his estrangement from his kids. However, under my tactful direction, he gradually acknowledged his own responsibility for his distant relationship with his children. It was critically important for him to admit his role in his unhappy state of affairs so that he did not unconsciously or automatically transfer or scapegoat (O'Reilly & Morrison, 1993) his past mistaken parenting habits (he attributed these habits as good parenting techniques used by his parents when raising him) on to his step-grandson.

Again, I confronted and disputed his mistaken beliefs regarding his parents' rearing practices. I asked him to reflect on how he experienced punishment (e.g., harsh spanking) as a child and asked if it worked. Had it changed his behavior in a positive way? He reflected for a moment and said ruefully, I think, surprising himself, "Not really!"

Recommendations to the court system. Clinicians who assist grandparent caregivers also frequently find themselves dealing with the court system to advocate on behalf of grandparents' legal rights. Virtually all states have laws that grant grandparents limited visitation with their grandchildren under certain situations such as a family crises or in the case of divorce (Thompson, Tinsley, Scalora, & Parke, 1989). However, most judges are reluctant to use the power of the court to compel compliance for adult parents who deny the grandparents visitation. We can understand the court's desire not to interfere in these family matters. Furthermore, we recognize that identifying who is right and who is wrong in these contentious and bitterly fought custody battles frequently becomes murky or lost in the avalanche of accusations and counter accusations. Moreover, to complicate matters further, the adult child (generally the son) of the parents will switch his loyalty back to his former spouse or significant other and support her efforts to deny his parents visitation.

Two of my patients, Lucy and Tom, a married couple, attempted to obtain custody of their 8-year-old biological grandson because his mother had a serious alcohol and drug problem. She frequently left the child home alone or with her 13-year-old delinquent son (his step-brother), who also had alcohol and substance abuse problems of his own. On two occasions, the grandparents were on the verge of being awarded custody of their grandson when the adult son, the child's father, became at his former girlfriend's invitation romantically entwined with her, and informed the court that he favored the child's mother as guardian. Once his former girlfriend regained custody of their child, she ditched him once again. On a third occasion, the court denied the grandparents custody on a technicality—their lawyer inexplicably failed to file a paper within a set date. Now, the grandparents are regrouping for yet a fourth try to obtain custody of their grandson.

On the positive side, they have been receiving regular visitation with their grandson, although the mother still balks on occasion. In the interim I work with Lucy, focusing on helping her enjoy the time she has with her grandson, and supporting her efforts as she once again wrestles with the court system. When the grandson comes to counseling, I build on his burgeoning self-control to help him cope with the resentments he feels in being shuttled back and forth between these families and to cope with their diametrically opposed value systems. His mother provided him with little or no supervision—he did whatever he wanted to do—whereas his grandparents monitored his behavior and imposed consequences for inappropriate behavior. I would like to say the above scenario is unusual in this type of therapy; unfortunately, it is all far too common.

The power of nurture. The above case study involved a grossly impaired parent who abused alcohol and drugs. Other cases we see frequently involve parents who have been incarcerated for engaging in egregious illegal activities, who have a history of sexual misconduct, or who are severely mentally ill or cognitively impaired. Given the level of impairment of the biological parents in these scenarios, one cannot help but wonder if these children have any chance at all of overcoming their genetic inheritance.

For example, I have as patients a paternal grandmother, Sally, and her granddaughter, Marlena. Marlena's mother has a long history of involvement with the courts, CPS, and the police. On several occasions, mental health specialists have diagnosed Marlena's mother as exhibiting the symptoms of paranoid schizophrenia. Some of her difficulties included sharing her sexual fantasies and paranoid view of society with her daughter. Marlena's mother, who was about 5'8" and thin, was constantly battling the courts and the county's social service system. Because of her frustration, she frequently threatened to leave the state with her daughter even though she was under the supervision of CPS and not allowed to leave the county. CPS eventually deemed her an unfit mother and transferred her parental rights to Marlena's paternal grandmother, Sally.

The court did not consider awarding custody to Marlena's father, who lived in another state a considerable distance away, because he had been accused (by Marlena and her mother) of sexually molesting Marlena when she was 6 years old. As part of a plea-bargain arrangement, Marlena's father agreed to live in another state and not to have any contact with his daughter until she attained adulthood status, which in New York is defined as 21 years old.

The first time I met Marlena she was 8 or 9 years old, a diminutive but stocky child. I was charged by the court to conduct a psychological evaluation on Marlena and her parents. At the time, she was living with her mother and her mother's third husband—a quiet, reserved individual who appeared to be very passive and ineffectual. In my report, I noted that Marlena clearly exhibited prodromal signs of schizophrenia and had a tenuous grasp on reality. She was withdrawn, manifested odd conversations with herself, had no friends in school or in her neighborhood, was failing all her grades (although a standardized cognitive assessment indicated she scored in the low-average range of intelligence), and was verbally and physically aggressive toward her peers in school (Gottesman & Erlenmeyer-Kimling, 2001).

When she was 11 years old, I saw Marlena again, after the court had named her grandmother her guardian and recommended counseling. Her grandmother,

Sally, a short woman in her mid-50s, scheduled an appointment with me for both of them to receive individual and family counseling. Because of Marlena's unstable mental health, I considered ancillary services and referred her to her family physician for medication. Marlena's medical doctor prescribed Risperdal 1.25 mg once a day. I discovered that Sally was quite different in temperament and discipline from Marlena's mother. Unlike Marlena's mother, Sally possessed traits that could provide a beneficial environment for Marlena (Jones & Hanson, 1996). She was calm, down to earth, supportive, tolerant, humorous, strict, consistent, and rather on the prim and proper side. Marlena often complained acrimoniously to me about her grandmother's strictness, especially when it came to being with boys.

I would occasionally intervene on Marlena's behalf when the grandmother's injunctions appeared to be too strict (e.g., no overnights at a girlfriend's house, no use of the computer, and so on). I always conducted these conversations individually with Sally when Marlena was out of the room so as not to undermine Sally's authority with her granddaughter. Furthermore, when I met with Marlena, I would validate the parenting of the grandmother and indicated to Marlena that her grandmother's rules were there to protect her and that her grandmother had only her best interest at heart. Marlena was skeptical, but she did listen to me.

Sometimes, Sally could not afford to purchase something Marlena wanted badly, as Sally lived off a disability check, was quite poor, and received no financial assistance from either of the child's parents. As a third party and seemingly outside the family system from Marlena's perspective (although theoretically, I was a participant in the family system when I interacted with it in therapy), I could reframe the situation and help Marlena understand that her grandmother was not being mean or stingy when she did not purchase what she wanted but that her grandmother truly was unable to pay for the desired object. Again, Marlena was skeptical, but she listened. Moreover, Sally, the school system, and I worked closely with Marlena to improve her academic performance. Academic progress was slow. Yet, after 2 ¾ years, sMarlena's academic work improved remarkably, and she received several certificates for excellence in various academic subjects. She was justifiably quite proud of her achievement. In addition, Marlena began to appreciate and even openly endorse her grandmother's strict set of rules regarding her behavior.

Helping Marlena cope with her mother's abandonment of her was another area of clinical concern that I actively focused on. Upon losing custody of Marlena, her mother left town without saying a word to anyone. To Marlena, it was as if her mother had fallen off the face of the earth. Many months later, out of the blue, she phoned Marlena and said she was living somewhere in the Midwest. Unfortunately for Marlena, her mother's phone calls came sporadically without rhyme or reason and always had the effect of upsetting her. Marlena's mother would promise to come to see her or buy her birthday or Christmas gifts, which she would fail to do or the gifts would arrive in the mail months later. Moreover, Marlena's mother never visited when she said she would. She would show up unexpectedly. She arrived with no forewarning on two different occasions over the past 3 years. Her visits left Marlena a bundle of nerves and confusion. For some reason, the court has been reluctant to sever the mother's visiting rights, but she inexplicably decided to stop contacting her daughter on her own. After a while, Marlena became less stressed and more tranquil.

Fortunately, regular individual and family therapy and the stability of living with her grandmother led to good results. Of late, Marlena has begun to exhibit emotional stability, maturity, and improved decision making. When she first arrived to live with Sally, she was extremely anxious, avoidant, and ambivalently bonded to her. She now feels less anxious, less vulnerable, and more securely and psychologically attached to Sally. Although these changes in Marlena's emotionality and personality are still weakly established, they go a long way in reducing her risk of decompensating (Rutter, 1987). Marlena is getting stronger every day. It appears unlikely, although it is too early to prognosticate for sure, that Marlena will ever fully develop into a paranoid schizophrenic, as likely would have been her fate if she had remained with her mother. Residing with her grandmother has helped Marlena to feel safer and become more emotionally stable. Moreover, as Marlena continues to internalize her secure psychological bond with her grandmother, it will fortify and strengthen her so she will be able to cope better with the difficulties and challenges she will inevitably experience in her future relationships (Krause & Haverkamp, 1996).

Marlena is currently close to 14 years old and continues to improve. She is even beginning to make some headway on the social front with her peers. Marlena's sense of self-control and self-efficacy has also increased. I am increasingly becoming optimistic about Marlena's future chances although I suspect she will always manifest difficulties in her day-to-day functioning and engage in odd thinking and, as is true in most of these cases, require long-term therapy and medication.

Treating both the grandparent and the grandchild. As is clear from the above case studies, the astute practitioner addresses the emotional concerns of both the grandchild and grandparent, although the grandchild is most often the identified patient (Emick & Hayslip, 1999; Glass & Huneycutt, 2002). Both the grandchild and grandparent are experiencing grief at the loss of a significant relationship: one has lost a parent, the other, a child. Moreover, grandparents have lost their social role as grandparent, and the child has lost his or her special role as grandchild in which the traditional grandparent dotes on him or her. Likewise, the surrogate grandparent has lost the benefits of being a traditional grandparent, and the child has lost the dream of being part of a normal family with a mother or father. These are traumatic loses and the participants require prolonged treatment to manage and resolve their complicated grief and associated feelings such as intense anger (Pinson-Millburn, Fabian, Schlossberg, & Pyle, 1996).

Much of this anger is misplaced, as we alluded to earlier. The grandparent feels angry at being forced to give up the grandparent's role (although virtually all of them say they would do it in a heartbeat if they had to do it all over again) and resents the grandchild for imposing on their way of life and exhausting their financial resources. Most grandparents take on the mantle of responsibility reluctantly (Hayslip et al., 1998). They feel cheated; they are angry with themselves for their perceived failure in raising their own children, who turned out to be incompetent or neglectful parents, drug abusers, or immersed in inappropriate relationships. The grandchild, in turn, may blame the grandparents for their current predicament and resent being taken away from their parents. The sensitive clinician helps both the grandparent and grandchild express their rage, identify their feelings and irrational thoughts, and will assist in processing them in a safe and supportive environment (Glass & Huneycutt, 2002).

Further ancillary referrals. Grandparents might also benefit with a referral to a support group (Dannison & Smith, 2003; Whitley, Kelly, & Sipe, 2001). Typical curriculum for a therapeutic support group includes providing an opportunity for grandparents to engage in mutual storytelling, psychoeducational intervention to improve stress management, highlighting appropriate role models for group members, in-service training, mental health resources, health care, parent training, and information on legal issues (Dannison & Smith, 2003). The model developed by Dannison and Smith (2003) includes concurrent support groups for grandparents and grandchildren.

Results of a pilot study completed by Kelly, Yorker, Whitley, and Sipe (2001) suggest that Sally and other grandparents might benefit as well from a multi-modal intervention plan that included a six-session social support group coupled with individual in-home social work and problem-solving sessions, and which resulted in improvements in grandparents' mental health, reduced psychological distress and anxiety on the part of grandparents, improved perception of parenting, and confidence in parenting knowledge and ability to provide adequate care for their grandchildren. However, this type of approach is generally beyond the scope of the individual or even group practitioner.

Summary and conclusions. Clinicians are currently witnessing an explosion of referrals of grandparents who are parenting their grandchildren. The grandparents are often reluctant to take on the role of parenting, but are willing to do so to provide a safe haven for their neglected or abused grandchild or to keep their grandchild out of foster care (Minkler, 1994). These families enter therapy with a plethora of challenging problems. For example, the grandchildren have ever-evolving educational needs. The challenge of comprehending modern curricula may strain the grandparents' ability to help with homework. Grandchildren who have special education requirements and academic accommodations are a contributing factor to further stress. Involvement in the legal system can also be daunting. In the face of competing in courts with their own adult children, grandparents must work cooperatively with law guardians who represent their grandchildren, their own attorneys, and social workers that represent the Department of Social Services. Interacting with the Department of Social Services and family courts can be time consuming, emotionally draining, and financially costly. The stressors grandparents face frequently cause them to be depressed and in poor health. The clinician requires solutions that are multilayered and complex. A family systems approach is most productive in treating multigenerational families. Despite the trials and tribulations these grandparents are experiencing, they are proud to help their grandchildren and find their role meaningful and worthwhile. The astute practitioner initiates psychotherapy by developing rapport and trust in the family members, advocates on behalf of the grandchild with a wide array of social service and governmental organizations, intervenes cautiously and respectfully, utilizes all available family members, and generally makes gains in small graduated steps. Ultimately, the successful transactions and resolutions of these cases can be profoundly meaningful to the family and clinician alike.

REFERENCES

Aldous, J. (1995). New views of grandparents in intergenerational context. *Journal of Family Issues, 16*, 104–122.

Barranti-Ramirez, C. C. (1985). The grandparent/grandchild relationship: Family resource in an era of voluntary bonds. *Family Relations, 34*, 343–352.

Clarke, E. J., Preston, M., Raksin, J., & Bengtson, V. L. (1999). Types of conflicts and tensions between older parents and adult children. *The Gerontologist, 39*(3), 261–270.

Dannison, L., & Smith, A. B. (2003). Custodial grandparents' community support program: Lessons learned. *National Association of Social Workers*, 87–95.

Denham, T. E., & Smith, C. W. (1989). The influence of grandparents of grandchildren: A review of the literature and resources. *Family Relations, 38*, 345–358.

Elgar, F. J., McGrath, P. J., Waschbusch, D. A., Stewart, S. H., & Curtis, L. J. (2004). Mutual influences on maternal depression and child adjustment problems. *Clinical Psychology Review, 24*, 441–459.

Emick, M., & Hayslip, B., Jr. (1999). Custodial grandparenting: Stresses, coping skills, and relationships with grandchildren. *International Journal of Aging and Human Development, 48*, 35–61.

Fraenkel, P., & Markham, H. (2003). Preventing marital disorder. In Leonard A. Jason & David S. Glenwich (Eds.), *Innovative strategies for promoting health and mental health across the life span* (pp. 245–264). New York: Springer.

Ghuman, H. S., Weist, M. D., & Shafer, M. E. (1999). Demographic and clinical characteristics of emotionally disturbed children being raised by grandparents. *Psychiatric Services 50*, 1496–1498.

Glass, C. J. J., & Huneycutt, T. L. (2002). Grandparents parenting grandchildren: Extent of situation, issues involved, and educational implications. *Educational Gerontology, 28*, 139–161.

Goldenberg, I., & Goldenberg, H. G. (1985). *Family therapy: An overview.* Belmont, California: Wadsworth.

Goodman, C. C. (2003). Intergenerational triads in grandparent-headed families. *Journal of Gerontology: Social Sciences, 58B*(5), S281–S289.

Gottesman, I. I., & Erlenmeyer-Kimling, L. (2001). Family and twin strategies as a head start in defining prodromes and endophenotypes for hypothetical early-interventions in schizophrenia. *Schizophrenic Research, 51*, 93–102.

Hackney, H. L., & Cormier, S. L. (2005). *The professional counselor: A process guide to helping.* Boston, MA: Allyn and Bacon.

Hayslip, B., Jr., Shore, J., Henderson, C. E., & Lambert, P. L. (1998). Custodial grandparenting and the impact of grandchildren with problems on role satisfaction and role meaning. *Journal of Gerontology: Social Sciences, 53B*(3), S164–S173.

Jendrek, M. (1993). Grandparents who parent their grandchildren: Effects on Lifestyle. *Journal of Marriage and the Family, 55*, 609–621.

Johnson, C. L. (1998). Active and latent functions of grandparenting during the divorce process. *The Gerontologist, 28*(2), 185–191.

Jones, M. R., & Hansen, C. (1996, August). *Caregiving behaviors which predict adjustment of children raised by grandparents.* Presented at Annual Meeting of the American Psychological Association. Toronto, Ontario, Canada.

Kelley, S., Yorker, B., Whitley, D., & Sipe, T. (2001). A multimodal intervention for grandparents raising grandchildren: Results of an exploratory study. *Child Welfare League of America, LXXX*, 27–50.

Krause, A. M., & Haverkamp, B. E. (1996). Attachment in adult child-older parent relationships: Research, theory, and practice. *Journal of Counseling and Development, 75*, 83–92.

Minkler, M. (1994). Grandparents as parents: The American experience. *Aging International, 21*, 24–28.

Minkler, M., Fuller-Thomson, E., Miller, D. & Driver, D. (1997). Depression in grandparents raising grandchildren: Results of a national longitudinal study. *Archives of Family Medicine, 6,* 445–452.

Minkler, M., Roe., K. M., & Price, M. (1992). The physical and emotional health of grandmothers raising grandchildren in the crack cocaine epidemic. *The Gerontologist, 32*(6), 752–761.

Nichols, M. P., & Schwartz, R. C. (1995). *Family therapy: Concepts and methods.* Needham Heights, MA: Simon & Shuster.

Okum, B. F., & Rappaport, L. J. (1980). *Working with families: An introduction to family therapy.* North Scituate, MA: Duxbury Press.

Ooms, T. (1990). Keeping troubled families together: Promising programs and statewide reform. *The Family Impact Seminar,* 1–29.

O'Reilly, E., & Morrison, M. (1993). Grandparent-headed families: New therapeutic challenges. *Child Psychiatry and Human Development, 23,* 147–159.

Pinson-Millburn, N. M, Fabian, E. S., Schlossberg, N. K., & Pyle, M. (1996). Grandparents raising grandchildren, *Journal of Counseling and Development, 74,* 548–554.

Premack, D. (1959). Toward empirical behavior laws: pt. 1, Positive reinforcement. *Psychological Review, 66,* 219–233.

Premack, D. (1962). Reversibility of the reinforcement relation. *Science, 136,* 255–257.

Rutter, M. (1987). Children's behavior questionnaire for completion by teachers: Preliminary findings. *Journal of Child Psychology and Psychiatry, 8,* 1–11.

Thompson, R. A., Tinsely, B. R., Scalora, M. J., & Parke, R. D. (1989). Grandparents' visitation rights: Legalizing the ties that bind. *American Psychologist, 44*(9), 1217–1222.

Tinsley, B. R., & Parke, R. D. (1984). Grandparents as support and socialization agents. In M. Lewis (Ed.), *Beyond the dyad* (pp. 161–195). New York: Plenum.

Troll, L. E. (1985). The contingencies of grandparenting. In V. L. Bengstrom & J. F. Robertson (Eds.), *Grandparenthood* (pp. 135–149). Beverly Hills, CA: Sage.

Uhlenberg, P. (1996). Mutual attraction: Demography and life-course analysis. *The Gerontologist, 36*(2), 226–229.

Weber, J. A., & Waldrop, D. P. (2000). Grandparents raising grandchildren: Families in transition. *Journal of Gerontology: Social Sciences, 33*(2), 27–45.

Whitley, D. M., Kelly, S. J., & Sipe, T. A. (2001). Grandmothers raising grandchildren: Are they at increased risk of health problems? *Health & Social Work, 26*(2), 105–114.

CHAPTER 14

Counseling Custodial Grandchildren

Patricia L. Kaminski and Amy R. Murrell

The suggestions for counseling custodial grandchildren (CGC) that we offer in this chapter are based on our clinical experiences (as psychologists), empirical work, and a review of the existing literature on populations of children with similar presenting problems or life experiences. Our discussion emphasizes certain experiences that are common in the lives of CGC and how those life experiences can help us understand how we might best serve these children and their families when they present for counseling.

Circumstances that create grandfamilies range from the practical (e.g., when a grandparent provides co-parenting help for a single parent who must work or go to school) to the tragic (e.g., when a child's parent dies) to the traumatic (e.g., when the court mandates that the grandparent care for the grandchild due to child abuse by the adult parent). Indeed, divorce, adult parent drug abuse, and child abuse or neglect most commonly lead to grandparent custody (Fuller-Thomson & Minkler, 2000; Goodman & Silverstein, 2002; Hirshorn, VanMeter, & Brown, 2000). When considering the circumstances that lead to a custodial grandparent acting as a parent, the mental or emotional disability of the adult child is also a common reason for a change in child custody (Goodman & Silverstein, 2002). However, teen pregnancy, or the incarceration, physical disability, or death of an adult child can also thrust grandparents into the custodial role. In this chapter, however, we are primarily concerned with those circumstances that lead to full-time guardianship of grandchildren by their grandparents. Circumstances that typically lead to co-parenting arrangements (e.g., divorce, teen pregnancy), therefore, are not considered.

Our discussion of the counseling needs of CGC is based on life experiences that are common in this population of children. These experiences include temporary or permanent loss of one or more primary attachment figures and, often, prenatal drug exposure, physical or emotional abuse, physical or emotional neglect, economic disadvantage, social stigma, or relocation. Given that, as a group, CGC are more likely than other children to have endured one or more of these adverse circumstances or events, it is not surprising that they are also at higher risk for certain cognitive, emotional, and behavioral difficulties.[1]

ASSEMBLING A TREATMENT TEAM

Before reviewing what is known about the specific counseling needs of CGC, we would like to address our approach to working with CGC more generally. While there is tremendous diversity among CGC, the majority of these children have unusually complicated lives. The children often have co-morbid difficulties in physical, psychological, or intellectual functioning, and the grandparents are often struggling with their economic or emotional unpreparedness to raise additional children. We have found, therefore, that—while it is not always pragmatically possible—a multidisciplinary treatment team approach far exceeds any single treatment modality. If we know from the outset what a best-case scenario would be, we can make better use of the resources that are available. Typically, the treatment team of a CGC in our community consists of at least two other professionals as well as regular consultation with the child's teacher and pediatrician.

Although the particular difficulties a child is facing determine the types of assessment needed, in general, CGC benefit from specialized assessments conducted by a team including a pediatrician, a child psychiatrist, and a family therapist, in addition to one of us. Very often those assessments will lead to referrals to a neuropsychologist or speech therapist.

The physician on the team assists by giving checkups that are often overdue, as well as updating vaccinations and, in cases of abuse or neglect, running any tests needed to rule out malnutrition, exposure to toxins, substance use, or untreated injuries. Family assessments typically indicate that family therapy is warranted, although sometimes it does not begin until other interventions have been implemented (e.g., individual counseling for family members, grief work, parent training, support groups, or marital therapy). Our role as psychologists typically leads us to give a battery of diagnostic tests to understand each child's current intellectual, academic, social, emotional, and behavioral strengths and challenges.

Enlisting the expertise of an experienced social worker when working with CGC is vital because grandfamilies too often fall between the cracks of agency responsibility (McCallion, Janicki, Grant-Griffin, & Kolomer, 2000). The absence of advocacy for grandparent caregivers as well as other barriers to service use have contributed to the underutilization of resources from which grandfamilies could benefit (Butts, 2000). For example, 90% of grandparent caregivers do not receive social security benefits and 85% do not receive any type of public assistance (Landry-Meyer, 2000). These statistics are surprising when one considers that CGC with certain disabling conditions or who have lost both biological parents may be entitled to Supplemental Security Income (SSI) or Medicaid benefits; children with certain types of medical conditions may also receive Medicare. Currently, many states also offer federally subsidized health insurance to uninsured families with income levels that are higher than allowed by Medicaid (i.e., State Children's Health Insurance Program or SCHIP). Finally, the addition of dependent children to a grandparent's household might make them eligible for various types of governmental assistance that they did not qualify for in the past (e.g., food stamps).

Another example of the underutilization of resources among grandfamilies is that only a small number enjoy foster care status, which can provide child care, monetary remuneration, and tutoring (Dellmann-Jenkins, Blankemeyer, & Olesh, 2002). Finally, another reason to have a social worker on your team is that, compared to other types of mental health professionals, social workers often have working relationships with other people and agencies in the community with whom grandfamilies may already be involved (e.g., Child Advocates, Child Protective Services, Family Court, etc.).

LOGISTICAL CONSIDERATIONS

There are other logistical concerns to keep in mind when working with CGC. Becoming a custodial grandparent is associated with a variety of negative consequences; chief among these are poorer physical and mental health (Hayslip, Shore, Henderson, & Lambert, 1998). Indeed, the incidence of such illnesses as depression, diabetes, hypertension, and insomnia is greater among grandparent caregivers, who often report more difficulty than their age peers in performing activities of daily living (Minkler & Fuller-Thomson, 1999). In practical terms, many of these health problems can interfere with a custodial grandparent's ability to bring their grandchild to counseling on a regular basis. Counselors who can be mobile might consider meeting the child at their home or school. Another option is to work with the grandparent to find a relative, friend, or neighbor who might be willing to transport their grandchild to your office. If this is the case, we find that it is important to schedule regular phone check-ins with the grandparent so that they are actively involved in their grandchild's treatment.

Another serious impediment to the acquisition of essential services for CGC is the burden of poverty. The percentage of grandparent caregivers living below the poverty line (19%) is greater than that for other types of families with children (14%; U.S. Census Bureau, 2000). Contributing to this dire situation, many grandparents must reduce or give up paid work to raise a grandchild. In addition to a loss of income, the less tangible benefits of employment—for example, better health and less parenting stress—may also be sacrificed (Musil, Schrader, & Mutikani, 2000). Other factors also contribute to the financial burden of grandfamilies. For example, one-quarter of the custodial grandparents in one sample reported paying for their adult child's living expenses (Waldrop & Weber, 2001). Grandparents also commonly provide financial assistance for their adult child's psychiatric care, substance abuse treatment, and legal expenses. When a grandparent has to choose between the cost of a counseling session (even if you offer a sliding scale reduced fee) and groceries, the latter is clearly more urgent. Once again, the participation of a skilled social worker on the treatment is invaluable, as they can assist low-income grandfamilies in applying for food stamps and other types of assistance.

Not only do a disproportionate number of grandfamilies live below poverty level, but only one in three CGC is covered by health insurance (see Kirby & Kaneda, 2002). Furthermore, CGC who have recently been in the custody of an impaired parent may be undernourished and overdue for medical, dental, and vision checkups. (See Landry-Meyer, 1999, for a summary of grandparent caregivers' identified needs and concerns.)

When grandfamilies are bearing the burden of poverty, certain practical impediments to attending counseling are ubiquitous. For example, even if session fees are considerably reduced, the cost of reliable transportation as well as child-care expenses (for CGC siblings who are not in treatment) may still prohibit regular participation in counseling. Although we are not suggesting that transportation can be realistically provided in most cases, counselors should think about logistics such as public transportation schedules in addition to considering their own mobility. With respect to child care, we are fortunate in our clinic to have graduate student trainees available to supervise our clients or their siblings when we need to work with custodial grandparents directly. We have also worked with grandfamilies who solved their transportation and child-care problems by carpooling to our clinic and supervising one another's CGC before or after their own sessions.

COMMON PRESENTING PROBLEMS AND DISORDERS AMONG CUSTODIAL GRANDCHILDREN

School-aged custodial grandsons are the most frequent type of custodial grandchild to present at our community mental health center. Most often their custodial grandparents are concerned with aggressive and defiant behavior or academic problems. We consider psychological testing indispensable, as these boys would be overdiagnosed (with ADHD in particular) if we relied on caregiver report alone.

Although the research in this area is fairly limited, several authors have reported atypically high rates of cognitive, emotional, and behavioral difficulties (e.g., hyperactivity, learning disorders, oppositionality, depression) among CGC (Edwards, 1998; Hayslip & Shore, 2000). While there is at least one exception (i.e., Solomon & Marx, 1995), several authors have reported high rates of grade retention (e.g., 23%–63%) and special-education placement (e.g., 26%–28%) among custodial grandchildren (see Sawyer & Dubowitz, 1994). One often overlooked factor that likely plays a role in academic performance problems among CGC is residential relocation, which often requires the grandchild to change schools (see Scanlon & Devine, 2001, for a review). In addition, some researchers report exceptionally high rates of "special needs" classifications (e.g., cerebral palsy, pervasive developmental disorder, serious emotional disturbance) among CGC (i.e., 40% [Grant, 2000] and 52% [Blackburn, 2000]). In another sample of 170 inner-city grandchildren (M age = 7.4 years) in kinship care, the most common reasons for referral to school personnel were (from most to least common): poor concentration, hyperactivity, depression, oppositional-defiant behavior, ADHD, temper tantrums, mood swings, and social isolation (Grant & Kucera, 1998).

It is vital to mention, however, that the adjustment reactions of some CGC may be misdiagnosed as more severe psychopathology. When children have not yet developed a broad array of coping skills (many of which cannot be employed until a certain level of cognitive or verbal development is reached), their attempts to cope with life stressors may resemble symptoms of more chronic conditions. For example, a child who is coping with a chaotic home life may express her anxiety in the form of hyperactivity or communicate her feelings of frustration and anger by being aggressive with her peers. It is important that mental health professionals consider the context of the child's life and complete a thorough assessment before assigning diagnostic labels that have the potential to bring about more harm than good.

By definition, one factor that plays a critical role in the context of all CGC is the temporary or permanent loss of a parent or parents. This adverse life event challenges the coping resources of people of all ages (e.g., Brown, Harris, &

Bifulco, 1986; Lloyd, 1980; Mack, 2001; Parker, Barrett, & Hickie, 1992) and can be especially traumatic for children. Given the frequency of *additional* stressful and traumatic experiences (e.g., abuse, custody battles) that CGC have commonly encountered, it is not surprising that a disproportionately high number of these children exhibit symptoms of emotional, behavioral, and learning problems. To date, however, no longitudinal studies have been conducted to determine if such symptoms were preexisting (e.g., secondary to prenatal drug exposure or parental abuse), relatively normative temporary reactions to the immediate crisis, or psychopathology precipitated by the crisis.

As is the case with many clients, it is our experience that the number and intensity of adverse life events a custodial grandchild has endured is often a good predictor of the extent and severity of symptoms he is likely to have (Turner & Lloyd, 1995). Moreover, the knowledge that certain risk factors almost inevitably co-occur can assist with treatment planning. For example, a child who becomes a CGC following the incarceration of her single parent related to a drug offense will most likely also have suffered emotional and physical neglect and, often, one or more types of child abuse. Even if child neglect or abuse were not documented in a situation like this, it is a fairly safe assumption given what is known about the nature of addiction and its effect on parental functioning (e.g., see Vrasti & Eisemann, 1994, for a review of parenting and alcoholism). Just as there is significant overlap between parental drug abuse and child neglect or abuse, those risk factors increase the likelihood that the child was exposed to drugs in utero. Prenatal drug exposure increases the risk for every child problem that has been mentioned thus far in this chapter (see Zuckerman, Frank, & Brown, 1995, for a review) and may be a seriously underacknowledged risk factor in the lives of CGC.

Another set of risk factors tends to co-occur when parents have been declared incompetent due to mental illness. Specifically, their children almost certainly have endured other stressors such as neglect, social stigma, and, possibly, economic disadvantage (Perris, Arrindell, & Eisemann, 1994). Thus, some of the most important questions to ask custodial grandparents when conducting intakes for CGC clients will relate to the circumstances that led them to assume the custodial role.

THE IMPORTANCE OF UNDERSTANDING THE CIRCUMSTANCES THAT LED TO GRANDPARENT CUSTODY

When interviewing grandparents in the context of counseling CGC, however, clinicians should remain aware of the social stigma that often haunts these nontraditional families. It is vital to keep in mind that custodial grandparents describe feeling judged, misunderstood, socially isolated, and ashamed (Joslin, 2002; Kolomer, McCallion, & Overeynder, 2003; Miltenberger, Hayslip, Harris, & Kaminski, 2003–2004; Wohl, Lahner, & Jooste, 2003; also see Hipple & Hipple, this volume), largely related to the particular circumstances that led to them having custody of their grandchildren. Questions about why their adult child can no longer care for his or her own children are vital, but also likely to elicit guilt and shame in custodial grandparents. These questions are hard to ask without inadvertently putting custodial grandparents on the defensive as they face what is often a parent's worst fear (i.e., "What did I do to cause my (adult) child to fail in life?").

Thus, it is paramount for counselors to work through their own biases and challenge their preconceived notions in order to be authentic, empathic, and supportive of grandfamilies. Although "blame the parent" explanations for various negative outcomes among adult children can be appealing in their simplicity, in reality, the empirically supported models that predict adult behavior—whether divorce, substance abuse, or child abuse—are complex and multidetermined. Moreover, while no parent is perfect, very few we have encountered ever set out to intentionally harm their children.

In our experience, the most effective work with CGC can only occur within the context of a strong therapeutic alliance with the custodial grandparents who, undeniably, are making many sacrifices to assist their grandchildren in having healthier and happier lives. As such, your child clients will reap the most benefit from caregivers who cope with any self-doubt or guilt by actively working toward a better future for their family, rather than getting mired in fruitless self-recrimination and regret. While attending to those latter feelings may make up a phase of custodial grandparents' grieving and healing process in their individual counseling, as child clinicians we find that modeling empathy (without denying personal responsibility) is more helpful to grandparent caregivers. Statements such as "parents tend to do the best the can at any given time" and "the important thing now is that you are consistently working to gain the skills and resources to improve your parenting" are worth repeating until custodial grandparents internalize them. Among the healthiest responses we have seen are custodial grandparents who turn their guilt and regret (which are nearly inevitable for parents in general) into a strong motivation to do a better job as a second-time parent.

Gaining a clear understanding of the circumstances under which children arrive in the custody of their grandparents is also important because some circumstances are more socially stigmatizing than others and, therefore, predict different counseling needs and possible impacts on the psychosocial adjustment of CGC. For example, the permanency of the grandfamily arrangement and whether its length can even be predicted are likely to influence a child's adjustment to it.

Certain CGC are also more likely to feel particularly alone in their grief related to parental loss (e.g., if the circumstances that precipitated that loss are socially stigmatizing, such as a parent's death due to AIDS or overdose, or parental absence due to child abuse or incarceration). Even under the best circumstances, however, simply being raised by one's grandparents at all affects children in that they are apt to feel different from their age peers. For example, many things related to their living situation—from the older appearance of their caregivers to the practical consequences of caregivers who may not drive—tend to make them feel different from their peers. Feeling singled out is likely to be particularly stressful for children who are required to transition to a new school as a result of their new custody arrangement. Moreover, especially in cases where the grandchild must relocate to a different city or state to live with a grandparent, friendship networks and other sources of stability are likely to be disrupted, leaving many children feeling acutely lonely and displaced, adding to the sense of loss and abandonment that they already experience.

When a custodial grandchild client feels particularly embarrassed or ashamed of their nontraditional family constellation, we engage in creative therapeutic activities to address that. For example, one 14-year-old custodial granddaughter (who we will call LaKisha) was given a homework assignment to conduct research and identify successful people that spent at least some of their childhood as a custodial grandchild. LaKisha's sense of shame was quickly transformed into pride when she discovered that one of her role models, Oprah Winfrey, had been primarily raised by her grandmother. Edwards (1998) notes that many other high-profile people (e.g., Bill Clinton and Mary Tyler Moore) were also CGC at one point in their lives. A more recent Internet search reveals that Eric Clapton, Willie Nelson, and Jack Nicholson were also raised by their grandparents (Talarico, 2007).

DIFFICULT EXPERIENCES IN THE LIVES OF CUSTODIAL GRANDCHILDREN

Loss of Primary Attachment Figures

The loss of an attachment relationship is widely recognized as one of the most emotionally painful experiences human beings endure (e.g., Brown, Harris, & Bifulco, 1986; Lloyd, 1980; Parker, Barrett, & Hickie, 1992). Unfortunately, such a significant loss may also be the most universal of the life experiences shared by CGC.

As understood from the framework of John Bowlby's attachment theory (1969/1982, 1973, 1980), an attachment figure is a person to whom an infant has an inherent motivation to stay physically close to and whose absence causes intense psychoemotional distress (e.g., sadness, anxiety, anger). In most circumstances, as long as they are physically present, an infant's biological mother or parents become his primary or most important attachment figure(s). Importantly, although the quality of the attachment depends largely on the way the attachment figure responds to the infant, an attachment bond can still form even in poor circumstances. That is, even infants and children who are mistreated or abused by their caregivers will typically have an attachment relationship with them. The loss of *any* attachment figure, therefore, is significant and painful. Thus, despite all the other issues CGC may present with, counselors should keep in mind that most CGC are also parentally bereaved.

Children's attachment relationships with their caregivers can be categorized as secure, insecure, or absent. Secure attachment relationships result from sensitive and responsive parenting and are associated with a variety of positive outcomes in childhood and adulthood, such as effective emotional regulation, social competence, and reduced risk for psychopathology (e.g., Cassidy, 1994; Dozier, Stoval, & Albus, 1999; Fonagy et al., 1996; Greenberg, 1999). Insecure attachments are considered the product of insensitive, rejecting, or inconsistent parenting and, especially when studied in concert with other risk factors, are associated with a variety of negative outcomes in childhood (e.g., problematic peer relationships, symptoms of depression and aggression, mood lability) and adulthood (e.g., anxiety and affective disorders, unstable romantic relationships; Egeland & Sroufe, 1981; Lyons-Ruth, Alpern, & Repacholi, 1993). In cases of profound maltreatment by caregivers, children may not form an attachment at all. The serious problems that result from such nonexistent or seriously impaired caregiver-child relationships are best subsumed under the diagnostic category of Reactive Attachment Disorder (American Psychiatric Association, 2000), which will be discussed later in this chapter.

Given the importance of a custodial grandchild's history of attachments in understanding the way she is likely to feel about herself, significant others, and relationships, attachment history is another sensitive area of inquiry that needs to be addressed with grandparent caregivers. Importantly, even in highly dysfunctional family environments, children can be resilient if they have been able to find a trustworthy adult with whom they could form a secure attachment. Grandparents often fill this role, so assessing the grandparent-grandchild relationship over the course of the child's entire life is advisable. Observing the custodial grandparent and grandchild directly is also useful for developing hypotheses about the strengths and challenges of any given dyad. One assessment tool that allows clinicians to efficiently observe caregiver-child dyads across multiple contexts is the Parent-Child Interaction Assessment-II (Holigrocki & Kaminski, 2002; Holigrocki, Kaminski, & Frieswyk, 1999, 2002).

Not surprisingly, a child with a history of insecure attachments is also likely to have difficulty bonding with their therapist. How to address this in counseling will depend on the age of the child and the severity of their attachment problems. In general, however, the type of therapeutic approach that is effective for children with attachment problems is one that is emotionally warm (without being intrusive), consistent, predictable, patient, and structured (for more information on working with children with attachment problems, see Sameroff & Emde, 1989).

Inconsistent Primary Attachment Figures

Understanding a custodial grandchild's life context and likely attachment pattern are important factors in treatment planning. In cases where there is still contact with a surviving parent, a custodial grandchild may have a sense of divided loyalties; they may feel emotionally torn between a grandparent and a parent, even when the latter drifts unpredictably in and out of their life. The ill-defined nature of the child's relationship to both parent and grandparent can also inhibit the child's processing of her feelings of grief regarding the loss of the relationship with a parent who has either willingly given up his parental rights or who has had such rights rescinded by the court. Continuing questions regarding legal custody and patterns of visitation by the child's parents, as well as what is communicated to the child by the grandparent regarding the role that a parent is likely to fill in the child's life, can either undermine or enhance the child's emotional well-being, social relationships, and school performance (Hayslip & Kaminski, 2005).

Sometimes it may be beneficial for counselors of CGC to play a role in helping a grandparent and grandchild forge a new relationship with the adult parent that permits some contact, yet does not interfere with the quality of the relationship that has been established between grandparent and grandchild. (For discussions of family therapy approaches with custodial grandparents, parents, and children, see Brown-Standridge & Floyd, 2000, and Heywood, 1999.) In many cases, however, a grandchild's well-being can be harmed by renewing a relationship with their parent, particularly when physical, emotional, or sexual abuse has occurred.

Even parents who have not been abusive can inordinately harm a child when they unpredictably enter and exit the lives of their children (Smith &

Dannison, 2001). Depending on the circumstances surrounding the custody arrangement, the relationships between the grandparent, parent, and child, the parent's emotional stability, and other factors, even the sudden presence of a biological parent can cause significant distress. For CGC, that distress will often appear as a change in mood or behavior at school. When this is the case, it is important for custodial grandparents and school personnel to be in communication. Clear communication from the school can help custodial grandparents understand the possible impact of parental visitation or absence, which may affect their decisions about parental contact in the future. Similarly, clear communication with the school can help the child's teachers anticipate and potentially minimize negative consequences of parental visitation or absence.

Parental Bereavement

No matter what the circumstances of a parent's temporary or permanent absence, children will be bereaved, requiring more emotional resources from grandparents and often necessitating the guidance of a child counselor. While in many ways the grief process of CGC will follow a course similar to that of other parentally bereaved children, CGC are also unique in ways in which counselors should remain aware.

First, complications related to parental bereavement (i.e., complicated bereavement) are especially likely to occur when children feel stigmatized (as when a parent has died of AIDS or a drug overdose) and when they have not been afforded the opportunity to express their feelings related to the parent's leaving or dying. The latter factor often varies with the grandparent's own openness to doing so, especially if the abandoning or deceased parent was a son or daughter. In families where the reality of a parent's absence is denied or avoided, CGC are likely to need interventions that allow them to face reality and express feelings ranging from sadness to anger, guilt, regret, and anxiety.

A grandparent's ability and willingness to attend to a grandchild's feelings over the loss of a parental relationship can be compromised by the fact that many custodial grandparents are also simultaneously grieving over the losses that placed them in that role, such as the disappearance, death, or incarceration of their adult child (Baird, 2003; Pinson-Millburn, Fabian, Schlossberg, & Pyle, 1996). Moreover, grandparents often express shame, guilt, and anxiety over an adult child's abandonment, criminal behavior, or death due to AIDS (Joslin, 2002). Thus, many grandparent caregivers must also cope with secondary losses linked to their child's temporary or permanent physical (or emotional) absence, as well as with their grandchild's grief related to parental loss. Recent evidence (Miltenberger et al., 2003–2004) suggests that grandparent caregivers' grief may be disenfranchised (i.e., not publicly recognized or acknowledged by others), undermining their opportunities to express themselves, receive social support, and inquire about their grandchildren's feelings. Thus, it is likely that the grief of CGC is also disenfranchised.

As is developmentally normative for young children, most prepubescent CGC have not developed the abilities to verbalize complex feelings and tolerate intensely painful emotional experiences such as grief. What complicates this process for many CGC, however, is that children who have not been adequately emotionally nurtured may experience developmental delays in their social-emotional skills, such that even adolescent CGC may have difficulty working through their grief in talk therapy. As such, grief may initially be expressed in any number of other ways (e.g., somatic and depressive symptoms, irritability, aggression, academic problems; see Webb, 1993, for a primer on working with bereaved children). A vital role for any child or adolescent counselor, therefore, is to meet the child where they are (developmentally) and assist them in processing their feelings in ways that are most beneficial to them.

Childhood Abuse or Neglect

Recall that children who have no attachments—neither secure nor insecure—may be best described as having Reactive Attachment Disorder (RAD; see American Psychiatric Association, 2000). RAD is, by definition, associated with grossly pathological care (e.g., severe physical or emotional neglect, physical or emotional abuse, or frequent changes in primary caregiver such that a stable attachment relationship cannot be formed) in the first five years of life. Children with RAD have been deprived of opportunities to learn how to relate to other people, which is typically achieved through relationships with primary attachment figures. As a result, children with RAD are either excessively inhibited or disinhibited in their social relationships. In the former, they do not initiate or respond to social interactions in ways that are expected for their developmental level. Disinhibited children with RAD, on the other hand, tend to be indiscriminate in their sociability, such as being overly affectionate with relative strangers.

It is imperative that children with RAD receive intense and specialized intervention to assist them in forming selective attachments. A review of those interventions is beyond the scope of this chapter. Clinicians who do not have expertise in treating RAD should make an appropriate referral as soon as possible, as early intervention with this serious disorder is essential.

Fortunately, most abused and neglected children do not develop RAD. Somehow they are able to form an attachment, albeit an insecure one, with an abusive caregiver or find another person in their life that can become a secondary attachment figure. Many times the available adult in the child's life was their grandparent, with whom they may have a secure pattern of attachment. In those cases, the transition to a grandparent-headed family may be relatively unproblematic for a child.

Counselors should be aware, however, that many children will experience intense grief in response to the loss of an abusive parent. One explanation for this is that the "traumatic [attachment] bonds" that result from extremely unpredictable relationships (e.g., episodes of affection interspersed with episodes of abuse) can be *stronger than* the secure bonds that are associated with emotionally sensitive and responsive interactions (Dutton & Painter, 1981). In these situations, CGC will benefit from supportive interventions *first* (vs. trauma recovery work) until their grief is more manageable. Counselors will likely have to educate custodial grandparents about the nature of traumatic bonds so that they can understand and accept their grandchildren's fierce loyalty to attachment figures who may have been abusive.

ADDITIONAL THERAPEUTIC INTERVENTIONS FOR CUSTODIAL GRANDCHILDREN

Strengthening the Caregiver-Child Relationship

In addition to individual child psychotherapy, there are numerous other interventions that can assist CGC. For example, efforts to foster a warm and mutually fulfilling relationship between custodial grandparents and grandchildren constitute a primary form of intervention (Keller & Stricker, 2003). A custodial grandchild's secure relationship with her grandparent may help compensate for earlier parental failures and serve as a protective factor against depression, low self-esteem, and low social acceptance. A psychologically healthy caregiver-child relationship can be reparative, helping the child to develop attachment security despite their initial insecure attachment with a primary caregiver. Indeed, for children who internalize their feelings, focusing on building the quality of the grandchild-grandparent relationship may be more effective than focusing on ameliorating behavior problems or impaired school performance (Keller & Stricker, 2003).

The mechanisms for facilitating a secure custodial grandparent–custodial grandchild attachment have yet to be empirically tested. In a recent paper, however, Poehlmann (2003) proposes that factors that are likely to predict relationship quality in these dyads include the age of the child at placement, the sensitivity with which grandparents respond to their grandchildren, and the quality of the grandparents' marital relationship.

CGC who had insecure attachments or traumatic bonds to their parents are likely to have more difficulty in developing trusting relationships with grandparent caregivers. For example, it is normal for a child who has been abandoned by an attachment figure (either literally or figuratively) to fear abandonment in the future. Children's fears of abandonment are likely to be exacerbated when their custodial grandparents are in poor health or elderly. From the grandchild's perspective, wondering when a single or widowed 80-year-old grandparent will die is a real concern, and most likely exacerbates her fears of abandonment.

Another potentially problematic interpersonal dynamic that is sometimes observed among custodial grandparent-grandchild dyads is called role reversal. Role reversals occur when children in a family system are expected to take care of adults (either physically or emotionally), instead of the adults taking care of the children. CGC who did not experience appropriate caregiver-child boundaries with their parents are particularly vulnerable to role reversals with their grandparents. Thus, it is important to monitor CGC for signs that too many emotional or physical caretaking demands are being placed on them (Kaminski & Hayslip, 2004). Such role reversals can be detrimental to children, for the real "work" of childhood (i.e., intellectual, psychological, and spiritual development) cannot optimally occur when pseudo-adult behavior is required.

Improving Parenting Skills Among Custodial Grandparents

A crucial role that counselors may play in the lives of grandchildren being raised by their grandparents is to assist custodial grandparents with their parenting. This is especially important for those grandparents who are raising grandchildren with emotional or behavioral difficulties that bring them into conflict with teachers, school officials, other parents, or peers. Depression, ADHD, drug or alcohol abuse, or disruptive behavior disorders are likely to pose many challenges to the behavior-management skills of teachers as well as the parenting skills of grandparents. Grandparents may need to be educated about such difficulties as well as know when problem behaviors in their grandchildren warrant a referral to a mental health professional.

In coordinating parental-skills training for custodial grandparents, psychologists should advocate for the inclusion of a variety of topics. Such content might include: (1) parenting skills such as discipline styles (and their outcomes), setting limits, and providing consequences; (2) communication skills on topics such as how to talk to a teenager or to a child's teacher; (3) advocacy issues that include legal or custody questions and becoming knowledgeable about one's rights; (4) drug use and sexuality; and (5) grief and related issues of loss (Wohl et al., 2003). This is especially important as grandparents may lack knowledge about mental health care for themselves or their grandchildren, and may also be unfamiliar with STDs, drug use, school violence, or peer influences on their grandchildren (Silverthorn & Durant, 2000).

One innovative approach to improving parenting skills is based on an empowerment model (Cox, 2002). Custodial grandmothers were involved in designing a 12-class curriculum. In addition to modules on parenting, communication, and related topics, the program covered topics such as "developing advocacy skills" and "making presentations." Furthermore, each participant also became an expert on a topic of her choice and presented the material she learned to other grandparents in the community.

It is important to point out that parenting-skills training, despite its potential benefits for grandparents and grandchildren, may be resisted by grandparent caregivers because it may imply they have not adequately parented their adult children. Prefacing this training with a caveat that stresses how times have changed may help decrease grandparents' defensiveness about this issue.

Custodial grandparents report that a primary obstacle to participation in parenting programs in not having time to attend (Kaminski & Hayslip, 2004). We encourage practitioners to develop creative solutions to these problems. For example, time-crunched custodial grandparents might benefit from either audiotaped or videotaped parent training materials they can use at home.

PROGRAMS AND SUPPORT GROUPS FOR CUSTODIAL GRANDPARENTS AND CUSTODIAL GRANDCHILDREN

While the quality of the grandchild-grandparent relationship is paramount, it is also important to make sure that both the child and the grandparent have sources of social-emotional support and companionship outside of their relationship with each other. In particular, increasing social-emotional support may be especially helpful for those custodial grandparents who unduly rely on their grandchild to meet their needs, perhaps borne of their isolation from age peers or friends.

School psychologists may be helpful in coordinating the formation of educational programs and support groups to assist custodial grandparents (see Smith, 2003). Model programs typically employ a professional facilitator and incorporate both didactic sessions and peer support for custodial grandparents (e.g., Glass & Huneycutt, 2002) and grandchildren (e.g., Dannison & Smith, 2003; Rogers & Henkin, 2000).

One school-based intervention for school-aged CGC ("Grandma's Kids," Rogers & Henkin, 2000) aims to teach life skills (e.g., empathy training, anger management, impulse control). The program includes information about drug abuse, provides academic tutoring, and engages CGC in group counseling to help them build self-esteem, manage conflict, increase coping, and improve their relationships with others. Through this program, grandchildren can also interact with other children living with their grandparents and gain access to many activities (e.g., arts and crafts, summer camps and workshops, sports, tutoring, mentoring; see Rogers & Henkin, 2000).

Support groups have been demonstrated to provide needed information and emotional support to grandparent caregivers, and such benefits seem to be especially important for minority grandparents (AARP, 2003), as well as for grandparents who are either isolated or live in rural areas. While support groups likely mitigate some of the distress grandparent caregivers experience, it is important to point out that they sometimes merely allow group members to vent endless frustrations without moving to a more positive and constructive focus (Strom & Strom, 2000). However, support groups do provide the opportunity for expressing feelings and receiving empathy from others, especially important in light of the fact that grandparents report feeling invisible and judged by others as parental failures (Wohl et al., 2003). By disclosing how they became custodial grandparents, talking about their families, and comparing the memories of raising their adult children with their current experiences, custodial grandparents can bring closure to unfinished business and work through feelings of guilt and regret (Smith, 2003; Wohl et al., 2003).

Through their participation in support groups, grandparents can socialize, provide reassurance to one another, share needed resources, and exchange information about legal assistance, financial aid, and personal counseling (Cohen & Pyle, 2000; Smith & Monahan, 2004). KinNet is a project that was funded in 2000 through the Adoption and Safe Families Act (ASFA), created through Generations United. It established a national network of support groups for grandparent caregivers in the formal foster care system. Recent evidence suggests that KinNet is effective in imparting information and providing needed social networking support to custodial grandparents (Generations United, 2004).

STRENGTHS OF GRANDFAMILIES

Despite the challenges faced by grandfamilies, they have many strengths; indeed, it is these resources that allow them to function and even prosper despite the disruptions they have experienced in their personal and family lives. First, grandparents have a wealth of life experience that they can use in their newly assumed roles of parents to their grandchildren. They can draw upon a lifetime of coping with life stresses both within and outside the context of their marriages and their relationships with their adult children and grandchildren. They can serve as role models, influence the values and life choices made by their grandchildren, and otherwise impart a sense of stability in the lives of children who typically have suffered the loss of their family of origin and a disrupted relationship with one or both parents. In fact, there is some cross-cultural evidence that speaks to the resilience of grandchildren raised in extended families who have experienced high levels of involvement by grandparents (see Hirshorn, 1998).

Raising a grandchild can afford grandparents a second chance at parenting as well as numerous other benefits (see Reynolds, Wright, & Beale, 2003). Reflecting a strengths-based perspective, Ruiz (2004) described African American grandmothers raising their grandchildren as purveyors of moral, spiritual, and family values. Moreover, the perspectives of Cox (2000) and Whitley, White, and Kelley (1999), emphasizing the empowerment of custodial grandparents and stressing the promotion of independence, self-confidence, and self-assurance among grandparent caregivers, respectively, reflect the assumption that grandfamilies are better thought of as having resources and strengths, rather than deficiencies and shortcomings. When conducting therapy with CGC, this is the posture that we choose to take, and it has thus far been highly rewarding work.

REFERENCES

American Association of Retired Persons. (2003). *Financial assistance for grandparent caregivers: TANF.* Retrieved June 15, 2007 from http://www.aarp.org/confacts/money/tanf.html

American Psychiatric Association. (2000). *Diagnostic and statistical manual of mental disorders* (4th ed., text revision; DSM-IV-TR). Washington, DC: Author.

Baird, A. (2003). Through my eyes: Service needs of grandparents who raise their grandchildren, from the perspective of a custodial grandmother. In B. Hayslip, Jr., & J. Patrick (Eds.), *Working with custodial grandparents* (pp. 59–68). New York: Springer.

Blackburn, M. L. (2000). America's grandchildren living in grandparent households. *Journal of Family and Consumer, 92,* 30–36.

Bowlby, J. (1969/1982). *Attachment and loss: Vol. 1. Attachment.* New York: Basic Books.

Bowlby, J. (1973). *Attachment and loss: Vol. 2. Separation.* New York: Basic Books.

Bowlby, J. (1980). *Attachment and loss: Vol. 3. Loss.* New York: Basic Books.

Brown, G. W., Harris, T. O., & Bifulco, A. (1986). Long-term effects of early loss of parent. In M. Rutter et al. (Eds.), *Depression in young people: Clinical and developmental perspectives* (pp. 251–296). New York: Guilford Press.

Brown-Standridge, M. D., & Floyd, C. W. (2000). Healing bittersweet legacies: Revisiting contextual family therapy for grandparents raising grandchildren in crisis. *Journal of Marital & Family Therapy, 26,* 185–197.

Butts, D. M. (2000). Organizational advocacy as a factor in public policy regarding custodial grandparenting. In B. Hayslip, Jr., & R. Goldberg-Glen (Eds.), *Grandparents raising grandchildren: Theoretical, empirical, and clinical perspectives* (pp. 341–350). New York: Springer.

Cassidy, J. (1994). Emotional regulation: Influences of attachment relations. In N. A. Fox (Ed.), The development of emotion regulation: Biological and behavioral considerations. *Monographs of the Society for Research in Child Development, 59,* 228–249.

Cohen, C. S., & Pyle, R. (2000). Support groups in the lives of grandparents raising grandchildren. In C. Cox (Ed.), *To grandmother's house we go and stay: Perspectives on custodial grandparents* (pp. 235–252). New York: Springer.

Cox, C. (2000). Empowering grandparents raising grandchildren. In C. Cox (Ed.), *To grandmother's house we go and stay: Perspectives on custodial grandparents* (pp. 253–267). New York: Springer.

Cox, C. (2002). Empowering African American custodial grandparents. *Social Work, 47,* 45–54.

Dannison, L. L., & Smith, A. B. (2003). Custodial grandparents community support program: Lessons learned. *Children & Schools, 25,* 87–95.

Dellmann-Jenkins, M., Blankemeyer, M., & Olesh, M. (2002). Adults in expanded grandparent roles: Considerations for practice, policy, and research. *Educational Gerontology, 28,* 219–235.

Dozier, M., Stoval, K. C., & Albus, K. E. (1999). Attachment and psychopathology in adulthood. In J. Cassidy & P. R. Shaver (Eds.), *Handbook of attachment: Theory, research, and clinical applications* (pp. 497–519). New York: Guilford.

Dutton, D., & Painter, S. L. (1981). Traumatic bonding: The development of emotional attachments in battered women and other relationships of intermittent abuse. *Victimology, 6,* 139–155.

Edwards, O. W. (1998). Helping grandkin—Grandchildren raised by grandparents: Expanding psychology in the schools. *Psychology in the Schools, 35,* 173–181.

Egeland, B., & Sroufe, L. A. (1981). Developmental sequelae of maltreatment in infancy. *New Directions for Child Development: No. 11,* 77–92. San Francisco: Jossey-Bass.

Fonagy, P., Leigh, T., Steele, M., Steele, H., Kennedy, R., Mattoon, G., Target, M., & Gerber, A. (1996). The relation of attachment status, psychiatric classification, and response to psychotherapy. *Journal of Consulting and Clinical Psychology, 64,* 22–31.

Fuller-Thomson, E., & Minkler, M. (2000). The mental and physical health of grandmothers who are raising their grandchildren. *Journal of Mental Health and Aging, 6,* 311–323.

Generations United. (2004, November). *Efficacy of support groups for grandparents raising grandchildren.* Paper presented at the Annual Scientific Meeting of the Gerontological Society of America. Washington, DC.

Glass, J. C. & Huneycutt, T. L. (2002). Grandparents raising grandchildren: The courts, custody, and educational implications. *Educational Gerontology, 28,* 237–251.

Goodman, C., & Silverstein, M. (2002). Grandparents raising grandchildren: Family structure and well being in culturally diverse families. *The Gerontologist, 42,* 676–689.

Grant, R. (2000). The special needs of children in kinship care. *Journal of Gerontological Social Work, 33,* 17–33.

Grant, R., & Kucera, E. (1998). *Social and environmental stressors affecting an inner city school population.* National Assembly on School Based Health Care, Washington, D.C.

Greenberg, M. T. (1999). Attachment and psychopathology in childhood. In J. Cassidy & P. R. Shaver (Eds.), *Handbook of attachment: Theory, research, and clinical applications* (pp. 469–496). New York: Guilford.

Hayslip, B., Jr., & Kaminski, P. (2005). Grandparents raising their grandchildren: A review of the literature and suggestions for practice. *The Gerontologist, 45,* 262–269.

Hayslip, B., Jr., & Shore, R. J. (2000). Custodial grandparenting and mental health services. *Journal of Mental Health and Aging, 6,* 367–384.

Hayslip, B., Jr., Shore, R. J., Henderson, C., & Lambert, P. (1998). Custodial grandparenting and grandchildren with problems: Their impact on role satisfaction and role meaning. *Journal of Gerontology: Social Sciences, 53B,* S164–S174.

Heywood, E. M. (1999). Custodial grandparents and their grandchildren. *The Family Journal: Counseling and Therapy for Couples and Families, 7,* 367–372.

Hirshorn, B. (1998). Grandparents as caregivers. In M. Szinovacz (Ed.), *Handbook on grandparenthood* (pp. 200–216). Westport, CT: Greenwood.

Hirshorn, B., VanMeter, J. V., & Brown, D. R. (2000). When grandparents raise grandchildren due to substance abuse: Responding to a uniquely destabilizing factor. In B. Hayslip, Jr., & R. Goldberg-Glen (Eds.), *Grandparents raising grandchildren: Theoretical, empirical, and clinical perspectives* (pp. 269–288). New York: Springer.

Holigrocki, R. J., & Kaminski, P. L. (2002). A structural and icroanalytic exploration of parent-child relational psychopathology. *Constructivism in the Human Sciences, 7,* 111–123.

Holigrocki, R. J., Kaminski, P. L., & Frieswyk, S. H. (1999). Introduction to the Parent-Child Interaction Assessment. *Bulletin of the Menninger Clinic, 63,* 413–428.

Holigrocki, R. J., Kaminski, P. L., & Frieswyk, S. H. (2002). *Parent-Child Interaction Assessment II (PCIA-II): Directions for administration.* Available from the PCIA Web site at http://facstaff.uindy.edu/~rholigrocki/Downloads.htm

Joslin, D. (2002). *Invisible caregivers: Older adults raising children in the wake of HIV/AIDS.* Columbia, NY: Columbia University Press.

Kaminski, P. L., & Hayslip, B., Jr. (2004, August). *Parenting Attitudes of Custodial Grandparents.* Paper presented at the Annual Convention of the American Psychological Association. Honolulu, HI.

Keller, S., & Stricker, G. (2003). Links between custodial grandparents and the psychological adaptation of grandchildren. In B. Hayslip, Jr., & J. Patrick (Eds.), *Working with custodial grandparents* (pp. 27–44). New York: Springer.

Kirby, J., & Kaneda, T. (2002). Health insurance and family structure: The case of adolescents in skipped generation families. *Medical Care Research and Review, 59,* 146–165.

Kolomer, S., McCallion, P., & Overeynder, J. (2003). Why support groups help: Successful interventions for grandparent caregivers of children with developmental disabilities. In B. Hayslip, Jr., & J. Hicks-Patrick (Eds.), *Working with custodial grandparents* (pp. 111–126). New York: Springer.

Landry-Meyer, L. (1999). Research into action: Recommended intervention strategies for grandparent caregivers. *Family Relations, 48,* 381–389.

Landry-Meyer, L. (2000). Grandparents as parents: What they need to be successful. *Family Focus, 45,* F9–F10.

Lloyd, C. (1980). Life events and depressive disorder reviewed: I. Events as predisposing factors. *Archives of General Psychiatry, 37,* 529–535.

Lyons-Ruth, K., Alpern, L., & Repacholi, B. (1993). Disorganized infant attachment classification and maternal psychological problems as predictors of hostile-aggressive behavior in the preschool classroom. *Child Development, 64,* 572–585.

Mack, K. Y. (2001). Childhood family disruptions and adult well-being: The differential effects of divorce and parental death. *Death Studies, 25,* 419–443.

McCallion, P., Janicki, M., Grant-Griffin, L., & Kolomer, S. (2000). Grandparent caregivers II: Service needs and service provision issues. *Journal of Gerontological Social Work, 33,* 57–84.

Miltenberger, P., Hayslip, B., Jr., Harris, B., & Kaminski, P. (2003–2004). Perceptions of the losses experienced by custodial grandmothers. *Omega: Journal of Death and Dying, 48,* 245–261.

Minkler, M., & Fuller-Thomson. (1999). The health of grandparents raising grandchildren: Results of a national study. *American Journal of Public Health, 93,* 1384–1389.

Musil, C., Schrader, S., & Mutikani, J. (2000). Social support stress and the special coping tasks of grandmother caregivers. In C. Cox (Ed.), *To grandmother's house we go and stay: Perspectives on custodial grandparents* (pp. 56–70). New York: Springer.

Parker, G. B., Barrett, E. A., & Hickie, I. B. (1992). From nurture to network: Examining links between perceptions of parenting received in childhood and social bonds in adulthood. *American Journal of Psychiatry, 149,* 877–885.

Perris, C., Arrindell, W. A., & Eisemann, M. (Eds.) (1994). *Parenting and psychopathology.* Chichester, England: John Wiley & Sons.

Pinson-Millburn, M., Fabian, E., Schlossberg, N., & Pyle, M. (1996). Grandparents raising grandchildren. *Journal of Counseling and Development, 74,* 548–554.

Poehlmann, J. (2003). An attachment perspective on grandparents raising their very young grandchildren: Implications for intervention and research. *Infant Mental Health Journal, 24,* 149–173.

Reynolds, G. P., Wright, J. V., & Beale, B. (2003). The roles of grandparents in educating today's children. *Journal of Instructional Psychology, 30,* 316–325.

Rogers, A., & Henkin, N. (2000). School-based interventions for children in kinship care. In B. Hayslip, Jr., & R. Goldberg-Glen (Eds.), *Grandparents raising grandchildren: Theoretical, empirical and clinical perspectives* (pp. 221–238). New York: Springer.

Ruiz, D. (2004). *Amazing grace: African American grandmothers as caregivers and conveyors of traditional values.* New York: Praeger.

Sameroff, A. J., & Emde, R. N. (Eds.). (1989). *Relationship disturbances in early childhood: A developmental approach.* New York: Basic Books.

Sawyer, R., & Dubowitz, H. (1994). School performance of children in kinship care. *Child Abuse & Neglect, 18,* 587–597.

Scanlon, E., & Devine, E. (2001). Residential mobility and youth well-being: Research, policy, and practice issues. *Journal of Sociology and Social Welfare, 28,* 199–138.

Silverthorn, P., & Durant, S. (2000). Custodial grandparenting and the difficult child: Learning from the parenting literature (pp. 47–64). In B. Hayslip, Jr., & R. Goldberg-Glen (Eds.), *Grandparents raising grandchildren: Theoretical, empirical, and clinical perspectives* (pp. 47–64). New York: Springer.

Smith, A. B., & Dannison, L. L. (2001). Educating educators: Programming to support grandparents-headed families. *Contemporary Education, 72,* 47–51.

Smith, G. (2003). How grandparents view support groups: An exploratory study. In B. Hayslip, Jr., & J. Patrick (Eds.), *Working with custodial grandparents* (pp. 69–92). New York: Springer.

Smith, C. J., & Monahan, D. J. (2004, November). *Evaluating kinship care: Practice and policy implications.* Paper presented at the Annual Scientific Meeting of the Gerontological Society of America. Washington, DC.

Solomon, J. C., & Marx, J. (1995). "To grandmother's house we go:" Health and school adjustment of children raised solely by grandparents. *The Gerontologist, 35,* 386–394.

Strom, R., & Strom, S. (2000). Goals for grandparent caregivers and support groups. In B. Hayslip, Jr., & R. Goldberg-Glen (Eds.), *Grandparents raising grandchildren: Theoretical, empirical, and clinical perspectives* (pp. 171–218). New York: Springer.

Talarico, D. (2007, May 7). *Celebrities who are adopted: A look at famous adoptees.* Retrieved October 6, 2007, from http://www.associatedcontent.com/article/233335/celebrities_who_are_adopted_a_look.html

Turner, R. J., & Lloyd, D. A. (1995) Life-time traumas and mental health: The significance of cumulative adversity. *Journal of Health Social Behavior, 36,* 360–376.

U.S. Census Bureau. (2000). *Current population survey.* Washington, DC: U.S. Government Printing Office.

Vrasti, R., & Eisemann, M. (1994). Perceived parental rearing behaviour in alcoholics. In C. Perris, W. A. Arrindell, & M. Eisemann (Eds.), *Parenting and psychopathology* (pp. 201–218). Chichester, England: John Wiley & Sons.

Waldrop, D., & Weber, J. (2001). From grandparent to caregiver. *Families in Society: The Journal of Contemporary Human Services, 82,* 461–472.

Webb, N. B. (1993). *Helping bereaved children: A handbook for practitioners.* New York: Guilford.

Whitley, D. M., White, K. R., & Kelley, S. J. (1999). Strengths-based case management: The application to grandparents raising grandchildren. *Journal of Families in Society, 80,* 110–119.

Wohl, E., Lahner, J., & Jooste, J. (2003). Group processes among grandparents raising grandchildren. In B. Hayslip, Jr., & J. Patrick (Eds.), *Working with custodial grandparents* (pp. 195–212). New York: Springer.

Zuckerman, B., Frank, D., & Brown, E. (1995). Overview of the effects of abuse and drugs on pregnancy and offspring. *National Institute of Drug Abuse Research Monographs, 149,* 16–38.

NOTE

1. This higher risk does *not* mean that clinically significant problems are inevitable among CGC; given the focus of this chapter, however, we will focus our discussion on CGC who could clearly benefit from intervention.

CHAPTER 15

Preschool Children and Caregiving Grandparents: Enhancing Family Strengths

Andrea Smith and Linda Dannison

$\mathbf{P}$rogramming for multigenerational families typically focuses on community services, parenting information, and respite for custodial grandparents. There may be many reasons for initially developing programming for adult family members, including their ability to independently assent to services, transport themselves to group settings, and participate in group services without second-party assistance. These groups have become numerous in the past decade and provide valuable services and support to participants (Vacha-Haase, Ness, Dannison, & Smith, 1999). For maximum effectiveness, however, a multifaceted approach, emphasizing holistic programming to all grandparent-headed family members, is useful (Dannison, Smith, & Vacha-Haase, 1999). In 1996, more than half of the children residing in grandparent-headed households were under age 6 (U.S. Census Bureau, 1996). In addition, 75% of custodial grandchildren began living with their grandparents when they were younger than 5 years of age (Fuller-Thomson, Minkler, & Driver, 1997). Many children in the care of grandparents experience common emotional themes that can be addressed within a group setting (Smith & Dannison, 2003). An understanding of these themes, as well as additional information about the family circumstances that led to the formation of a grandparent-headed household, are essential for professionals working in this arena.

Circumstances and family configurations in grandparent-headed homes are diverse and can be depicted on a continuum of involvement (see Figure 15.1) that ranges from less involved to highly involved. Families represented on the far left of this model, Parental Apprentice, often maintain the goal of having the adult child (parent) take increasing responsibility for parenting the grandchild. Examples of this family typology include teen parents, cognitively and mentally impaired parents, and parents who are physically ill. Grandparents who provide substantial day care for their grandchildren may also fall into this category. Grandparents typically play an essential role in providing daily care for the grandchildren while simultaneously teach the adult child how to assume parental responsibilities. Moving along the continuum are grandparents who provide substantial assistance (Parental Support) to their adult children and grandchildren. Examples here are very diverse and might include parents who are substance abusers, have mental illness, are incarcerated, or work in other locations. Military parents who are deployed for duty would fall into this category. These parents typically come and go, entering their children's lives and then often abruptly leaving again. At this point, grandparents often assume increasing amounts of responsibility for daily care and financial support. The final category, Parental Replacement, represents the highest level of grandparental involvement. At this stage, grandparents have assumed fulltime care for grandchildren and have assumed guardianship or become foster or adoptive parents.

Preschool children in the care of grandparents differ from those in parent-maintained homes in many ways. Their grandparents are less likely to have graduated from high school, less likely to be employed, and more likely to be economically disadvantaged (Casper & Bryson, 1998). Many preschool children in grandparent-headed homes have experienced prenatal drug or alcohol exposure and may have experienced neglect and abuse as a result of living in a drug-involved household. Poor nutrition, lack of preventive and routine medical and dental care, and inconsistent and often dangerous living circumstances present conditions well below expected or even marginal levels of care. Young children in kinship care may also face developmental challenges related to physical, cognitive, or emotional delays. Difficulties communicating their feelings to others may be complicated by slow-to-emerge verbal skills. Past traumatic events, including frequent disruptions in living environments, lack of dependable daily schedules, and inconsistent access to caregivers, can often impact children's coping mechanisms (deToledo & Brown 1995; Smith,

◄ . . . . . . *less involved*. . . . . *more involved* . . . . ▶

Parental Apprentice   Parental Support   Parental Replacement

FIGURE 15.1 Continuum of involvement for grandparent-headed families.

Dannison, & Vacha-Haase, 1999). These children may face continuing challenges as they enter formal school environments. Grandparented children experience higher levels of behavioral and emotional problems when compared to children living with their biological parents. Additionally, approximately 30% of children in grandparent-headed homes show learning difficulties or mental impairment and over 60% of school-age children repeat at least one grade (Sawyer & Dubowitz, 1994).

Children in grandparent-maintained homes may come to their current living situation from diverse circumstances, but most share a lack of consistency in their early lives (Dannison & Smith, 2003; Smith & Dannison, 2002). Inconsistent and inappropriate discipline, sporadic meals, and lack of daily routines are common life experiences. These factors contribute to emotions experienced by many grandparented children. Feelings of grief and loss are common as grandchildren struggle to adapt to the losses in their lives. They have not only lost a parent but have also lost a traditional grandparent. Grandchildren often find it difficult to give up their special relationships with "grandma" or "grandpa" when he or she becomes the primary caregiver. Grandchildren in the care of grandparents may also feel high levels of guilt. They may view their parents' absence as proof that they did not measure up or had misbehaved in some way. Grandchildren may even verbalize that they wish they were prettier, smarter, or in other ways different so that their mom or dad would still be living with them. Grandchildren may experience additional guilt as they realize they prefer living in their new kinship environment. Fear is another emotion common in the lives of custodial grandchildren. The many inconsistencies in their early environments and interactions, combined with a sometimes-abrupt change in living situations, contribute to feelings of fear in many grandchildren. They may have never had the opportunity to effectively bond with a consistent and nurturing adult caregiver. Some grandparented children are unable to form relationships and cannot effectively maintain reciprocal relationships. Others become insecurely attached to the grandparent or an older sibling. They may experience great difficulty separating from their trusted caregiver and may be fearful about reaching out or trusting others. Not wanting to be different from their peers, custodial grandchildren may also be embarrassed about their unique family configuration and living environment. They may feel exposed or sensitive about their family composition, and comments and questions from peers may be difficult for them to manage. Children living with grandparents have often experienced major changes in their lives and usually had little control over the contributing circumstances. This lack of empowerment often results in feelings of anger. Angry behaviors may take many forms, including threats, destructive behaviors, and violence and aggression toward self or others (Smith et al., 1999).

CASE STUDY SCENARIOS

The following case studies were developed to help professionals conceptualize the continuum of care represented by grandparent-headed households. Professionals will also benefit from increasing their understanding and empathy related to the strengths and challenges inherent in second-time-around families. Emotional themes common in grandparented children's lives and accompanying behaviors are also illustrated in these scenarios. Professionals are encouraged to consider the following questions when reading these case studies:

1. What strengths does this family bring to this situation?
2. What challenges does this family face?
3. What services would benefit this grandchild?
4. What services and/or information would be beneficial to this family?

Case Study 1: Parental Apprentice

> LaKisha, age 4, lives with her mother, Crystal, age 18, and her maternal grandmother, Carla, age 37. Carla's oldest daughter attends college and does not live at home, but two younger daughters still reside with the family. Carla works two part-time jobs to provide for the family and is often away from home. Crystal spends little time with LaKisha. She maintains an active social life and often goes out with friends. LaKisha is frequently left in the care of her 10-year-old aunt. Crystal's interactions with LaKisha show inconsistency and impatience. She has unrealistic expectations for her daughter's developmental level and often resorts to threats and physical punishment. LaKisha's behavior is sometimes problematic. She is hesitant to interact with other children and refuses to try new experiences. She refuses to eat most foods, frequently sucks her thumb, and is frightened of the dark. She loves spending time with her grandmother Carla and cries when Carla leaves for work. Her aunts sometimes play with her and LaKisha appears to have good verbal skills; she knows colors and shapes and is beginning to recognize some letters and numbers. Carla worries about Crystal's lack of involvement with LaKisha and tries to encourage her to take more responsibility. However, Carla's random work schedules make it difficult for her to be around on a regular basis.

LaKisha lives with people who care about her. Her grandmother, an experienced parent of four children, is aware and concerned about Crystal's approach to parenting. In addition, Carla is employed and works hard to provide for her family's financial needs. Other family strengths include La-Kisha's aunts, who enjoy playing with her and provide LaKisha with individual attention.

This family's challenges include Crystal's negative interactions with La-Kisha, Carla's erratic work schedule, lack of reliable and responsible child-care providers, and an inconsistent schedule at home. Additionally, Crystal's age and developmental level make it difficult for her to parent effectively and fully meet LaKisha's needs. Crystal's reliance on physical punishment and her unrealistic view of LaKisha's developmental level also impact negatively on both LaKisha and the entire family.

Services that could be beneficial to LaKisha include opportunities to socialize with other preschool-aged children in a safe and nurturing setting. Small group size and low adult-to-child ratios are often advantageous for children in the care of grandparents (Dannison & Smith, 2003a, 2003b, 2003c). Increased consistency in LaKisha's home environment, emphasizing routines for separating from her grandmother, may also be helpful. Receiving positive reinforcement for "brave" behaviors (i.e., trying new foods, sleeping with a nightlight or flashlight) may also assist LaKisha to conquer some of her fears and enhance her view of self. A holistic family systems perspective (Dannison et al., 1999) highlights services for other family members. Parenting classes and a relationship with a trained parent mentor could be useful for Crystal. She might also benefit from counseling and vocational training, with the future goal of being able to live independently and support herself and her daughter. Carla would feel less challenged if she could access financial support for custodial grandparents currently available in some states. Involvement in a support group for grandparents, where she would be reinforced in her role to teach Crystal parenting and independent-living skills, would also be beneficial. A second function of this support group could be to assist this family in prioritizing goals and increasing effective communication. Respite services could be a welcome outlet for Carla as she continues to juggle her multiple roles. Access to consistent and affordable child care for LaKisha is an additional consideration. Although LaKisha enjoys her play times with her aunts, they should not be routinely expected to provide child-care services.

Case Study 2: Parental Support

> Joe is a 5-year-old boy living with his maternal grandmother, Joan, and her husband, Ben. His mother, Dawn, is currently in a mandated residential treatment program for substance abusers. Dawn became pregnant at age 20 and continued a long pattern of drug and alcohol usage throughout her pregnancy. During her teen years

she repeatedly ran away from home and had only sporadic contact with her mother and stepfather. Joan and Ben were unaware that she was pregnant until she returned home with Joe when he was 4 months of age. Dawn and Joe lived with Joan and Ben for about 6 months, until she met a man and moved to another state to be with him. Joe was left in the care of Joan and Ben. It was nearly a year before Dawn returned and again moved into her parents' home. During the next two years Dawn did not abuse drugs but continued to have problems with drinking. She got a first-shift job at a factory but spent time with Joe in the afternoons and evenings. Her parents continued to help support the family. There was a great deal of tension and conflict between Joan and Dawn as they struggled to negotiate responsibilities for Joe's care. Dawn continued to assert that she was "the mom" but Joan felt Dawn did not do an appropriate job of raising her son and often criticized Dawn. Additionally, Ben and Joan began having problems in their marriage. Ben left for a few months but eventually moved back home. When Joe was 4, Dawn again began going out with friends and was re-exposed to the drug culture. She lost her job and was often gone from home for weeks at a time with no contact. She was placed in a residential treatment program following her arrest for prostitution.

Joe's preschool teacher is concerned about his slow development. His teacher provided them with ideas for activities to do at home with Joe. Despite their best efforts, Joe has made little progress. He struggles academically and physically, displaying poor coordination and delayed motor skills. He is easily distracted and cannot stay on task. He has few friends and seems to shy away from social interactions, is unable to initiate or maintain eye contact, and nearly always prefers to play alone. He sleeps poorly, often waking and coming into his grandparents' bedroom describing nightmares. Recently, he has begun to wet the bed almost nightly. His grandparents are concerned about his developmental delays and his recent regression. They worry that he will be even more negatively affected when his mom returns from residential treatment. They are unsure where to go for help.

Joe's grandparents have been involved throughout his entire life. His relationship with Joan and Ben has continued through the periods when his mother entered and exited the home. Joan and Ben appear to have a caring and committed relationship with Joe. They are aware of his developmental delays and devote time and energy to helping him. Joe attends preschool and a home-school partnership has been established. Joe's recent regressive behaviors concern Joan and Ben and they are willing to seek additional help.

Challenges this family faces include Joan and Ben's strained relationship with Dawn and her inconsistent presence in Joe's early life. Joan and Ben may be struggling to cope with feelings of anger and resentment over Dawn's inabilities to effectively parent her son. Their marital relationship has been stressed. Ben may find it difficult to resolve conflicting feelings related to the fact that he is not Joe's biological grandfather. Joe is facing significant developmental delays. His mother's involvement with drugs and alcohol indicates that Joe is at risk for prenatal exposure to these substances. He is cognitively, socially, and physically delayed. Dealing with challenges associated with a special needs child frequently places additional stress on families.

Joe's inconsistent relationship with his mother presents multiple challenges. Joe may be grieving the loss of Dawn's presence in his life and also may feel self-imposed guilt related to her absence. Many grandparented children feel they are somehow responsible for their parents' absence and have low self-esteem. Joe's guilt may be exacerbated by his recognition that his life with his grandparents, and without his mother, is improved (Smith et al., 1999).

Obtaining a comprehensive evaluation that would include psychological testing for identifying fetal alcohol syndrome or prenatal drug exposure is an important first step in developing a service plan for Joe. Additionally, Joe would benefit from individual counseling that would enable him to process feelings related to his relationship with his mother and to develop strategies to deal with his anxiety. Services tailored to enhancing his self-esteem, improving his social skills, and developing anger management strategies will also be useful. Counseling may also be effective in controlling Joe's enuresis; if symptoms continue after a few months his primary care physician should be consulted to rule out physiological causes. His academic needs could be more effectively met by designing an educational plan that is tailored to his cognitive abilities. Testing to determine Joe's level of cognitive functioning or the presence of learning disabilities will be helpful in determining other essential services. Joe's level of diagnosed disability will determine if he is eligible for financial benefits, including SSDI.

Joan and Ben might benefit from involvement in a Grandparent Support Group where they could meet and interact with other kinship care providers. This would provide them with respite, a social network, and education and information about raising their grandson (Dannison & Smith, 2003; Hayslip & Kaminski, 2005; Smith & Dannison, 2003; Vacha-Haase et al., 1999). Additional information about parenting a special needs child would also be useful. Joan and Ben need opportunities for individual respite but would also benefit from time together as a couple. Marital counseling might be helpful as they continue to deal with the stresses associated with raising a special needs grandchild.

Dawn's presence in Joe's life has been inconsistent but it remains probable she will attempt to reconnect with her son following release from her residential treatment program. Dawn would benefit from supportive services including parenting classes, individual counseling to assist with personal mental health issues, and family counseling focused on improving her relationship with Joe and assisting her in assuming an effective parental role. Vocational education could provide Dawn with access to education that will help her get a job. This is an important step in developing independence and self-sufficiency. Joan will need to remain involved in Dawn and Joe's lives to provide assistance and needs to be ready to step in if Dawn resumes her former lifestyle.

Case Study 3: Parental Replacement

Juan, age 4 1/2, came into his paternal grandmother Elizabeth's care approximately 6 months ago. His mother, Christina, abandoned him shortly after birth, and Juan lived with his father Mike and Mike's new girlfriend. Elizabeth saw Juan only infrequently during the first 3 years of his life, as she did not approve of Mike's lifestyle. When Juan was 4, Elizabeth was informed by the police that Mike had been arrested for attempted murder following a fight in a bar. His girlfriend wanted no part of caring for Juan and Elizabeth was told that he would go into foster care unless she agreed to raise him. Mike was found guilty and sentenced to 12–15 years in prison. Elizabeth, who had recently retired, took on a part-time job to pay for the additional expenses associated with raising a grandchild. Between working and caring for Juan she has little time to see her friends or do any of the things she used to enjoy.

Juan hardly knew his grandmother when he began living in her home. He frequently engages in violent temper tantrums, often hitting or kicking at anyone who attempts to control his actions. He challenges the rules Elizabeth tries to enforce, has difficulties staying in bed for an entire night, and prefers junk food and soda to regular meals. His teeth are decayed, but Elizabeth is having difficulty locating a dentist who will assist with this problem. Elizabeth wonders about Juan's health history, as she had no records related to early medical care. Juan appears to be of above-average intelligence and his child-care provider describes him as "bright." He is cute, personable, and has an engaging personality. Other children sometimes look to him as a leader. However, his behavior at day care is as disruptive as it is at home. Juan has difficulties playing with other children and inconsistently follows directions and rules. Juan continues to get into Elizabeth's things and is sometimes destructive. He scratched her car with a set of keys and laughed when she attempted to punish him. Lately, he has become increasingly physical toward the family dog, causing Elizabeth to intervene and stop him from hitting and kicking their pet. Elizabeth is committed to providing Juan with a supportive home but is beginning to report personal health issues that appear related to the stress she is encountering.

Juan's grandmother appears highly committed to providing a nurturing and supportive home environment for her grandson. He has only been in her care for 6 months but she has established rules, provided nutritious food, and secured child care. In addition, Elizabeth sought out employment to ensure that she had adequate finances to support her grandson. Juan is an attractive and bright child who displays some leadership qualities. He engages readily with other people.

Juan and Elizabeth face significant challenges as they attempt to establish a sense of family. Elizabeth lacks a history with Juan, as she had little contact with him during the first 3 1/2 years of his life. She is adjusting to many things, including parenting a young child, re-employment, altered finances, changes in her daily schedule, and social isolation. Elizabeth is beginning to feel the stress of this lifestyle and is reporting health concerns. Her conflicted feelings about her son may be contributing to the stress she is feeling. After years of not approving of his lifestyle, Elizabeth now is openly angry about his imprisonment and subsequent inability to raise Juan. She is unprepared for the challenges Juan presents and is at a loss on how to parent him. Parenting strategies she has used in the past are not successful with her grandson. Elizabeth is concerned about Juan's medical and dental health and is unsure of where to obtain appropriate care.

Juan's behaviors are consistent with feelings of intense anger and rage common to many children in grandparent-headed homes (Dannison & Smith, 2004). He recognizes that he has been abandoned by many significant adults, including his mother, his father, and his father's girlfriend. Juan has experienced major changes in his life and has had no control over the related circumstances. He misses his father and is grieving this loss in his life. His destructive behaviors, temper tantrums, and defiance represent the depth of the grief and anger he feels.

Juan needs immediate psychological and medical attention. His destructive behaviors, including defacing possessions and cruelty toward animals, are dangerous to him, his grandmother, and to the other children in his day-care setting. His unreported health history, coupled with severe tooth decay, makes it critical to obtain a comprehensive medical evaluation. Social, emotional, cognitive, and physical needs of custodial grandparents and grandchildren require specialized attention and services within the medical arena. Health care professionals often occupy a unique position for assisting grandparents at teachable moments (Grinwys, Smith, & Dannison, 2004; Smith & Dannison, 2006b). Mental health counseling, which would assist Juan with his feelings of grief, provide anger management, and increase his tolerance to frustration, would be beneficial. In addition, an adult male mentor who is willing to commit to a long-term supportive relationship with Juan should be located. Juan would also benefit from continued consistency in his home environment. Family counseling sessions, involving both Elizabeth and Juan, with a focus on prioritizing rules, setting realistic limits, and defining appropriate consequences, could be advantageous. Elizabeth, struggling to adjust to the many demands on her time and energy, would benefit from respite, support, and education. Elizabeth can be assisted in recognizing that she needs to provide Juan with consistency, patience, realistic expectations, and love. Helping her to recognize and appreciate small gains may assist her in not being overwhelmed by the task ahead.

PROFESSIONALS AND CUSTODIAL GRANDPARENT FAMILY MEMBERS

Custodial grandparents, wherever they may fall on the continuum of care, need to maintain a consistent, nurturing home environment for preschool-aged grandchildren. Simple things such as ensuring predictability in daily routines, positive communication that enhances grandchildren's feelings of self worth, and reassurance that grandparents will remain a caring presence in their lives can go a long way toward enhancing development in young children. Providing acceptable outlets for emotional expression and modeling appropriate behaviors are helpful strategies. Additionally, grandparented children benefit from repeated conversations recognizing that everyone feels sad, angry, or guilty at times and that these feelings are both natural and acceptable.

Professionals working with kinship care families can help grandparents refine their parenting skills through involvement in support groups or one-on-one educational opportunities (Dannison & Smith, 2003). Grandparents may initially be overwhelmed by the tasks ahead of them and can benefit from assistance in prioritizing goals and strategies. Kinship care providers can be encouraged to create a caring home environment where grandchildren know they are unconditionally loved and accepted. Consistent modeling of loving behaviors, recognition of the grandchild's needs and emotions as valid, and ample positive feedback are essential first steps toward establishing a loving home environment. These practices must become routine for them to be effective. Grandchildren need to believe that their grandparents' love will remain strong, no matter what they say or do. Grandchildren benefit from being shown how much they are loved, both verbally and physically. Professionals may need to assist grandparents in building sensitivity to their grandchild's earliest experiences and taking cues from their responses (Dannison & Smith, 2006b). Most young children respond positively to lots of kind words, hugs, and kisses. However, some children in the care of grandparents may react more slowly to grandparents' verbal and physical overtures and grandparents need to be patient.

Children in kinship care benefit from consistency and predictability (Dannison & Smith, 2003). Establishing routines for daily tasks is an essential first step. This provides the message that the home environment is supportive and trusting. Establishing routines for daily activities such as meals, dressing, brushing teeth, and going to bed will set the tone for larger transitions including separation routines and atypical days. Grandparents, overwhelmed with the immediacy of many changes, may attempt to change too many things too quickly. Assisting grandparents to prioritize one or two routines and ensuring that they are established habits before setting other goals is an important role for involved professionals (Dannison & Smith, 2006b). Established routines and trust take time to develop. Grandparents benefit from professional involvement and support if their initial efforts are not immediately successful.

Custodial grandparents can also be assisted in ensuring that grandchildren feel they are valued members of the new family unit. Inconsistencies in their early environments may leave grandchildren feeling disconnected and unnoticed. They often miss out on being part of and hearing about treasured family stories and experiences. Special personal items, including baby books, photo albums, family videos, and keepsake boxes may not be part of their lives. These oral traditions and historical mementos are vital in enhancing personal identify and self-esteem in young children. Simple and inexpensive strategies such as Saturday morning pancake breakfasts and Tuesday afternoon library dates are effective first steps in developing family traditions. Grandparents may need assistance in understanding the importance of developing personal mementos, such as photo albums or scrapbooks, that focus special attention on their grandchild's place in the newly established family (Dannison & Smith, 2006a).

Professionals need to acknowledge grandparents' prior experiences and expertise in parenting before expanding their knowledge and skills (Dannison & Smith, 2003; Smith & Dannison, 2003). Role modeling, sharing specific examples, and providing positive feedback and reinforcement are strategies that may be useful. Many kinship providers can enhance interactions with grandchildren by focusing on positive communication. Life with young grandchildren can be hectic and fast paced. In spite of good intentions, it's often easier to tell children what *not* to do. Simple strategies such as positive statements ("Please use your inside voice" instead of "Shut up!"), anticipating transitions ("Bedtime in ten minutes" or "At the end of the game it will be time for dinner"), and positive reinforcement ("I like how you remembered to say please" or "Thank you for remembering to put away your boots") are an effective means toward establishing positive family communication. Grandchildren who see themselves as valued and worthy of positive communication from others have increased self-concept and more positive behavior (Dannison, Smith & Nieuwenhuis, 2007).

Raising a young child is a big job and grandparents should not be expected to do it in isolation. Professionals can guide grandparents in assessing personal needs for social interaction, support, and respite. Custodial grandparents who are juggling multiple roles on a daily basis may benefit from periodic breaks from the intensity of their involvement with their preschool-aged grandchild. Many grandparents are so busy that they may need professional "permission" to actually do good things for themselves. Similarly, professionals can assist grandparents in assessing their grandchildren's needs for outside-the-home activities. Grandchildren will enhance skills in all developmental domains through participation in both formal and informal group activities. The importance of play in enhancing development is unfamiliar to many grandparents. They can benefit from increased knowledge on the importance of play in young children's lives and assistance in developing strategies for organizing high-quality play opportunities (Lally, Lerner, & Lurie-Hurvitz, 2001; Smith & Anderson, 1996; Smith & Dannison, 2004).

The diverse and ongoing needs of grandparent-headed family members necessitate sensitive and effective responses from professionals. Recognizing a family's prior history and focusing on their unique strengths can assist professionals in providing services that are individualized and supportive. Feedback and recommendations tailored to kinship families' specific needs will enhance grandchildren's development. Awareness of community programs and resources can assist kinship-care family members in accessing vital services. Additionally, identifying grandparents' involvement along the continuum of involvement is essential. Most important, however, is recognition that grandparents can make a real difference in their grandchildren's lives. The effort of supporting professionals in enhancing grandchildren's development increases the likelihood that, in time, these grandchildren will become effective parents of their own children.

REFERENCES

Casper, L., & Bryson, K. (1998). *Co-resident grandparents and their grandchildren: Grandparent-maintained families.* (Population Division technical working paper, 26). Washington, DC: U.S. Census Bureau.

Dannison, L., & Smith, A. (2003a). Lessons learned from a custodial grandparent community support program. *Children and Schools, 25*(2), 87–95.

Dannison, L., & Smith, A. (2003b). *Building resiliency in children who are in the care of grandparents.* Family Information Services. Retrieved April 12, 2007 from http://familyinfoserv.com

Dannison, L., & Smith, A. (2003c). *Can we talk about family? Commentary.* Family Involvement Network of Educators, Harvard Family Research Project. Retrieved april 12, 2007 from www.hs.harvard.ed/hffp/projects/fine.resources/teaching-case/grandparent.htm

Dannison, L., & Smith, A. (2004). *Understanding emotional issues in your grandchildren's lives.* Family Information Services. Retrieved April 12, 2007 from http://family infoserv.com

Dannison, L., & Smith, A. (2006a). *Managing the holidays: Strategies for families in transition.* Family Information Services. Retrieved April 12, 2007 from http://family infoserv.com

Dannison, L., & Smith, A. (2006b). *Restructuring rules: When "save room for dessert" becomes "eat your broccoli."* Family Information Services. Retrieved April 12, 2007 from http://familyinfoserv.com

Dannison, L., Smith, A., & Nieuwenhuis, A. (2007). *Second time around: Grandparents raising grandchildren* (2nd ed.). Kalamazoo, MI: Western Michigan University Press.

Dannison, L., Smith, A., & Vacha-Haase, T. (1999). Grandparents as parents: An ecological approach to programming. *Michigan Family Review, 4*(1), 37–45.

deToledo, S., & Brown, D. (1995). *Grandparents as parents: A survival guide for raising a second family.* New York: The Guilford Press.

Fuller-Thomson, E., Minkler, M., & Driver, D. (1997). A profile of grandparents raising grandchildren in the United States. *The Gerontologist, 37,* 406–411.

Grinwys, B., Smith, A., & Dannison, L. (2004). Custodial grandparent families: Steps for developing responsive health care. *Michigan Family Review, 9,* 37–44.

Hayslip, B., Jr., & Kaminski, P. (2005). Grandparents raising their grandchildren: A review of the literature and suggestions for practice. *The Gerontologist, 45*(2), 262–269.

Lally, J., Lerner, C., & Lurie-Hurvitz, E. (2001). Public policy report: National survey reveals gaps in the public's and parents' knowledge about early childhood development. *Young Children, 56*(2), 49–53.

Sawyer, R., & Dubowitz, H. (1994). School performance of children in kinship care. *Child Abuse and Neglect, 18,* 587–597.

Smith, A., & Anderson, A. (1996). The importance of lay in children's lives: Parents and teachers as partners in providing play opportunities for children. *Ohio Journal of the IXKE,* 58–63.

Smith, A., & Dannison, L. (2002). Educating educators: Programming to support grandparent-headed families. *Contemporary Education, 72*, 47–51.

Smith, A., & Dannison, L. (2003). Grandparent-headed families in the United States: Programming to meet unique needs. *Intergenerational Programming Quarterly, 1*(3), 35–47.

Smith, A., & Dannison, L. (2004). *Activities for grandchildren: Discovering local opportunities.* Family Information Services. Retrieved April 10, 2007 from http://family infoserv.com

Smith, A., & Dannison, L. (2006). *Health care for grandparent-headed families.* Family Information Services. Retrieved April 10, 2007 from http://familyinfoserv.com

Smith, A., Dannison, L., and Vacha-Haase, T. (1999). When grandma is mom: What today's teachers need to know. *Childhood Education, 75*, 12–16.

U.S. Census Bureau (1996). *Current population reports: Marital status and living arrangement.* U.S. Government Printing Office.

Vacha-Haase, T., Ness, C., Dannison, L., & Smith, A. (1999). Families in society: Grandparents raising grandchildren. *The Journal for Specialists in Group Work, 25*(1), 67–78.

CHAPTER 16

School-Based Support Group Intervention for Children in the Care of Their Grandparents

Stacey Kolomer, Phillip McCallion,
and Cara Van Voorhis

Increasing numbers of children in America are residing with grandparents, as this skipped-generation family form is becoming a growing phenomenon. According to Casper and Bryson (1998), there were 3.9 million grandchildren living in grandparent-headed households in 1997. Currently, according to the 2000 census, over 4.5 million infants, children, and teens live in households headed by one or more grandparents (U.S. Census Bureau, 2000). This represents 5% of all children in the United States. Children enter the custody of their grandparents for a variety of reasons including parental death, divorce, substance abuse, neglect, unemployment, or teenage pregnancy (Dubowitz, Feigelman, Harrington, Starr, & Zuravin, 1994; Edwards, 2006; Minkler, Roe, & Robertson-Beckley, 1994; Pinson-Millburn, Schlossberg, & Pyle, 1996). Ultimately, the traumatic experiences faced by many of these children, including the separation from their parents, can increase their susceptibility to a number of social and emotional problems throughout childhood (Edwards, 2006).

There are differences experienced by children raised in relative-headed households as compared to children reared by their parents (Dubowitz, Feigelman, Zuravin, Tepper, Davidson, & Lichenstein, 1992; Sawyer & Dubowitz, 2004). The problems facing these children may include a greater risk for developmental delays and emotional problems, dealing with neglectful or absent parents, a higher incidence of Attention Deficit Hyperactivity Disorder, and serious medical concerns often related to parental substance abuse (Janicki, McCallion, Grant-Griffin, & Kolomer, 2000; Kolomer, McCallion, & Janicki, 2002; Myers, Kropf, & Robinson, 2002).

Financial concerns are also prevalent in grandparent-headed households. The available research indicates that children are the most underprivileged population in the country followed by adults over the age of 65 (Myers et al., 2002). These findings support that children living in grandparent-headed families, when compared to children living in families led by biological parents, are more likely to be underprivileged to begin with and to become even poorer over time. Casper and Bryson (1998) agree, finding that children living in households maintained by grandparents were more likely to be poor, receiving public assistance, and without health insurance as compared to children in parent-maintained households.

Furthermore, problems in school such as reduced attention and concentration, poor work-study habits, and an increase in failed grades also burden these children (Myers et al., 2002). One-third of children residing with grandparents live in a home where no one has a high school diploma (Casper and Bryson, 1998). A portion of their school-related problems therefore may be due to the likelihood that some children living in grandparent-headed households live in a family where there is a lack of influence in terms of educational achievement. School-related problems have been highlighted as continuing to increase among children in grandparent-headed households, and teachers are identifying the need for school-based interventions (Edwards, 2006).

SUPPORT GROUPS FOR CHILDREN IN SCHOOLS

"Children who live in environments of chronic poverty, poor early parent-child relationships, family conflict or disorder, negative life events, and abuse, and who endure childhood trauma are vulnerable to maladjustment" (Edwards, 2006, p. 570). The hardships experienced by children in grandparent-headed households often develop into emotional and behavioral problems that adversely affect their school functioning. These children are likely to require extra support and stability within the school system in order to overcome their disadvantages (Edwards, 2006). Group counseling theory suggests participation in a group can help children feel less isolated, normalize their experiences, and gain support from peers (Gladding, 1991).

Schools have become a common setting for group work with children because the children are observed for long periods of time in a variety of activities. Students in need of help are able to gain the attention of school administrators who have access to resources that can assist them (O'Rourke, 1990). Support groups established in the school setting begin with the goal that children can build self-esteem regardless of the circumstances within their family. In the context of the group, children ultimately learn that they are not alone in their situation or with their problems. Children are able to learn from one another how to manage different situations within their lives (DeLucia-Waack & Gerrity, 2001). Through these groups children are able to explore feelings, manage stress, and develop coping skills (O'Rourke, 1990).

BANANA SPLITS SUPPORT GROUP MODEL

Group work is an accepted and professional method of providing assistance to children experiencing the effects of divorce. (DeLucia-Waack & Gerrity, 2001). One of the most notable support groups established for children within the school system is known as Banana Splits, a support group for children of divorcing parents. This group was first established in 1978 by Elizabeth McGonagle in upstate New York as ongoing therapeutic support for children to assist them with parental separation, divorce, and new relationships (Tucker, 1995). This group method is ideal for children ages 6 to 12 (Bonkowski, 1997). Participation in Banana Splits is voluntary, although children must obtain permission from a guardian in order to participate. In addition, confidentiality is a key component of the group and helps the children recognize the group leader as a trustworthy adult, an experience that group members may not have previously had (Lawson, 1991).

The Banana Splits group usually meets once per week during lunch or recess and is facilitated by a psychologist, social worker, counselor, school nurse, or teacher (Lawson, 1991). During the group meetings, children are encouraged to express their thoughts and feelings through the utilization of role-playing, puppets and art projects, posting thoughts on a bulletin board, and talking with peers experiencing similar situations (Lawson, 1991). Ultimately, the concept behind the Banana Splits support group is that of shared experiences, and it highlights the importance of exploring feelings and receiving emotional support and validation from others in similar situations.

APPLYING THE BANANA SPLITS GROUP MODEL TO GRANDCHILDREN LIVING IN GRANDPARENT-HEADED HOUSEHOLDS

A team of social workers testing case management and support group strategies for custodial grandparents chose to pilot an intervention for children living in grandparent-headed households. In other programs, grandparent caregivers were benefiting from the support of their peers and it seemed that children in grandfamilies might also gain from peer support. After reviewing models of support groups for children, Banana Splits appeared to be a natural fit. The focus of the Banana Splits intervention is on the child's management of his or her changing family situation. This model seemed ideal to adapt for children in grandfamilies. Most of the adaptations to the intervention were around issues of language. For example, rather then talking about what it was like to live with their mother or father, discussions focused on what it was like to live with grandparents.

The social-work study team approached an elementary school (K–5) principal and school counselor in the Bronx, New York, to discuss the possibility of conducting a pilot support group based on the Banana Splits model with children whose primary caregivers were their grandparents. The principal and counselor were both supportive of having the group although could not provide any assistance with supplies or personnel.

Nearly 70% of the approximately 800 students in the school are African American and 24% are Hispanic. There was no obvious way to know which children were being raised in grandparent-headed households due to inaccuracies in the way many children were registered for school (e.g., children registered by one parent with a no-longer-valid address of the other parent and actually living somewhere else with a grandparent). School personnel, however, were aware that large numbers of their students were from such households. The children that were recommended for participation were sufficiently well known to the principal, because of their behavior problems in the classroom, that she knew that the grandparent was the primary caregiver.

Seven children were interviewed individually by a social worker to assess for appropriateness for participation in a support group for children being raised by a grandparent. The social worker met with each child for approximately 20 minutes. Ultimately, two girls and four boys were invited to participate. The children's ages ranged from 7 to 10 years old (grades 2–5) and all were African American. The one child who was not invited to join had great difficulty concentrating and sitting in place for more than 2 minutes at a time. He was also only 6 years old and the sibling of another child being interviewed. For this type of intervention it is recommended that siblings not be in the same group (DeLucia-Waack & Gerrity, 2001). For the above reasons it was determined that it would be better for him not to participate in this group.

The intervention. The Banana Splits Model was adapted to address the issues concerning children in grandparent-headed households. The group met weekly for eight 35-minute-sessions. This pilot group was led by a certified social worker with 8 years experience. The social worker provided the supplies, which included chart paper, magic markers, photocopies, scotch tape, masking tape, and scissors. A teacher in the school allowed the social worker to keep the supplies in his classroom.

Session one: The purpose of the first session was for the students to get acquainted with one another and begin to build an atmosphere of trust. It was an opportunity for the children to realize that living with a grandparent was common to all group members. During this first session the children introduced themselves to one another and then the facilitator assisted the children in establishing the ground rules of the group. The ground rules were written on a chart for future reference. Ground rules included:

- not sharing information about group members outside of the group; and
- no yelling, no fighting, no starting trouble, no arguing, no cursing, and no interrupting one another.

The children and facilitator then signed "contracts" stating that they would adhere to the ground rules of the group. In the beginning of every session the ground rules were revisited and they were always available, hanging in the room where the group was taking place.

Session two: The goal of the second session was to have the children realize that although some family members live in different homes, they are still a part of the family. The group discussed the definition of family. Following the discussion each child drew a picture of the number of homes it took to show all of the people in their family. The children then shared their pictures with the group and briefly discussed the commonalities of their families. Many of the children shared pictures that depicted three homes or more. In this drawing by Justin, for example, he drew his family residing in five different homes.

Session three: In the third session children were asked to provide written responses to the following questions or statements:

- What has changed about his/herself in the last year?
- Identify something good about living with the grandparent.
- What would he or she like to change about living with the grandparent?
- Identify a favorite memory experienced with the grandparent.

Some of the changes they saw in themselves included getting older, getting a dog, having a new sibling, and growing taller. The most common responses to the question of what was good about living with a grandparent were "being loved" and "being taken places." Some of the students also discussed feeling

"Justin" age 8

FIGURE 16.1 Justin's drawing.

lonely living with their grandparents. Examples of happy memories identified were Christmas, being picked up and carried, and going on trips with the grandparents. Love was a large theme of the discussion during this meeting about living in a grandparent's home.

Since the children had acclimated to the schedule of attending the group weekly, assignments were given for future meetings. Following the third session the children were asked to think about all of the feelings that they had experienced as a result of living with a grandparent.

Session four: The goal of the fourth meeting was for children to identify feelings they had related to living in a grandfamily. The children called out feelings while the social worker wrote them on a large sheet of chart paper that was taped to a wall. Then the children chose a feeling from the chart that they had experienced personally and wrote it down on the index card. Some good feelings included being happy, excited, and feeling loved. Some bad feelings the children identified included feeling sad, angry, misunderstood, and frustrated.

Each group member then shared a personal incidence when they had experienced the feeling that they chose. Common positive experiences among the children included, again, being able to go places, being well fed, being helped with homework, playing with grandparents, and having permission to do special activities such as going on the internet or jumping on the bed. General negative experiences included coping with an angry grandparent, being yelled at, and dealing with an ill grandparent. Each child then designed a grandparents' feeling journal. Despite the children's range of writing abilities, even the children who had difficulty constructing sentences were able to complete this task. It was established that, as with almost everything, there are positives and negatives to living with a grandparent. The session concluded with a discussion about ways to cope with difficult feelings.

Session five: The fifth meeting also focused on the children's feelings. The goal was for students to identify stressful situations. The children were asked to discuss stressful events that they had experienced. Children openly shared events where they felt anxiety or stress. The students were then instructed on how to design "stress meters." Stress meters were drawn much like rulers and scale was labeled 1 through 10. Each child then had to specify where the stressful events they had shared were on the scale of 1 to 10 (with 10 being the most stressful event). For one child much of her stress was around her pets and how others treated those pets. Another child shared that worrying about her family was stressful for her.

This group of children shared many of the same concerns about their grandparents. One common theme among the children was anxiety about the status of their grandparents' health and their ability to care for them until they reached adulthood. The children also expressed concern about who would care for them if something should happen to their grandparents. There was fear about not knowing who would take care of them should their grandparents be unable to. One young boy wrote that thinking about his mother being sick was very stressful. Some of the children speculated about who could step in to care for them if their grandparents were unable to, while others felt no one would be available.

A discussion followed about how stress is different for everyone. The children shared ideas about how to deal with potentially stressful situations. The facilitator then described relaxation techniques the children could try and use when confronted with a stressful event. The techniques included deep breathing and silently counting to 10 in their heads before expressing their anxiety. For the following week students were instructed to try these techniques and were asked to be willing to share at the next meeting what worked and what did not work in reducing their concerns.

Sessions six and seven: As well as hearing about how group members used relaxation techniques to reduce stress, the sixth session was designed to have the children participate in a project together. Following up on the previous week's discussion about coping strategies for dealing with stress, the children were asked to develop a newspaper about what life was like living in a grandparent-headed household. This activity allowed the children to express themselves creatively as well as further explore the issues related to living with a grandparent. The children chose to name their paper *Grandparent Times* and include articles, pictures, and interviews in it. The children were candid in their stories. For example, Shelly wrote the following story for her article:

> Once when my mom and grandpa was fighting and I was trying to break it up before my grandpa called the cops. I got punched in the mouth. My tooth came out. Grandpa reached for the phone and grabbed it. I was bleeding on my hand and leg and my teeth. I grabbed the phone and was crying. I begged for him not to do it [i.e. call the police]. Mom went downstairs and grandpa locked the door. She didn't come back for three months.

Another story written by Kwan tells about his upcoming family trip:

> My grandparents are nice. They love me a lot they are going to take me on a cruise ship. Then we might go to Florida too so I can go to the concerts.

At the end of the seventh session children were asked to describe what it was like to produce their own newspaper, what they learned about themselves and each other, if they were going to share it with their family, and, if so, what they thought their family would think about their contribution to the newspaper. Most of the children expressed pride in their work and felt that they would share their newspaper with their family members.

Session eight: The final meeting's purpose was to encourage the children to think about how their home lives could be enhanced for everyone living in the household. The children were given the opportunity to fantasize about how to make their lives more "perfect." The children were given a worksheet with outlines of gift boxes. The children were then asked to write or draw in the gift boxes what kind of qualities they would choose to give to members of their family. For example, they might wish for someone to have a certain skill or a personality trait. The participants were asked: "If you could give something to each member of the group, what would it be?" Children were then able to talk about their feelings about being a member of the group and how it felt to be leaving the group.

All of grandchildren expressed that being in a group with others who knew what it was like to live with a grandparent was helpful. Sharing their experiences

once when my mom and grandpa was fighting and was trying to break it up before grandpa called the cops, I got punched in the mouth, my tooth came out. Grandpa Reached for the phone and I grabbed it. I was bleeding on my hands and legs and my teeth. I grab the phone and crying I beg for him not to do it. Mom when downstairs and grandpa locked the door. she didn't come back up for 3 many?

"Shelly" age 9

FIGURE 16.2 Shelly's drawing.

with other children living with grandparents helped them to feel less isolated from others. Some experiences that they may not ordinarily share with others they felt comfortable disclosing in the group. Occasionally discussion drifted towards some painful family experiences (e.g., family violence). The group became a safe place for these children to talk about what it was like to live in their particular family.

LESSONS LEARNED

There were several challenges in facilitating this group. First, identifying which children were living in grandparent-headed households was difficult. The school administrators reported not having a clear way to identifying those children. The children who were referred by the principal were known to school administrators because of their classroom misbehaviors. Those children living in grandparent-headed households but not having difficulty in their classrooms could have also been referred if the children in the school were tracked more closely. These children may have benefited from being part of such a group. For future groups it may be advantageous to send notices home with all of the children in the school and allow the grandfamilies to self identify. Another option would be to meet with teachers. Teachers would be more likely to know their students' living situations and therefore would be able to make referrals to the group.

Ideally this group would have been comprised of children closer in age to one another. Based on how the referrals were made it was difficult to have a group of only 6- to 8-year-olds and then another group of 9- to 11-year-olds. The program could be modified depending on the ages of the participants. With a younger group more play activities could have been designed to help them express their feelings and thoughts while an older group could have had more verbal discussions. In addition, consideration should be made about the socioeconomic background of the participants. All of these children were living in a lower socioeconomic neighborhood and all were African American. If this intervention were going to be used with another population the facilitator may choose to make some adaptations.

Initially teachers were pleased to have the children participate in the support group, particularly because these children were disruptive in the classroom. As the intervention progressed, one teacher voiced concerns that allowing her disruptive students to attend an enjoyable support group might inadvertently reward the child's poor behavior. On at least one occasion a teacher did not allow her student to attend group because the child had been having "a bad day" in the classroom.

Getting teacher support is critical to any therapeutic group in a school. Meeting with the teachers in advance, explaining the purpose of the group, and ensuring a shared understanding of agreed rules for participation may have garnered teacher support. In addition, meeting with the teachers would offer an opportunity to inform them how a child's misbehavior in a classroom may be a possible symptom of emotional distress.

Having space for a group to meet in schools is a continuing challenge. Most social workers or counselors do not have a classroom. If their office is small or shared it is not easy to facilitate a group in that space. In this case, the group had to change rooms several times during the 8-week period. Most sessions occurred in the cafeteria and gymnasium, but one session had to be conducted in a quiet hallway. Ensuring the availability of large private space is critical for the success of a support group, particularly when the children are talking about personal matters. More widespread use of such interventions will be difficult if appropriate meeting spaces are not available.

Ensuring confidentiality in this type of group is critical to the trust among the members and facilitators. However, at times confidentiality must be violated if the child reveals that his or her safety is in jeopardy. The social worker who facilitated the group and the school counselor had an agreement that the social worker would report to the counselor and the principal if any child was being harmed either in or outside of the group. Fortunately this did not occur, although the student Shelly did share a violent story that had occurred in her home. The social worker shared her knowledge of that incident with the principal after having a discussion with Shelly about having to disclose that information. Indeed, the school had been aware of that incident and Shelly was aware that the school knew.

In retrospect, rather then creating a newsletter during sessions six and seven, the children could have continued to write in the journals that were started in session four. These journals would only be shared within the group. There was a risk that students or teachers could have seen the newsletter and a possibility of negative repercussions for the children if sensitive information was shared with others outside of the group. In addition, some grandparents may not have been pleased with what his or her grandchild revealed in the newsletter. Having the social worker keep the journals at the end of every session would have decreased the risk of confidentiality being broken.

This was a pilot intervention in an inner-city school where an additional criterion for participation was being such a behavior problem in class that the principal knew the child's family circumstances well. As such, the child participants were complex clients with a variety of issues. Despite the complexities of their lives and significance of their problems, the children were active and cooperative, had relatively good attendance (when teachers allowed), and appeared to enjoy and benefit from the intervention. While Banana Splits intervention and the adaptation presented here draw heavily from well-established group work and therapeutic principles, the absence of a literature and an evidence base can make it difficult to secure the support needed for staff time, space, and the release of students from the classroom. The decision of one teacher to withhold the "reward" of the group in many ways speaks to these groups being viewed as recreational, rather than as therapeutic and helpful to academic performance. Thus, it will be important for researchers and clinicians to work together and test the efficacy of this and other school-based support group interventions.

If Banana Splits is easily adaptable to a variety of school and nontraditional family situations, it suggests that training and expertise both in the traditional delivery of Banana Splits and on systematic approaches to its adaptation may be important for school social workers, nurses, and psychologists. As schools and other agencies respond to the needs of children cared for by grandparents and the realities of the additional difficulties endemic to many of these caregiving situations, it is vital to increase the availability of effective interventions that were specifically developed for these children and families.

REFERENCES

Bonkowski, S. (1997). Group work with children of divorce. In G. L. Grief & P. H. Ephross (Eds.), *Group work with populations at risk* (pp. 94–104). New York: Oxford University Press.

Casper, L. M., & Bryson, K. R. (1998). *Co-resident grandparents and their grandchildren: Grandparent maintained families.* (U.S. Bureau of the Census Population Division Working Paper 26).

DeLucia-Waack, J. L., & Gerrity, D. (2001). Effective group work for elementary school-age children whose parents are divorcing. *The Family Journal, 9*(273), 273–284.

Dubowitz, H., Feigelman, S., Harrington, D., Starr, R., Jr., & Zuravin, S. (1994). Children in kinship care: How do they fare? *Children and Youth Services Review, 16*(1–2), 85–106.

Dubowitz, H., Feigelman, S., Zuravin, S., Tepper, V., Davidson, N., & Lichenstein, R. (1992). The physical health of children in kinship care. *Archives of Pediatric and Adolescent Medicine, 146*(5), 603–610.

Edwards, O. W. (2006). Teachers' perceptions of the emotional and behavioral functioning of children raised by grandparents. *Psychology in the Schools, 43*(5), 565–572.

Gladding, S. T. (1991). *Group work: A counseling specialty.* New York: Macmillan.

Janicki, M. P., McCallion, P., Grant-Griffin, L., & Kolomer, S. R., (2000). Grandparent caregivers I: Characteristics of the grandparents and the children with disabilities they care for. *Journal of Gerontological Social Work, 33*(3), 35–55.

Kolomer, S. R., McCallion, P., & Janicki, M. P. (2002). African American grandmother caregivers of children with disabilities: Predictors of depressive symptoms. *Journal of Gerontological Social Work, 37*(3/4), 45–63.

Lawson, C. (1991). School club for children of divorce eases the pain of family separation. *Curriculum Review, 30*(7), 191–199.

Minkler, M., Roe, K. M., & Robertson-Beckley, R. J. (1994). Raising grandchildren from crack cocaine households: Effects on family and friendship ties of African-American women. *American Journal of Orthopsychiatry, 64*, 20–29.

Myers, L. L., Kropf, N. P., & Robinson, M. (2002). Grandparents raising grandchildren: Case management in a rural setting. *Journal of Human Behavior in the Social Environment, 10,* 53–71.

O'Rourke, K. (1990). Recapturing hope: Elementary school support groups for children of alcoholics. *Elementary School Guidance and Counseling, 25*(2), 107–115.

Pinson-Millburn, N. M., Schlossberg, N. K., & Pyle, M. (1996). Grandparents raising grandchildren. *Journal of Counseling and Development, 74*(6), 548–555.

Sawyer, R., & Dubowitz, H. (2004). Child abuse and neglect. *The International Journal, 18*(7), 587–597.

Tucker, L. (1995). *Banana Splits: A group for kids.* Retrieved March 13, 2007, from http://www.nymetroparents.com/newarticle.cfm?colid=6893

U.S. Census Bureau. (2000). *Grandparents living with grandchildren.* Retrieved February 1, 2006, from http://www.census.gov/prod/2003pubs/c2kbr-31.pdf

Adjusting and Succeeding in School: Helping Grandparent Caregivers and Their Grandchildren

Rick Mauderer

It was still class time, and the teacher was reviewing for a test. Addy didn't know why her phone kept vibrating or who was calling her for the third time, but if it continued, she would get in trouble and her phone would be taken up. School rules as well as state law forbid cell phone use during school hours. Addy didn't have the resources to pay the $15 the state allows schools to charge in order to retrieve her cell phone from the office if it was taken up. She ignored the silent vibrating of the phone while the teacher droned on. When class was over, she went into a restroom and risked calling the number on her phone. To her surprise, on the other end a Dallas detective answered the phone. They had found her picture on the dresser in a dead man's motel room in Dallas. On the back of that picture was her phone number. The police could not identify the man's body, as there was no ID. The only bit of information they could find was a picture with a phone number. It was her father—dead of a drug overdose. Addy was asked to come and ID the body.

She cried and called her grandmother. They wept together, and made plans to go to the Dallas morgue in the morning. As long as she could remember, her father had struggled with a drug addiction. Her mother also struggled with addictions as well as prostitution. The arrangement for her to live with her grandparents had been made years ago. It was the best option at the time as there were no aunts or uncles that volunteered to step up to the plate. Addy's grandparents loved her greatly, but they were tired. They had already raised children once, and the money they made at their jobs was supposed to go to their retirement, not raising a grandchild. On top of having already raised children, they had to fight their children's drug addictions. Their house had been broken into, their cars stolen, and they had loaned money more times than they cared to think about. Then, there was the anger they felt toward their son for abandoning their granddaughter for the drug world. Now he was dead.

Addy returned to school the next week after the funeral. Her teachers were very merciful and understanding, even though she already had accrued over 50 absences earlier that semester. Addy had trouble getting to school on a regular basis, and her grandparents had trouble getting her there and keeping her there. She was not rebellious, just very passive about school. Looping in her mind was the endless thought asking the same questions: Why do my parents not love me? Why don't my grandparents care more? Why is my life so messed up? Am I going to end up like my parents? Will my grandpa be around to walk me down the aisle when and if I get married? When will the pain end? She was a frequent flier to the school's crisis counselor. If the crisis counselor were busy, she would visit her assistant principal, who always had time to listen and offer healthy perspectives.

Addy's grandparents gave her lots of freedom. It was that same freedom that had allowed her parents to venture into the drug world. Addy does not want anything to do with drugs, even though many of her friends are users. Because of Addy's freedoms, she has a great number of school absences. Along with those absences come low and often failing school grades. She qualified for special education services years ago and has some special education classes because she is missing a lot of foundational knowledge upon which to build further learning.

THE IMPACT OF THE SCHOOL ON CUSTODIAL GRANDCHILDREN

In 1969, the U.S. Government released the Coleman Report on the status of education in America. Among other things, the report stated that who a child's parents were, what happened in the home, and what the family's socioeconomic status was had a greater impact on the educational outcome of students than a school did. Hence, for years, little emphasis was placed upon what actually happened within a school. Laws and taxes were adjusted to socially engineer educational justice and equality. However, with the advent of better computers that are able to conduct more sophisticated statistical analysis at a much quicker rate, it has become quite obvious that schools and individual teachers have a profound impact on the educational outcome of a student.

In 1994, Sanders and Horn released a seminal study based in Tennessee, which held that, "The most important factor affecting student learning is the teacher. In addition, the results show wide variation in effectiveness among teachers" (Sanders & Horn, 1994). Not long after, Robert Mendro, in the Dallas Independent School District (ISD), released a study with similar results. Mendro tracked first-grade students for 3 years and observed that students who had 3 consecutive years of strong teachers grew, on average, from the 63rd to the 87th percentile (a 24-point growth) on the Iowa Test of Basic Skills in math. He then compared their growth with students who had 3 consecutive years of weak teachers, who had an observed decline in growth from 58th to 40th percentile (an 18-point decline) on the same test. Comparing the two groups of children, there was an observed achievement gap of 42 percentile points. Moreover, after 3 more years of intervention, the children with the weak teachers still had not caught up to where their strong-teacher counterparts were. Accounting for family income, race, and gender of the students, Mendro found conclusive evidence that teachers have a profound impact on the growth and ultimate success of children (Mendro, 1998).

Contrary to the Coleman Report, strong teachers clearly make an impact on the lives of children, and it is important that students, regardless of background or guardianship, have a strong connection to their teacher and their school. Those strong connections are made possible by guardians getting their students to school daily and to classes on time. In addition to getting the children into the classes of strong teachers, it is important for guardians to realize that schools have an academic culture that is also a strong source of proper socialization for children. The social culture of schools is also a strong influence on the socialization of children—both positively and negatively. It is for this reason that guardians must maintain a connection with the school and the current culture to see what those influences are and if they are healthy or not for the children in their care.

There are also many positive school organizations that are powerful influences on children due in part to the strength of character of the adult sponsoring the organization—the assumption being that only a person who cares about kids would commit even more of their own time, without additional pay, to sponsor a student organization in order to invest in the lives of children. The other part of the powerful influence is due to the generally altruistic type of child that gets involved in a club or organization, and the commitment to a cause higher than themselves by being part of such a group.

Group membership builds a positive esprit de corps and a healthy social network of support. Anecdotal evidence is also manifold that school grades and accomplishments are generally greater while involved in school activities and organizations.

It is the intent of this chapter to show the data associated with grandparents raising grandchildren in a school setting and to suggest ideas to improve school-guardian relationships, and, ultimately, student success not only in school, but in life generally. Practical advice will be shared as well as common things to observe when working with children from families where the primary guardian is the grandparent.

THE PRESENT STUDY

An analysis of school achievement was conducted in a large suburban high school in Texas, with a grade 9–12 student population of 2,649 for the school year 2006–2007. Of particular interest was the achievement of children raised by grandparents compared to those raised by mothers, fathers, both, or others. Enrollment data was gathered where custodial guardians were identified as father, mother, grandparent, or other (cousin, brother, sister, aunt, uncle, or relative). Each course grade earned by a child was linked to whether the student's primary guardian was identified as father, mother, grandparent, or other. In addition, the race of the child, attendance, semester grade, rigor-level of the course, and whether or not the child was in special education was identified. Records omitted were those where the course was identified as merely pass/fail. Students had anywhere from three to seven classes within a traditional seven-period-day schedule. A series of one way ANOVAs were conducted to measure grades, attendance, and tardies comparing children raised by fathers, mother, grandparents, and others.

A one-way ANOVA was used to compare first semester grades of children with various types of guardians (father, mother, grandparent, and other). Table 17.1 shows that there is a statistically significant difference ($F(3, 15062) = 18.71, p < .001$) for the first semester average of children raised by grandparents and other subgroups. Similar but even more striking results were obtained looking at the second semester averages ($F(3, 14999) = 24.83$, $p < .001$), indicating that children being raised by grandparents achieve lower semester grades than children raised by other categories of guardians.

Another comparison was made with regard to attendance. Is there a difference in attendance patterns between children raised by grandparents and those raised by other categories of guardians? Absences at the school are recorded by classroom teachers as a "U" (unexcused absence) as policy. The absence gets changed to an "A," an excused absence, by the attendance office if and only if a guardian calls, or a guardian provides a legitimate note explaining the absence. To reduce the chances of fraudulent notes or calls by the child, a follow-up call is always made to the child's legal guardian verifying the veracity of the call or note. However, an analysis of excused absences reveals a different situation. Children raised by grandparents suffer from a greater incidence of excused absences ($F(3, 13468) = 18.94$, $p < .001$), as shown in Table 17.1. This seems to indicate that children raised by grandparents have a great incidence of seeing a health care provider than children raised by other groups. However, caution must be exercised in the assumption of who is visiting the healthcare provider—the child, or the grandparent? Documentation provided by the attendance office does not specify whom the appointment was for, only that a legitimate note was provided.

A more telling analysis was completed indicating the attitude of the child toward her or his classes. Tardies are recorded by individual teachers when a child arrives to the class after the tardy bell rings. Table 17.1 reveals that there is a significant difference in the number of tardies when comparing children raised by grandparents and children raised by other groups ($F(3, 14802) = 9.39$, $p < .001$). If school is important, kids will show it by their involvement. Tardiness to class is an area where kids vote with their feet. When they are engaged in the learning process, excited about learning, and have a connection with their teacher, they tend to get to class on time. When students are disconnected from class or their teacher they have little motivation to get to class, let alone on time. Children raised by grandparents apparently struggle with this area.

Finally, course rigor is an important arena to gauge success in life after high school. Students who take courses that are more rigorous are more likely to not only go to college, but to do well in college. There are three levels of courses in most high schools: regular, pre-Advanced Placement, or PAP, and Advanced Placement, or AP. For the purposes of this analysis, regular classes were given a value of 1, PAP a value of 2, and AP a value of 3. A one-way ANOVA was conducted to determine if there were any differences between groups of guardians. A significant difference was found ($F(3, 20315) = 26.44$, $p < .001$) between the groups, with the children raised by grandparents having the lowest level of rigor in their coursework. These results are illustrated in Table 17.1.

CAUSES OF DIFFICULTIES EXPERIENCED BY CUSTODIAL GRANDCHILDREN

There are several causes and reasons for the struggles indicated above. Many times, a student does not have the academic support at home to help with rigorous

TABLE 17.1 Means, Standard Deviations, and One-way Analysis of Variance (ANOVA) for Result of Primary Guardian on Academic Success of Students

	Primary Guardian									
	Father		Mother		Grandparent		Other			
Variable	μ	SD	μ	SD	μ	SD	μ	SD	$F(df1, df2)$	$\acute{\eta}$
1st semester grades	85.04	11.33	83.71	11.36	81.1	11.44	83.36	11.62	18.71(3, 15062)	.37
2nd semester grades	84.23	12.65	82.63	12.64	78.66	13.65	81.88	12.7	24.83(3, 14999)	.49
Unexcused absences	5.89	6.94	6.30	6.84	4.99	3.28	6.85	6.29	9.52(3, 16127)	.18
Excused absences	2.70	2.09	3.06	2.93	3.48	2.40	2.81	2.32	18.94(3, 13468)	.42
Tardies	8.19	10.66	8.84	10.74	12.82	13.84	8.31	10.02	9.39(3, 14802)	.19
Course rigor	1.19	0.52	1.14	0.45	1.02	0.13	1.11	0.41	26.44(3, 20315)	.39

Note. $\acute{\eta}$ = effect size
$p < .001$

classes. Often, grandparents themselves never had algebra, chemistry, physics, or any of the other high-level classes. If they did have the class, it has been a long time since they had it, and knowledge or methodology may have changed significantly. For example, in 1975, a biology class recognized only two kingdoms in the ecosphere of planet earth—plant and animal. Today, in 2008, biologists recognize six kingdoms (Bacteria, Archaea, Protista, Plantae, Fungi, and Animalia) that are further reduced into three domains (Bacteria, Archaea, and Eukarya). The new system of biological organization is quite foreign and substantially more complex than 33 years ago. DNA was not even discovered until the mid 1960s, yet today middle and high school students are expected to be very familiar with its chemical structure and the nucleotides that make up the DNA double helix. A second reason is a breakdown of communication between school and home. Many times, the grandparent simply does not know if the child has homework or not, and the child will lie to them. A third reason is that there are psychosocial issues involving the child that the grandparent may be unaware of. The child may be disconnected from school for a variety of reasons, or may be resistant to the grandparents. The child may be suffering from depression, bipolar disorder, or any other of a number of issues. A fourth issue is substance abuse. A child with a lot of pain in their life may try to self-medicate by using illegal drugs, prescription drugs, alcohol, or over-the-counter drugs. A fifth cause is peer associations. Even King Solomon in his wisdom stated over 3,000 years ago, "He who walks with the wise grows wise, but a companion of fools suffers harm" (Proverbs 13:20). While poor friendships have caused trouble over the ages, negative people have become more commonplace given the toxicity of modern culture. Finally, a sixth cause of poor performance at school is a genuine learning disability. Learning disabilities can be screened for and, if identified, addressed by special education. While a child may struggle at school with low grades, they may not, however, actually have a learning disability such as dyslexia or dysgraphia. They may struggle with two other common problems: (a) lack of motivation, or (b) lack of study skills.

INTERVENTION STRATEGIES: ACADEMIC SUPPORT

Children raised by grandparents are known to struggle academically more than children raised by other types of guardians. While the reasons are many, there are specific interventions that may help a great number of these children. Intervention is very important. Intervention is key to changing the academic direction of a student. There are several tools and resources within a school to help guardians of any child who is struggling. In some states, teachers are required to schedule tutorial times to assist struggling students. A wise student would take advantage of those opportunities. Parents and grandparents alike can communicate with their child's teachers via email, voicemail, and during their daily scheduled conference times, though it may be necessary to call ahead to schedule a time to meet with the given teacher. In addition, most schools have academic counselors to aid in getting educational help. As the instructional leader of the school, any assistant principal or principal should be able to offer varied solutions to academic trouble. Most schools have a Web site that guardians can study to find programs, teacher information, counselor information, and a host of other items the guardian may find useful.

When helping with homework, it is important to offer as many avenues for information to get into the brain as possible. For example, there comes a time when science classes study liquid solutions. Inevitably, they will study how impurities will lower the freezing point or raise the boiling point of a liquid. A great home activity to help reinforce the concept is to boil water, take the temperature, and then add salt and take the temperature again. When the water again actually boils, the temperature of the actual water will have increased a few degrees. The salt is an impurity in the water, and introducing the salt to the water will raise the boiling point of the water. Making home-made ice cream is a great example of salt lowering the freezing point of water. Ice cream is made by adding ice and water around the cream cylinder; the cream will not freeze as easily until the salt is added. Taking the temperature of the water will confirm that the addition of the salt has indeed lowered the freezing point of the water so the cream will now freeze. In doing one or both of these activities, the guardian will have provided several avenues into the brain for the concept of solutions and impurities—visual, kinesthetic, tactile, experiential, olfactory, even verbal and auditory if it is discussed. The concept will be much easier to recall on a test with multiple neural pathways involved in its memory structure.

DEALING WITH COMMUNICATION BREAKDOWNS

It is difficult when the only link of communication between the school and the home is the child. Things get lost, forgotten, or thrown away. During progress-report or report-card time, many teachers have found that such reports given to students end up in the trash bin after school as opposed to taken home. An effective school has many avenues of communication that the parent can pursue at their leisure. Less effective schools will place the burden of ensuring timely and accurate communication on the shoulders of the guardian.

Most schools have Web sites with school calendars on them. Those calendars will contain important information, from lunch menus to report-card or progress-report times. It will also contain important dates regarding testing, school pictures, even school registration. The Web sites will also contain contact phone numbers and email addresses, even homework helps and teacher homework pages.

Schools also often have phone callout systems (e.g., "Phonemaster"). However, those systems of calling are only as accurate as the information stored within them. If a family changes their phone number or address, they must notify the school to ensure that they are kept in the loop of important school happenings. Additionally, it is recommended that the phone number kept on file in the office for automated callout purposes not be the phone number to the home address. Such calls can be intercepted or erased. Guardians should list their cell phone numbers as the primary contact number. Such calls are rarely intercepted or erased, and if the phone is off or charging a message can be left that can easily be checked later. Automated callout systems have sensors that wait until any greeting message is over before leaving a message.

One communication tool that can be utilized for struggling students is a quick feedback form for each teacher to sign (see Figure 17.1). If the child is in elementary school, the teacher can sign it for any content area that is needed. If the child is in secondary school, it is easily used for a traditional seven-period day, and can easily be modified for any variation of block schedules. Some guardians have elected to implement a token economy based upon points earned in the behavior category. Some guardians give 10 points per day or per period for each completed homework assignment their child presents to them. The points are lost if the sheet is not turned in the next day. At the end of the week, points can be redeemed to "purchase" certain privileges or opportunities. Some guardians will combine behavior and homework points. Many permutations can be utilized to make the homework log an effective tool of communication between school and home. Consistent, daily utilization is key to effective use of the homework log.

PSYCHOSOCIAL ISSUES

Psychologist Jean Twenge did a remarkable study where she carefully examined children's records from the 1950s to present. She found that the *average* child today is more anxious than a child in the 1950s and 1960s that was referred to a psychiatrist for mental illness (Twenge, 2000). Indeed, children in today's schools are faced with a greater amount of stress than their parents or grandparents when they were in school.

Family of origin is a helpful concept when looking at some of the forces causing stress to children being raised by grandparents. Situations such as

Student: _____ Phone: _____
Date: _____ email: _____

Daily Homework Log

	Class:	Teacher:	Behavior: (circle)	Behavior Notes:	Homework:	Homework Notes:
Period 1			5 4 3 2 1		yes ____ no ____	
Period 2			5 4 3 2 1		yes ____ no ____	
Period 3			5 4 3 2 1		yes ____ no ____	
Period 4			5 4 3 2 1		yes ____ no ____	
Period 5			5 4 3 2 1		yes ____ no ____	
Period 6			5 4 3 2 1		yes ____ no ____	
Period 7			5 4 3 2 1		yes ____ no ____	

5 = Excellent
4 = Good
3 = Fair
2 = Not so good
1 = Please call me

FIGURE 17.1 Teacher's feedback form.

anger, alcoholism, abuse, learned helplessness, and depression are often seen in students and can be traced back to families. Most schools have a crisis counselor or social worker that is specifically designated to help deal with psychosocial issues.

One of the largest and fastest-growing problems facing adolescents is self-mutilation ("carving" or "burning"). Researchers have theorized that shame, guilt, self-hatred, self-blame, and self-punishment are important reasons for self-mutilation and suicide. Though there are many possible causes for self-mutilation, it appears that one recurrent underlying issue is internalized anger. This issue, if not intervened quickly, can lead to problems that are more serious. There are treatment centers that specialize in the treatment of self-mutilation. (A valuable Web site to begin a search for a treatment program is http://www.athealth.com/Consumer/tcenter/tcenter.html.)

Most assuredly, whatever critical psychosocial issues face the child, they can probably be traced back to the event that necessitated the grandparents raising the children instead of the natural parents. Case after case in the school in this study are due to parents in jail due to drugs, or one or both parents dead due to murder. In two unrelated circumstances, children were present and witnessed one parent murder the other. In one case, a male child and his brother both spent the night at two separate friends' homes, only to return in the morning to high levels of carbon monoxide in the house due to a faulty furnace, and the rest of the family (dad, brother, little sister) dead in their beds and their mother in a coma with brain damage. Mostly, however, grandparent custody is due to parents in jail or prison, or just absent due to persistent drug use.

Teachers and staff need to be told by the child's therapist or family when a parent is being released from jail so they can be on the lookout for abnormal behaviors due to anxiety or fear. When an educator sees those behaviors occurring they can notify a crisis counselor, social worker, or school counselor to help deal with the issues emerging from the child's heart. Another organization that is a help to grandparents raising grandchildren whose parents are incarcerated is Prison Fellowship (http://www.prisonfellowship.org), which has a host of resources for all parties involved.

SUBSTANCE ABUSE

Teens are increasingly being exposed to drugs and alcohol in our society. Moreover, their leaders and heroes are using drugs and alcohol. It has become an epidemic in our society to be unable to face our pain and to turn to secondary sources to help dull the sting of a toxic society. Teens are increasingly being taken to treatment centers for substance abuse.

In 1986, the drugs of choice for teens in high school were alcohol, stimulants, cocaine, hallucinogens (e.g., LSD), sedatives or barbiturates, inhalants, tranquilizers, and opiates (Beschner, 1986). In 2007, according to the National Institutes of Health (NIDA, 2006), the drugs of choice are acid/LSD, alcohol, club drugs, cocaine, ecstasy/MDMA, heroin, inhalants, marijuana, methamphetamine, and PCP/Phencyclidine. There are also a number of prescription drugs that being abused. These include oxycodone (OxyContin), propoxyphene (Darvon), hydrocodone (Vicodin), hydromorphone (Dilaudid), meperidine (Demerol), and diphenoxylate (Lomotil).

Schools can be a place of education or a place of drug access. According to the National Institutes of Health, 72.7% of seniors have abused alcohol and even more have tried drugs at some point in their lives. For many students, unsupervised weekends are times for parties and drug use. The disease of addiction can remain undetected, much like termites, unless a parent knows what to look for. The warning signs of teenage alcohol and drug use include social withdrawal, decline in school performance, resistance to authority, behavior problems, high-risk behavior (shoplifting, excessive speeding, reckless driving, etc.), extreme mood swings, sexual promiscuity, physical complaints, changes in relationships, extended time away from home, changes in eating patterns, and the more obvious signs of alcohol on the breath, slurred speech, staggering, dilated pupils, pipes, pill boxes, straws, spoons, and clothing depicting drug and alcohol themes. One of the worst things a teen can have at their disposal is unsupervised, unaccountable time. To know if marijuana has recently been smoked all one has to do is sniff the hands of the suspect. The odor will be obvious. Teens using hand lotion or eye drops excessively may be trying to cover up the symptoms of drug use.

Many police departments, crisis counselors, and school nurses will have resources to help a parent detect drug use or intervene. To search a child's room is not an invasion of their privacy—it is an act of love by looking for things that can harm the child. For a parent to allow a poisonous snake to sneak into the playpen of a toddler would be unthinkable. The child lacks the judgment to know that the snake can kill them. That same child, 16 years later, may still lack the judgment to know that drugs (a different form of poison) will kill them. A parent should search inside the insoles of shoes, secret pockets in pants, CD-carrying cases, and innocent-looking plumber's fittings, and should be on the lookout for folded foil or aluminum soda cans with holes in the sides. A good Web site to consult is the National Institute for Drug Abuse for Teens Web site (http://www.teens.drugabuse.gov/parents/index.asp).

Helpful organizations include Tough Love (http://www.toughlove.com/), 4 Troubled Teens, (http://www.4troubledteens.com/wilderness-therapy.html), and Alateen (http://www.al-anon.org/alateen.html). It has been said, "It's hard to con a con." Alateen is a 12-step program rooted in Alcoholics Anonymous (AA) and consists of recovering addicts that meet for mutual support and encouragement. They are also a good group of peers for exposing a teen addict's rationalizations and lies. If a teen wonders what damage certain drugs, alcohol, or even smoking does to their brains, they need look no further than Dr. Daniel Amen's Web site. Dr. Amen is a psychiatrist and neuro-imaging pioneer in the field of brain scans. He has a library of hundreds of brain scans that show brains on most anything one can imagine. Many teens like hard evidence. This Web site can show it to them: http://www.brainplace.com/bp/atlas/.

PEER ASSOCIATIONS

One of the natural trends that occurs in a child's maturation process is a gradual movement away from parents as their locus of esteem and significance and toward peers. The child will still value the parents' values, but will shift their energies to making relationships with others as they develop autonomy. Autonomy is vital to a functional adult. It is a critical asset to be formed during adolescence. However, it is in the formation of building this autonomy that kids can enter a world of darkness and hurt. If they have not developed a good filter (value system) with which to sort out good friends and bad friends, then those bad friends will have a harmful effect upon the child.

A study conducted by the Maryland School of Social Work in 2003 concluded that "an inverse relationship exists between parental monitoring and [deviant peer associations], even after statistical adjustments are made for multiple covariates" (Lloyd, 2003). The earlier a guardian intervenes in problematic peer associations, the better the probability of preventing trouble at a later date. Parents are the people who instill values in their children, and, hence, provide the filter with which their children select their friends. In the absence of parents, grandparents have the double job of un-training possible bad values, or filters, and instilling a new set of values that will serve as the new filters for selecting peers.

Once a bad peer association has begun, many grandparents ask how it can be terminated. Even the strongest of parents has had to deal with this. The parents of Cassie Bernal, a victim of the Columbine school shooting in April of 1999, had to deal with this very problem. Their daughter, Cassie, had formed relationships with the goth group within Columbine High School in ninth grade. The mother found letters that spoke of satanic ritual, suicide, even the murder of Cassie's own parents. Cassie had also gotten into drugs, sex, and occult practices.

Her parents intervened by transferring Cassie to a local private school, demanding she change her friends, and making sure it happened by putting her under a strict grounding as soon as school was over each day. They searched her and her belongings daily. They also made sure the only music she listened to was music they had first screened and found appropriate for their value system. She was also barred from watching TV. Cassie's anger flared and things got worse for a short while. Her friends even vandalized their house. However, the Bernals did not give up. They stuck to their course of action, and began to see a change come over Cassie in the months that followed. Within a year, Cassie was back to the healthy and trustworthy state she had been in before her deviant peer associations had formed. She had earned such trust with her parents that they allowed her to transfer back to Columbine High School the next school year. Cassie was a model student, both academically and socially. This was put to the test on April 20, 1999, when the two gunmen broke into the school and, among others, shot and killed Cassie for telling them that she believed in God.

Before her death, the transformation of her life was complete and genuine. It took strong intervention on the part of her parents, and it took time for those changes to produce effect.

LEARNING DISABILITIES

Custodial grandchildren with learning disabilities can be helped. If a guardian suspects that a learning problem exists, they should contact the school's counselor or assistant principal to request a special education screening. By federal law, this can be done as early as age 3. Whether the child is home schooled, enrolled in a private school, or in public school, the local public school is required to screen the child within 60 days of a request by a parent. The school then has 30 days to report those findings.

The end result, in many cases, will compare the child's IQ with their performance IQ. If there is more than a 16-point lag in performance behind the actual IQ, the child qualifies for special education services. They will then schedule an ARD (a committee meeting which stands for Admission, Review, and Dismissal—relating to the child's possible placement into special education services). Sometimes it is referred to as an IEP meeting (Individual Education Plan meeting). At the ARD meeting, there will be the diagnostician or counselor who did the testing, an administrator, one or more of the child's teachers, and the child's parents. The testing will be discussed, and dependent upon the outcome of the testing, additional services or testing may be requested, or a new schedule will be developed with one or more special education classes instead of regular education classes.

If the special education program is a good one, the child should begin progressing nicely to eventually get back to the same level as their peers, assuming they work hard at their schoolwork.

NOT YOUR FATHER'S OLDSMOBILE

Schools are a mirror of the culture. Every culture has heroes. Heroes have a powerful impact on those who follow them in shaping their values and morals. Those values and morals determine what people believe and how they live. Hence the power of cultural heroes, also known as singers, movie stars, and athletes. These superstars are powerful in their effect on culture. Culture creates them, and is supported and perpetuated by them. If a parent wants to know what is going on in the hearts and minds of their child, they need look no further than the music they listen to, the programs they watch, and the posters they post on their walls for a glimpse into their child's inner being.

Clearly, the popular media culture in the United States is substantially different than it was 40 years ago. Culture, and hence schools, are fed and supported by the popular media. The media of 40 years ago set a tone and value system in which many of the parents of current high school students were raised. The news headlines on June 19, 1967, read that Paul McCartney actually admitted to using LSD. That was a shocking revelation to the country—an indication of where the cultural values resided at the time. The culture yielded popular TV programs such as *Bonanza, Gilligan's Island, The Avengers, The Man*

From U.N.C.L.E., Mission: Impossible, Gunsmoke, Get Smart, Hogan's Heroes, The Monkees, The Andy Griffith Show, The Beverly Hillbillies, The Fugitive, Lost in Space, The Carol Burnett Show, and *Dragnet* (dMarie, 2007). There was no reference to drug, drug use, nudity, or sex on TV. Even profanity was rare. Parents did not have to be wary of what their children watched on TV.

The songs of the era also reveal a pulse of the cultural values of the time. Top songs were "Groovin'" by the Young Rascals, "Daydream Believer" by the Monkees, "Somethin' Stupid" by Nancy and Frank Sinatra, "To Sir with Love" by Lulu, and "Roses Are Red" by Bobby Vinton. A quick look at the lyrics of "Roses Are Red" shows what made the song popular in the 1960s. The song is about a man who lost his true love to another man, and yet still he wished her all of the best. The third verse of the song says,

> Then I went far away and you found someone new.
> I read your letter dear, and I wrote back to you.
> Roses are red, my love, violets are blue.
> Sugar is sweet, my love, good luck—may God bless you. (Songfacts, 2007)

If the same circumstance were written about in today's culture, there would be a significant shift in the reaction of the writer. Compare the number one song downloaded during the month of June in 2001. The lyrics reveal a very different type of song. The author was Eminem (real name Marshall Mathers), and the song was "Public Service Announcement" from the album Slim Shady. The lyrics (there is no melody as it is a rap) are replete with profanity that would be inappropriate to publish in a public book of any kind.

There has been a substantial shift in what is socially acceptable lyrical verbiage over the last 4 decades. The lyrics come from a value system that is prevalent in the culture. The impact upon culture and schools is also quite clear. Sony music reveals the following about the life and character of Bobby Vinton:

> This success afforded Bobby the opportunity to help the struggling people of Poland, a country that his grandparents had taught him to love. Telethons that Bobby hosted and supervised gave the men, women and children the much needed relief that was long overdue. Hundreds of thousands of dollars were raised. (Sony, 2007)

But more than just through song lyrics, the actual character of a person has an effect on the behavior of their teen followers. Values are shaped by unconscious imitation of a role model, often by engaging in reward and punishment and reflective thinking. Just as thinking of a song's lyrics repetitively can shape what a child thinks, values, and believes, so can emulating how their hero lives. What are the effects of the character and lyrics of Eminem (Marshall Mathers) on his followers?

At the time of the release of his song "Public Service Announcement," Eminem had been sentenced to 2 years probation. Some of the terms of his probation were no alcohol, the requirement to undergo regular drug testing, and the limitation to only tour within the contiguous United States. He also was awaiting trial on a second weapons charge, stemming from an incident the prior summer outside the Hot Rocks Cafe in Warren, Michigan. Mathers was accused of clubbing another man with a handgun. What were his fans' responses? Not a TV telethon to raise money for needy people—"You'll be dropping the charges [or] we'll coming uptown with 20 oz Mountain Dew bottles full of gas and charcoal lighting fluid and matches" was just one of the threats made in a letter to City Attorney George Constance in Warren, Michigan, by fans of Eminem after the star's arrest on assault and weapons charges (RollingStone.com, 2007).

Cultural values truly have changed in 40 years, as has the need for parents and grandparents to monitor the media intake of their children. However, many times grandparents do not monitor their grandchildren's media intake, or if they do, they lack enforcement authority. As a result, grandchildren who have been entrusted to today's media are subject to being duly poisoned in attitude, values, and beliefs. Furthermore, grandchildren's school achievement and progress will be evidence of culture's negative academic impact.

CONCLUSIONS

Many factors contribute to the difficulties custodial grandchildren experience at school. Adolescents who have difficulty with schoolwork bring together a unique combination of causes. The behavioral and attitudinal patterns that result from these influences may persist throughout young people's lives and govern their opportunities for future work if intervention is not sought out. As has been seen, the quicker and sooner the intervention the better.

All interventions need to be carried out in an attitude and atmosphere of love. The foundation for any work with adolescents who have trouble at school must be to encourage an "I can" attitude. Adolescents must be able to sense acceptance of themselves by their guardians and counselors, and guardians and counselors must avoid criticism, sarcasm, and teasing at all costs. Criticism of any kind will most likely squelch any opportunity for effective intervention. Effective counselors and guardians work diligently to distinguish personal worth of the child from academic performance.

Literally dozens of effective interventions are available to help adolescents having problems with schoolwork. An excellent online resource for help and support is from the Northwest Regional Literacy Web site (http://www. nwlincs.org/NWLINCSWEB/StuSuccess.htm). Another place one might begin is with the Skills for Classroom Success Checklist (SCSC), or the Skills for Study Success Checklist (SSSC). Both are available from Research Press, 2612 North Mattis Avenue, Champaign, Illinois 61821. Both are copyrighted by Rosemarie S. Morganett.

In helping grandparents raise grandchildren who are able to adjust and succeed in school, remember the following:

Consider the family context. Adolescent anxiety, anger, or depression about home life drains young people emotionally and makes concentration at school next to impossible. Additionally, young people who feel they must compete with successful siblings may opt for failure as a means to either gain attention or to relieve the competitive tension.

Focus on encouragement. All of the intentions for intervention should be to build successes and achievements, small as they may be, in order to build an "I can do it" attitude. Negativity should not exist in any intervention. Research by Willner, Braukman, Kirigin, Fixsen, Phillips, and Wolf (1977) found that children preferred being taught by adults who gave positive feedback, set clear expectations with reasons to back them up, and showed enthusiasm and concern. Other studies have also shown that students are more positive and friendly with others in their classrooms and develop more positive attitudes when they experience warm and accepting relationships with their teachers. Encouragement increases learning as well as students' behavioral options.

Examine study conditions. Students should have a clear, unobstructed, organized, and well-lit study area in the home, free from interruptions and background noise. A bright light should come from the direction opposite the writing side in order to avoid shadows. Telephone calls should not be accepted during study time. The key is having a regular place that is their own in order to study free from interruptions.

Make sure children know how to study. There are several ways to do this. Use the 30–3–2 schedule. Study or work for 30 minutes, then take a 3-minute break to do something other than think about work. When returning to the study area, take an extra 2 minutes to quickly review mentally what was just studied, and preview what is coming up in order to be prepared. Another help is the SQ3R method of studying. SQ3R stands for Survey the material or assignment, Question what you need to know or learn, Read and pay special attention to the main idea in each paragraph and to italicized words, Recall roughly every 15–30 minutes what you have read or done and write it down.

Finally, Review your work to make sure all questions on the assignment were answered and goals were met.

Explore getting a tutor. If a child is behind academically, and the grandparent is behind the times educationally, a tutor may well be worth their money. Tutoring should first come from the school in the form of before- or after-school help. Many colleges offer tutoring programs for children. Many high schools have National Honor Society Members who need community service hours and can meet those requirements by tutoring children. Many students embrace success in the one-on-one atmosphere of a tutoring relationship.

Children are trainable and moldable. The process of raising and educating children can be compared to putting braces on teeth. At first it is very painful to have such implements on, restricting the teeth when there was nothing in the first place. Then, each month the orthodontist tightens the braces to achieve optimal stress. After years of optimal stress and lots of pain, the teeth are straightened. Even then, however, the process is not over. At night the child typically wears a retainer to prevent the teeth from moving during their sleep. This is typically worn for a few years until their jawbones mature. After that long and unloved process, the teeth are straight and functional. Much the same is true of children. The intervention strategies in this chapter will hopefully be a help for a child who is in need of such help.

REFERENCES

Beschner, G. (1986). Understanding teenage drug use. In G. Berschner & S. Friedman (Eds.), *Teen drug use.* Lexington, MA: Health.

dMarie Direct. (2007). dMarie Time Capsule. Retrieved June 18, 2007, from http://dmarie.com/timecap/step1.asp

Lloyd, J. J. (2003, July). *Hanging out with the wrong crowd: Do parents really matter?* University of Maryland School of Social Work, College Park, MD.

Mendro, R. (1998). Student achievement and school and teacher accountability. *Journal of Personnel Evaluation in Education, 12,* 257–267.

National Institute of Drug Abuse (NIDA). (2006, December). *NIDA InfoFacts: High School and Youth Trends.* Retrieved June 25, 2007, from http://www.drugabuse.gov/infofacts/HSYouthtrends.html

RollingStone.com. (2007). Michigan prosecutor threatened by Eminem fans. *RollingStone.com.* Retrieved June 18, 2007, from http://www.rollingstone.com/news/story/5924449/michigan_prosecutor_threatened_by_eminem_fans

Sanders, W., & Horn, S. (1994). The Tennessee Value-Added Assessment System (TVAAS): Mixed-model methodology in educational assessment. *Journal of Personnel Evaluation in Education, 8*(3), 299–311.

Songfacts. (2007). *Songfacts*. Retrieved June 18, 2007, from http://www.songfacts.com/ lyrics.php?findsong = 1889

Sony. (2007). *Sony Music USA*. Retrieved June 18, 2007, from http://www.sonymusic. com/artists/BobbyVinton/aboutbv.htm

Twenge, J. (2000). The age of anxiety? Birth cohort change in anxiety and neuroticism, 1952–1993. *Journal of Personality and Social Psychology, 79,* 1007–1021.

Willner, A. G., Braukman, C. J., Kirigin, K. A., Fixsen, D. L., Phillips, E. L., & Wolf, M. M. (1977). The training and validation of youth-preferred social behaviors of child care personnel. *Journal of Applied Behavior Analysis, 10*(2), 219–230.

CHAPTER 18

Epilogue

Bert Hayslip, Jr., and Patricia L. Kaminski

Most custodial grandparents would likely endorse the notion that raising a grandchild is the most important task before them. Relative to parents who are raising their children, however, custodial grandparents often have little time to prepare for this tremendous responsibility, assume it under socially stigmatizing and often negative family circumstances, and frequently have had little direct or ongoing responsibility for raising a child for many years. Yet, their deep commitment to establishing and maintaining fulfilling relationships with the grandchildren they are raising and ensuring that their grandchildren are happy and healthy may exacerbate the parenting challenges they face, even while such dedication can make their economic, physical, social, and emotional sacrifices palatable.

One goal of this edited volume was to share what is known about the central tasks of parenting grandchildren and establishing meaningful relationships with them in ways that are accessible to a wide range of people—from health care providers and researchers, to educators, policymakers, and custodial grandparents themselves. As such, we aimed to offer scientifically informed chapters filled with practical ideas that could be readily applied to assist grandfamilies. Thus, in this text, the choice was made to emphasize the importance of developing new knowledge about parenting the custodial grandchild and applying that knowledge in ways that not only assist the grandparents themselves, but also help those who interact with them on a daily basis (family, neighbors, grandparent peers) and those who may provide services and support to them (e.g., counselors, educators, social workers, school nurses, social service personnel). This dual emphasis reflects a *scientist-practitioner* perspective on issues pertaining to parenting and intergenerational relationships. That is, research and practice can be mutually influential and informative. New knowledge not only stimulates novel theoretical and empirical work, but it is also driven by the choices practitioners must make in treating and providing services for grandparent caregivers and their grandchildren. It is our hope that both researchers and professionals in the field will benefit from this scientist-practitioner orientation to understanding custodial grandparenting and intergenerational relationships.

Despite the diverse professions and perspectives represented by the contributors to this volume, common themes emerged across their empirical, theoretical, and applied chapters.

- Grandparents and grandchildren are best thought of in dyadic terms; their influence on one another is dynamic and bidirectional. Indeed, a family systems approach to understanding such relationships is not just beneficial, but indispensable. Indeed, grandchildren have for the most part been ignored in work to date. Many chapters (Campbell & Miles; Goodman & Hayslip; Hayslip, King, & Jooste; Kaminski & Murrell; Letiecq, Bailey, & Dahlen; Maiden & Zuckerman) reflect this necessary attention to multigenerational family systems dynamics in understanding custodial grandparenting. These chapters rest upon the assumption that there is a mutually interactive relationship between grandparent caregiver physical and mental health and grandchild health outcomes (Goodman & Hayslip; Ramaswamy, Bhavnagri, & Barton; Roberto, Dolbin-MacNab, & Finney; Smith & Richardson). Likewise, grandparents' parenting practices may contribute to or be reactions to their grandchildren's emotional or behavioral difficulties (Hayslip & Glover; Ramaswamy et al.; Smith & Richardson). Indeed, understanding custodial grandparents and grandchildren at the *level of their relationships* is key to effective case conceptualization and clinical work with each member of the dyad.
- Parenting grandchildren does not occur in a cultural, historical, or interpersonal vacuum. For example, despite their focus on the grandchild, grandparents do continue to have concerns about relationships with adult children who may not be physically present, but are nevertheless influential (Musil, Warner, McNamara, Rokoff, & Turek). Likewise, they have concerns about relationships with adult children born of ambivalence about being caught between the desires of an adult child and a grandchild (Letiecq, Bailey, & Dahlen); with grandparent peers, who might otherwise provide needed social and emotional support (Hayslip & Glover); with school personnel

(Kolomer, McCallion, & Voorhis; Mauderer; Musil et al.); and with health care providers (Roberto, Dolbin-MacNab, & Finney), which are all important interpersonal dimensions of the context in which grandparents raise their grandchildren. In this respect, in a poignantly written chapter, Hipple and Hipple discuss the difficulties they faced in dealing with the legal system (e.g., CPS) as well as in processing their feelings about the insensitive and judgmental words of others. Reflecting the larger context in which grandfamilies must be understood, therapists may be drawn into the role of representing grandparent caregivers to the court system in cases where legal custody of the grandchild is an issue (Maiden & Zuckerman). Targeting the larger societal context in which custodial grandparenting can be understood, it is important to realize that custodial grandparents' feelings of being stigmatized as parental failures are likely rooted in the stereotypes others have about them (Hayslip & Glover). These contextual forces must be acknowledged by professional helpers and educators in order to better understand the grandchild as well as what the custodial grandparent is up against, especially with regard to older grandchildren (Mauderer). Helpers should also be prepared to contend with cultural or historical changes (Jooste, Hayslip, & Smith) giving rise to the availability of social services and with the influence of the culture per se in terms of providing healthy role models (Mauderer).

- The construct of levels of intervention, as well as taking a flexible, multimodal approach to intervention, is critical in helping grandparents and their grandchildren. In this respect, taking into consideration the degree and nature of grandparental involvement in the grandchild's life is key to designing and providing social services for grandparents, intervening with the adult child, or helping grandparents create a home environment that is both consistent and nurturing (Smith & Dannison). Alternatively, for some custodial grandparent-grandchild dyads, accessing support groups in the community (Jooste, Hayslip, & Smith; Kaminski & Murrell) or school system (Kolomer & McCallion), participating in educational programs (Kaminski & Murrell), attending individual or family counseling (Kaminski & Murrell), enhancing the availability of social support from friends, neighbors, or grandparent peers (Hayslip & Glover; Ramaswamy, Bhavnagri, & Barton), evoking the resources of the school system (Mauderer), acquiring parent-skills training (Campbell & Miles; Kaminiski & Murrell; Smith & Richardson), and improving grandparents' health and access to health services (Roberto, Dolbin-MacNab, & Finney) all reflect a multileveled, multimodal approach to intervention with grandparents and grandchildren. The very diversity of grandparent-grandchild dyads demands such an approach. In light of the likely stigma associated with raising a grandchild in today's culture (Hayslip & Glover; Hipple & Hipple), interventions in the form of marshalling social support and educating the public about the issues facing grandfamilies may be equally effective relative to those solely targeting grandparent caregivers and their grandchildren. In this light, attention to (1) the pre-morbid circumstances giving rise to the emotional, behavioral, and health-related problems reported by grandfamilies; (2) factors giving rise to the phenomenon of custodial grandparenting per se; and (3) phenomena contributing to the adverse financial, housing-related, and social service–oriented conditions with which grandfamilies must cope, are all central to designing and implementing effective interventions with grandfamilies.

- In some respects and not others, custodial grandparents and grandchildren are best understood in unique terms, relative to parents raising their own children. Seeing grandfamilies in this manner helps depathologize the experience of both grandparent and grandchild, leading to more productive efforts at intervention by framing one's situation from being problem oriented to being strengths oriented (Kaminski & Murrell; Servaty-Seib & Wilkins). At the same time, it is important to acknowledge that feeling stigmatized and isolated are realities for many grandfamilies (Hayslip & Glover; Hipple & Hipple), as is experiencing the loss of a primary attachment figure via parental abandonment, abuse, drug use, death, or divorce (Hipple & Hipple; Kaminski & Murrell). As is true for parents, both strengths/gains and weaknesses/losses in terms of views of self, relationships, and assumptions about the world should be recognized in the grandparent and grandchild (Servaty-Seib & Wilkins); this would encourage a proactive stance toward involvement in grandchildren's peer relationships and school performance by grandparents by empowering them to do so (Musil et al.). Focusing on both gains and losses can also be valuable in guiding both assessment and intervention with grandfamilies (Kaminski & Murell; Servaty-Seib & Wilkins; Smith & Richardson). Not unlike parents who feel as if they should be an omnipotent force in their children's lives, grandparents may feel they can mitigate the negative impact of adverse family circumstances on their grandchildren (Maiden & Zuckerman). Encouraging a proactive stance toward parenting their grandchildren would build on such feelings. We argue here that to the extent it is possible to do so, drawing on what we know about parenting in general can aid us in understanding and assisting grandparent caregivers. In this context, it may be that parental styles (i.e., authoritarian, laissez-faire, authoritative) that have permeated the parenting literature may exist in parallel form among grandparent caregivers. Yet this parallel has yet to be demonstrated, as have the consequences for grandchildren who have been raised by a grandparent with a given parental style. Importantly, both grandparents and grandchildren are best understood along a continuum of both separateness/independence to interdependence regarding one another, and more generally along a continuum of normalcy to pathology.

- The above issues reflect very diverse methodological approaches to gathering information about intergenerational and parental concerns among grandfamilies: case studies, original empirical data, and secondary data can each inform important clinical insights. In this manner, too, a rich theoretical framework, which may either already exist to inform both research and practice (e.g., attachment theory), or arise out of the necessity to better understand grandfamilies' functioning (e.g., intergenerational ambivalence), is essential. In this respect, there is virtually no long-term empirical data speaking to the impact on both grandparent and grandchild of having raised a grandchild or having been raised by a grandparent, particularly if such work is theoretically driven.

- The above themes speaking to research and practice with grandfamilies will hopefully signal the beginning of a beneficial partnership between researchers and practitioners. Thus, the interface between those who generate new knowledge and those who apply it is an evolving one. In fact, while these chapters both generate new knowledge about parenting grandchildren and can inform practice, such collaboration is in its youth. It is hoped that both custodial grandparents and custodial grandchildren will benefit from this partnership.

Index

AARP. *See* American Association of Retired Persons Grandparent Information Center
Abandonment, 116, 151, 158, 225, 228
Academic counselors, 272
Academic performance problems, 219
Academic support, 271–272
Activities of daily living, 189, 217
Adjustment of children and grandparent caregivers in grandparent-headed families, 17–39
  dependent variables, 22–23
    caregiver mental health, 22
    caregiver parental aggravation, 22
    child's behavior problems, 23
    child's school engagement, 23
  discussion, 29–37
    behavior problems in children aged 6 to 11 years, 33
    behavior problems in children aged 12 to 17 years, 33–34
    caregiver aggravation, 32–33
    caregiver mental health, 29–32
    implications of findings for counseling and interventions with grandfamilies, 34–37
    school engagement, 34
  education, socioeconomic status, and grandparent age, 18
  ethnicity, 17–18, 24–25, 30–31
  family structure, 19–20, 35
  grandchild's developmental level, 18–19
  historical effects, 21–22
  independent variables, 21–22
    age, 20
    ethnicity, 20, 21–22, 24–25, 28
    family type, 20, 21, 25–26, 27–29, 29
    gender, 20, 25–26, 28–29, 31–32
  method in study, 20–23
  National Survey of America's Families (NSAF) national database, 20, 23
  one-way analysis of covariance (ANOVA), 23
  purpose of study, 20
  results, 23–29
  school-related difficulties, 19
Adjustment reactions, 219
Admission, Review, and Dismissal (ARD) meetings, 278
Adoption, 103, 124, 238
Adoption and Safe Families Act (ASFA), 230
Adult children, 105–107, 113, 191
  AIDS in, 222, 225
  biological mothers, 106–107, 131, 132, 223
  circumstances leading to grandparent custody, 3, 215, 216, 220–222, 237, 239, 251
  divorce, 116, 150, 158, 215, 253
  financial support for, 218
  incarceration of, 54, 106, 116, 150, 151, 158, 215, 222, 275